Man
May Know
For Himself

Man May Know For Himself

Teachings of
President David O. McKay

Compiled by Clare Middlemiss

Published by
DESERET BOOK COMPANY
SALT LAKE CITY, UTAH
1967

Printed by

DESERET NEWS PRESS

in the United States of America

YOU

By Edgar A. Guest

You are the fellow who has to decide
Whether you'll do it or toss it aside.
You are the fellow who makes up your mind
Whether you'll lead or will linger behind.
Whether you'll try for the goal that's afar
Or just be contented to stay where you are.
Take it or leave it. Here's something to do!
Just think it over—It's all up to you!

What do you wish? To be known as a shirk,
Known as a good man who's willing to work,
Scorned as a loafer, or praised by your chief,
Rich man or poor man or beggar or thief?
Eager or earnest or dull through the day?
Honest or crooked? It's you who must say!
You must decide in the face of the test
Whether you'll shirk or give it your best.

Nobody here will compel you to rise;
No one will force you to open your eyes;
No one will answer for you, yes or no,
Whether to stay there or whether to go;
Life is a game, but it's you who must say
Whether as cheat or as sportsman you'll play.
Fate may betray you, but you settle first
Whether to live to your best or your worst.

So, whatever it is you are wanting to be,
Remember, to fashion the choice you are free.
Kindly or selfish, or gentle or strong,
Keeping the right way or taking the wrong,
Careless of honor or guarding your pride,
All these are questions which you must decide.
Yours the selection, whichever you do;
The thing men call character's all up to you.

Reprinted by permission of Reilly & Lee, Publishers, Chicago, Ill.

PREFACE

The will to survive is said to be the most powerful of all human impulses. But how we live from day to day is quite another matter.

To live without purpose, for example, is to drift with the current.

To live without hope of constant improvement is a barren existence indeed.

To live without faith is to encase oneself in a prison which shuts out the only light which can pierce the uncertainty of tomorrow and make today worth all of our efforts.

But to live without God is to erase all meaning from our existence.

In God we find the purpose, faith and hope which give our daily lives a depth of joy and satisfaction that can be obtained in no other way.

At a vantage point that few ever attain, President David O. McKay has acquired a perspective which has turned hope into faith, and faith into such reality that God, through his Holy Spirit, is a daily companion to him.

His intellectual and spiritual achievements have given him such a view of life that he sees in their proper relationships the good and the evil, and the areas in between. Seeing them clearly as he does, he evaluates each of them accurately.

He recognizes true values for what they are.

He understands their significance, and finds the niche where each one belongs, seeing them as building stones essential to the development of a great soul.

It is this soul-building which catches his interest, for he sees in every individual a limitless potential, and seeks to bring it to fruition.

As an educator he knows that understanding must precede accomplishment, and that understanding comes only through learning. So he teaches his fellowmen.

As the Lord's mouthpiece on earth—a prophet and a seer—he knows that each soul is a child of God, so with divine assistance he gives inspiration.

He realizes that the spark of divinity inherent in us all may be made to glow with an eternal power capable of helping us to perfect ourselves, even as our Father in Heaven.

With a concept of such a goal, how can we fail to appreciate the means of achieving it?

But every one of us needs encouragement and guidance in obtaining it. This President McKay has provided abundantly over a life span of nearly a century.

He teaches and he inspires!

His lessons are clear and uplifting. They enlighten the mind and invigorate the soul.

But great as his precepts are, his personal example seems even greater. It is his most convincing teaching medium.

"Do as I do" has always preceded "Do as I say." Together they have been a beacon in a world of confusion and darkness to the millions who have known him.

It is such guidance which provides the motif for his book. Reproduced from his editorials published in the Instructor Magazine, as well as from his addresses and other public utterances, a wealth of inspiration is now provided in this volume.

Each chapter bears evidence of his prophetic calling, and every one testifies of his matchless teaching skill.

President McKay continues to be a great light to his people because of his constant alertness to current needs. Still young at heart he lives completely in the present and constantly plans for the future. His eyes are ever on the horizon of tomorrow. The past is but a foundation on which to build.

This remarkable compilation of so many of his finest writings is made possible in large measure through the untiring efforts of his devoted secretary, Sister Clare Middlemiss, who has assembled an entire library on the life and works of President McKay.

In this permanent form his editorials and other works will become a continuing blessing to Church members throughout the world.

Mark E. Petersen

CONTENTS

YOUTH, LOVE, AND MARRIAGE

SUCCESS IN THE HOME

HOLIDAY THOUGHTS

The Religious Life

1

Man
May Know
for Himself

RECENTLY I was reminded of
an incident that occurred on City Road in old Glasgow, Scotland, when I was on my first mission. It was about the last
night that I was in the mission field.

As my companion and I approached the place of the
open-air meeting, we were met by a motherly woman whom
I had never seen before and have never seen since, who said,
"The minister wi' a' his congregation is here this nicht to
break up your meetin'. Stand close taegither, so he canna get
in the circle." And she and some of her friends loyally joined
in that circle and helped us to keep it.

When the first speaker began to testify of the restoration
of the gospel, this minister cried out, "These men are 'Mormons.'" The elder, who at that time was giving his first
address in public out in the field, became somewhat confused, said a few more words, and stepped back in the ring.
Then this interrupter had the crowd, and among other things,
he said, "These men come from Salt Lake City. They are
after your daughters, and they want to take them out there
and hitch them to the plow and make them work, and make
slaves out of them!"

We then called on Brother Joseph Legget, who was a
resident of Glasgow. He stepped out in the ring and said,

"Fellow townsmen," which gave the lie right at once to the minister's statement that we were all from Salt Lake City; and then Brother Legget bore his testimony in an excellent address. Well, that man continued his railing against us until our meeting was about half over, at which time the crowd began to realize that his heart was filled with animosity. They silenced him and listened to the message which the elders had to give.

This misguided brother, and those who joined with him, did not realize the importance of the message which those humble boys—for some of us were mere boys—had to give to the world. He thought, and those who sympathized with him thought, the men holding that meeting were represen-tatives of an organization whose purpose was to injure the people. They did not know that the message which those elders had to give to the world was indeed, and is, the mes-sage of life, a philosophy which is the true science of living.

The gospel of Jesus Christ, as revealed to the Prophet Joseph Smith, is in very deed, in every way, the power of God unto salvation. It is salvation here and now! It gives to every man the perfect life here and now as well as hereafter.

Life is the dearest thing in all the world to us. Nothing else do you cherish as you cherish your life. You would give your life today for someone else, would give it in order to save the life of one who is dearer to you than your own life. So life is the one thing we hold to. It is the one thing we desire here and hereafter. Eternal life is God's greatest gift to man!

What is eternal life? In that glorious prayer of inter-cession offered by Jesus, our Redeemer, just before he crossed the brook Cedron and received the traitor's kiss that betrayed him into the hands of the soldiers, we find these words: "And this is life eternal, that they might know thee the only true God, and Jesus Christ, whom thou hast sent." (John 17:3.) To know God and his Son is eternal life. There is the key. Life eternal is what I desire. I desire it more than

I desire anything else in the world—life eternal for me, mine and all the world. And there in the words of the Redeemer we have the secret given to us in a simple sentence —To know God and Jesus Christ, whom thou has sent, is eternal life.

But how may we *know* him? That is the next question. Has he, at any time, or on any occasion, answered that question? If so, we want the answer, because it is vital. In searching the record as it is given to us by men who associated daily with the Lord, we find that upon one occasion men who were listening to him cried out against him. They opposed his works, as men today oppose him. And one voice cried out and said, in effect, "How do we know that what you tell us is true? How do we know that your profession of being the Son of God is true?" And Jesus answered him in just a simple way—and note the test—"If ye will *do* the will of my Father, which is in heaven, ye shall know whether the doctrine is of God, or whether I speak of myself." (See John 7:17.) That test is most sound. It is most philosophical. It is the most simple test to give knowledge to an individual of which the human mind can conceive. *Doing* a thing, *introducing* it into your very being, will convince you whether it is good or whether it is bad. You may not be able to convince me of that which you know, but *you* know it because you have *lived it*. That is the test that the Savior gave to those men when they asked him how they should know whether the doctrine was of God or whether it was of man.

What Is "the Will"?

But in considering his answer, another question arises. "If ye will do *the will*"—what is "the will"? We can see what conditions will bring eternal life. We have the spoken statement that if we will do his will we shall know; but now comes the question, what is "the will"? And therein is the whole essence of the gospel of Jesus Christ. Just as plainly as Jesus stated and defined what eternal life is, or how we should

5

know it, just as plainly as he laid down that test, just as plainly has he expressed what his will is.

It is impossible to give here all the principles that constitute that will; but they are so simple that, as the scriptures say, a wayfaring man though a fool need not err therein.

The Church of Jesus Christ of Latter-day Saints bears testimony to the world that this will of God has been made manifest in this dispensation; that the principles of the gospel, the principles of life, have been revealed. They are in harmony with the principles which Christ taught in the Meridian of Time. They are the same because they are eternal, as are the principles given in all dispensations of the world: *Faith*—who can dispute that faith is an eternal principle? You cannot live without it. It is as eternal as love; eternal, active, and may be as constant as the force of gravity that is acting every day. *Repentance*—it is not just in the scriptures that you find that repentance is an eternal principle. Read Carlyle, you who take him as a guide and like his reasoning. Do you know that in contemplating this principle of repentance, he makes this statement: "The man who cannot repent is dead"? And he is right. He felt the eternal element in that saving principle. It is part of life. It is a fatal condition to reach when one cannot repent.

"The Will" Is To Serve

So we might go on with our principles. It may be summed up this way—that after obeying the principles and ordinances of the gospel, "the will" of God is to serve your fellowmen, benefiting them, making this world better for your being in it. Christ gave his all to teach us that principle. And he made the statement, ". . . Inasmuch as ye have done it unto one of the least of these my brethren, ye have done it unto me." (Matthew 25:40.) This is the message which God has given to us. This Church is God's Church, which is so perfectly organized that every man and every woman, every child, may have an opportunity to do something good for somebody else. Such is the perfect organization of our Church, and it is the obligation of our priesthood members—the high priests, seventies, elders, priests, teachers, and deacons—it is the responsibility of auxiliary organizations to serve and do God's will; and if we do, the more we do it, the more we shall become convinced that it is the work of God, because we are testing it. Then by *doing* the will of God, we get to know God and get close to him, and to feel that life eternal is ours. We shall feel to love humanity everywhere, and we can cry out with the apostles of old, "We know that we have passed from death unto life, because we love the brethren. . . ." (I John 3:14.)

May we have the sincere determination to do what the poet has said she would like to do:

It may not be on the mountain height
Or over the stormy sea;
It may not be on the battle's front
My Lord will have need of me;
But if, by a still, small voice he calls
To paths that I do not know,
I'll answer, dear Lord, with my hand in thine;
I'll go where you want me to go.

There's surely somewhere a lowly place
In earth's harvest fields so wide,
Where I may labor through life's short day
For Jesus, the Crucified;
So trusting my all to thy tender care,
And knowing thou lovest me,
I'll do thy will with a heart sincere;
I'll be what you want me to be.

I'll go where you want me to go, dear Lord,
Over mountain, or plain, or sea;
I'll say what you want me to say, dear Lord;
I'll be what you want me to be.[1]

—Mary Brown.

------

[1]*Hymns—Church of Jesus Christ of Latter-day Saints*, (Salt Lake City: Deseret News Press, 1948) No. 75.

7

Chapter Two

The Value of True Religion and Right Thinking

TRUE religion has three manifestations: *first,* the thought, the feeling, the mental and *spiritual attitude of the individual toward his God; second, worship;* and *third, service to one's fellowmen.* Evidently a man must be religious if he directs his thoughts and his words toward God, and his worship and acts among his fellowmen should follow in accordance therewith.

Charles Foster Kent, in his *Life of Jesus,* speaks of "the fatal crime of wrong thinking"; and approximately three thousand years ago one of the greatest teachers, and one of the ablest and wisest of men said: "For as he thinketh in his heart, so is he. . . ." (Proverbs 23:7.) No one emphasized this truth more strongly than did Jesus. "With Him," says Kent, "the deadly sins were, not neglect of the ritual nor even crimes punishable by the laws of all civilized nations, *but wrong ideas, motives, and feelings. He decried the fatal effects of hatred and jealousy in the mind of the individual more vehemently than He did the acts that hate and jealousy prompt.*"

Proper Direction of the Mind

The Savior knew that if the mind could be directed rightly; if the evil thought and tendency could be resisted, the evil act would be minimized. Jesus does not lessen the seriousness of these acts, nor say that we should not punish them; but he emphasizes the greater need of keeping the thought clean, the mind pure. An evil tree will bring forth evil fruit; a good tree will bring forth good fruit. Keep the tree pure, the thoughts pure, and the fruit will be pure and the life pure.

We are living in an age which, measured by the standards of the gospel, is full of unstable opinions, and into that world of shifting uncertainty our young people are thrown. Think for a moment how their thoughts are diverted from our standards as they read some of the articles in current magazines. In customs and fashions, what was considered bad taste yesterday has become quite acceptable today. In regard to the ideals of success and the standards that lead to success, I quote this surprising statement: "Success is not the result of hard work, clean living, and personal integrity. The vulgar, proud, haughty, not the meek, inherit the earth." Young men and young women read these things, and their minds are diverted from the channel of right thinking and right living.

Wholesomeness Is Questioned

The wholesomeness of our ancestral home life is questioned. That thought, too, is leading our young people to think in a wrong direction.

Modesty, "that diamond setting to female beauty," is in some circles considered prudish, puritanic; and the influence is leading astray some of our girls who are susceptible to the influence of society.

What are we doing to counteract this tendency toward fatal wrong thinking?

The first duty that rests upon every parent and upon every teacher within this Church is *to arouse within the mind of the child a sense of responsibility toward other individuals and toward society*. The sacredness of personality is a fundamental teaching of Jesus Christ. One writer, Harry Emerson Fosdick, is right when he says, "Christ thought of personality as the central fact in the universe, and used it as a medium of interpretation of all other parts." In that thought, he approaches the more sublime teaching of the Lord given through the Prophet Joseph Smith: "For behold, this is my work and my glory—to bring to pass the immortality and eternal life of man." (Moses 1:39.)

In this truth is found a fundamental principle of true religion, and it touches the very heart of the government of society and the peace of the home. Let the child in the home realize that there are certain things which he cannot do to gratify his own appetite, if in doing so he brings sorrow or inconvenience to other members of the household. A sense of duty to others should be a governing factor in his actions.

O, youth of the land, think of the responsibility of keeping your name unsullied! Think of bringing comfort and happiness to the mother who bore you! There is the fundamental thought that will lead you toward God. He is recreant indeed who, to gratify his appetite or his passions, will bring a stain upon the honored name he bears or sorrow to the heart of his mother.

Prayer—Basic Force for Good

The second principle I name is *Prayer*. There are men who say that prayer is not efficacious. Unfortunately some of our young people believe such fallacious remarks. Prayer is a fundamental principle of religion and is a force for good. A praying man is a growing man. He is a powerful man.

Every day that we start out on our daily work and mingle with our fellows we enter into conflict; and it is the appropriate thing for every young man in the world to say in secret, to think and feel in his heart, "O, let me not lose my head this day as I meet temptation, as I am tempted to misjudge my fellows. Keep me from trespassing upon the rights of others."

Reverence

A third principle that contributes to a right religious attitude is *Reverence—reverence for the Sabbath day* and all things sacred. Reverence directs thought toward God. Without it there is no religion. Let us not make Sunday a holiday. It is a holy day, and on that day we should go to the house of worship and seek our God. If we seek him on the Sabbath day, come into his presence on that day, we shall find it less difficult to be in his presence the other days of the week.

There should be more reverence for the house of worship. All are supposed to have come to meet him and worship him, and there should be present that spirit of order and reverence which will direct the worshiper's thoughts in the right channel.

God help us to serve him with our minds, might, and strength. With kind consideration for all mankind, and particularly for those who have given us honored names and pure lives, with prayer and reverence in our hearts, may we seek first the kingdom of God and his righteousness.

Chapter Three

How to
Gain a
Testimony

Several years ago a stranger sat in the gallery of the Salt Lake Tabernacle and listened to the testimony of one of the elders of the Church. He accompanied a man who had been excommunicated from the Church. As they were walking out of the grounds, the stranger said, referring to the testimony of the speaker that day, "Do you know, I would give all I possess if I knew that what that speaker said today is true."

The Most Valuable Possession

There is nothing a man can possess in this world which will bring more comfort, more hope and faith, than a testimony of the existence of a Heavenly Father who loves us, or of the reality of Jesus Christ, his Only Begotten Son, that those two heavenly personages appeared to the Prophet Joseph Smith and established the Church of Jesus Christ, and that men are officially authorized to represent Deity.

Scientists are seeking that knowledge, some of them in vain. One of them not long ago declared that he had failed to find it; that he had lost his faith even in God. However, Dr. Cressy Morrison, eminent scientist and author of the book, *Man Does Not Stand Alone,* impressively leads the world to accept the existence of God's guidance. You who have heard missionaries return and bear witness that they know this gospel is true will remember, probably, when as boys and girls, you, too, would have given anything if you could so testify to the truth.

Our young men and women are eagerly longing to have that testimony. Of its value, there is no question. Of its reality, too, there is no question in the minds of leaders and members of the Church who possess an absolute knowledge of these things.

What Is a Testimony?

But as I have listened to the testimonies that have been borne, I have often wondered how many of us are showing our young people *how* they may know, and if we are sufficiently emphasizing the fact that they will never gain a testimony if they indulge in sin; that they will never know if they live to gratify their passions and appetites. "My spirit shall not always strive with man." (Genesis 6:3; see D.&C. 1:33; Moses 8:17.) His spirit will not dwell in unclean tabernacles. ". . . The Spirit of the Lord doth not dwell in unholy temples." (Helaman 4:24.) Do they know that one cannot have a testimony without the Spirit of God?

I shall just name three steps that will aid our young people in obtaining this priceless possession, and ask that they follow them.

On the night of Gethsemane, Jesus offered a great prayer in which he said: "And this is life eternal, that they might know thee the only true God, and Jesus Christ, whom thou hast sent." (John 17:3.)

That is what a testimony means. To know God, and Jesus Christ, is to have life eternal, the great possession of eternal life.

A Step Toward Testimony

But the question arises—How may I know? Jesus has answered it, as he has shown the way in every aspect of life.

One day, when he bore testimony to his divinity, and that his teachings were of God, the Pharisees and others around him said, "How knoweth this man letters, having never learned?" How do we know you are divine?—that was their question. And Jesus gave them a simple answer: "If any man will do his will, he shall know of the doctrine, whether it be of God, or whether I speak of myself." (John 7:15, 17.) There is a definite answer—a clear-cut statement for our young people seeking a testimony: *If ye will do the will, ye shall know.* And, *to know God, and Jesus Christ, whom he has sent, is eternal life.*

However, there still remains unanswered the question: What is God's will? On one occasion several thousand people asked that question, saying: "Men and brethren, what shall we do?" It was on the Day of Pentecost, and Peter, who had received a testimony and instructions from the Savior, answered:

. . . Repent, and be baptized every one of you in the name of Jesus Christ for the remission of sins, and ye shall receive the gift of the Holy Ghost. For the promise is unto you, and to your children, and to all that are afar off, even as many as the Lord our God shall call. (Acts 2:38, 39.)

Did you note that first sentence, that first condition? Repentance, which is a changing of life. If you have been swearing, stop it. That is what repentance means. If you have been disobeying father and mother, cease your disobedience. If you have been thinking impure thoughts, substitute for them noble ideas. Repentance means ever to change your thoughts and acts for the better.

Developing Testimony

A lawyer, a Pharisee, asked Christ, on one occasion, "Which is the great commandment in the law?" (Matthew 22:36.) And in answer, most profound, Jesus said the first fundamental law is to "love the Lord thy God with all thy heart, and with all thy soul, and with all thy mind, and with all thy strength." (Mark 12:30.) "And the second is like unto it, Thou shalt love thy neighbour as thyself." (Matthew 22:39.) And the Pharisee admitted that Jesus had spoken wisely.

Analyze that and you will find it means that instead of centering your thoughts on self, God becomes the center of your existence; your thoughts will be—what you are going to do for him. You will pray to him at night. You will pray to him when you have some heavy task to perform. Even in your school work you should pray. I know you may not hear his voice always, and you may feel that he did not answer your question in your prayer; but in youth, keep praying and holding to the assurance that God is near you to help you.

The Holy Ghost a Reality

Christ has given us "all things that pertain unto life and godliness, through the knowledge of him that hath called us to glory and virtue: Whereby are given unto us exceeding great and precious promises: that by these ye might be partakers of the divine nature" (II Peter 1:3-4); that is, the Holy Ghost promised by Peter, to live in this world and be a partaker of the divine nature of our Father in heaven.

I bear witness to you that that is a reality. I ask our young men and women never to lose sight of it. And then, after Peter bore witness that that is a reality, he said this:

. . . Add to your faith virtue; and to virtue knowledge;

And to knowledge temperance [note the words]; and to temperance patience; and to patience godliness;

And to godliness brotherly kindness; and to brotherly kindness charity [*love*].

Now, note the promise:

For if these things be in you, and abound, they make you that ye shall neither be barren nor unfruitful in the knowledge of our Lord Jesus Christ [of the things of God]. (II Peter 1:5-8.)

15

And to know God is eternal life!

These are divine steps that lead back to the presence of God, our Eternal Father, and I trust that our young people and all in the Church will follow those steps and that each one will gain the precious gift of a knowledge of the divinity of this work.

Chapter Four

Reverence:
A Sign of Nobility
and Strength

As we enter into the New Year, there is one message which I should like to stress, and one appeal I should like to make to the leaders and membership of this Church. I have in mind the need of more reverence in our houses of worship, better order and discipline in our classrooms, in quorum meetings, and in auxiliary groups.

The more we try to cultivate the attributes of the Savior, the stronger we become in character and in spirituality. We should so live that we may be susceptible to the inspiration of the Holy Ghost and to his guidance.

I do not know who it was who wrote that the whole purpose of life might be summed up: "to subdue matter that we might realize the ideal." When I first read that, I thought I could paraphrase it and say: The whole purpose of life is to bring under subjection the animal passions, proclivities, and tendencies, that we might realize the companionship always of God's Holy Spirit.

One chief purpose of life is to overcome evil tendencies, to govern our appetites, to control our passions—anger, hatred, jealousy, immorality. We have to overcome them, to conquer them, because God has said: "My spirit will not dwell in unclean tabernacles, nor will it always strive with man." (See Genesis 6:3; D.&C. 1:33.)

Self-control the Basis of Reverence

The principle of self-control lies at the basis of reverence and good order in classrooms. I do not know how to define reverence, but I do know how to classify or to place it as one of the objectives of nobility; indeed, one of the attributes of Deity.

Love is the divinest attribute of the human soul. I am not so sure but sympathy is next to it—sympathy for the afflicted, for our brethren and sisters, for suffering animals. That is a Godlike virtue!

Kindness is also a sublime virtue. The first sentence in what is now known as the Psalm of Love is this: "Charity suffereth long, and is kind. . . ." (I Corinthians 13:4.)

However, in my thinking, I am prompted to place reverence next to love. Jesus mentioned it first in the Lord's prayer: ". . . Our Father which art in heaven, Hallowed be thy name . . ." (Luke 11:2.) Hallowed—to make holy—to hold in reverence.

When Jesus cleansed the temple, he was filled with reverent indignation because men were desecrating his father's house, selling doves and lambs to be offered as sacrifice. Money-changers were there for the convenience of those who came from other countries so they could give in local currency their temple contributions. Seemingly, in their own eyes, they were justified, but they were doing these things in the house of God. We are told that he overturned the money-changers' tables and said to the sellers of doves, ". . . Take these things hence; make not my Father's house an house of merchandise." (John 2:16.) Ruskin wrote:

Reverence is the noblest state in which a man can live in the world. Reverence is one of the signs of strength; irreverence, one of the surest indications of weakness. No man will rise high who jeers at sacred things. The fine loyalties of life must be reverenced or they will be foresworn in the day of trial.

Charles Jefferson, the author of *The Character of Jesus*, writes:

18

Men in many circles are clever, interesting, brilliant, but they lack one of the three dimensions of life. They have no reach upward. their conversation sparkles, but it is frivolous and often flippant. Their talk is witty, but the wit is often at the expense of high and sacred things.

You can tell a true soul of wit by the things of which he makes light. The best humorous writers avoid making light of religion or of sacred things. Jefferson continues:

One finds this lack of reverence even in the church. In every community there are those who treat the house of God as they treat a streetcar, entering it and leaving it when they please. Even habitual church attendants often surprise and shock one by their irreverent behavior in the House of Prayer. Those persons are not ignoramuses or barbarians; they are simply undeveloped in the virtue of reverence.

Order Important in Classrooms

Our classrooms are sometimes places of boisterousness. Here is where we need good teachers. A teacher who can present a lesson interestingly will have good order, and when he or she finds students who are rebellious, flipping papers, paying no attention, stumbling, kicking one another, he or she may know that the lesson is not being properly presented. Perhaps it was not even properly prepared.

One of our mothers recently went to a Sunday School class to try to find out why her son was losing interest. There was so much boisterousness, so much confusion, so much noise, that she felt heartsick; and as she arose to leave, she said to the teacher: "I thought this was a Sunday School class, not a bedlam!"

Self-control, self-mastery, is one of the fundamental purposes of life. You see it exemplified in the life of the Savior on the Mount of Temptation when he resisted the tempter. There is a lesson of life to us all in the temptation which he withstood. Satan tauntingly tempts us, and unless we resist and have in mind a higher goal than the mere indulgence or gratification of the physical, we are going to weaken, and the tempter will gain in strength.

19

Self-control Begins at Home

The lesson of self-control should begin in childhood in the home. Little children should have a sense of freedom to do as they wish up to a certain point. Beyond that point, they cannot go; and that is when that freedom interferes with the rights, comfort, or convenience of another member of the family.

I have referred before to an incident that occurred in a zoo. It is simple, and some may think we should not go to monkeys for lessons. I think they can teach us something. Sister McKay and I stood one day, I believe it was at San Diego, watching a mother monkey with a newborn babe. She was guarding it, her quick eye watching the other monkeys in the cage; but the little babe was free to do just as it pleased, hopping around, weak in its infancy, getting hold of the bars, starting to climb, etc. However, when it would reach a certain place, the mother would reach up and bring it back. When it got into a danger point, that mother instinctively guarded it, and said, "Back this way"; and then the babe was free again, but only within certain limits.

I said to Sister McKay, "There is a lesson of life in guiding children."

In the classrooms children should be taught, should be free to discuss, free to speak, free to participate in classwork, but no member of the class has the right to distract another student by jostling or making light and frivolous remarks. I think in this Church, in the priesthood quorums and classes, and in auxiliaries, teachers and leaders ought not to permit it. Disorder injures the child who makes it. He should learn that when he is in society there are certain things which he cannot do with impunity. He cannot trespass upon the rights of his associates.

Let children learn this lesson in youth, because when they get out in society and try to trespass against the law, they will feel restraining hands and probably suffer punishment.

Good Order Develops Self-control

Good order in the classroom is essential to instill into the hearts and lives of young men and young women the principle of self-control. They want to talk and they want to whisper, but they cannot do it because it will disturb somebody else. Learn the power and lesson of self-mastery.

Reverence should be particularly manifest in sacrament meeting, in quorum meetings, in Sunday School, in MIA, in Primary, yes, and in Relief Society. This is a missionary church. People come to our houses of worship for light and knowledge, for instruction; and they have a right to find it when they come. Disorder and irreverence should not interfere with that right.

I plead with you stake presidents, bishops, and auxiliary leaders to develop a Christ-like attribute of reverence in our houses of worship and better discipline in our classrooms; and I believe you can lead in it.

It is said: "For where two or three are gathered together in my name, there am I in the midst of them." (Matthew 18:20.) And I tell you when he is present, we should be reverent.

Someone said that if Shakespeare were to enter one of our houses of worship, we should all stand up to greet him, but if Christ entered, we should fall on our knees and worship him.

God bless our leaders as guides to youth, to increase their influence with those among whom they labor. The Lord help us all during the coming New Year to sanctify our houses of worship, that our chapels may indeed be sacred places in which we meet to worship God!

Chapter Five

Meditation, Communion, Reverence

THE greatest comfort in this life is the assurance of having a close relationship with God. It has been said that "consciousness of God is the highest achievement in human experience and is the supreme goal of human life. This is true religion. It is a mental, spiritual experience of the highest order." Many of our members know what that experience is.

The Value of Meditation

A house of worship furnishes an opportunity to commune with one's self and to commune with the Lord, especially during the sacrament period. Sunday is a day of worship which we turn over to him. We may rest assured that he will be there in that house of worship to inspire us if we come in proper attunement to meet him. We are not prepared to meet him if we bring thoughts regarding business affairs, and especially if we bring feelings of hatred towards our neighbor, or enmity and jealousy toward the authorities of the Church. Most certainly no individual can hope to come into communion with the Father if that individual entertains any such feelings, as they are foreign to worship and particularly out of tune with the partaking of the sacrament.

I think we pay too little attention to the value of meditation, a principle of devotion. In our worship there are two elements: One is spiritual communion arising from our own meditation; the other, instruction from others, particularly from those who have authority to guide and instruct us. Of the two, the more profitable introspectively is *meditation.* Meditation is the language of the soul. It is defined as "a form of private devotion or spiritual exercise, consisting in deep, continued reflection on some religious theme. Meditation is a form of prayer. We can say prayers without having any spiritual response. We can say prayers as the unrighteous king in *Hamlet,* who said: "My words fly up, my thoughts remain below: Words without thoughts never to heaven go."[1]

The poet, contrasting the outward form of worship and the prayer of the soul, said:

> The Power, incens'd, the pageant will desert,
> The pompous strain, the sacerdotal stole;
> But haply in some cottage far apart,
> May hear, well-pleas'd, the language of the soul,
> And in His Book of Life the inmates poor enroll.[2]

Inner Power of Meditation

Meditation is one of the most secret, most sacred doors through which we pass into the presence of the Lord. Jesus set the example for us. As soon as he was baptized and received the Father's approval, "This is my beloved Son, in whom I am well pleased" (Matthew 3:17), Jesus repaired to what is now known as the Mount of Temptation where, during the forty days of fasting, he communed with himself and his Father and contemplated the responsibility of his own great mission. One result of this spiritual communion was such strength as enabled him to say to the tempter: "Get thee hence, Satan: for it is written, Thou shalt worship the Lord thy God, and him only shalt thou serve." (Matthew 4:10.)

----

[1] William Shakespeare, *Hamlet,* Act III, Scene 3.
[2] Robert Burns, "The Cotter's Saturday Night," verse 17.

Before he gave to the Twelve the beautiful Sermon on the Mount, he was in solitude, in communion. He did the same thing after that busy Sabbath day, when he arose early in the morning after having been the guest of Peter. Peter undoubtedly found the guest chamber empty, and when he and others sought Jesus they found him alone. It was on that morning that they said: "All men seek for thee." (Mark 1:37.)

Again, after Jesus had fed the five thousand, he told the Twelve to dismiss the multitude. Then Jesus, the historian says, went to the mountain for solitude; and "when the evening was come, he was there alone." (Matthew 14:23.) Meditation! Prayer!

The Best Opportunity for Meditation

I believe the short period of administering the sacrament is one of the best opportunities we have for such meditation, and there should be nothing during that sacred period to distract our attention from the purpose of that ordinance.

One of the most impressive services I have ever attended was in a group of over eight hundred people to whom the sacrament was administered, and during that administration not a sound could be heard except the ticking of the clock—eight hundred souls, each of whom at least had the opportunity of communion with the Lord. There was no distraction, no orchestra, no singing, no speaking. Each one had an opportunity to search himself introspectively and to consider his worthiness or unworthiness to partake of the sacrament. His was the privilege of getting closer to his Father in heaven. That is ideal!

We recommend that this sacred ordinance be surrounded with more reverence, with perfect order; that each one who comes to the house of God may meditate upon and silently and prayerfully express appreciation for God's goodness. Let the sacrament hour be one experience of the day in which the worshiper tries at least to realize within himself that it is possible for him to commune with his God.

Great events have happened in this Church because of such communion, because of the responsiveness of the soul to the inspiration of the Almighty. I know it is real. You will find that when these most inspirational moments come to you, you are alone with yourself and your God. They come to you probably when you are facing a great trial, when a wall is across your pathway, and it seems that you are facing an insurmountable obstacle, or when your heart is heavy because of some tragedy in your life. I repeat, the greatest comfort that can come to us in this life is to sense the realization of communion with God.

Great testimonies have come in those moments. It is just such experience as that which came to my father in the north of Scotland when he prayed to God to remove from him the spirit of gloom and despondency that overwhelmed him. After a night of worry and restlessness, he arose at daylight and repaired to a cave on the shore of the North Sea. He had been there before in prayer. There, just as the rays of the morning light began to come over the sea, he poured out his soul to God as a son would appeal to his father. The answer came: "Testify that Joseph Smith is a prophet of God!" The cause of his discouragement flashing upon his mind, he said aloud: "Lord, it is enough!"

Those who knew my father could testify as to his integrity and his honesty. A testimony of that kind has one hundred percent value.

These secret prayers, these conscientious moments in meditation, these yearnings of the soul to reach out to feel the presence of God—such are your privilege and mine.

Only Silence During the Sacred Ordinance

Some think that music helps to intensify that feeling of communion. When you stop to consider the matter, you realize that there is nothing during the administration of the sacrament so important as remembering our Lord and Savior, nothing so worthy of attention as considering the value of the promise we are making. Why should anything distract us? Is there anything more sublime? We are witnessing there, in the presence of one another and before him, our Father, that we are willing to take upon ourselves the name of Christ, that we will always remember him, that we will keep his commandments that he has given us. Can you, can anybody living who thinks for a moment, place before us anything which is more sacred or more far-reaching in our lives? If we partake of it mechanically, we are not honest, or, let us say, we are permitting our thoughts to be distracted from a very sacred ordinance.

One man said, "Oh, but the beautiful music of the choir helps us to concentrate." Concentrate on what? The more beautiful the music, the more your attention is attracted to it, to the musician, or to the composer. If it is beautiful music poorly played, then the discord distracts your attention. Have that music in preparation up to the moment, yes; but when the prayer is said, and that young priest speaks for us, as he does, then remember that we are placing ourselves under covenant. It will be ideal if, during the fifteen minutes, every man, woman, and child will think as best he can of the significance of that sacred ordinance.

The lesson I wish to leave is: Let us make that sacrament hour one of the most impressive means of coming in contact with God's spirit. Let the Holy Ghost, to which we are entitled, lead us into his presence, so that we may sense that nearness, and have in our hearts a prayer which he will hear.

Reverence Is Spirituality

Inseparable from the acceptance of the existence of God is an attitude of reverence. The greatest manifestation of spirituality is reverence; indeed, reverence is spirituality. Reverence is profound respect mingled with love. It is a "complex emotion made up of mingled feelings of the soul." Carlyle says it is "the highest of human feelings." If reverence is the highest, then irreverence is the lowest state in which a man can live in the world. Be that as it may, it is nevertheless true that an irreverent man has a crudeness about him that is repellent. He is cynical, often sneering, and always iconoclastic.

Reverence embraces regard, deference, honor, and esteem. Without some degree of it, therefore, there would be no courtesy, no gentility, no consideration of others' feelings or of others' rights. Reverence is the fundamental virtue in religion. It is one of the signs of strength; irreverence, one of the surest indications of weakness. "No man will rise high," says one man, "who jeers at sacred things. The fine loyalties of life," he continues, "must be reverenced or they will be foresworn in the day of trial."

Churches Are for Meeting God

Churches are dedicated and set apart as houses of worship. This means that all who enter do so, or at least pretend to do so, with an intent to get nearer the presence of the Lord than they can in the street or amidst the worries of a workaday life. In other words, we go to the Lord's house to meet him and to commune with him in spirit. Such a meeting place, then, should first of all be fitting and appropriate in all respects, whether God is considered as the invited guest, or the worshipers as his guests.

Whether the place of meeting is a humble chapel or a "poem in architecture" built of white marble and inlaid with precious stones makes little or no difference in our approach and attitude toward the Infinite Presence. To know that God is there should be sufficient to impel us to conduct ourselves orderly, reverently. Presiding authorities in stake, ward, and quorum meetings, and especially teachers in classes, should make a special effort to maintain better order and more reverence during the hours of worship and study. Less talking behind the pulpit will have a salutary effect upon those who face it. By example and precept, children should be impressed with the inappropriateness of confusion and disorder in a worshiping congregation. They should be impressed in childhood, and have it emphasized in youth, that it is disrespectful to talk or even to whisper during a sermon, and that it is the height of rudeness, except in an emergency, to leave a worshiping assembly before dismissal.

Prepare and Become Reverent

Reverence for God's name should be dominant in every home. Profanity should never be expressed in a home in this Church. It is wrong; it is irreverent to take God's name in vain. There is no provocation which will justify it. Let us apply that quality and that virtue of reverence at all times.

If there were more reverence in human hearts, there would be less room for sin and sorrow and increased capacity for joy and gladness. To make more cherished, more adaptable, more attractive, this gem among brilliant virtues is a project worthy of the most united and prayerful efforts of every officer, every parent, and every member of the Church.

May we through worship, meditation, communion, and reverence sense the reality of being able to have a close relationship with our Father in heaven. I bear you my testimony that it is real; that we can commune with our Heavenly Father, and if we so live to be worthy of the companionship of the Holy Spirit, he will guide us into all truth; he will show us things to come; he will bring all things to our remembrance; he will testify of the divinity of the Lord Jesus Christ and of the restoration of the gospel.

Chapter Six

Obedience
Develops
Character

WHAT is the end and purpose of religion, "swaying the lives of men the centuries through"? Members of The Church of Jesus Christ of Latter-day Saints answer in the words of the Lord revealed through the Prophet Joseph Smith, that the end and purpose of true religion, which is the work of God, is ". . . to bring to pass the immortality and eternal life of man." (Moses 1:39.)

And what is the crowning glory of man in this earth so far as his individual achievement is concerned? It is *character —character developed through obedience to the laws of life as revealed through the gospel of Jesus Christ, who came that we might have life and have it more abundantly.* Man's chief concern in life should not be the acquiring of gold nor fame nor material possessions. It should *not* be the development of physical prowess nor of intellectual strength, *but his aim, the highest in life, should be the development of a Christlike character.*

Four Pictures of Importance and Beauty

There are four pictures upon which I always love to look. Three are imaginary; one is real. The first of these is the picture of Christ before Pilate when that Roman official said to the angry mob, "Behold, the Man!" As he said it, he pointed to Jesus, crowned with thorns, and bearing upon his shoulders a purple robe. The angry mob sneered and condemned him as a felon and blasphemer; and yet when Pilate said, "Behold, the Man!" he described one who was perfect in character; one who was a conqueror over weaknesses and temptations, and one who could say, and did say, to his fellow workers, "Peace be unto you! I have overcome the world." He is our pattern!

The other picture is Christ in his youth. Have you not admired the paintings of the best artists who have tried to picture purity and strength in that young boy of 12 years? I have; and I never look upon one of the choicest of these without feeling that I am looking upon one who is the embodiment of youthful strength, vigor, and purity.

The third picture is of a boy described by Nathaniel Hawthorne who looked upon the great stone face, and, while thinking of the ideals and virtues characterized in that great work of nature, developed those same virtues in his own life.

The fourth is a picture in real life, a youth whose clear eyes picture the strength of young manhood and the purity of the life he has led. What more beautiful thing can one see in nature than that? We love beauty in womanhood; we also love beauty and strength in young manhood, and that strength and beauty come as a result of true living.

I am grateful to be associated with the members of the priesthood of The Church of Jesus Christ of Latter-day Saints, the greatest organization in the world for the building of character; an organization which is striving to bring to pass the end and purpose of true religion, which is the immortality and eternal life of man. This earth life is the probationary state through which every soul must pass. By overcoming difficulties and temptations, and by rendering service to others, each may develop toward the Christ-character as he revealed it among men. It is a glorious ideal; it is inspiring!

Two Ways in Which Character Is Built

There are two ways in which we build this character in the youth of our Church. One is positive. In that positive development we ask our boys and young men to participate in the various organizations and quorums of the priesthood. Fathers, do we realize what this means in the development of the character of our boys? I ask that we go from this meeting with a determination to unite with the officers and teachers in these associations in helping them to win the interest of our children who participate in these organizations —the Sunday School, the Mutual Improvement Association, the Primary. These organizations, with our seminaries and church schools, are but auxiliaries in this great organization of character-building. They are but helps to the priesthood. No youth in the Church who reaches the age of 12 should be excluded from membership in the deacons quorum; and that membership should signify a clean life, a prayerful life, and faith in the gospel of Jesus Christ. Every bishop should ask the boys of his ward what their attitude is in regard to these things before he ordains them to the priesthood. This is true of the teachers quorum and the priests quorum. That is but a glimpse of the positive means of character-building, and the bringing of our children to Christ.

Now, there is alongside these positive means, a *negative means*. All through life the Latter-day Saint child is asked to refrain from indulgence in things that will tend to weaken character. He is asked to keep the Word of Wisdom; he is asked to keep himself pure and unspotted from the sin of immorality. That is a wonderful thing, especially when the community and the Church uphold that teaching.

In the Church we have long known of the evils and detrimental effects of cigarette smoking, and I ask that all these auxiliary forces in the Church cooperate in assisting youth to resist the evil of cigarette smoking. This habit is an indulgence which tends to weaken manhood and to undermine character.

One of the most significant statements in the Word of Wisdom, *one which carries with it evidence of the inspiration of the Prophet Joseph Smith*, is found in the following statement ". . . In consequence of evils and designs which do and will exist in the hearts of conspiring men in the last days, I have warned you, and forewarn you, by giving unto you this word of wisdom by revelation." (D.&C. 89:4.) *"Evils and designs which do and will exist in the hearts of conspiring men"*—the purport of that statement impressed me way back in the twenties and thirties of this century.

I ask you to recall the methods employed by certain tobacco interests to induce women to smoke cigarettes. You remember how insidiously they launched their plan: First, by saying that smoking would reduce weight. Their slogan was: "Take a cigarette instead of a sweet." Later, some of us noticed in the theater that they would have a young lady light the gentleman's cigarette. Following this, a woman's hand would be shown on billboards lighting or taking a cigarette. A year or two passed, and soon they were brazen enough to show the lady on the screen or on the billboard smoking the cigarette.

I have a newspaper clipping I set aside in 1931 which corroborates this idea. It reads: "It is well known that the cigarette manufacturers are now after the young women and girls. They say there are twenty-five million of these in the United States, and if they can popularize smoking among them, they will be able to increase their sales from three billion, six hundred million dollars annually, to six billion dollars. This is their claim and their aim."

Now, as you all know, it is common to see beautiful young women depicted on billboards and in magazine advertisements smoking cigarettes; and now, most insidious of all, are the cigarette advertisements which come into our homes by way of television and are viewed by our boys and girls, of young men and young women smoking in the most enticing scenes possible.

Our youth should be taught the hazards of cigarette smoking to health. They should be taught that doctors and scientists now have established a direct tie to cancer in cigarette smoking.

Smoking Brings Disability and Death

Emerson Foot, chairman of the National Interagency Council on Smoking and Health, has testified that:

it has been concluded by responsible scientific authorities that cigarette smoking is responsible for at least 125,000 and possibly 300,000 deaths a year in this country. But death is not the only thing, it is beyond doubt that there are millions of people who suffer varying degrees of disability brought on by cigarette smoking. (Deseret News, March 23, 1965, p. A7.)

Somewhere between sixty and eighty percent of boys and men, and a somewhat lesser number of girls and women, are already habituated to cigarettes, or they are confirmed addicts.

The high death rates from cigarette smoking have created a demand from many interested groups for positive action that will lessen the dangers to health. The Royal College of Physicians of Great Britain, the American Cancer Society, and the United States Public Health Service have led the way in creating public reaction against smoking. The American Cancer Society has supported research generously and has kept the public and the medical profession informed on the problems connected with smoking. The Surgeon General of the Public Health Service has used his official and moral influence in emphasizing the dangers involved in smoking.

These agencies, as well as the great body of research scientists, have compiled the evidence and stated the facts so clearly that every reasonable mind is fully aware of the danger entailed in smoking.

Advertising Stepped Up

Notwithstanding the admission of danger from smoking, the advertising of cigarettes by the tobacco companies has been stepped up to an all-time peak. Yet there is never a hint that smoking is already a major threat to life. Instead, the advertising constantly emphasizes the mildness of the cigarette and its pleasurable qualities. This cigarette advertising is promoted with such reckless abandon, in spite of what research has already proved regarding the dangers from smoking, that the most charitable conclusion to be drawn is that the promoters have no regard whatever for the value of human life. It seems that success for the tobacco industry is more important than avoiding suffering and death.

One hundred and thirty-two years ago a 27-year-old youth told the world that tobacco was harmful for the human body. Members of The Church of Jesus Christ of Latter-day Saints were given by divine revelation the Word of Wisdom, in which they were advised to refrain from the use of tobacco in any form. They were promised better health as a result. This was strange, as no one knew of any danger from smoking at that time. Most of the members accepted and applied the instructions given. The demonstration presented today by more than two million people of the Church should be impressive to any skeptic. Hundreds of thousands of teenage youths have never smoked. They know that smoking is a destructive habit that mars the human body, as well as the mind.

Our homes should establish the fact that the boy who indulges in cigarettes is not contributing to his advancement and growth in the Church and kingdom of God, neither is he preparing himself for his responsible place in society. The word of God to the Prophet Joseph Smith is that tobacco is not good for man. The statement is not qualified in any way. Scientists have demonstrated it; men who have tried to disprove it have failed, and we as a people stand committed

to that command from God. Keep the habit of smoking and
the use of tobacco in any form out of the lives of our boys.
Resistance of the appetite will react upon the character and
strengthen it, and just because a man has developed the
habit is no justification for his continuing it. Just because
some man may think he is immune to the ill effects of tobacco
is no justification for its use in the priesthood of God.

Fathers and mothers and leaders in the Church have
the obligation of setting an example worthy of imitation to
the youth. Remember, even though you may have the habit,
overcoming it will make you stronger.

> It is easy enough to be virtuous
> When nothing tempts you to stray,
> When without or within no voice of sin
> Is luring your soul away.
> But it is only a negative virtue
> Until it is tried by fire,
> And the soul that is worth the honor of earth
> Is the soul that resists desire.

To our boys I would say that if they want to live physically, if they want to be men strong in body, vigorous in
mind; if they want to be good in sports, enter the basketball
game, the football game, the contest in running and jumping;
if they want to be good scouts; if they want to be good
citizens, in business, anywhere, they should avoid tobacco
and live strictly the religious life.

May God help us as leaders in the Church, as fathers
and mothers, to reach our boys and girls, our young men and
women, and impress upon them this great lesson, this divine
truth, that to be carnally minded is to be miserable, unhappy;
but to be spiritually minded, which means to obey the principles of the gospel in all that it means, is to have life, life
eternal, and peace.

Chapter Seven

Treasures
of Truth in
Modern Revelation

THE gospel and spiritual things should ever be uppermost in the minds of members of the Church. If we would devote more time to the real things in life and less time to those things that will perish, if we would resist the various temptations that are in our midst and adopt the teachings of the gospel in our lives, we should really become a light upon a hill, a light that could not be hid.

If we would devote more study to modern revelations as contained in the Doctrine and Covenants, we would grow in appreciation of the magnitude of the great work that has been established in this dispensation. It is often said that the Church is the greatest thing in the world. It is—but the more we give attention to it and realize how well adapted it is to our individual life, to our home life, to our social life; when we study it from the standpoint of our environment, from the standpoint of scientific discoveries, our hearts are made to rejoice because of God's goodness to us in giving us the privilege of knowing the gospel of Jesus Christ.

Revelation Replete with Admonitions

Nearly every passage in the Doctrine and Covenants is replete with admonitions, and is full of inspiration and wonderful revelations to men. Sometimes those revelations are couched in but few words, but by careful study one sees how closely related they are to all truth. Take for example that wonderful, simply expressed revelation in regard to government by the priesthood: "No power or influence can or ought to be maintained by virtue of the priesthood, only by persuasion, by long-suffering, by gentleness and meekness, and by love unfeigned." (D.&C. 121:41.) Just think of the word "unfeigned."

Love *pretended* has no influence. Love *unfeigned* always has the power to reach the heart. The revelation continues: "Reproving betimes with sharpness, . . . and then showing forth afterwards an increase of love toward him whom thou hast reproved, lest he esteem thee to be his enemy." (D.&C. 121:43.) What a wonderful admonition and lesson in regard to government, not only in the quorums of priesthood in the Church, but also in our home life and in all phases of association in society!

Consider the statement of the Lord in regard to the worth of souls—"Remember the worth of souls is great in the sight of God." (D.&C. 18:10.) Also the revelation in regard to true riches—"Seek not for riches but for wisdom, and behold, the mysteries of God shall be unfolded unto you, and then shall you be made rich. Behold, he that hath eternal life is rich." (D.&C. 6:7.)

Adherence Yields Faith, Rejoicing

We might continue, revelation after revelation, as given in the Doctrine and Covenants, which if studied and heeded by the Latter-day Saints would establish faith in their hearts and make them rejoice at this great and wonderful organization placed among men for their salvation.

Not the least among these by any means is that revelation on the Word of Wisdom. There are just one or two little paragraphs in it that refer to the use of strong drink: "That inasmuch as any man drinketh wine or strong drink among you, behold it is not good. . . ." (D.&C. 89:5.) Just a simple statement; it is unqualified, but there it stands. Strong drinks are not good for the body! That revelation was given in 1833—the word of God, not only to the people who are members of the Church, but to the inhabitants of the world wherever that book has been published; wherever it has been distributed by the elders of the Church, the word of God has been sounded to the world.

People have thus been told by revelation that it is not good to indulge in these intoxicating beverages, but they have wavered; and some Latter-day Saints have wavered. They have been very much as ancient Israel with the gods of Baal. Elijah came amongst them and denounced their worship of idols, and said, ". . . How long halt ye between two opinions? if the Lord be God, follow him: but if Baal, then follow him. And the people answered him not a word." (1 Kings 18:21.) There, too, the people were halting; many of them knew in a way that Israel's God was omnipotent; that he it was who could save them, and yet the other gods offered pleasure, offered indulgence; and the people halted, some trying to serve and yield obedience to both. The Prophet Elijah told them to stop trying to serve one God today and then fall back in obedience to the teachings of the other on the morrow. You know the test that was decided upon; you know the result, and the death that came to the priests of Baal.

Multitudes Halt between Two Opinions

For more than a century the word of God has been given to the people of this day to refrain from indulgence in tobacco and to refrain from indulgence in strong drink, and still many falter in obedience. How long, Israel, halt ye between two opinions? The Lord has said that strong drink is not good. Men are declaring, "We don't want the people to drink more beer, but we want *more people* to drink beer." Which teaching, will the people heed? One declared in the voice of Omnipotence that beer, alcoholic beverages, are not good;

the other declared it is good, and he wants to develop the appetite of the people so more people will drink. "How long halt ye between two opinions?"

What does it mean *to obey God's word,* to refrain from indulgence in narcotics and alcoholic beverages? It means stronger manhood; it means brighter intellects; it means stronger and more perfect physical organisms; it means better and truer husbands, more devoted and affectionate fathers; it means parenthood that will transmit to children clean habits, and power in the will to resist temptation of appetite and greater temptations of passion that may come to them; it means happy homes, contented wives; well-dressed and better-educated children; it means a safe and sound citizenship which goes for the buliding of a safe and sound nation; it means salvation for the individual in the kingdom of God. A little thing?

Indulgence Induces Depravity

On the other hand, what does *indulgence mean?* Weakened manhood, a weakened will, a physical organism that will transmit weakness to unborn generations; it means the cutting off of life by slow suicide; it means the derangement of mental faculties; it means the breaking up of homes; it means broken-hearted wives, destitute children, a weakened society; it means the maiming and killing of people on our highways—that is what it means!

Members of the Church should be determined to live in accordance with the teachings and admonitions given us. We should be strong enough to introduce the principles given into active life; and after doing that as individuals, we should see that we use our influence with our children; and remember, example in the home will go further in helping our children than will our teaching. Children are entitled to a kingly birth, whether they must live in a mud hovel or in a palace, it makes no difference—a kingly birth, inherited strength, physical strength, moral strength, and spiritual up-lift.

"Why halt ye, Israel, between two opinions? if the Lord be God, follow him: but if Baal, then follow him."

Chapter Eight

Necessity
of
Repentance

THERE are many people in the world who doubt that the ordinance of baptism is essential to salvation; but it is inconceivable to think that anyone can even question the essentiality of repentance. Every principle of the gospel when studied carefully reveals a harmony with truth that is simply sublime. Each seems to be all-comprehensive, either leading into or embracing other principles. Thus faith in a perfect being, inspiring one to live righteously, seems to include repentance. So, forgiveness may encompass charity, love, forbearance, etc.

This harmony, or rather this oneness of all fundamental principles of the gospel, is indicative of their being elements of eternal truth. Truth, being "the sum of existence," is all-comprehensive! Faith, repentance, charity, forgiveness, and every other element of truth will of necessity show a close relationship not only to each other, but also to the whole of which they are a part.

It is difficult, therefore, to designate any one principle as being *the* most important. One student may name this, and another name that as being chief, the choice of each being determined by the amount of study and attention given to the favorite principle. When comparing eternal principles, it is more nearly correct to say that each is equal to any other.

This thought, however, does not lessen the significance of the great Thomas Carlyle's forceful remark about repentance. "Of all acts of man," he says, "repentance is the most divine. The deadliest sin, I say, were that same supercilious consciousness of no sin; that is death; the heart so conscious is divorced from sincerity, humility and, in fact, is dead." Plainly, the penetrating mind of the Scottish philosopher glimpsed the eternal nature of this divine principle.

Know What Faults You Have

What progress can there be for a man unconscious of his faults? Such a man has lost the fundamental element of growth, which is the realization that there is something bigger, better, and more desirable than the condition in which he now finds himself. In the soil of self-satisfaction, true growth has poor nourishment. Its roots find greater succor in discontent.

> Our pleasures and our discontents
> Are rounds by which we may ascend.

Heaven pity the man who is unconscious of a fault! Pity him also who is ignorant of his ignorance! Neither is on the road to salvation. "The greatest of faults is to be conscious of none."

The first step to knowledge is a realization of the lack of it; and the first step toward spiritual growth is the belief in a higher and better life, or conversely, a realization of the meanness of one's present state. Repentance is the turning away from that which is low and the striving for that which is higher. As a principle of salvation, it involves not only a desire for that which is better, but also a sorrow—not merely remorse—but *true sorrow* for having become contaminated in any degree with things sinful, vile, or contemptible.

Change in Conduct

It is not uncommon for people to have remorse for mistakes made, for follies and sins committed, but to have *no turning away* from such frailties and evils. They may even feel penitent; but "penitence," we are told, "is transient, and may involve no change of character or conduct." Repentance, on the other hand, "is sorrow for sin with *self-condemnation, and complete turning away from the sin.*" It is, therefore, more than mere remorse; "*it comprehends a change of nature befitting heaven.*"

Every principle and ordinance of the gospel of Jesus Christ is significant and important in contributing to the progress, happiness, and eternal life of man; *but there is none more essential to the salvation of the human family than the divine and eternally operative principle, repentance.* Without it, no one can be saved. Without it, no one can even progress. Its sublimity and essentiality stirred the Prophet Alma's soul when he exclaimed:

O that I were an angel, and could have the wish of mine heart, that I might go forth and speak with the trump of God, with a voice to shake the earth, and cry repentance unto every people!

Yea, I would declare unto every soul, as with the voice of thunder, repentance and the plan of redemption, that they should repent and come unto our God, that there might not be more sorrow upon all the face of the earth. (Alma 29:1, 2.)

Avoid Ignorance and Sin

Ignorance and sin are man's worst enemies. They are barriers to salvation. Only through repentance and obedience to the gospel can these be eradicated. In the repentant man's soul, these evils are supplanted by light and knowledge. From him who will not repent ". . . shall be taken even the light which he has received; for my Spirit shall not always strive with man, saith the Lord of Hosts." (D.&C. 1:33.)

It is the duty of the elders of the Church, first, to apply to their own lives this eternal principle; and, secondly, to "go forth and speak with the [power] of God . . . and cry repentance unto every people." (See Alma 29:1.)

For all men must repent and be baptized, and not only men, but women, and children who have arrived at the years of account-ability. (D.&.C. 18:42.)

Chapter Nine

The Lord's Sacrament

Wherefore whosoever shall eat this bread, and drink this cup of the Lord, unworthily, shall be guilty of the body and blood of the Lord. But let a man examine himself, and so let him eat of that bread, and drink of that cup. (1 Corinthians 11:27, 28.)

No more sacred ordinance is administered in the Church of Christ than the administration of the sacrament. It was initiated just after Jesus and the Twelve had partaken of the last supper, and the saints in the early days followed that custom. That is, they ate before they administered the sacrament; but that custom was later discontinued by instruction from Paul to the saints to eat their meal at home so that when they met for worship they might meet as a body of brethren and sisters on the same level to partake of the sacrament in remembrance of the life and the death, particularly the death of their Lord.

Evaluate, Covenant, and Commune

There are three things fundamentally important associated with the administration of the sacrament. The first is self-discernment. It is introspection. "This do in rememberance of me," but we should partake worthily, each one examining himself with respect to his worthiness.

Secondly, there is a covenant made; a covenant even more than a promise. You have held up your hand, some of you; or, if in England when signing a document, put your hand on the Bible, signifying the value of your promise or of the oath that you took. All this indicates the sacredness of a covenant. There is nothing more important in life than that. Until the nations realize the value of a covenant and a promise, and conduct themselves accordingly, there will be little trust among them. Instead there will be suspicion, doubt, and signed agreements, "scraps of paper," because they do not value their word. A covenant, a promise, should be as sacred as life. That principle is involved every Sunday when we partake of the sacrament.

Thirdly, there is another blessing, and that is a sense of close relationship with the Lord. There is an opportunity to commune with oneself and to commune with the Lord. We meet in the house that is dedicated to him; we have turned it over to him; we call it his house. Well, you may rest assured that he will be there to inspire us if we come in proper attune to meet him. We are not prepared to meet him if we bring into that room our thoughts regarding our business affairs, and especially if we bring into the house of worship feelings of hatred towards our neighbor, or enmity and jealously towards the authorities of the Church. Most certainly no individual can hope to come into communion with the Father if that individual entertains any such feelings. They are so foreign, particularly, to the partaking of the sacrament.

The Value of Meditation

I think we pay too little attention to the value of meditation, a principle of devotion. In our worship there are two elements: One is spiritual communion arising from our own meditation; the other, instruction from others, particularly from those who have authority to guide and instruct us. Of the two, the more profitable introspectively is the meditation. Meditation is the language of the soul. It is defined as "a form of private devotion, or spiritual exercise, consisting in deep, continued reflection on some religious theme." Meditation is a form of prayer. We can say prayers without having any spiritual response. We can say prayers as the unrighteous king in *Hamlet* who said: "My words fly up, my thoughts remain below: Words without thoughts never to heaven go."

The poet, contrasting the outward form of worship, and the prayer of the soul, said:

> The Power, incensed, the pageant will desert,
> The pompous strain, the sacerdotal stole;
> But haply, in some cottage far apart,
> May hear, well-pleased, the language of the soul,
> And in His Book of Life the inmates poor enroll.[1]

Meditation is one of the most secret, most sacred doors through which we pass into the presence of the Lord. Jesus set the example for us. As soon as he was baptized and received the Father's approval, "This is my Beloved Son, in whom I am well pleased," Jesus repaired to what is now known as the mount of temptation. I like to think of it as the mount of *meditation* where, during the forty days of fasting, he communed with himself and his Father, and contemplated upon the responsibility of his great mission.

Before he gave to the Twelve the beautiful sermon on the mount, he was in solitude, in communion. He did the same thing after that busy Sabbath day, when he arose early in the morning after having been the guest of Peter. Peter and others undoubtedly found the guest chamber empty, and when they sought him they found him alone. It was on that morning that Peter and others said: ". . . All men seek for thee." (Mark 1:37.)

-----

[1] Robert Burns, "The Cotter's Saturday Night."

Again, after Jesus had fed the five thousand he told the Twelve to dismiss the multitude, but Jesus went to the mountain for solitude. The historian says, ". . . when the evening was come, he was there alone." (Matthew 14:23.) Meditation! Prayer!

Meditation in Prayer

I once read a book written by a very wise man, whose name I cannot now recall, which contained a significant chapter on prayer. The author was not a member of the Church, but evidently had a desire to keep in close communion with God, and he wanted to find the truth. Among other things he said in substance:

> In secret prayer go into the room, close the door, pull down the shades, and kneel in the center of the room. For a period of five minutes or so, say nothing. Just think of what God has done for you, of what are your greatest spiritual and temporal needs. When you sense that, and sense his presence, then pour out your soul to him in thanksgiving.

I believe the short period of administering the sacrament is one of the best opportunities we have for such meditation, and there should be nothing during that sacred period to distract our attention from the purpose of that ordinance.

Reverence during Meditation

One of the most impressive services I have ever attended was in a group of over 800 people to whom the sacrament was administered, and during that administration not a sound could be heard excepting the ticking of the clock—800 souls, each of whom at least had the opportunity of communion with the Lord. There was no distraction, no orchestra, no singing, no speaking. Each one had an opportunity to search himself introspectively and to consider his worthiness or unworthiness to partake of the sacrament. His was the privilege of getting closer to his Father in heaven. That is ideal!

Brethren, we recommend that we surround this sacred

ordinance with reverence, with perfect order; that each one who comes to the house of God may meditate upon his goodness, and silently and prayerfully express appreciation for God's goodness. Let the sacrament hour be one experience of the day in which the worshiper tries at least to realize within himself that it is possible for him to commune with his God.

Great events have happened in this Church because of such communion, because of the responsiveness of the soul to the inspiration of the Almighty. I know it is real. President Wilford Woodruff had that gift to a great extent. He could respond; he knew the "still small voice" to which some are still strangers! You will find that when these most inspirational moments come to you that you are alone with yourself and your God. They come to you probably when you are facing a great trial, when the wall is across your pathway, and it seems that you are facing an insurmountable obstacle, or when your heart is heavy because of some tragedy in your life. I repeat, the greatest comfort that can come to us in this life is to sense the realization of communion with God.

Blessings from Meditation

Great testimonies have come in those moments. It is just such an experience as that which came to my father in the north of Scotland when, as I have told some of you before, he prayed to God to remove from him a spirit of gloom and despondency that overwhelmed him. After a night of worry and restlessness, he arose at daylight and repaired to a cave on the shore of the North Sea. He had been there before in prayer. There, just as the rays of the morning light began to come over the sea, he poured out his soul to God as a son would appeal to his father. The answer came: "Testify that Joseph Smith is a prophet of God!" The cause of his discouragement flashing upon his mind, he said aloud: "Lord it is enough!"

There are those who knew my father and can testify to

his integrity and his honesty. A testimony of that kind has 100-per cent value.

These secret prayers, these conscientious moments in meditation, these yearnings of the soul to reach out to feel the presence of God—such is the privilege of those who hold the Melchizedek Priesthood.

The Sacredness of the Sacrament

There should be nothing during the administration of the sacrament of an extraneous nature that would prevent us from *remembering* our Lord and Savior, nothing so worthy of attention as considering the value of the promise we are making. Why should anything distract us? Is there anything more sublime? We are witnessing there, in the presence of one another, and before him, our Father, that we are willing to take upon ourselves the name of Christ, that we will always remember him, that we will keep his commandments that he has given us. Can you, can anybody living, who thinks for a moment, place before us anything which is more sacred or more far-reaching in our lives? If we partake of it mechanically, we are not honest; or, let us say, we are permitting our thoughts to be distracted from a very sacred ordinance.

Have sacramental music in preparation up to the moment, yes, but when the prayer is said, and that young priest speaks for us, as he does, then remember that we are placing ourselves under covenant. It will be ideal if, during the fifteen minutes, every man, woman, and child will think as best he or she can of the significance of that sacred ordinance.

Proper Administration

There is one other point which might be associated with the passing of the sacrament. It is a beautiful, impressive thing to have our boys administer it. They are the servants; they are waiting upon the Lord; and have come there because they are worthy to officiate if the bishop has spoken to them properly. ". . . be ye clean, that bear the vessels of the Lord." (Isaiah 52:11.) If every deacon could sense this, quietly and with dignity he would pass the sacrament to us.

The Aaronic Priesthood bearer should carry the sacrament to the presiding officer, not to honor him, but the office, as you would honor the presidents of the Church. That presiding officer may be the bishop of the ward; if so, let the young man carry the sacrament first to the bishop. After that, pass it to one after the other who sit either on the left or the right of the presiding officer, not going back to the first and second counselors and then to the superintendent. The lesson is taught when the sacrament is passed to the presiding officer. The next Sunday the president of the stake may be there, who is then the highest ecclesiastical authority Do you see what the responsibility of the deacons and the priests is? There is a lesson in government taught every day. It is their duty to know who is the presiding officer in that meeting that day. Next Sunday there may be one of the general authorities. Those young men will have in mind the question, "Who is here today, and who is the presiding authority?"

Aspire to Spiritual Communion

But the lesson I wish to leave is: Let us make that sacrament hour one of the most impressive means of coming in contact with God's Spirit. Let the Holy Ghost, to which we are entitled, lead us into his presence, and may we sense that nearness, and have a prayer offered in our hearts which he will hear.

God help us so to live that we may sense the reality, as I bear you my testimony it is real, that we can commune with our Father in heaven; and if we so live to be worthy of the companionship of the Holy Spirit, he will guide us into all truth; he will show us things to come; he will bring all things to our remembrace; he will testify of the divinity of the Lord Jesus Christ, as I do, and of the restoration of the gospel.

51

Chapter Ten

The
Reality of
the Resurrection

. . . Ye seek Jesus of Nazareth
which was crucified: he is risen; he
is not here: behold the place where
they laid him. (Mark 16:6.)

THROUGHOUT Christendom we
are celebrating, this Eastertide, the greatest event of all
history—the literal resurrection of Jesus Christ. For over
four thousand years, man had looked into the grave and had
seen only the end of life. Of all the millions who had entered
therein, not one person had ever returned as a resurrected,
immortal being. "There was in all earth's area, not one
empty grave. No human heart believed; no human voice
declared that there was such a grave—a grave robbed by the
power of a victor stronger than man's great enemy, death."

It was, therefore, a new and glorious message that the
angel gave to the women who fearfully and lovingly had approached the sepulcher in which Jesus had been buried:
". . . Ye seek Jesus of Nazareth, which was crucified: he is
risen; he is not here: behold the place where they laid him."
(Mark 16:6.)

If a miracle is a supernatural event whose antecedent
forces are beyond man's finite wisdom, then the resurrection
of Jesus Christ is the most stupendous miracle of all time.

In it stand revealed the omnipotence of God and the immortality of man.

The resurrection is a miracle, however, only in the sense that it is beyond man's comprehension and understanding. To all who accept it as fact, it is but a manifestation of a uniform law of life. Because man does not understand the law, he calls it a miracle. There are many people who reject the reality of the resurrection of Jesus. They believe, or profess to believe, in the teachings of Christ, but do not believe in the virgin birth, nor in his literal resurrection from the grave; yet, this latter fact was the very foundation of the early Christian church. Even some of the religious leaders of the present day are claiming that Jesus is dead.

Someday man's enlightenment may bring the momentous event of the resurrection out of the dusk of mystery into the broad day of understanding.

Just recently a scientist, in speaking before a university audience, said, "Man has only begun the search. I cannot stop being amazed and reverent at the wonders of the universe around me. It is hard to imagine that this just happened without the intervention of a power beyond man's comprehension. Anyone who denies the existence of a power beyond man's specific knowledge, lacks the necessary humility and objectivity which is vital for good scientific work."[1]

Establish it as a fact that Christ did take up his body and appeared as a glorified, resurrected being, and you answer the question of the ages: "If a man die, shall he live again?" (Job 14:14.)

That the literal resurrection of Christ from the grave was a reality to the disciples who knew him intimately is a certainty. In their minds there was absolutely no doubt. They were witnesses of the fact; they knew because their eyes beheld, their ears heard, their hands felt the corporeal presence of the risen Redeemer.

------

[1]Dr. Elie A. Shneour, quoted in *Church News*, March 12, 1966.

Peter, the chief apostle, on the occasion when the eleven had met to choose one to take the place of Judas Iscariot, said, "Wherefore of these men . . . must one be ordained to be a witness with us of his resurrection." (Acts 1:21, 22.)

It always interests me to study about the class of men who surrounded the apostles at that time, from whom the apostles chose this special witness. They were men who had been "witnesses" of the resurrection. Only such a one was considered eligible and worthy to be chosen as one of the Twelve Apostles.

On another occasion Peter declared before their enemies, the very men who had put Jesus to death on the cross: "Ye men of Israel, hear these words . . . . This Jesus hath God raised up, whereof we all are witnesses." (Acts 2:22, 32.)

Of the value and significance of the nearness and intimacy of the authors of the epistles, the author Beverly Nichols writes:

[They] were within hailing distance, historically, of Christ; at any rate, when their ideas, which they afterwards transmitted to paper, were formed. The winds had hardly had time to efface the sacred print of his steps in the sands over which He walked. The rain had hardly had time to wash away, with its callous tears, the blood from the rotting wood of the deserted cross.

Yet these men knew—I can't go on using the word "believe," which is far too vapid and colourless—that God had descended to earth in the shape of a certain man, that this man had met an obscene and clownish death, and that the grotesque mode of his dying had redeemed mankind from sin. They knew, moreover, that He had risen from the dead on the third day and ascended into heaven.[2]

Nearness to the event gives increased value to the evidence given by the apostles. A deeper value of their testimony lies in the fact that with Jesus' death the apostles were stricken with discouragement and gloom. For two and one-half years they had been upheld and inspired by Christ's

---

[2]Beverly Nichols, *The Fool Hath Said* (New York: Doubleday, 1936.), pp. 56-57.

presence. But now he was gone. They were left alone, and they seemed confused and helpless. Not with timidity, not with feelings of doubt, gloom, and discouragement is a skeptical world made to believe. Such wavering, despairing minds as the apostles possessed on the day of the crucifixion could never have stirred people to accept an unpopular belief and to die martyrs to the cause.

What, then, was it that suddenly changed these disciples to confident, fearless, heroic preachers of the gospel of Jesus Christ? It was the revelation that Christ had risen from the grave. "His promises had been kept, his Messianic mission fulfilled."

I urge all to consider carefully the testimonies of these eyewitnesses as recorded in the New Testament, whose honesty is not questioned even by skeptical criticism.

That the spirit of man passes triumphantly through the portals of death into everlasting life is one of the glorious messages given by Christ, our Redeemer. To him this earthly career is but a day and its closing but the setting of life's sun. Death, but a sleep, is followed by a glorious awakening in the morning of an eternal realm. When Mary and Martha saw their brother only as a corpse in the dark and silent tomb, Christ saw him still a living being. This fact he expressed in the two words: ". . . Lazarus sleepeth. . . ." (John 11:11.)

If everyone participating in Easter services knew that the crucified Christ actually rose on the third day—that after having greeted others and mingled with others in the spirit world, his spirit did again reanimate his pierced body, and after sojourning among men for the space of forty days, he ascended a glorified soul to his Father—what benign peace would come to souls now troubled with doubt and uncertainty!

The Church of Jesus Christ of Latter-day Saints stands with Peter, with Paul, with James, and with all the other early apostles who accepted the resurrection not only as being literally true, but as the consummation of Christ's divine mission on earth.

Eighteen hundred years after Jesus died upon the cross, the Prophet Joseph Smith declared that the risen Lord appeared to him, saying: ". . . I saw two Personages, whose brightness and glory defy all description, standing above me in the air. One of them spake unto me, calling me by name and said, pointing to the other—*This is My Beloved Son. Hear Him!*" (Joseph Smith 2:17.)

Later, speaking of the reality of this vision, he testifies as follows: ". . . I had seen a vision; I knew it, and I knew that God knew it, and I could not deny it, neither dared I do it; at least I knew that by so doing I would offend God, and come under condemnation." (Joseph Smith 2:25.)

If Joseph Smith's testimony stood alone, it would be, as Christ said of his testimony when he spoke of himself, of no avail; but Jesus had God's testimony and that of the apostles. And Joseph Smith had other witnesses, whose testimonies cannot be questioned. Three witnesses corroborated Joseph Smith's testimony, the truth of which was made known by the appearance to them of the Angel Moroni.

Confirming the irrefutable testimony of Christ's early apostles, The Church of Jesus Christ of Latter-day Saints proclaims the glorious vision of the Prophet Joseph Smith:

> And now, after the many testimonies which have been given of him, this is the testimony, last of all, which we give of him: That he lives!
> For we saw him, even on the right hand of God; and we heard the voice bearing record that he is the Only Begotten of the Father—
> That by him, and through him, and of him, the worlds are and were created, and the inhabitants thereof are begotten sons and daughters unto God. (D.&C. 76:22-24.)

In the light of such unimpeachable testimonies as given by the ancient apostles—testimonies dating from a few years subsequent to the event itself—in the light of that most marvelous revelation in this age of the living Christ, it seems difficult indeed to understand how men can still reject him and can doubt the immortality of man.

An unwavering faith in Christ is the most important need of the world today. It is more than a mere feeling. It is power that moves into action, and should be in human life the most basic of all motivating forces.

It was in this sense that an eminent doctor of medicine, who had but recently lost his mother in death, admonished his students to keep their faith. Said he,

Those of you who have discarded faith will live to regret it. There are times such as this when you lose a loved one by death that science is entirely inadequate. I commend you to think seriously about these matters. They give comfort and solace which can be obtained in no other way. Many have discarded religion because it appears unscientific. I believe you will find in the last analysis that Faith is scientific.

There is no cause to fear death; it is but an incident in life. It is as natural as birth. Why should we fear it? Some fear it because they think it is the end of life, and life often is the dearest thing we have. Eternal life is man's greatest blessing. If only men would "do his will," instead of looking hopelessly at the dark and gloomy tomb, they would turn their eyes heavenward and know that Christ is risen!

No man can accept the resurrection and be consistent in his belief without accepting also the existence of a personal God. Through the resurrection Christ conquered death and became an immortal soul. "My Lord and my God" (John 20:28) was not merely an idle exclamation of Thomas when he beheld his risen Lord. Once we accept Christ as divine, it is easy to visualize his Father as being just as personal as he; for, said Jesus, ". . . he that hath seen me hath seen the Father. . . ." (John 14:9.)

The Church of Jesus Christ of Latter-day Saints declares to all the world that Christ is the Son of God, the Redeemer of the world! No true follower is satisfied to accept him merely as a great reformer, the ideal teacher, or even as the one perfect man. The Man of Galilee is—not figuratively, but *literally*—the Son of the living God.

Belief in the resurrection connotes also the immortality of man. Jesus passed through all the experiences of mortality just as you and I. He knew happiness, he experienced pain. He rejoiced as well as sorrowed with others. He knew friendship. He experienced, also, the sadness that comes through traitors and false accusers. He died a mortal death even as you will. Since Christ lived after death, so shall you, and so shall I, and so shall your soldier boy who gives his life on the battlefield.

Jesus was the one perfect man who ever lived. In rising from the dead, he conquered death and is now Lord of the earth. How utterly weak, how extremely foolish is he who would willfully reject Christ's way of life, especially in the light of the fact that such rejection leads only to unhappiness, misery, and even to death!

No man can sincerely resolve to apply in his daily life the teachings of Jesus of Nazareth without sensing a change in his whole being. The phrase "born again" has a deeper significance than what many people attach to it. This changed feeling may be indescribable, but it is real. Happy is the person who has truly sensed the uplifting, transforming power that comes from this nearness to the Savior this kinship to the living Christ. I am thankful that I know that Christ is my Redeemer.

When Christians throughout the world have this faith coursing in their veins, when they feel a loyalty in their hearts to the Resurrected Christ and to the principles connoted thereby, mankind will have taken the first great step toward the perpetual peace for which we daily are praying. Reject him and the world will be filled with hatred and drenched in blood by recurring wars.

Members of the Church of Christ are under obligation to make the sinless Son of Man their ideal. He is the one perfect being who ever walked the earth; the sublimest example of nobility; godlike in nature; perfect in his love; our Redeemer; our Savior; the immaculate Son of our Eternal Father; the Light, the Life, the Way.

As Christ lives after death, so shall all men, each taking that place in the next world for which he is best fitted.

The message of the resurrection, therefore, is the most comforting, the most glorious ever given to man, for when death takes a loved one from us, our sorrowing hearts are assuaged by the hope and divine assurance expressed in the words: *"He is not here; he is risen!"*

With all my soul I know that death is conquered by Jesus Christ, and because our Redeemer lives, so shall we. I bear you witness that he does live. I know it, and I hope you know that divine truth.

May all mankind some day have that faith, I pray in the name of Jesus Christ. Amen.

Chapter Eleven

Responsibility
of the
Priesthood

A great responsibility rests upon the priesthood of this Church to teach the truths of the gospel, and the members should be aroused to the realization that the enemies of truth are just as active today as they were when two powers stood before the Creator and each presented his plan, and when Christ was on earth and tempted on the mount.

Nearly two thousand years ago Peter, the chief apostle, addressed the elders of the Church in that day. He said:

I . . . am also an elder, and a witness of the sufferings of Christ, and also a partaker of the glory that shall be revealed.

Then he said to the elders,

Feed the flock of God . . . being ensamples to the flock. (1 Peter 5:1-3.)

Be sober, be vigilant: because your adversary the devil, as a roaring lion, walketh about, seeking whom he may devour:

Whom resist stedfast in the faith, knowing that the same afflictions are accomplished in your brethren that are in the world. (1 Peter 5:8-9.)

These quotations give an insight into the troubles they had in that day.

Testimony That Came from Home

The older I grow the more grateful I am for my parents, for their example in that old country home; both father and mother lived the gospel.

I realize, as perhaps never before, that my testimony of the reality of the existence of God dates back to that home when I was a child, and it was through my parents' teachings and their examples that I received as a child the absolute knowledge that God is my Father; that I received then the knowledge of the reality of the spiritual world; and I testify that it is so, that it is a reality.

It is easy for me to accept as a divine truth the fact that Christ preached to the spirits in prison while his body lay in the tomb. His body was silent; his spirit was in the spiritual realm with his Father. It is true!

It is just as easy for me to realize that one may so live that he may receive impressions and direct messages through the Holy Ghost. The veil is thin between those who hold the priesthood and those on the other side of the veil. That testimony began in the home in my youth because of the example of a man — a father who lived the priesthood — and his wife, who sustained him and lived it in the home.

I do not know that Peter had that in mind particularly when he mentioned being an example to the flock, but I know that such a home is a part of that flock. The influence you spread in your home will go throughout the town, will go throughout the country, the wards, and the stakes.

My testimony was increased and strengthened through the training and teaching I received in the auxiliary organizations and priesthood quorums of the Church.

By Those In Authority

The most precious thing in the world is a testimony of the truth. Truth never grows old, and the truth is that God is the source of your priesthood and mine.

May 15 marks the anniversary of the restoration of the

Aaronic Priesthood. On that day in the year 1829, John the Baptist came to earth as a heavenly messenger and conferred this authority upon Joseph Smith and Oliver Cowdery. John, the son of Zacharias, was probably the last among the Jews to hold the keys of the Aaronic Priesthood, which continued among the children of Israel from the time that Moses and the higher priesthood were taken from their midst until the coming of Christ in the meridian of time. From the standpoint of direct authority, therefore, it is highly fitting that John should be the messenger to restore this authority in this dispensation. He held it not only by right of lineage, but also by special ordination when he was eight days old.

This question of divine authority is one of the important factors which distinguish the Church of Jesus Christ from the Protestant creeds of Christendom. In plain, unmistakable terms, the Church declares that "a man must be called of God, by prophecy, and by the laying on of hands, by those who are in authority to preach the gospel and administer in the ordinances thereof."[1] In this declaration, the Church but reiterates the words of one who bore Christ's authority in the meridian of time, and who, in writing upon this very question, said, "And no man taketh this honour unto himself, but he that is called of God, as was Aaron." (Hebrews 5:4.)

The Order and Will of Christ

Herein lies one secret of the strength of this great latter-day work. Its origin consists not in the whims, the desires, or the aspirations of men, but in the order and the will of Christ himself, the author of our eternal salvation. If one man could assume the right to speak in the name of the Lord, other men would have the same privilege. If these many men all presumed to say, "Thus saith the Lord," yet did not see "eye to eye" on important elements of God's kingdom, the inevitable result would be confusion, and sincere men and women would be driven from, not attracted to, Christ's

---

[1]Articles of Faith No. 5.

Church, yet these eventually would be made to suffer for not having obeyed the principles of life and salvation.

Yet the real cause of their failure to accept these eternal principles would be the fact that unauthorized men arrogated to themselves the right to officiate in things pertaining to God. Herein lies the explanation of the discordant condition existing among jarring creeds in the so-called Christian world today. Men who have no right so to do are officiating in the name of Christ. The result, of course, is confusion. Whatever else may be said of the Prophet Joseph Smith, the strength of his position in regard to divine authority must be recognized.

If the world could but realize the full significance of the Angel John's coming again to earth, May 15, 1829, multitudes who are praying for the kingdom of God to be established among men would gratefully join in the commemoration of that heavenly manifestation. Their souls would respond to the ecstatic joy that Oliver Cowdery expresses in his description of the event as follows:

On a sudden, as from the midst of eternity, the voice of the Redeemer spake peace to us, while the veil was parted, and the angel of God came down clothed with glory, and delivered the anxiously looked-for message, and the keys of the gospel of repentance. What joy! what wonder! what amazement! While the world was racked and distracted—while millions were groping as the blind for the wall, and while all men were resting upon uncertainty, as a general mass, our eyes beheld, our ears heard, as in the "blaze of day"; yes, more—above the glitter of the May sunbeam, which then shed its brilliancy over the face of nature! Then his voice, though mild, pierced to the center, and his words, "I am thy fellow-servant," dispelled every fear. We listened, we gazed, we admired! 'Twas the voice of an angel from glory, 'twas a message from the Most High! And as we heard we rejoiced, while his love enkindled upon our souls, and we were wrapped in the vision of the Almighty! Where was room for doubt? Nowhere; uncertainty had fled, doubt had sunk no more to rise, while fiction and deception had fled forever! [2]

---

[2]Pearl of Great Price, p. 57.

Who Stands at the Head of The Church?

Christ did not confer the Aaronic Priesthood direct, but recognized John the Baptist, by whose authority Jesus himself had been baptized, and in the case of the Melchizedek Priesthood, it was restored through Peter, James, and John, unto whom Christ himself had given authority when he established his Church at Jerusalem.

Jesus the Christ is the source of the power of the priesthood. As long as members of the priesthood merit the guidance of Christ by honest and conscientious dealing with their fellowmen, by resisting evil in any of its forms, by the faithful performance of duty, there is no opposing power in this world which can stay the progress of the Church of Jesus Christ.

Jesus Christ, the great High Priest, stands at the head of this Church, and every man who holds the priesthood, if he lives properly, soberly, industriously, humbly, and prayerfully, is entitled to the inspiration and guidance of the Holy Spirit.

God help us to defend the truth—better than that, to live it. Exemplify it in our homes. What we owe to our parents we cannot express. Are you going to have that same influence on your children, parents—mothers—fathers, bearers of the priesthood?

Standing
and Speaking
for the Right

If any man offend not in word, the same is a perfect man, and able also to bridle the whole body.

Behold, we put bits in the horses' mouths, that they may obey us; and we turn about their whole body.

Behold also the ships, which though they be so great, and are driven by fierce winds, yet are they turned about with a very small helm, withersoever the governor listeth.

Even so the tongue is a little member, and boasteth great things. Behold, how great a matter a little fire kindleth!

And the tongue is a fire, a world of iniquity: so is the tongue among our members, that it defileth the whole body, and setteth on fire the course of nature; and it is set on fire of hell.

For every kind of beasts, and of birds, and of serpents, and of things in the sea, is tamed, and hath been tamed of mandkind:

But the tongue can no man tame; it is an unruly evil, full of deadly poison.

Therewith bless we God even the Father; and therewith curse we men, which are made after the similitude of God.

Out of the same mouth proceedeth blessing and cursing. My brethren, these things ought not so to be.

Doth a fountain send forth at the same place sweet water and bitter?

Can the fig tree, my brethren, bear olive berries? either a vine, figs? so can no fountain both yield salt water and fresh.

Who is a wise man and endued with knowledge among you? let him shew out of a good conversation his works with meekness of wisdom.

But if ye have bitter envying and strife in your hearts, glory not, and lie not against the truth.

This wisdom descendeth not from above, but is earthly, sensual, devilish.

For where envying and strife is, there is confusion and every evil work.

But the wisdom that is from above is first pure, then peaceable, gentle, and easy to be intreated, full of mercy and good fruits, without partiality, and without hypocrisy.

And the fruit of righteousness is sown in peace of them that make peace. (James 3:2-18.)

So wrote the Apostle James many hundred years ago, but I feel that, like all truth, what he expresses in these lines is applicable today. The tongue is but a little member, yet a most effective means of giving wings to our thoughts and of influencing one another.

Then let us speak well of everyone when we can do it truthfully!

> Nay, speak no ill; a kindly word
> Can never leave a sting behind;
> And, oh, to breathe each tale we've heard
> Is far beneath a noble mind.[1]

Then, say you, would you not speak of evil conditions? Must we not raise our voices in denouncing conditions and men who are bringing evil upon us? Yes, speak of conditions; but do not falsely revile the character of men. We cannot do

-----

[1]*Hymns—Church of Jesus Christ of Latter-day Saints*, No. 116.

it as true Latter-day Saints; we must rise above it. There is a trait in the heart of the world to pick at their fellowmen. Emerson says that so pronounced is this tendency that an accident cannot happen in the street without the bystanders becoming animated with a faint hope the victim will die. We cannot encourage that tendency. As James says, it is "earthly, sensual, devilish."

We must not pick out that which will tear down a brother's character, nor the character of our Founding Fathers, nor the works of those great men who founded the Constitution of the United States. Let us be true to our nation! There is every reason to be true to it.

If we see a condition in a town that endangers the lives of our fellow citizens, we meet that condition. If it is a washout, a cave, a hole in the roadway, there is a warning lamp or sign placed there to keep the travelers from falling into it; and as soon as possible the dangerous condition is remedied. That is proper.

You will remember when Napoleon's cuirassiers made the fatal charge against Wellington, that there lay between them and the English soldiers a sunken road. Napoleon stood away off and could not see it. He had asked a man if there were any obstacles and had received no as the answer; trusting to that, he gave the command for the brigade to charge. The "Invincible Column" rushed on, until they came, it is said, to a sunken road, and then horse and rider piled one upon another till the whole abyss was filled with a living debris that made a bridge of the broken bodies of horse and man.

There are, perhaps, sunken roads in our communities. Let us see them and not stand off and say that they are all right when our young people by the score are rushing headlong into them. It is our duty to meet these conditions, but let us do it calmly; let us do it determinedly, and take the high stand of right. Let the men whom you elect and appoint to represent you in your communities know that you desire to have these "sunken chasms" closed before more human beings are piled or dragged down to destruction. But, I repeat again, in meeting these conditions, we can take the high stand of truth.

The gospel is our anchor. We know what it stands for. And knowing this, let us do forthrightly what should be done, avoiding irresponsible gossip and evil speaking. Let us be what we should be and do what we should do—and keep control of our tongues.

Chapter Thirteen

Something
Higher
than Self

It is difficult for me to put even in outline the message that I have in my heart for the people of the Church and the people of the world. There is a saying by Paul, that "to be carnally minded is death; but to be spiritually minded is life and peace." (Rom. 8:6.)

Carnal relates, as you know, to the physical. It includes sensual. But we have in mind this morning the physical surroundings and our animal instincts, the anger that comes to us, the unpleasant words that are spoken, making life unpleasant, rather than emphasizing the spiritual side, the real side of our nature.

The text was suggested several weeks ago, particularly emphasized at that time, by a report that came to me of unpleasantness in a home, and I wondered why we cannot emphasize spiritual attitudes in our homes instead of unpleasant attitudes; why, having before us all the admonitions of the Lord, all the opportunities offered by the Church, we cannot express spiritual attitudes every day of our lives. What good is religion if it does not make our daily lives better? Why need there be emphasis put upon the carnal side of our natures? True, that is the natural reaction for all animals. But having in our possession the high principles of the gospel as revealed through Christ, why cannot members of the Church at least in the home, in school, in all their associations, emphasize the spiritual side of their natures instead of the carnal side?

I learned through a letter of a condition which I think, so far as members of the Church are concerned, is absolutely inexcusable. A husband and wife quarreling—the husband demeaning himself to such an extent as to curse his wife, and in a mad fit of anger overturning a table spread with dishes— a creature in the form of a man harboring the nature of an animal! A man in such a mental state that the anger itself does him more harm than the condition which aroused his anger, and in reality, brothers and sisters, he suffers more from the vexation than he does from the acts that aroused that vexation.

I wonder how long it will take us to realize that in matters of temper nothing can bring us damage but ourselves— we are responsible for what helps us and for what injures us— that the harm that each one sustains he carries about with him, and never is he a real sufferer but by his own fault. I think you get that thought, and yet the tendency of each one is to blame somebody else, the wife blaming the husband, the husband blaming the wife, children finding fault with the parents when the fault lies with themselves. If in the dignity of manhood such a man would cease to magnify his troubles; would face things as they really are; recognize blessings that immediately surround him; cease to entertain disparaging wishes for another; how much more of a man he would be, to say nothing about being a better husband and a more worthy father! A man who cannot control his temper is not very likely to control his passion, and no matter what his pretensions in religion, he moves in daily life very close to the animal plane.

Religion is supposed to lift us on a higher level. Religion appeals to the spirit in man, the real person, and yet how often notwithstanding our possessing a testimony of the truth, we yield to the carnal side of our nature. The man who quarrels in his home, banishes from his heart the spirit of religion. A mother in this Church who would light a cigarette in the home is yielding to the carnal side of her nature. How far below the ideal of the Church! Any quarreling in the home is antagonistic to the spirituality which Christ would have us develop within us, and it is in our daily life that these expressions have their effect.

Man is making great progress in science and invention, greater perhaps than ever before, but is not making comparable progress in character and spirituality.

I read awhile ago of a remark of General Omar N. Bradley, formerly Army's Chief of Staff, who on one occasion said:

> With the monstrous weapons man already has, humanity is in danger of being trapped in this world by its moral adolescence. Our knowledge of science has clearly outstriped our capacity to control it. We have too many men of science; too few men of God. We have grasped the mystery of the atom and rejected the Sermon on the Mount. Man is stumbling blindly through a spiritual darkness while toying with the precarious secrets of life and death.
>
> The world has achieved brilliance without wisdom, power without conscience. Ours is a world of nuclear giants and ethical infants. We know more about war than we know about peace, more about killing than we know about living.

Our living comes hourly and daily in the home, in our association in business affairs, in our meeting strangers. It is the attitude of the person during the daily contacts by which we show whether we are appealing to the carnal or to the spiritual within us and within those with whom we associate. It is a daily matter. I do not know whether we can get the thought over or not. And it is within the power of each one, especially members of the Church who make such pretensions. You cannot imagine a real, true Christian, and especially a member of the Mormon Church, swearing at his wife. Why, it is inconceivable that such a thing as that could be in a home and especially with children around. How can anyone justify parents quarreling in front of children! In the instance to which I have referred the man (I should say the *brute*) even struck his wife. Such a thing should never be. That is out of the life of Church members.

Christ has asked us to develop the spiritual within us.

Man's earthly existence is but a test as to whether he will concentrate his efforts, his mind, his soul upon things which contribute to the comfort and gratification of his physical nature or whether he will make his life's purpose the acquisition of spiritual qualities.

Every noble impulse, every unselfish expression of love, every brave suffering for the right; every surrender of self to something higher than self; every loyalty to an ideal; every unselfish devotion to principle; every helpfulness to humanity; every act of self-control; every fine courage of the soul, undefeated by pretence or policy, but by being, doing, and living of good for the very good's sake—that is spirituality.

The spiritual road has Christ as its ideal—not the gratification of the physical, for he that will save his life, yielding to that first gratification of a seeming need, will lose his life, lose his happiness, the pleasure of living at this present time. If he would seek the real purpose of life, the individual must live for something higher than self. He hears the Savior's voice, saying: "I am the way, the truth, and the life." (John 14:6.) Following that voice he soon learns that there is no one great thing which he can do to attain happiness or eternal life. He learns that "life is made up not of great sacrifices or duties, but of little things in which smiles and kindness and small obligations given habitually are what win and preserve the heart and secure comfort."

Spirituality, our true aim, is the consciousness of victory over self, and of communion with the Infinite. Spirituality impels one to conquer difficulties and acquire more and more strength. To feel one's faculties unfolding, and truth expanding in the soul, is one of life's sublimest experiences.

"The thing a man does practically lay to heart," says Carlyle, "and know for certain concerning his vital relations to this mysterious Universe, and his duty and destiny there, that is in all cases the primary thing for him, and creatively determines all the rest. . . . And, I say, if you tell me what that is, you tell me to a very great extent what the man is, what the kind of things he will do is."

The man who sets his heart upon the things of the world, who does not hesitate to cheat his brother, who will lie for gain, who will steal from his neighbor, or, who, by slander, will rob another of his reputation, lives on a low, animal plane of existence, and either stifles his spirituality or permits it to lie dormant. To be thus carnally minded is to be spiritually dead.

On the other hand, keeping in mind our daily vocations, the man who tills the soil, garners his fruit, increases his flocks and his herds, having in mind making better the world in which he lives, desiring to contribute to the happiness of his family and his fellows, and who does all things for the glory of God, will, to the extent that he denies himself for these ideals, develop his spirituality. Indeed, only to the extent that he does this will he rise above the plane of the animal world.

Years ago we read in school the following from Rudolph Eucken:

"I cannot," he says, "conceive of the development of a powerful personality, a deep-rooted, profound mind, of a character rising above this world, without his having experienced a divinity in life above, beyond the world of sensible reality, and as surely as we create in ourselves a life in contrast to pure nature, growing by degrees and extending to the heights of the true, the good, and the beautiful, we may have the same assurance of that religion called universal."

Paul, you will remember, expresses it more specifically:

But if ye bite and devour one another, take heed that ye be not consumed one of another.

This I say then, Walk in the Spirit, and ye shall not fulfil the lust of the flesh.

For the flesh lusteth against the Spirit, and the Spirit against the flesh: and these are contrary the one to the other: so that ye cannot do the things that ye would.

But if ye be led of the Spirit, ye are not under the law.

Now the works of the flesh are manifest, which are these; Adultery. . . .

The young man who leaves his home at night having in

73

mind anything that would injure either the character or the life or the reputation of a young woman with whose company he is entrusted, is carnal-minded instead of spiritual-minded.

> . . . fornication uncleanness. . . .
>
> . . . hatred, variance, emulations . . . strife, seditions. . . .
>
> Envyings . . . drunkenness, revellings, and such like: of the which I tell you before, as I have also told you in time past, that they which do such things shall not inherit the kingdom of God.
>
> But the fruit of the Spirit is love, joy, peace, longsuffering, gentleness, goodness, faith,
>
> Meekness, temperance: against such there is no law.
>
> And they that are Christ's have crucified the flesh with the affections and lusts.
>
> If we live in the Spirit, let us also walk in the Spirit, daily, hourly. (Gal. 5:15-25.)

It can be done, and it should be done in every home of the Latter-day Saint Church.

With all our boasted civilization there never was a time when spiritual awakening and spiritual ideals were more needed. Civilization has grown too complex for the human mind to visualize or to control. Unless mankind come to a speedy realization that the higher and not the baser qualities of man must be developed, the present status of civilization is in jeopardy. Life on the animal plane has as its ideal the survival of the fittest, crush or be crushed, mangle or be mangled, kill or be killed. For man, with his intelligence, this is a sure road to anguish and death.

About fifty years ago, Lord Balfour, Prime Minister of Great Britain, delivered a lecture in the McEwen Hall of the University of Edinburgh on the subject "The Moral Values Which Unite the Nations." In an interesting and convincing manner, the gentleman presented four fundamental ties that unite the different nations of the world: (1) "Common Knowledge"; (2) "Common Commercial Interests"; (3) "The Intercourse of Diplomatic Relationship"; (4) "The Bonds of Human Friendship." The audience greeted his masterful address with a great outburst of applause.

As the presiding officer arose to express his appreciation and that of the audience, a Japanese student who was doing graduate work at the University stood up, and leaning over the balcony, said, "But, Mr. Balfour, what about Jesus Christ?"

Mr. Robin E. Spear, to whom Professor Lang related this incident, writes:

One could have heard a pin drop in the hall. Everyone felt at once the justice of the rebuke. The leading statesman of the greatest Christian empire in the world had been dealing with the different ties that are to unite mankind, and had omitted the one fundamental and essential bond. And everyone felt, too, the dramatic element in the situation—that the reminder of his forgetfulness had come from a Japanese student from a far-away non-Christian land.

Life, brethren and sisters, is an everflowing river on which one embarks at birth and sails, or is rowed for fifty, seventy, eighty, or more years. Every year that passes goes into an eternity, never to return; yet each carries with it into the past no personal weakness, no bodily ailment, no sorrow, no laughter, no thought, no noble aspirations, no hope, no ambition: all these with every trait of character, every inclination, every tendency remain with each individual. In other words, our lives are made up of daily thoughts and actions. We may resolve to let all our sorrows and weaknesses go with the passing time, but we know that every thought, every inclination has left its indelible impression upon our souls, and we shall have to deal with it today.

So live, then, that each day will find you conscious of having wilfully made no person unhappy. No one who has lived a well-spent day will have a sleepless night because of a stricken conscience. Daniel Webster once said that the greatest thought that had ever occupied his mind was the realization of the fact that, and I quote,

. . . there is no evil we cannot face or flee from but the consequences of duty disregarded. A sense of obligation pursues us ever. It is omnipresent like the Deity. If we take to ourselves the wings of the morning and dwell in the uttermost parts of the sea, duty performed, or duty violated is still with us, for our happiness or our misery. If we say that night shall cover us, in the darkness as in the light, our obligations are yet with us. We cannot escape their power nor fly from their presence. They are with us in this life, will be with us at its close, and in that scene of inconceivable solemnity which lies yet farther on, we shall find ourselves followed by the conciousness of duty—to pain us forever if it has been violated, and to console us so far as God has given us grace to perform it. Weighed against conscience the world itself is but a bubble. For God himself is in conscience lending it authority.

Mankind needs a spiritual awakening, brethren and sisters; the carnal minded are causing heartaches and threatening the extinction of the race.

But the sun of hope is rising. Thinking men and women are recognizing the need of man's looking up towards the heavens instead of groveling in response to the animal instinct. One man, commenting upon this, said that if all the destroyers of civilization could be eliminated, and the traits of the rest of us that come from destructive strains could be eliminated, an approach to the millennium some hundred years hence is by no means inconceivable.

"Can you imagine," he continues, "what this country would be like if ten or twenty billion dollars a year" (that is the amount expended to take care of our criminals)

were added to our national income? That would mean five hundred dollars, or one thousand dollars per family; but the average today, even if we include Henry Ford, is only twenty-five hundred, or three thousand dollars. What would happen if that sum were increased by twenty or even forty percent all around? Even if you cannot imagine the result, do you realize what it would be like to feel no need of locking doors and windows, no fear of leaving your car unprotected, no danger that your wife or daughter would be insulted, or you yourself sandbagged if you went out at night, no fear that you would have any uncollectable bills except through accident or unpreventable misfortune, no fear that in political election there would be any bribery, or in politics any graft, and no fear that anyone anywhere was trying to "do you"—can you imagine all that? It would almost be heaven on earth. Of course, it cannot happen (someday it will have to happen) . . . and yet if all the destroyers of civilization could be elimin-inated, and if the traits of the rest of us that come from destructive strains could be eliminated, an approach to such a state some hundred years hence is by no means inconceivable.

Spiritual awakening in the hearts of millions of men and women would bring about a changed world. I am hopeful, my brethren and sisters, that the dawning of that day is not far distant. I am conscious, as I hope all of you are, that the responsibility to try to bring about such a day rests upon the priesthood of the Church of Jesus Christ and upon the membership and upon husbands and wives and upon children in Mormon homes.

My faith in the ultimate triumph of the gospel of Jesus Christ assures me that a spiritual awakening must come. It will come through the acceptance of Jesus Christ and obedience to his gospel and in no other way completely. I believe there never was a time in the history of the world when there was such a need for a united, determined stand to uphold Christ and the restoration of the gospel through the Prophet Joseph Smith as there is today.

Chapter Fourteen

Gaining
the Abundant
Life

At Jacob's well in Samaria, Jesus
said to the woman, "But whosoever
drinketh of the water that I shall
give him shall never thirst."
(John 4:14.)

These are perilous times, but
they can be weathered if youth will but aspire to high ideals.
Degenerating forces in the world are rampant, but they can
be resisted if youth will cherish right thoughts. The age-old
conflict between truth and error is being waged with acceler-
ating fury, and at the present hour error seems to be gaining
the upper hand. Increasing moral turpitude and widespread
disregard for the principles of honor and integrity are undermining influences in social, political, and business life.

I believe with all my heart that most young people want
to live the abundant life; they want to live and have a good
time and not be deceived by an improper way of getting that
good time. They need teachers and leaders who live the
upright life and who conform to the highest ethical standards.
The religious teacher has the greater responsibility; for in addition to his belief in the efficacy of ethical and moral precepts, he assumes the responsibility of leading youth into the
realm of spirituality! Jesus prayed to the Father,

And now I am no more in the world, but these are in the world, and I come to thee. . . .

I have given them thy word; and the world hath hated them, because they are not of the world, even as I am not of the world.

I pray not that thou shouldest take them out of the world, but that thou shouldest keep them from the evil. (John 17:11, 14, 15.)

Thus, in perhaps the most impressive prayer ever offered Jesus prayed for his disciples on the night that he faced Gethsemane. Nor did he plead for his disciples alone, but, as he said,

Neither pray I for these alone, but for them also which shall believe on me through their [the disciples] word. (John 17:20.)

In this text is a clear implication of the divine purpose for man's being in this mortal probation. This purpose is expressly stated in the Book of Abraham by the Eternal Father to his fellow intelligences:

. . . We will make an earth whereon these [organized intelligences] may dwell; And we will prove them herewith, to see if they will do all things whatsoever the Lord their God shall command them. (Abraham 3:24, 25.)

And so our place in this world is divinely appointed. We are not to be out of it. Christ himself prayed that we should not be taken out of it.

Man a Dual Being

Man is a dual being; and his life, a plan of God. Man has a *natural* body and a *spiritual* body. Man's body is but the tabernacle in which his spirit dwells. Too many, far too many, are prone to regard the body as the man, and consequently to direct their efforts to the gratifying of the body's pleasures, its appetites, its desires, its passions. Too few recognize that the *real man is an immortal spirit*, which "intelligence or the light of truth," animated as an individual entity before the body was begotten, and that this *spiritual entity with all its distinguishing traits will continue after the body ceases to respond to its earthly environment*. Said the Savior: "I came

79

forth from the Father, and am come into the world: again, I leave the world, and go to the Father." (John 16:28.)

As Christ's pre-existent spirit animated a body of flesh and bones, so does the pre-existent spirit of every human being born into this world. This is the first basic truth of life.

The question, then, is: Which will give the more abundant life—pampering our physical natures, or developing our spiritual selves?

Man Has Free Agency

Man's greatest endowment in mortal life is the power of choice—the divine gift of free agency. No true character was ever developed without a sense of soul freedom. If a man feels circumscribed, harassed, or enslaved by something or somebody, he is shackled. That is one fundamental reason why Communism is so diabolically wrong.

Indulgence

Equal in importance to the consciousness of soul-freedom is the consciousness of self-mastery. Indulgence in appetites and desires of the physical man satisfy but for the moment and may lead to unhappiness, misery, and possible degradation; spiritual achievements give "joy not to be repented of."

Spiritual Progress Demands Effort

From the 40 days' fast on the mount of temptation to the moment on the cross when he cried in triumph, "It is finished," Christ's life was a divine example of subduing and overcoming. Full of significance are his words spoken in his farewell address to his disciples:

> These things I have spoken unto you, that in me ye might have peace. In the world ye shall have tribulation: but be of good cheer; I have overcome the world. (John 16:33.)

One scientist who has just glimpsed these eternal truths says this about keeping the moral law:

> Moral Law imposes disinterestedness; it orders that which is disagreeable, hard and painful. Its requirements often revolt the flesh

whose sole ambition is to persist and to enjoy. It demands the throttling of selfish sentiments for the sake of something which is still obscure to those who do not have faith, but which is even more powerful than the instinct of self-preservation: human dignity. The profound awareness of this dignity imposes a highly moral existence and paves the way to spirituality. And the greatest miracle is that this cruel law has won the universal respect of man who sometimes uses his intelligence to combat it, thus affirming its reality.

The joys it procures compensate for the sacrifices it demands. The sentiment of duty accomplished is accompanied by a kind of total satisfaction which alone gives true peace of soul. The moral man—in olden days one would have said the virtuous man—spreads happiness and good will around him, or, if happiness is impossible, the resignation which takes its place.[1]

There are thousands, millions, of men and women who have high standards, and we do not have to yield to the few who fail.

Now, having in mind these four fundamental facts of life—(1) the dual nature of man; (2) his freedom of choice and his responsibility therefor; (3) indulgences contrary to one's conscience leave heaviness of heart and unhappiness, while spiritual achievements always give joy; and (4) spiritual progress demands effort. There are eight difficulties to consider.

1. The Sabbath Day

Is it better to cherish Church ideals on Sunday or to indulge in Sunday sports? This is simply a question of physical pleasure or spiritual development; and in that regard we should keep in mind the following: First, it is a day of rest, essential to the true development and strength of the body, and that is a principle we should publish more generally abroad; and we should practice it. A second purpose for keeping holy the Sabbath day is mentioned in one sentence of modern revelation: ". . . That thou mayest more fully keep thyself unspotted from the world. . . ." (D.&C. 59:9.) That is a glorious sentence!

---

[1]Lecomte de Nouy, *Human Destiny* (Mentor Books, New York, N. Y., 1947).

Third, keeping the Sabbath day holy is a law of God, resounding through the ages from Mount Sinai. You cannot transgress the law of God without circumscribing your spirit.

Finally, our Sabbath, the first day of the week, commemorates the greatest event in all history—Christ's resurrection and his visit as a resurrected being to his assembled apostles.

Now, if a person wants to indulge in bodily exercises and amusements, he cannot do it on the Sabbath day with impunity.

2. Choosing Companions

Having in mind our basic truths, this question is a simple one—whether to choose companions who appeal to our baser natures, or those who inspire us always to be at our best.

Choose good companions, and find among them those with whom you should like to go through life and eternity.

3. Observing the Word of Wisdom

Obedience to the Word of Wisdom develops greater spiritual power—that spiritual power which comes from resistance. Of the virtue of self-control, consider the following:

> The soul that is worth the honor of earth,
> Is the soul that resists desire.

It is better in youth to say, "No, thank you," when tempted to indulge in things which create an appetite for themselves. Be a master, not a slave. Look around you, and you will see the slaves to appetite; unfortunately, women are numbered among them. Where is the spiritual power in these future mothers?

4. Does Active Membership in the Church Inhibit or Enhance One's Freedom and Development

Can you think of any organization in the world in which a person can serve more effectively in an organized way than he can in The Church of Jesus Christ of Latter-day Saints? Now I mention service and character because those are the only two things which we can take with us in a few years when we leave this world.

The question is: What have you made of yourself—your character? And what service have you rendered to others?

> Supposing today were your last day on earth,
> The last mile of the journey you've trod;
> After all of your struggles, how much are you worth,
> How much can you take home to God?
>
> Don't count as possessions your silver and gold,
> Tomorrow you leave these behind,
> And all that is yours to have and to hold
> Is the service you've given mankind.
>
> Anonymous

5. Chastity

The dominant evil in the world today is unchastity. He who is unchaste in young manhood is untrue to a trust given him by the parents of the girl; and she who is unchaste in maidenhood is untrue to her future husband and lays the foundation of unhappiness, suspicion, and discord in the home. Do not worry about these teachers who say something about inhibitions. Just keep in mind this eternal truth that chastity is a virtue to be prized as one of life's noblest achievements. It contributes to the virility of manhood. It is the crowning virtue of womanhood, and every red-blooded man knows that is true. It is a chief factor to a happy home; it is the sources of strength and perpetuity of the nation.

6. In the World but Not of the World

There is no loss of prestige in maintaining in a dignified way the standards of the Church. You can be "in" this world and not "of the world." Keep your chastity above everything else!

7. The Value of Doing Right

"Tell me what you think about when you do not have to think, and I will tell you what you are."

Temptation does not come to those who have not thought of it before. Keep your thoughts clean, and it will be easy to resist temptations as they come.

8. Getting Back on the Moral and Spiritual Highway

Think of the prodigal son who first "came to himself" before he turned his face homeward. Come back home, back to the path of virtue; but sense your own evil, and remember that there might be many who have been hurt on your way down.

When a man asked how he could help those he had injured, particularly in slander, a good wise old man took a sack of feathers, scattered them, and then said: "Now, try to gather them up."

He said, "Oh, I cannot!"

That is just it. Let us be careful that we have not wounded people, and hurt them as we have been going down selfishly on the road of indulgence.

Young people: Is it the body you are going to serve and be a slave to, or is it the spirit you are going to develop and thus live happily in this life and in the world to come?

Resist evil, and the tempter will flee from you. Keep your character above reproach no matter what others may think or what charges they make; and you can hold your head erect, keep your heart light, and face the world undauntedly because you, yourself, and your God know that you have kept your soul untarnished!

Chapter Fifteen

The Gospel and the Individual

What is man, that thou art mindful of him? and the son of man, that thou visitest him?

For thou hast made him a little lower than the angels, and hast crowned him with glory and honour. (Psalm 8:4-5.)

Since the dawn of civilization, leaders in organized society have sought the answer to the age-old question: "What is the chief end of man?" Carlyle answered it by saying, "To glorify God and enjoy him forever."

The Prophet Joseph Smith gave through revelation from the Lord the following:

That mine everlasting covenant might be established,
That the fulness of my gospel might be proclaimed by the weak and the simple unto the ends of the world, . . . (D.&C. 1:22-23.)

He further brought to light the great truth that God's work and glory is: "to bring to pass the immortality and eternal life of man." (Moses 1:39.)

Throughout the centuries there have been leaders and socially minded men who have desired the better way of living than that which was theirs. The good life, so important to man's happiness, has been the quest of the ages. To sense the need of reform has been easy, but to achieve it has been difficult and well nigh impossible. Ideas suggested by the wisest of men have often been impractical, sometimes fantastic, yet in many cases the world in general has been made better by the dissemination of new ideas even though the experiments proved failures at the time.

In this respect the first half of the nineteenth century was particularly marked by the feeling of social unrest, and many observing people became dissatisfied with social and economic conditions, and thinking men sought for remedial changes. In France, for example, the fanciful theories of Francois Marie Charles Fourier were circulated. He attempted to outline the future history of our globe and of the human race for eighty thousand years. Today, his books are seldom, if ever, read.

Later, Robert Owen, a man of exceptional ability and insight, when about nineteen years of age, became dissatisfied with the churches of his day. He decried their departure from the simple teachings of Jesus and was disturbed also by economic conditions. With a fortune back of him, and with the confidence of the Duke of Kent, Queen Victoria's father, Owen came to the New World in America about 1823. He purchased twenty thousand acres of land in what later became New Harmony, Indiana. He established what he hoped to be an ideal society. Within three years he lost two hundred thousand dollars of his fortune, and his experiment failed.

A few years later, George Ripley, a Unitarian minister, conceived a plan of plain living and high thinking. He and his associates became the founders of what is known now as "The Great Experiment." He had as his associates such able men as Nathaniel Hawthorne and Charles A. Dana, who afterwards became Assistant Secretary of War in the Cabinet of the President of the United States. This "Great Experiment" came to an end in 1846.

I believe with others that government, institutions, and organizations exist primarily for the purpose of securing to the individual his rights, his happiness, and proper development of his character. When organizations fail to accomplish this purpose, their usefulness ends. "So act," says Kant, "as to treat humanity, whether in your own person or that of another, in every case as an end, never as a means only."

In all ages of the world men have been prone to ignore the personality of others, to disregard men's rights by closing against them the opportunity to develop. The worth of man is a good measuring rod by which we may judge the rightfulness or the wrongfulness of a policy or principle, whether in government, in business, or in social activities.

Theories and ideologies exploited during the last half century present challenges more critical and dangerous than mankind has ever before faced.

This present world conflict, affecting the minds and souls of men today, is set forth by a prominent statesman of our country in the following succinct summary:

> On one side are those who, believing in the dignity and worth of the individual, proclaim his right to be free to achieve his full destiny—spiritually, intellectually, and materially. And—on the other side—there are arrayed those who, denying and disdaining the worth of the individual, subject him to the will of an authoritarian state, the dictates of a rigid ideology, and the ruthless disciplines of a party apparatus.
>
> This basic conflict—so deeply dividing the world—comes at a time when the surge of other changes and upheavals staggers the mind and senses. Whole nations are trying to vault from the Stone Age to the twentieth century.[1]

Thus, today, brethren, we are in danger of actually surrendering our personal and property rights. This development, if it does occur in full form, will be a sad tragedy for our people. We must recognize that property rights are essential to human liberty.

Former United States Supreme Court Justice George Sutherland, from our own State [Utah], carefully stated it as follows:

-----

[1] *The Future of Federalism,* pp. 60-61.

It is not the right of property which is protected, but the right *to* property. Property, per se, has no rights; but the individual—the man —has three great rights, equally sacred from arbitrary interference: the right to his life, the right to his liberty, and the right to his property. The three rights are so bound together as to be essentially *one* right. To give a man his life, but deny him his liberty, is to take from him all that makes life worth living. To give him liberty, but take from him the property which is the fruit and badge of his liberty, is to still leave him a slave.[2]

The bond of our secular covenant is the principle of constitutional government. That principle is, in itself, eternal and everlasting, despite the pretensions of temporary tyrannies. The principle of tyranny maintains that human beings are incurably selfish and therefore cannot govern themselves. This concept flies in the face of the wonderful declaration of the Prophet Joseph Smith that the people are to be taught correct principles, and then they are to govern themselves. Dictatorship, however, argues that the people should be governed by the individual or a clique who can seize power through subversion or outright bloodshed. Further, the people are declared to be without guarantees or rights, and the regime is claimed to exist beholden only to the plans and whims of the ruling tyrant.

Our Founding Fathers, despite some natural fears, clearly regarded the promulgation of the Constitution of the United States as their greatest triumph.

On June 12, 1955, Sir Percy Spender, Australian Ambassador to the United States, delivered a speech at the Union University at Schenectady, New York, at the time they conferred an honorary degree of Doctor of Civil Laws upon him. I agree with what he said in that speech, relating to present-day efforts, and I quote part of it as follows:

Today, freedom—political, economic, and individual freedom—lies destroyed or is in the course of being destroyed over great areas of the globe. And it has been destroyed and is being destroyed in the

---

[2]George Sutherland, speech before the New York State Bar Association, January 21, 1921.

name of freedom. *A vast struggle for the mind of man is now being waged—a struggle in which I hope each of you with all your heart will take part. In this struggle truth is distorted by those who have not the slightest regard for truth.* All the words which mean so much to us—like Liberty, Freedom, Democracy—are being despoiled and prostituted by the enemies of Liberty, Freedom, and Democracy. A ruthless dialectical battle is being waged against the Christian way of life, against political liberty, against individual freedom, and it is being waged in the name of Freedom. Black becomes White; Tyranny becomes Freedom; The Forced Labor Camp stands for Liberty; The Slave State is represented as Democracy. *This is the deadly challenge of Communism.* And in this challenge those who put their emphasis upon man as an economic being—and there are plenty in every so-called free country in the world today who do just that—those who explain man in terms of scientific and chemical facts and the accident of circumstance, those who treat human beings as so many "bodies," those who deny man's spiritual and individual existence—each of them aids and hastens the destruction of the political institutions on which our free society rests, and whether he knows it or not, supports the dialectics and the aims of International Communism.[3]

Jesus always sought the welfare of the individual; and individuals, grouped and laboring for the mutual welfare of the whole in conformity with the principles of the gospel, constitute the kingdom of God. Many of the choicest truths of the gospel were given in conversations with individuals when Jesus was on the earth. It was while Jesus talked with Nicodemus that he gave us the message relative to baptism and of being "born again." From the conversation with the woman of Samaria, we have disclosed the truth that they who worship God must worship him "in spirit and in truth." From Jesus' conversation with Mary and Martha, we hear the divine declaration, "I am the resurrection and the life: he that believeth in me, though he were dead, yet shall he live: . . ." (John 11:25.)

Jesus' regard for the personality was supreme!

To the members of The Church of Jesus Christ of Latter-day Saints the worth of the individual has special meaning.

---

[3]Sir Percy Spender, speech at the Union University, Schenectady, N. Y., June 12, 1955.

Quorums, auxiliaries, wards, stakes, even the Church itself, are all organized to further the welfare of man. All are but a means to an end, *and that end is the happiness and eternal value of every child of God.*

With wards, quorums, organizations, and auxiliaries in mind, I suggest three major means of winning souls to Christ. These three conditions are: one—enrollment in the Church of every individual; two—personal contact; three—group service.

These three plans, or conditions, are already operating in the Church, but unless they function, they will be ineffective in accomplishing the purposes for which they have been established.

It is the duty of each of these organizations to enroll every individual who belongs to it, not only to enroll, but to know by personal contact the conditions under which each person lives. It is not enough to know, and it is not sufficient to visit, for no person can become enthusiastic with the principles and doctrines of the gospel unless he or she lives them. "If ye will do the will, ye shall know" is a fundamental law of spiritual growth. (See John 7:17.)

If each of the thousands of officers and teachers in the ward, stake, and auxiliary organizations; if each of the many thousands of priesthood members were to influence for better living one individual, and should labor all his days "and bring save it be but one soul unto me," says the Lord, "how great shall be his joy with him in the kingdom of my Father!" (See D.&C. 18:15.)

Today, many nations have lost their independence; men, defeated, have been compelled to labor for their conquerors, property has been seized without recompense, and millions of people have surrendered all guarantees of personal liberty.

Force and compulsion will never establish the ideal society. This can come only by a transformation within the individual soul—a life redeemed from sin and brought in harmony with the divine will. Instead of selfishness, men must be willing to dedicate their ability, their possessions, their lives, if necessary, their fortunes, and their sacred honor for the alleviation of the ills of mankind. Hate must be supplanted by sympathy and forbearance. Peace and true prosperity can come only by conforming our lives to the law of love, the law of the principles of the gospel of Jesus Christ. A mere appreciation of the social ethics of Jesus is not sufficient—men's hearts must be changed!

In these days of uncertainty and unrest, liberty-loving people's greatest responsibility and paramount duty is to preserve and proclaim the freedom of the individual, his relationship to Deity, and the necessity of obedience to the principles of the gospel of Jesus Christ. *Only thus will mankind find peace and happiness.*

Let us strive to support good and conscientious candidates of *either party* who are aware of the great dangers inherent in communism, and who are truly dedicated to the Constitution in the tradition of our founding fathers. They should also pledge their sincere fealty to our way of liberty —a liberty which aims at the preservation of both personal and property rights. Study the issues, analyze the candidates on these grounds, and then exercise your franchise as free men and women. Never be found guilty of exchanging your birthright for a mess of pottage!

God enlighten our minds to comprehend our responsibility, to proclaim the truth and maintain freedom throughout the world.

Chapter Sixteen

The Spiritual Life, the True Life of Man

If we are true within, if we remain steadfast in integrity, we are rich in the eyes of God who sees the heart and judges therefrom. The true life within is largely the measure of what we are. But we are dual beings—our body, the outward part is the temple, if you please; and the spirit within, the true life. We cannot ignore the importance of the complete picture as suggested by the Apostle Paul (in speaking of the Church) in the twelfth chapter of Corinthians:

> For the body is not one member, but many.
>
> And the eye cannot say unto the hand, I have no need of thee: nor again the head to the feet, I have no need of you. (1 Corinthians 12:14, 21.)

I like this comparison because it suggests the importance of inward and outward "completeness." The healthy man, who takes care of his physical being, has strength and vitality — his temple is a fit place for his spirit to reside.

There are many things which attack the vitality of the body. We are exposed to disease which may make its inroads in one organ, which, being weakened, weakens and impairs other organs, the result being that the body succumbs to the attack. Thus bodily ailments deprive us of the full exercise of our faculties and privileges, and sometimes of life itself.

It is necessary, therefore, to care for our physical bodies and to observe the laws of physical health and happiness.

Here is a selection of Edward Everett Hale reflecting his views on some of the physical factors of life, and written a half century or so ago:

> The peril of this century is physical decay. This peril is gravely eminent with respect to all who dwell in our great cities. All the conditions of life in the modern American city favor it; wealth or the accumulation of the wherewith to gratify the desire is the great incentive of our contemporaneous life, and under its fevered stimulation, vast numbers of men and women, utterly careless of the body's needs or demands, struggle in the great conflict and eventually go down victims of the unchangeable law of nature. . . . There is a great natural truth, universally demonstrated, with regard to the various forms of living organisms, and that is when all the function of the body work together harmoniously . . . there is found a normal, strong, healthy organism, capable of existing under conditions that would mean the quick dissolution of one in which there was a derangement of the natural functions.

But, great as is the peril of physical decay, greater is the peril of spiritual decay. The peril of this century is spiritual apathy. As the body requires sunlight, good food, proper exercise and rest, so the spirit of man requires the sunlight of the Holy Spirit, proper exercise of the spiritual functions, the avoiding of evils that affect spiritual health, that are more ravaging in their effects than the dire diseases that attack the body.

I am greatly concerned over the conditions that are existing today in the world about us. Never before have the forces of evil been arrayed in such deadly formation as they are now. Few will question the fact that we are living in critical times. Satan and his forces are attacking the high ideals and sacred standards which protect our spirituality. One cannot help but be alarmed to note the ever-increasing crime wave. Even children are being corrupted by it, and youth are caught in its whirpool and are being contaminated overwhelmingly by it. Too many of our young folk respond to the call of the physical because it seems the easy and natural thing to do. Too many of our young people are vainly seeking shortcuts to happiness, and are often tempted to indulge in the things which appeal only to the baser side of humanity, five of the most common of which are: (1) vulgarity and obscenity, (2) drinking and the using of the narcotics, (3) unchastity, (4) disloyalty, and (5) irreverence.

Physical diseases may stop the manifestations of life in the body, but the spirit lives on; but when disease of the spirit conquers, life ebbs eternally. When men become spiritually sick they do not care much for religion. They think it is not necessary for them to attend to their spiritual wants. Dissatisfied with themselves, they find fault with those who do enjoy the true life of spirituality. Why? Because they do not know what real spiritual life is. They succumb to the diseases that are attacking the spirit.

I have in mind young people who become associated with the wrong kind of company, and who spend their time in wanton and wasteful ways. They withdraw themselves from the things of the spirit, and in doing so invite into their souls a malady that is more fatal than a wasting fever. They become infected with the virulent germs of spiritual disease. This condition keeps them from their quorum meetings, from Sunday School and sacrament meetings, and from other church associations. They lose the moral strength to go to these places for spiritual sunlight and for the healthful exercise of the spirit.

There are other manifestations of spiritual poisoning: The man who hates his brother has in his spirit a disease which will impair his spiritual life. The man who cheats his neighbor (I care not whether anyone else knows it or not) is weakening his spirituality. Dishonesty is a spiritual disease. The man who steals is inviting into his soul that which will prevent him from growing to the perfect stature of Christ. The man who fails in any way to live up to that which God and conscience tell him is right is weakening his spirituality

—in other words, is depriving himself of the sunlight in which his spiritual nature will grow.

If we are true within, if we are pure, if we are sincere, God is our stay and our inspirer, and the outward attacks and temptations cannot hurt us any more than Daniel of old was hurt in the lions' den when God protected him. We are outwardly strong only to the extent that we are pure and true as individuals, by seeking the truth and living in harmony with it, and by resisting every influence, every power that tends to destroy or to dwarf in any way the spiritual life.

I appeal to all members of the Church, and especially to the youth, to be courageous in maintaining the moral and spiritual values of the gospel of Jesus Christ. After all, "For what is a man profited, if he shall gain the whole world, and lose his own soul? or what shall a man give in exchange for his soul?" (Matthew 16:26.)

Chapter Seventeen

Manhood -
Honor -
Integrity

T͟HERE is nothing in life so admirable as true manhood; there is nothing so sacred as true womanhood. Manhood! Oh, what that means—to be a man, to be worthy of the honor that Anthony gave to Brutus when he pointed and said:

> This was the noblest Roman of them all:
> All the conspirators save only he
> Did that they did in envy of great Caesar;
> He only, in a general honest thought
> And common good to all, made one of them.
> His life was gentle, and the elements
> So mix'd in him that Nature might stand up
> And say to all the world "This was a man!"[1]

We delight in associating with true men; it is good to be in their presence. "A great man," says Carlyle, "is the living light-fountain, which it is good and pleasant to be near." I often think that it is easy to be honest. To be honest means that we are in harmony with divine law; that we are in keeping with the noblest work of God.

All men who have moved the world have been men who could stand true to their conscience—not only James, not only Paul, Peter, and all those ancient apostles, but all other

[1]Shakespeare, *Julius Caesar*, Act V, Scene V.

96

great men in history. I often admire Martin Luther. I cannot help feeling uplifted when I read his words to the Assembly at the Diet of Worms with all the Catholic Church opposing him, and all the powers of the land staring him in the face:

> Let me then be refuted and convinced by the testimony of the scriptures or by the clearest arguments, otherwise I cannot and will not recant, for it is neither safe nor expedient to act against conscience. Here I take my stand; I cannot do otherwise, so help me God!

It was Joseph Smith who, after having received a fervent testimony of the Lord Jesus Christ, declared to the men who said to him "It is from the devil"—ministers who before had influence with him, and whom he respected and believed were attempting to teach the word of God—"I had seen a vision; I knew it, and I knew that God knew it."[2] And just before his death he declared to all the world: "I have a conscience void of offense toward God and toward all men." Why? Because he had been true to it. He was a man possessing divine manhood, for true manhood is divine.

The man who is true to his manhood will not lie against the truth. We are told that we can crucify the Lord afresh. If that be true, we can betray the Lord afresh. There is that within every man which is divine, a divinity within every man's soul—it cannot die. God renews it, inspires it, works to keep it alive. The man who will be true to the divine within is true to his Lord, and is true to his fellowmen. The man who betrays that divinity within and is untrue to that which he knows to be right, wavers and is weak. God pity him; he may go so far that he will step out of the Light, out of that divine presence, and woe be unto him when he does!

In the following words from the 53rd Chapter of Alma is the account of young men who were exceedingly valiant:

> And they were all young men, and they were exceedingly valiant for courage, and also for strength and activity; but behold, this was

-----

[2]*Pearl of Great Price*, Joseph Smith, 2:25.

Man May Know for Himself

not all—they were men who were true at all times in whatsoever thing they were entrusted.

Yea, they were men of truth and soberness, for they had been taught to keep the commandments of God and to walk uprightly before him. (Alma 53:20-21.)

Who were these young men? They were sons of parents who were equally true to every trust. Their parents were converted Lamanites who, when the Spirit of God came upon them, devoted their lives to the service of their fellowmen, and in their ministry in the Church covenanted that they would never more take up arms against their brethren. Such was their oath; such was their covenant; and they were true to it even unto death.

One of the most moving accounts in literature is the account of these parents going out to meet enemies who came against them with swords, and of their sacrificing their lives rather than to uncover the swords they had buried and given their word not to unearth. A thousand of them suffered death rather than violate their covenant. Meeting no resistance, the enemy, being conscience-stricken, stopped the massacre after a thousand men had proved that they preferred death to the violation of a trust.

I mention this because parenthood has much to do in inculcating courage and trustworthiness in children. The law of cause and effect is working in parenthood as it is in any other law of nature. There is a responsibility upon all, especially upon fathers and mothers, to set examples worthy of imitation to children and young people.

Parents must be sincere in upholding the law and the priesthood in their homes that children may see a proper example. Respect for law and order, as charity, begins at home.

Many are familiar with a comment on this fundamental principle by Mr. Roger W. Babson, the great statistician:

The things which we look upon as of great value: the stocks, bonds, bankbooks, deeds, mortgages, insurance policies, etc. are merely nothing. While fifty-one percent of the people have their eyes on the goal of integrity, our investments are secure; but with fifty-one percent of them headed in the wrong direction, our investments are valueless. So the first fundamental of prosperity is integrity. Without it there is no civilization, there is no peace, there is no security, there is no safety. Mind you, also, that this applies just as much to the man who is working for wages as to the capitalist and every owner of property.

Integrity, however, applies to many more things than money. Integrity requires the seeking after, as well as the dispensing of, the truth. It was this desire for truth which founded our educational institutions, our sciences and our arts. All the great professions, from medicine to engineering, rest upon this spirit of integrity. Only as they so rest, can they prosper or even survive.

Integrity is the mother of knowledge. The desire for truth is the basis of all learning, the value of all experience, and the reason for all study and investigation. Without integrity as a basis, our entire educational system would fall to the ground; all newspapers and magazines would become sources of great danger, and the publication of books would have to be suppressed. Our whole civilization rests upon the assumption that people are honest. With this confidence shaken, the structure falls. And it should fall, for unless the truth be taught, the nation would be much better off without its schools, newspapers, books, and professions. Better have no gun at all, than one aimed at yourself. The cornerstone of prosperity is the stone of integrity.[3]

George Washington, the father of our country, said:

I hope that I may ever have virtue and firmness enough to maintain what I consider to be the most enviable of all titles—the character of an honest man.

And from the Doctrine and Covenants:

We believe that governments were instituted of God for the benefit of man; and that he holds men accountable for their acts in relation to them, both in making laws and administering them, for the good and safety of society.

We believe that all governments necessarily require civil officers and magistrates to enforce the laws of the same; and that such as will administer the law in equity and justice should be sought for and upheld by the voice of the people. (D.&C. 134:1, 3.)

-----

[3]Roger W. Babson, *Fundamentals of Prosperity* (Fleming H. Revell Co., N.Y., 1920, pp. 16-18. Used by permission.)

No member of the Church can be true to his country, true to his Church, true to his God, who will violate the laws which relate to the moral welfare and spiritual advancement of mankind. Members of the Church should uphold the law everywhere. And it is time all of us—the leaders of this country, the politicians, the statesmen, the leaders in civic affairs in the state and in the cities, as well as parents and private citizens—should so speak of and so uphold the constitutional law of the land that everywhere there will be a renewal of respect for it and a revival of the virtues of honor, honesty, and integrity.

All of us should take pride in making Mormonism a synonym for trustworthiness, temperance, chastity, honesty, justice. These are fundamental principles of the gospel of Jesus Christ and of The Church of Jesus Christ of Latter-day Saints. By exemplifying them in our lives we contribute to the transformation of society; we translate our religion into better social conditions, and bring salvation and peace to men everywhere here and now.

Chapter Eighteen

"What
Is a Man
Profited..."

A FEW YEARS ago when Sister McKay and I were riding down the valley of the Rhine, we saw farmers, men and women, out gathering hay because a storm threatened. The men were carrying the hay on their backs. We were told that each canvas-like bag, in which they had put the hay, weighed approximately two hundred pounds. Farther down, we saw a cow hitched to a cart, and some of these bags were put on the cart—a little more modern method of handling the hay. I remember when I returned home and went to the farm in Huntsville, I saw the hay cut, raked, baled, and placed in the barn by modern machinery. Later, I noticed, as I came through the valley on my way to Salt Lake City, piles of baled hay which told the same story. It had not even been touched by hand—hay and grain were threshed in the field, emptied into a wagon, and then elevated into the bin.

I wondered as I passed by if all these modern inventions of the past century had contributed to increase in character, in honesty, in upright living, in a more sacred and reverent devotion to Christ and his gospel. I wondered if the character of the men who were profiting by these wonderful inventions was any stronger and better than the character of the men who carried that hay on their backs. Were the men any better than the tall, handsome, upstanding young Swiss who graciously stood by his cow and cart to let my son take his photograph—a young man in whom I thought I saw reflected the pride of the Swiss; the love of freedom and independence. After all, it is what is within a man that counts—"For what is a man profited, if he shall gain the whole world, and lose his own soul?" (Matthew 16:26.)

The Paramount Purpose of Life

On the deck of the battleship *Missouri* in Yokohama Bay, when Japan surrendered, General Douglas MacArthur made this remarkable statement:

> If we do not now devise some greater and more equitable system, Armageddon will be at our door. The problem basically is theological and involves a spiritual recrudescence and improvement of human character. . . . It must be of the spirit if we are to save the flesh.[1]

I do not know that the problem is basically theological; we can have a study of theology without having character, without having religion; but the true meaning of that great general is in the sentence—*It involves a spiritual renaissance and improvement of human character. It must be of the spirit if we are to save the flesh.*

More recently, a man teaching physical science in one of our leading universities, studying, evidently, the same great problem as it applies to humanity today, said:

> I have come to three conclusions—the first is that salvation is not to be found in science. Secondly, we must have a moral revival. Thirdly, we can have no moral revival without a living religion.

That is one reason why we build our church edifices, because we believe in the spiritual development of man; because we believe this development to be the first and paramount purpose of life.

That we must make a living is evident to everyone. We are placed here to deal with the earth and earthly problems.

---

[1]Courtney Whitney, *MacArthur, His Rendezvous with History* (Alfred A. Knopf, New York, N. Y., 1956), p. 223.

Multiply, replenish, subdue, have dominion over the earth. These were the original commands given to man. Nature's first law is self-preservation—to gratify the flesh, satisfy the appetite, gain physical comfort and physical enjoyment— these things occupy the time and attention of the majority of the people of the world. No one can gainsay that. "He who will not provide for his loved ones is worse than an infidel"; and so it is a virtue to provide for loved ones. It is a necessity to preserve life.

Realize the Ideal

I remember reading many years ago that "the purpose of life may be summed up in one sentence—to subdue matter that we might realize the ideal!" Conquer the earth; conquer the roaring streams that come out of the canyons in the springtime; harness them instead of letting them destroy the land below by floods. Hold back that mighty torrent, bring it down to irrigate the orchards and the fields, and thus furnish livelihood for thousands, tens of thousands, in fact, millions. Subdue and conquer, yes, *that we might realize the ideal.*" Men and women, what is it? I cannot think of any higher and more blessed ideal than so to live in the spirit that we might commune with the Eternal.

There is a passage in one of Peter's epistles which I hope you will read and contemplate. It is found in 2 Peter 1:4. Peter had only two and a half years with Jesus. He was a good, practical man. He owned his own house, was a good fisherman, owning his own nets and boats. After two and a half years, and after the Savior had been crucified and the Twelve had filled the vacancy left by Judas Iscariot, with the responsibility of leadership upon him, Peter wrote a letter to some of the saints in which he used this phrase, that: "*. . . ye might be partakers of the divine nature.*" That hard, practical fisherman had realized the ideal of life. He had subdued, had conquered. That meant something more than conquering his own feelings, for he realized early in his life as a leader, the ideal of life.

103

Consider the Lilies of the Field

Jesus at one time said:

. . . Consider the lilies of the field, how they grow; they toil not, neither do they spin: And yet I say unto you, that even Solomon in all his glory was not arrayed like one of these. (Matthew 6:28-29.)

I have heard skeptics, guided by their reason, say, "How foolish, how impractical that injunction is!" And I say to them, all right. Let us consider the lily in the field. It is buried in the ground with a root, which strikes out in the darkness to receive strength and moisture from the soil; and soon a stalk pushes its way through the earth, and pushes it up and up until finally the lily blooms in the sunshine and produces its kind.

So man lives on the earth. His tentacles are his hands; his nervous system, his brain. From the earth he produces his living. For what purpose? That he, too, might realize the ideal—not the gratification of the appetite; not the gratification of passions; *but that the spirit might move in the sunshine of the Holy Ghost; that he might be, as Peter said, a "partaker of the divine nature."*

Control Is the First Virtue

In subduing matter, we have other things to subdue before we realize the ideal.

We must bring into subjection our appetites; the control of our passions; the keeping in mind the harnessing of these physical attributes and physical abilities, that we might use them for the development of the spirit. Subjecting, getting control, is the first virtue we should learn in this fight with nature and with mankind. How does it apply to members of the Church? Control your temper in the home. He is a weak man who will curse or condemn a loved one because of some little incident or accident. What good does it do him to lose control of himself? He would be a man if he would develop his spirit and subdue his anger and control his temper. Many a woman's heart is broken because a man has not learned to subdue that part of his nature. Many a husband's heart is broken because a wife has not learned to hold in subjection her temper, or her thoughts and feelings. A little thing you say? Analyze it, and you will find that yielding and *not controlling your temper* brings many an unhappy hour in your home.

In one general statement—most of our troubles here in this life in trying to subdue nature and subduing our appetites all come within the suggestion of *limitation.* Many things are right up to a certain point, beyond which they become evils or vices. Members of the Church should learn to control, to live within that proper limit.

On Conditons—The Fullness of the Earth Is Ours

It is our duty to seek to acquire the art of being cheerful.

A cheerful spirit is one of the most valuable gifts ever bestowed upon humanity by a kind Creator. It is the sweetest and most fragrant flower of the spirit that constantly sends out its beauty and fragrance and blesses everything within its reach. It will sustain the soul in the darkest and most dreary places in the world. It will hold in check the demons of despair and stifle the power of discouragement and hopelessness. It is the brightest star that ever cast its radiance over the darkest soul and one that seldom sets in the gloom of morbid fancies and foreboding imaginations. (Author unknown.)

Spirituality! Happiness is not found in material things.

If the experience of the past few years has taught us one thing more than another, it is that it is unwise to seek for happiness in worldly possessions only. I say *only* because I do not minimize the value of the good things of the world as contributing factors to man's peace, joy, and contentment. The Lord himself has said that if we worship him with rejoicing and prayer, with glad hearts and cheerful countenances, the fullness of the earth is ours.

. . . The fulness of the earth is yours, the beasts of the field and the fowls of the air, and that which climbeth upon the trees and walketh upon the earth;

Yea, and the herb, and the good things which come of the earth, whether for food or for raiment, or for houses, or for barns, or for orchards, or for gardens, or for vineyards;

Yea, all things which come of the earth, in the season thereof, are made for the benefit and the use of man, both to please the eye and to gladden the heart;

Yea, for food and for raiment, for taste and for smell, to strengthen the body and to enliven the soul.

And it pleaseth God that he hath given all these things unto man; for unto this end were they made to be used with judgment, not to excess, neither by extortion. (D.&C. 59:16-20.)

However, to seek joy and happiness or even contentment in the acquisition of these worldly things alone is to lose sight of the higher purpose of life—the spiritual development of man.

Recently I re-read an excellent book written by one of our leading educators, Dr. R. V. Chamberlain, as a tribute to his departed brother. It is a treatise on the philosophy of a good man's life. From it I quote the following:

The world has progressed because of people who cared but little for material rewards, people who knew that mortal self-denial is the only path to self-realization. By sacrificing for our ideals we do not throw ourselves away, but achieve the higher sides of ourselves. Civilization has come from the struggles of men and women in the past who risked all for ideals, for spiritual values, that they might become the common possession of the race. We who see the path today are unworthy if we do not take up the burden. The race goes down when it loses its sense of values, and the success of democracy depends upon the people's living in the understanding of the spirit and the obligations of righteousness. In the world today men have not advanced their ideals with an intensity commensurate with economics and material expansion. Wisdom has not kept pace with learning, nor righteousness with power.

Is it your purpose to get WORLDLY GAIN? You may obtain it! You may win in this world almost anything for which you strive. If you work for wealth, you can get it; but before you make it an end in itself, take a look at those who have desired wealth for its sake alone. Gold does not corrupt men; it is the *motive* of acquiring that gold that impairs or shrivels the soul. It is the *purpose* one has in acquiring it.

What a man is may be determined largely by his dominant quest. His success or failure, happiness or misery, depends upon what he seeks, upon what he chooses. Spirituality is the highest and best to which man can aspire! A spiritual awakening in the hearts of millions of men and women would bring about a changed world.

For what is a man profited, if he shall gain the whole world, and lose his own soul? . . .

Chapter Nineteen

Radiation
of the
Individual

E<small>VERY</small> <small>MAN</small> and every person who lives in this world wields an influence, whether for good or for evil. It is not what he says alone; it is not alone what he does. It is what he is. Every man, every person radiates what he or she really is. Every person is a recipient of radiation. The Savior was conscious of that. Whenever he came into the presence of an individual, he sensed that radiation—whether it was the woman of Samaria with her past life; whether it was the woman who was to be stoned, or the men who were to stone her; whether it was the statesman, Nicodemus, or one of the lepers. He was conscious of the radiation from the individual. And to a degree so are you, and so am I. It is what we are and what we *radiate* that affects the people around us.

As individuals, we must think nobler thoughts. We must not encourage vile thoughts or low aspirations. We shall radiate them if we do. If we think noble thoughts; if we encourage and cherish noble aspirations, there will be that radiation when we meet people, especially when we associate with them.

As it is true of the individual, so it is true of the home. Our homes radiate what we are, and that radiation comes from what we say and how we act in the home. No member of this Church—husband, father—has the right to utter an oath in his home, or ever to express a cross word to his wife or to his children. You cannot do it as a man who holds the priesthood and be true to the spirit within you by your ordination and your responsibility. You should contribute to an ideal home by your character, controlling your passion, your temper, guarding your speech, because those things will make your home what it is and what it will radiate to the neighborhood.

A City That Radiates Spirituality

I am reminded of a remark made by a man who came to Salt Lake City and attended the board meeting of the United States Steel Corporation in 1946. Some of the General Authorities were invited to attend a dinner of that board; and, at the conclusion of that entertainment, Mr. Irving S. Olds, the chairman of the board, who was the master of ceremonies on that occasion, said: "Now we are not going to have any set speeches, but here is an opportunity if any of you would like to express yourselves."

Mr. Nathan L. Miller, general counsel for that board, arose and in substance said, "I am one of those inquisitive, suspicious New Englanders; and I have been impressed with something in this city that seems to be different from any other city I have ever visited. I walked up and down Main Street and watched the people; and I tried to define that something, and wondered what it was, but during an interview in the president's office today (President George Albert Smith was their host then), I think I discovered what that difference is." (President Smith had called on some of the brethren to speak to these United States Steel board members who were sitting and standing around the First Presidency's board room in the Church Administration Building.) Mr. Miller continued, "I listened to what these men said. One of them had referred to the pioneers and the spirit of the pioneers; that before they started out across the plains, under the direction of President Brigham Young they first sought divine guidance. Second, under his direction, they

109

were prepared. Every man carried a gun and was prepared for an attack of savages or any other possible emergency that might come to the pioneers that day. And third, every man was required to take just as much care of his neighbor's cattle as he did his own." *Worship, Preparation, Service!*

I do not know whether it was that that answered this gentleman's curiosity or not; but he said, "I thought in that meeting in the President's office I detected what there is in this city which is different—it is spirituality! That's it—it is spirituality! I am wondering if you younger men (he spoke to those around him) can keep that spirituality with the installation of material things coming into your midst."

Mr. Miller was referring to that radiation of the group which we all feel. I repeat, every individual has it. Every home radiates it, and every Latter-day Saint home should have it.

A father visited his son's new home. The son was proud to show him the various rooms and the new installations in the kitchen. After they were through with their visit, the father said, "Yes, it is beautiful; but I see no signs of God in your home." And the son said, "I went back; and as I looked through the rooms, I noticed I had nothing suggestive of the presence of the Redeemer or the Savior."

Church Members Should Radiate Love and Harmony

As men of the priesthood, as women of the Church, we have greater responsibilities than ever before to make our homes such as will radiate to our neighbors harmony, love, community duties, loyalty. Let our neighbors see it and hear it. Never must there be expressed in a Latter-day Saint home an oath, a condemnatory term, an expression of anger or jealousy or hatred. Control it! Do not express it! You do what you can to produce peace and harmony, no matter what you may suffer.

The Savior set us the example. He was always calm, always controlled, radiating something which people could feel as they passed. When the woman touched his garment, he felt something go from him—that radiation which is divine.

Each individual soul has it. That is you! The body is only the house in which you live.

The Church is reaching out, radiating not only by its prayers, its houses of worship and meetings, but now through television and radio it is radiating throughout the whole world.

God help us as members of the priesthood, as members of the Church, to radiate faith, love of humanity, charity, control, consideration, and service!

Chapter Twenty

True
End of
Life

Eᴀʀᴛʜ ɪɴ ᴀʟʟ its majesty and wonder is not the end and purpose of creation. "My glory," says the Lord himself is ". . . to bring to pass the immortality and eternal life of man." (Moses 1:39.) And man, in exercising the divine gift of free agency, should sense an obligation to assist his Creator in the accomplishment of this divine purpose.

The true end of life is not mere existence, not pleasure, not fame, not wealth. The true purpose of life is the perfection of humanity through individual effort, under the guidance of God's inspiration.

Real life is response to the best within us. To be alive only to appetite, pleasure, pride, money-making; and not to goodness and kindness, purity and love, poetry, music, flowers, stars, God, and eternal hopes, is to deprive one's self of the real joy of living.

Two Phases of Activity

In this physical stage of existence, man finds activity in two phases: First, in the struggle for livelihood and comforts; and, second, in the tendency to grovel. The first is natural and most commendable. The second is debasing and, when unrestrained, leads one to the level of animals. When a man harbors the thought that he will obtain a liveli-

112

hood by injuring his neighbor, that moment he begins to circumscribe his life: bitterness replaces happiness; sordidness supplants generosity; hatred takes the place of love; and beastliness takes the place of humanity.

Generally, there is in man a divinity which strives to push him onward and upward. We believe that this power within him is the spirit that comes from God. Man lived before he came to this earth; and he is here now to strive to perfect the spirit within. At some time in his life, every man is conscious of a desire to come in touch with the Infinite. His spirit reaches out for God. This sense of feeling is universal; and all men ought to be, in deepest truth, engaged in the same great work—the search for and the development of spiritual peace and freedom.

Man Is Architect of His Fate

Each one of us is the architect of his own fate; and he is unfortunate indeed who will try to build himself without the inspiration of God, without realizing that *he grows from within,* not from without.

Trees that can stand in the midst of the hurricane often yield to the destroying pests that can scarcely be seen even with a microscope. Likewise, the greatest foes of humanity today are the subtle and sometimes unseen influences at work in society that are undermining the manhood and womanhood of today. The test, after all, of the faithfulness and effectiveness of God's people is an individual one.

Every temptation that comes to you and me comes in one of three forms:

(1) *A temptation of the appetite or passion;* (2) *A yielding to pride, fashion, or vanity;* (3) *A desire for worldly riches or power and dominion over lands or earthly possessions of man.*

Such temptations come to us in our social gatherings; they come to us in our political strivings; they come to us in our business relations, on the farm, and in the mercantile establishment. In our dealings in all the affairs of life, we find these insidious influences working. It is when they manifest themselves to the consciousness of each individual that the defense of truth should exert itself.

The Church teaches that life here is probationary. It is man's duty to become the master, not the slave of nature. His appetites are to be controlled and used for the benefit of his health and the prolongation of his life; his passions are to be mastered and controlled for the happiness and blessings of others.

Happiness Comes from Service

Man's greatest happiness comes from losing himself for the good of others. The advancement of science and the new discoveries from the dawn of history to the present are the results of the efforts of men who have been willing to sacrifice themselves, if necessary, for the cause of truth.

Today there are those who have met disasters which almost seem defeat and who have become somewhat soured in their natures; but if they would stop to think, even the adversity which has come to them may prove a means of spiritual uplift. Adversity itself may lead *toward* and not away from God and spiritual enlightenment; and privation may *prove a source of strength if we can but keep a sweetness of mind and of spirit.*

If you have lived true to the promptings of the Holy Spirit, and continue to do so, happiness will fill your soul. If you vary from it, and become conscious that you have fallen short of what you know is right, you are going to be unhappy even though you have the wealth of the world.

Spirituality—Victory Over Self

Spirituality is the consciousness of victory over self and of communion with the Infinite. Spirituality impels one to conquer difficulties and acquire more and more strength. To feel one's faculties unfolding and truth expanding the soul is one of life's sublimest experiences. Being true to self and being loyal to high ideals develop spirituality. The real test of any religion is the kind of man it makes. Being "honest, true, chaste, benevolent, virtuous, and . . . doing good to all men" is a virtue which contributes to the highest acquisition of the soul. It is the divine in man that makes him king of all created things. It is this one final quality that makes him tower above all other animals.

Let us ever keep in mind that life is largely what we make it, and that the Savior of men has marked clearly and plainly just how joy and peace may be obtained. It is in the gospel of Jesus Christ and adherence thereto. Do your duty no matter how humble, and resolve even in the face of difficulties and discouragements to be:

> Like a man who faces what he must
> With step triumphant and a heart of cheer;
> Who fights the daily battle without fear;
> Sees his hopes fail, yet keeps unfaltering trust
> That God is God.
> — Author unknown.

Chapter Twenty-one

Gratitude

Enter into his gates, with thanksgiving, and into his courts with
praise: be thankful unto him, and
bless his name.

Know ye that the Lord he is God;
it is he that hath made us, and not
we ourselves; we are his people,
and the sheep of his pasture.
(Psalms 100:4-3.)

M Y HEART is filled with gratitude
as I contemplate the opportunity I have had to meet with the
members of the Church in missions and stakes throughout
the world. It has been a great privilege to meet with them
in their worshipping assemblies, to dedicate their stake and
ward buildings; to mingle with the people and to shake hands
with them. I am most grateful for their faith and loyal
support through the years. Their prayers in my behalf during
the past two or three years have been a sustaining power
which I have felt as I have carried on the duties associated
with the office of the President of the Church.

Through the years, as I have traveled to the missions of
the world, I have listened with a great deal of comfort and
satisfaction to the testimonies borne by the missionaries.
Their expressions of gratitude for the opportunity of being
in the mission field; their appreciation for the gospel, which
they testified had enlarged their views and given them the
true philosophy of life, were heartwarming and faith pro-
moting. I wish the men and women of the world who are

uninformed, prejudiced or cynical about "Mormonism" could have heard these young men bear their testimonies and express gratitude for their parents, particularly for their mothers. They, the uninformed, would have had a clearer insight into the real purpose of the Church than they could have obtained in any other way, and would have had an insight also into the life of the members of the Church.

That which made those testimony meetings so impressive and memorable was the gratitude which the missionaries expressed for their parents and their mothers. Not one who, when he came to express what his mother had done for him, but broke down in tears and apologized. He did not need to. Those tears were merely the expression of a sincere soul.

I am grateful for the ideals of the Church, one of the most important of which is the establishing of an ideal home, the rearing of children, and the love for one another, for parents, and faith in God. A home in which family prayers are held—I know that they are out-of-date generally, even among Christian nations, and I know, too, that in our own Church there is a slackness in family prayer—but in the true Latter-day Saint home you will have a prayer every morning before a father and mother and children start out for work or for school, and a prayer of thanksgiving when night closes upon them.

I am grateful for home, where love and respect of children for parents exist. Blessed are parents and children where love and happiness reign in the home!

Gratitude is a deeper virtue than thanksgiving. You may express thanks by words, but gratitude is a feeling of the heart and the soul.

Many children and young people do not sense the importance of appreciation and gratitude. We pass through life without realizing what our blessings are. Not just the young folks, but those of us who have passed the three score years and ten. Daily there are things which we have which we take for granted without ever considering how important they are.

I have several times addressed groups of children and have said to them: "Well, I am happy to meet a group of millionaires." When they looked surprised and doubtful, I asked, "Are you not millionaires?"

No, they were very poor, some of them thought, and to accuse (I use that word advisedly), to accuse them of being millionaires, was an astonishing thought.

I asked them, "How many of you have a mother?" All hands of those who had mothers were raised. "Well, suppose I should like to purchase that mother. I will give you $1,000 for her." They shook their heads. By this time they were in business, real business. "I will give you $10,000—$100,000—$200,000." By this time they were almost indignant that I should try to purchase mother.

"How many of you have a father? Well, would you sell your father for $1,000? No? $10,000—$100,000? No?"

"How many of you have a little baby sister?" They had never thought of the value and the happiness that a little baby can bring into their lives, measured by money. How valuable, how sublimely valuable is that little babe!

Then I said to the children, "You could not sell your mother or your father, or that baby if you wanted to, even if I would give you a million dollars. You could not—mother would not let you."

Do you have something which is yours? One day I read of a man who was going to an execution. The criminal had promised to give to a blind man his eye, and how grateful that sightless man was that he was going to have an eye transplanted. You have two eyes. Have you ever knelt down and thanked the Lord that you have those eyes? Would you sell one of those eyes for $5,000, $10,000, or $100,000? No, you would not!

Let me take your hearing. Just sell your hearing. Then you never can hear a song of a bird. You cannot hear the sweet tones of the choir when you come to meeting. Never again can you hear your mother's voice. Would you sell your hearing for $5,000 or more? No!

We shall let you keep your eyes and your ears, just give me your arm. You can drive with your left arm. No? They will not let an arm go. We went on one by one, and soon we found out that every child is a millionaire, and that our real wealth is in what God has given us. Just count your blessings and see what the Lord has done.

Let me emphasize this by telling a true story. Years ago there came into an American home a sweet little baby girl, and when that little baby had been placed upon the mother's arm, the mother's first look was to see that she was physically perfect. That is what every mother looks for. There is the most inspiring, beautiful picture in all the world —a mother with her first babe on her arm and the baby perfect! It is a picture worthy of the greatest artist. And so this mother was happy, as are all mothers, forgetting the pain and the cost of bringing that little baby into the world and in the Church; for a baby is a gift from heaven.

That little baby girl grew in physical strength and a beauty until she was about two or two and one-half years of age. Then an intense fever seized the child. For days she hovered between life and death. Parents and other anxious loved ones almost despaired of her life; but one night at midnight the fever started to break, and shortly the child gave promise of recovery, and all were happy. The baby began to take a little nourishment and gained in strength, and all in the household rejoiced. But one day the mother was seized with a fearful thought. She waved her hand in front of the child's eyes and there was no blinking. The fever had destroyed the nerves of sight! Then a second fear gripped the mother's heart. She took the baby's rattle and rattled it behind her. But there was no response. The little girl was deaf, blind, and speechless. Now think what that mother would have given just to have either the hearing or the seeing back!

The father and mother were desperate. They sought advice and help from specialists, but all in vain. The little child grew until she was seven years of age without seeing, hearing, or speaking. The parents then sought a teacher who might break through that iron cage, for there was in that body, as a canary in a cage, a brilliant soul, striking, but with physical handicaps, unable to find expression. She would feel the heads of her little playmates, one whose hair was curly. She felt that and then her own and wondered why the difference. No expression. Her hand passed over the mother's face, but no designation of mother, no term to express that lovely countenance. A blind teacher, who came in response to the parents' call, said, "If she could hear, I could do something." They sent for a teacher of the deaf who said, "If she could see, I could teach her; but when she can neither see nor hear, we are helpless." Finally a young woman who had devoted herself to the blind and the deaf said, "I will see what I can do."

She took the little girl's doll and wrote in the palm of her hand D-O-L-L, and repeated it. And the little girl became impatient and dashed the doll to the floor. The teacher ·was wise. She did not lose her patience. She led the child out to the fountain and let the water run over her hand, and in her other hand wrote, W-A-T-E-R. Then the thought came to the child, "Do these marks in my hand name that something which I felt on my hand?", and she put her own hand out and received the same marks. Then, as she walked back to the house, she felt a rose, and had R-O-S-E spelled in her hand. She gathered fragments of the broken doll and put out her hand, and had D-O-L-L spelled. She then went to her mother and ran her hand over her face, and got, for the first time, M-O-T-H-E-R.

Years afterward, that little girl, in writing of the experience, said, that night as she climbed the stairway to her bedroom, *she was the happiest girl in all the world — she had learned three or four words!*

You know to whom I refer — Helen Keller, who is now over eighty years of age. She is named as one of the seven greatest women in all the world. I think she is the greatest. She learned those signs that teacher left with her day and night, and her teacher was her constant companion. Helen always called her "my teacher," and she learned to speak by putting her hand on the teacher's throat and feeling the movements of the throat and on the lips when the teacher was saying "Mother." Then she would try to reproduce those same sounds — Mother — and she learned to speak not only English, but French, and I think one other language.

When I was superintendent of Sunday Schools, we invited Helen Keller to come to Salt Lake City and speak to the children. She was blind and deaf, but not speechless, and she addressed more than seven hundred children in the Assembly Hall, and her speech was entitled "Happiness."

Later, she traveled throughout the world. She was received by kings and queens and the great of the earth. She has been entertained by presidents of the United States. Many honors and degrees have been conferred upon her.

She visited Salt Lake City several years later and spoke in the Tabernacle. As we were standing in the ante-room where the general authorities enter, prior to her appearing before the audience, the organ began to play, and, blind and deaf, but not speechless, she said, "The organ." She touched one of the pillars and listened to the strains of the organ through the sense of touch.

Young people, are you rich? Do you possess the wealth of the world? God has given you that which is far more valuable and worth more in treasure than any money in stocks or bonds. Day by day we go without thanking him for our blessings; without thanking God for mother and father, for our brothers and sisters, and for kind friends. Be grateful to God for his blessings. Give thankfulness to him for life and for health, vigor, for our faculties, and, above all, for the gospel which leads us into his presence. I testify to you that it is true. Declare it to the world!

So -

> When upon life's billows you are tempest tossed,
> When you are discouraged, thinking all is lost,
> Count your many blessings; name them one by one,
> And it will surprise you what the Lord has done.[1]

J. Oatman, Jr.

God help us to appreciate and be grateful for the blessings he has given us!

---

[1]*Hymns, The Church of Jesus Christ of Latter-day Saints.*

The Church and Daily Living

2

Chapter Twenty-two

Keeping
Ourselves
"Unspotted from the World"

JESUS in a wonderful prayer—
I think it must have been the most impressive ever offered
in this world—said these words:

And now I am no more in the world, but these [referring to the
members of the Twelve who knelt with Him] are in the world, and
I come to thee. Holy Father, keep through thine own name those
whom thou hast given me, that they may be one, as we are.

I pray not that thou shouldest take them out of the world, but
that thou shouldest keep them from the evil. (John 17:11, 15.)

A number of years ago a stake president, upon being
released from his position in which he had served well, made
the remark: "Now I am reduced to just a humble member."
Because he had been released, he felt that he had lost something. Well, he had. He had lost the privilege of serving the
members of his stake as president; for to be a stake president or to hold any other position in the Church is an honor
as well as a great responsibility. But to be a lay member is
also a great obligation, as well as a great opportunity.

Membership is obtained by baptism, which is at once a
burial and a birth—a burial of the old person, with all his
frailties, faults, and sins, if any, and a coming forth to walk
in a newness of life. Backbiting, faultfinding, slander, profanity, uncontrolled temper, avarice, jealousy, hatred, intem-

perance, fornication, lying, cheating are all buried. That is part of what baptism by immersion signifies. ". . . Except a man be born again, he cannot see the kingdom of God," (John 3:3) said Jesus to Nicodemus. A newly baptized person comes forth to walk in a newness of life, signifying that in the new life ahead there will be an effort to maintain honesty, loyalty, chastity, benevolence, and of doing good to all men.

Wordsworth once said of Milton: "Thy soul was like a star and dwelt apart." That is what membership in the Church does to those who keep the ideals they profess.

James said that "Pure religion and undefiled before God and the Father is this, To visit the fatherless and widows in their affliction, and to keep himself unspotted from the world." (James 1:27.)

It is in this sense of keeping ourselves "unspotted from the world" that the lay members, as all officers, are obligated.

Why Man Is in the World

In the Book of Mormon, in the forty-second chapter of Alma, we are told why the children of God are here in the world—namely, to mingle with the sons of men, to gain an experience that will bring them back to God, but not to partake of the sins of the world. The Savior said to his apostles on the same evening that he offered that beautiful prayer: ". . . Be of good cheer; I have overcome the world." (John 16:33.) Going soon to meet his Father, he admonished them to follow his example, praying that God should not take them out of the world, but should keep them from evil.

I have never met a member of the Church who would not express himself, and, if the occasion arose, who did not so express himself as being willing to defend his membership if this Church were attacked. I have seen boys, apparently indifferent to the Church, on occasions stand out and express defiance of an attack upon the Church. All very commendable, but perhaps at the very moment of that gallant defense there were encroachments upon their souls which weakened their power to defend the truth. Trees that can stand in the midst of the hurricane often yield to the destroying pests that can scarcely be seen with the microscope, and the greatest foes of humanity today are those unseen microscopic microbes that attack the body.

Undermining Influences

There are also influences at work in society which are undermining the manhood and womanhood of today. It is these unseen influences which come from the world that influence us when we are least prepared to defend ourselves. When we do not withstand the encroachments of these evil influences, we weaken the possibility of defending the Church of Jesus Christ. This is an individual work! What the individuals are, that the aggregate is. Jesus influenced individuals, knowing that if the individuals were pure and strong, a thousand individuals would make a strong community, and a thousand communities would make a strong nation. Individual responsibility!

The test of the efficiency of God's people is an individual one. What is each one doing to foster the group known as the Church of Christ in the world? Is he living so that he is keeping unspotted from the evils of the world? God wants us here. His plan of redemption, so far as we are concerned, is here; and we, my fellow workers in the Church of Christ, are carrying the responsibility of testifying to the world that God's truth has been revealed; that men and women can live in this world, free and uncontaminated from the sins thereof, following as nearly as humanly possible Jesus as he walked on earth thirty-two and one-half years in his day.

"The World"

What do we mean by "the world"? I take it that "the world" refers to the inhabitants who are alienated from the saints of God. They are aliens to the Church, and it is the spirit of this alienation from which we should keep ourselves free. We are told by Paul not to conform to the fashions of the world. Timothy was warned not to partake of the evils of the world. "Flee also youthful lusts: but follow righteousness, faith, charity, peace, with them that call on the Lord out of a pure heart." (2 Timothy 2:22.) Zion is the pure in heart, we have been told; and the strength of this Church lies in the purity of the thoughts and lives of its workers. Then the testimony of Jesus abides in the soul, and strength comes to each individual to withstand the evils of the world.

Temptations come in our social gatherings. They come to us at our weddings. They come to us in our politics. They come to us in our business relations, on the farm, in the mercantile establishments, in our dealings in all affairs of life. In our home associations we find these insidious influences working, and it is when they manifest themselves in the consciousness of each individual that the defense of truth should exert itself.

When that still, small voice calls us to the performance of duty, insignificant though it may seem, and its performance unknown to anyone save the individual and God, he who responds gains corresponding strength. Temptation often comes in the same quiet way. Perhaps yielding to it may not be known by anyone save the individual and his God; but if he does yield to it, he becomes to that extent weakened and spotted with the evils of the world.

A Glowing Countenance

Converts to the truth walk out of the waters of baptism with a glow upon their countenances, especially after confirmation, which they have never had before. They realize that they have taken upon themselves the name of Christ and have covenanted to walk in accordance with the ideals of his gospel. During Sunday School and sacrament meetings they are permitted to make a covenant, as does every lay member. In the presence of his fellow members of the Church, he covenants before God that he is willing to take upon him the name of the Son, always to remember him and keep his commandments which he has given him, and by so doing, always to have the Spirit of the Lord to be with him. That is true religion.

What a covenant for every lay member! Is he virtuous in thought and action? Is he dealing honestly with his neighbor in the horse and cattle trade, in the purchase of property, in any business transaction? If he believes in the covenants he has made, if he is true to the covenants he has made, if he believes in the efficacy of the Church to which he belongs, he has obligated himself to do these things. If called to a prominent position, it is his duty to be true; indeed, he is more obligated than ever to set an example to others. He may not be called, however; but his membership in the Church of Jesus Christ obligates him to these high ideals. Only in that way can religion become the most influential and potent power in life.

It is generally understood that every member of the Church should be a missionary. He is probably not authorized to go from house to house, but he is authorized by virtue of his membership to set a proper example as a good neighbor. Neighbors are watching him. He is a "light," and it is his duty not to have that "light" hidden under a bushel; but it should be set upon a hill that all men may be guided thereby.

The mission of the gospel of Jesus Christ is to make evil-minded men and women good, and to make good men and women better; in other words, to change men's lives, to change human nature.

Unspotted from Sins

Every member of the Church should keep himself unspotted from the sins of the world. To be just a lay member of the Church means that every man is a Christian gentleman; that every husband is true to the ideals of chastity;

that every young boy and every young girl refrains from indulgence in tobacco, in strong drink, and keeps himself or herself free from the sins of the world. That is what Mormonism means in daily life. If you are called upon to render service in any position, render it. If you are released, accept your release, always remembering that the Church is established for your benefit, and the benefit and happiness of your children and your children's children. If you will live in accordance with those humble principles under the covenants you made at the water's edge, and since that time in sacrament meetings, and many of you in the house of God, you will fill a noble mission; and God will reward you accordingly.

It is my fervent prayer and hope that every member of the Church will experience this transformation in his life, and so live that others, seeing his good deeds, may be led to glorify our Father in heaven.

Chapter Twenty-three

Cleanliness
Is Next to
Godliness

Wɪᴛʜ thoughts of the glorious dedication of the Oakland Temple still with me, and with the soul conviction of the blessings that await members of the Church, and especially our young people, when they enter the house of the Lord, I admonish youth to prepare to be worthy to enter the temples of the Most High.

There is one fundamental quality or virtue necessary to make that preparation complete. Of course, there are many virtues and principles of the gospel which should be lived up to as nearly as possible, as preparatory for entrance into the temple.

Many years ago this admonition was given by a servant of the Lord: ". . . Be ye clean that bear the vessels of the Lord. . . ." (D.&C. 38:42.) Every member of the Church should know that one of the very first requisites for entering the house of the Lord is *cleanliness*. You have heard it said that "Cleanliness is next to Godliness." It is a contributing virtue, not only as preparatory to entering the house of God, but as one that broadens, contributes to happiness and growth, to peace of mind in the individual, and to contentment in the home. Cleanliness contributes to health. Cleanliness contributes to sociability and pleasure of companionship.

Be Ye Clean

When the Lord said, "Be ye clean that bear the vessels of the Lord," I am sure he had in mind the necessity of *cleanliness of thought* as well as cleanliness of hands and of linen. The most powerful thing in the world is not the bomb that kills individuals and blows up cities—the most powerful thing in the world is an idea! It is the *thought* and the *idea* that discovered the bombs and other explosives.

"Tell me what you think about when you do not have to think, and I will tell you what you are." Latter-day Saints have the responsibility of thinking pure thoughts, of cherishing high ideals. As long as they do, their actions will be in accordance with those ideals. One writer has truly said:

> You never can tell what your thoughts will do
> In bringing you hate or love;
> For thoughts are things,
> And their airy wings
> Are swifter than carrier doves.
>
> They follow the law of the universe—
> Each thing must create its kind;
> And they sweep o'er the track
> To bring you back
> Whatever went out from your mind.
> — Author unknown.

Let me make it simple. Many years ago a young man came to me while I was president of the European Mission and made a confession of a wrong and sinful act. He justified himself by saying that he happened to be in a bookstore at the closing hour, and when the door was locked he yielded to temptation. He rather blamed the *circumstances* for his fall.

But I said, "It wasn't the circumstances; it wasn't the locked door, nor the enticement. You had thought of that before you went to that bookstore. If you had never thought of that act, there would have been no circumstance strong enough to entice or to tempt you, a missionary, to fall. The thought always precedes the act."

132

Clean thoughts, high ideals, thinking of love in the true sense, temperance, helpfulness, cheerfulness, all are principles that will contribute to development of character. Thinking of self, harboring ill will against a neighbor, thinking of some opportunity to gratify appetite by smoking or drinking, will lead the individual to commit those things.

The Lord's House Is Clean

Everything in the house of the Lord is clean, wholesome, and beautiful; that is as it should be, and those who enter should come with clean hands, clean thoughts, and pure hearts. I was deeply impressed once in the Salt Lake Temple when sitting with other members of the Council of the Twelve and in the presence of the First Presidency of the Church, at the time President Joseph F. Smith was president. He had told us of a dream he had had, which has since been published; and some of you may have read it.

He gave it more as a vision than a dream, and it seems such to me. He thought he was in the presence of other leaders of the Church who had died and gone to the other side. It seemed that he had been somewhat delayed in putting on his clean linen, and he was a little tardy when he entered the door in the presence of the leaders whom he named. There sat the Prophet Joseph Smith; the Prophet's brother, Hyrum; the patriarch, grandfather of President Joseph F. Smith; President Brigham Young; President John Taylor; President Wilford Woodruff; and other presidents and prominent leaders of the Church. At that time the realization came forcibly to President Joseph F. Smith of the privilege that was his to enter into this distinguished company. The thought of his being worthy to sit with that body of men rather overwhelmed him. He stood for a moment as he entered, and the Prophet Joseph looked up and spoke to him, saying, "Joseph, you are late."

And then a supreme satisfaction filled the president's soul, for he answered, "*Yes, President Smith, I am late, but I am clean!*" Not only was his linen clean, but also he could look in retrospect and have the realization that he had kept his soul unstained from sin.

I believe that will be the greatest satisfaction that can come to any of us when we, too, meet those of our loved ones who have gone before, and particularly when we enter the presence of our Lord and Savior.

We are in the midst of temptation here in mortality, but we can rise above it if we think noble thoughts, if we plan and pray for help to keep us above the low and the vulgar and the vile, and if we keep our bodies and thoughts pure and unsullied.

Let us practice these virtues in our homes, and in our daily lives wherever we may be, so that when we enter the house of the Lord we may say, *"I am clean."*

Chapter Twenty-four

True Beauty
and
Chastity

IN this day when modesty is thrust into the background and chastity is considered an outmoded virtue, I appeal to every girl and every woman in the Church to keep her soul unmarred and unsullied from the sin of unchastity, the consequence of which will smite and haunt her intimately until her conscience is seared and her character becomes sordid.

A young lady was once deploring the frequency of the changes in styles, when a young man to whom she spoke said, "Well, why do you women permit it? You do not have to adopt every suggestion of the fashion plate."

"If it were not for you men," she replied, "we wouldn't."

"For us men! How is that?"

"Yes, for you men; for, after all, to make an honest confession, one of the reasons for all this style in dress and complexion is to bring forth the admiration of you selfish 'lords of creation.' "

The conversation was carried on in a jocular vein and continued for some time. The thought that his opinion influenced the girl to make herself beautiful seemed to tickle the young man's conceit. However, the girl was the young man's superior and called forth his admiration, not merely by her outward beauty, but by a quality a thousand times more powerful and admirable.

135

True Beauty To Be Encouraged

Yes, men are attracted by beauty, and thousands are ensnared by it. There are thousands of men who look for nothing else and desire nothing else but to have their senses pleased or their passions gratified. These men, outward adornments will satisfy, and only outward adornment will retain. When beauty fades, the passion seeks for gratification elsewhere. "Beauty is only skin deep"; and when outward adornment is all a girl possesses, the admiration she calls forth is even more shallow than her beauty.

I do not discourage efforts to enhance physical beauty. When given by birth, it should be nurtured in childhood, cherished in girlhood, and protected in womanhood. When not inherited, it should be developed and sought after in every legitimate and healthful manner. However, I hope our girls will resist *all* the temptations of the world that may come under the heading of *vanity*, and that they will have the strength to resist all the allurements that come with wealth and worldly position, when they make those two things ends in themselves.

There is a beauty every girl has—a gift from God, as pure as the sunlight, and as sacred as life. It is a beauty that all men love, a virtue that wins all men's souls. That beauty is *chastity*. Chastity without skin beauty may enkindle the soul; skin beauty without chastity can kindle only the eye. Chastity enshrined in the mold of true womanhood will hold true love eternally.

As I have stated, chastity is a beauty that all men love. He who does not is not a real man, and as one has put it, "should be sent back to nature's mint and reissued as a counterfeit on humanity's baser metal." Such a one is not worth a pure woman's scorn, not to say smile.

Even vile men admire virtuous strength in woman. I am reminded of a great illustration of this in literature wherein a Jewish maiden won the respect of a profligate.

The True Beauty of Ivanhoe's Rebecca

Read the story of Rebecca, that beautiful character in Sir Walter Scott's *Ivanhoe*. She was the prisoner of Brian de Bois-Guilbert, who had chosen her for base reasons. Others of his crowd chose the old father to rob him of his wealth. When Brian de Bois-Guilbert came in to take charge of his prize, Rebecca "had already unclasped two costly bracelets and a collar, which she hastened to proffer to the supposed outlaw, concluding naturally to gratify his avarice was to bespeak his favor.

"Take these," she said, "and . . . be merciful to me and my aged father! These ornaments are of value, yet they are trifling to what he would bestow to obtain our dismissal from this castle, free and uninjured."

"Fair flower of Palestine," replied the outlaw, "these pearls are orient, but they yield in whiteness to your teeth: the diamonds are brilliant, but they cannot match your eyes; and ever since I have taken up this wild trade, I have made a vow to prefer beauty to wealth."

". . . Thou art no outlaw," said Rebecca; ". . . no outlaw had refused such offers . . .Thou art . . . a Norman—a Norman, noble perhaps in birth—Oh, be so in thy actions, and cast off this fearful mask of outrage and violence."

". . . I am not an outlaw, then fair rose of Sharon. And I am one who will be more prompt to hang thy neck and arms with pearls and diamonds, which so well become them, than to deprive thee of these ornaments."

"What would'st thou have of me?" said Rebecca, "if not my wealth?—We can have nought in common between us—you are a Christian—I am a Jewess—our union were contrary to the laws alike of the church and the synagogue."

"It were so, indeed," replied [Brian de Bois-Guilbert] laughing: "wed with a Jewess? . . . Not if she were the Queen of Sheba."

And then Rebecca knew his purpose. She threw open the latticed window, and an instant later stood on the verge of the parapet, with not the slightest screen between her and the tremendous depth below, and exclaimed:

"Remain where thou art, proud Templar, or at thy choice, advance!—one foot nearer, and I plunge myself from the precipice; my body shall be crushed out of the very form of humanity upon the stones of that courtyard, 'ere it become the victim of thy brutality!"

As she spoke thus, she clasped her hands and extended them towards heaven, as if imploring mercy on her soul before she made the final plunge. The Templar hesitated, and a resolution which had never yielded to pity or distress gave way to his admiration of her fortitude. "Come down . . . rash girl!" he said,— "I swear by earth, and sea, and sky, I will offer thee no offense."[1]

The reprobate for the first time in his life was taught respect for womanhood. Her beauty appealed to his passion; her chastity and honor to his soul.

Creation's Masterpiece

The indulgences and pleasures that lead girlhood away from the fundamental principles of happiness are shallow and shoddy, deceiving in their promises and ultimately disappointing.

The flower by the roadside that catches the dust of every traveler is not the one to be admired, and is seldom, if ever, plucked; but the one blooming way up on the hillside, protected by a perpendicular cliff, is the flower with the virgin perfume, the one the boy will almost risk his life to possess. Mere outside adornment may please the senses of many superficial admirers; the adornment of the soul and the chastity of pure womanhood will awaken in the soul of true manhood enduring life, that eternal principle.

The highest ideal of our young women today is love as it may be expressed in marriage and home-building, and this virtue in which love finds true expression is based upon the *spiritual* and not the physical side of our being. If marriage and home building be based upon physical attraction alone, your love will sooner or later become famished and home life a heavy, disheartening existence.

True joy is found, not in physical indulgence and excesses, but in clean living and high thinking; in rendering

---

[1]Sir Walter Scott, *Ivanhoe* (Airmont Publishing Company, Inc., New York, N. Y., 1964), pp. 211-217.

to others not inconvenience, injury, nor pain, but encouragement, cheer, and helpfulness.

The Church gives to woman a place of highest honor. To merit and maintain this high dignity, she must possess those virtues which have always, and which ever will, demand the respect and love of mankind. A beautiful, modest, chaste woman is creation's masterpiece. When to these virtues a woman possesses as guiding stars in her life righteousness and godliness and an irresistible impulse and desire to make others happy, no one will question if she be classed among those who are truly great.

Chapter Twenty-five

Honesty: A Fundamental Principle of the Gospel

Jesus the Christ lived a life of truth. Men have called him an enthusiast; they have accused him of being a dreamer, an ascetic, a recluse, and other epithets have they hurled at him, but they are loath ever to say that Christ, the Redeemer, was dishonest or untrue. His life was a life of honesty, honor, uprightness.

He was drawn to men who were honest themselves; whose hearts were pure and guileless. Witness how quickly he saw purity and guilelessness in Nathanael: "Behold," said he, "an Israelite indeed, in whom is no guile!" (John 1:47.) Their souls attracted each other as two drops of morning dew fall together on the same flower. So the purity of Christ seemed to absorb, to attract, the purity of Nathanael. Nathanael was honest and upright, as a follower of Christ should be. No guileless man can be dishonest. No guileless man can stoop to chicanery and fraud, deceiving a brother. Christ's life and his teachings always bore testimony to the truth.

"God Doth Not Walk in Crooked Paths"

In our day the Lord has said through the Prophet Joseph Smith:

For God doth not walk in crooked paths, neither doth he turn to the right hand nor to the left, neither doth he vary from that which he hath said, therefore his paths are straight, and his course is one eternal round. (D.&C. 3:2.)

To the Latter-day Saints, as God's people, he has declared that one of the fundamental principles of their belief is honesty. I rejoice in repeating our thirteenth Article of Faith:

We believe in being honest, true, chaste, benevolent, virtuous, and in doing good to all men; indeed, we may say that we follow the admonition of Paul—We believe all things, we hope all things, we have endured many things, and hope to be able to endure all things. If there is anything virtuous, lovely, or of good report or praiseworthy, we seek after these things.

"Let your light so shine before men, that they may see your good works, and glorify your Father which is in heaven." (Matthew 5:16.)

In probably no more effective way can the truth be witnessed before men than for every Latter-day Saint to maintain and foster the confidence of all men everywhere. Now, in order to do that we must be honest in all things. If we are contractors and agree to put certain materials into a building, let us use that material. If we agree to the stipulations of a contract, let us live up to what we agree. Such things may be considered only "details," but they are the "details" by which the men with whom we deal will judge our actions.

If we are taking potatoes of a particular grade to market, and we so describe that grade, let us know that an investigation will prove our statements to be true. I was grieved when once I heard a wholesale dealer say that he had opened sacks of produce brought in from the farm and found foreign material, such as rocks and dirt, placed in the sacks to make up the weight. I did not ask him for the religion of those men; I asked for no name; but such things are dishonorable, and no true member of the Church of Jesus Christ can stoop to such trickery.

How Common Is Insincerity?

In this world today there needs to be an ensign, a people standing out in bold relief as an example to the world in honesty and fair dealing. I shall not condemn the world, but to illustrate what I mean, I shall let a reverend gentleman give his opinion. I quote from Charles Edward Jefferson, author of *The Character of Jesus*. Speaking of the insincerity of the world, he says:

And yet how common insincerity is. What a miserable old humbug of a world we are living in, full of trickery and dishonesty and deceit of every kind. Society is cursed with affectation, business is honeycombed with dishonesty. The political world abounds in duplicity and chicanery, there is sham and pretense and humbuggery everywhere. Some use big words they do not understand, and some lay claim to knowledge which they do not have, and some parade in dresses which they cannot pay for; the life of many a man and many a woman is one colossal lie. We say things which we do not mean, express emotions which we do not feel, we praise when we secretly condemn, we smile when there is a frown on the face of the heart, we give compliments when we are really thinking curses, striving a hundred times a week to make people think we are other than we are. It is a penitentiary offense to obtain money under false pretenses. . . . But how many other things are obtained, do you think, by shamming and pretending, for which there is no penalty but the condemnation of Almighty God? Yes, it is a sad, deceitful, demoralized world in the midst of which we find ourselves; but thank God there are hearts here and there upon which we can ever more depend. We have tested them, and we know them to be true.[1]

That was written many years ago, and we all know that insincerity and dishonesty among peoples and among governments have increased.

Sincerity of International Relations

Referring to the necessity of moral integrity, sincerity, and honesty of purpose in "international relations, the signing of treaties, understandings, conventions, international

---

[1]Charles Edward Jefferson, *The Character of Jesus* (Thomas Y. Crowell Publishing Company, New York, N. Y., 1908), pp. 57-58.

policies," etc., Pierre Lecomte du Noüy, author of *Human Destiny*, writes as follows:

. . . We should know by this time that their effectiveness depends entirely on the moral character of the men who have draughted them or participated in them. We know that papers destined to settle for ten, twenty, or thirty years the relations between countries and the fate of their peoples, and signed in great pomp, often only engage the momentary responsibility of the signers and are sometimes nothing but short-lived "scraps of paper."

As long as there is no collective conscience, rendering the nations —that is, the citizens, not the governments—jointly liable for the engagements taken by their representatives, treaties will constitute a tragic comedy and it is surprising that anyone can still be their dupe. . . .

The problem of peace is far too grave and complex to be solved by such superficial methods. It will only be settled by systematic action on the minds of children and by imposing rigid moral structures, which, in the absence of real conscience, slower to erect, will render certain acts odious. Were the sense of human dignity spread universally, it would suffice to guarantee the respect *of the given word, of the signed engagement*, and consequently would confer a real value to all acts and treaties. Peace would be assured without effort, since every citizen would feel morally responsible for the fulfillment of the terms agreed upon. . . .

Every Promise Is Sacred

Children are trained to behave decently in public, but nobody dreams of making them repeat daily, as a prayer, "Every promise is sacred. No one is obliged to give a pledge, but he who breaks his given word is dishonored. He commits an unpardonable crime against his dignity, he betrays; he covers himself with shame; he excludes himself from society."

. . . Let every man remember that the destiny of mankind is incomparable and that it depends greatly on his will to collaborate in the transcendent task. Let him remember that the Law is, and always has been, to struggle, and that the fight has lost nothing of its violence by being transposed from the material onto the spiritual plane; let him remember that his own dignity, his nobility as a human being, must emerge from his efforts to liberate himself from his bondage and to obey his deepest aspirations. And let him above all never forget that the divine spark is in him, in him alone, and that he is free to disregard it, to kill it, or to come closer to God by showing his eagerness to work with Him, and for Him.[2]

Truth and Honesty Are Eternal Laws

How can peace and universal brotherhood be attained without truth and honesty in governments and individuals? The same laws of eternal progress are applicable to all of our Father's children. Such a universal requirement reflects divine justice. Only by compliance with the principles of the gospel can peace and universal brotherhood be attained and the soul of man progress throughout eternity, and such a plan is needed in this distracted world today.

If members of The Church of Jesus Christ of Latter-day Saints *believe*, not just think—*believe* must be stronger than *think*—if "we believe in being honest, true, chaste," and accept it as part of our lives, then our acts should so shine before men, that they, seeing our good works, will be led to glorify our Father in heaven.

May we be honest in our dealings; be true to ourselves; never be false to our honest convictions; be true to the Church; be true to the testimonies we possess. God help us in this and in all worthy things, to bear witness to the truth.

------

[2]Lecomte du Noüy, *Hymn Destiny,* pp. 187-189.

Chapter Twenty-six

The
Greatest
Possession

INDIFFERENCE toward religion is a dangerous state of mind. The most precious thing in all the world is to accept God as our Father, to accept his Son as our Redeemer, our Savior, and to know in one's heart that the Father and the Son appeared in this dispensation and gave the gospel of Jesus Christ for the happiness, salvation, and exaltation of the human family. To accept that as an eternal truth is to have the greatest possession that the human mind can possess.

I believe with the great English philosopher and scientist, Sir Humphrey Davy, that

> If I could choose what of all things would be at the same time the most delightful and the most useful to me, I should prefer a firm religious belief above every other blessing; for this makes life a discipline of goodness; creates new hopes when all earthly ones vanish; throws over the decay of existence the most glorious of all lights; awakens life even in death; makes every torture and shame the ladder of ascent to paradise; and far above all combinations of earthly hopes, calls up the most delightful visions of the future, the security of everlasting joys. . . .

That is the message we should like to give to all the world: that the most delightful, the most useful possession in life is a testimony of the truth of The Church of Jesus Christ of Latter-day Saints.

Jesus Saves Individuals

The gospel teaches that each individual is a child of our Father in heaven. Each one is precious in his sight. There are leaders of some nations today who do not believe that. The Communist leaders think that the state is the one thing that should be saved, and each individual man or woman is just a part of the whole to make that state supreme. That is false doctrine! The state exists for the good of each individual—to see that the individual has his rights as an individual. That is what the gospel teaches. You are baptized as an individual, not as a group; and the Father is interested in your salvation and in mine, and in the happiness and salvation of each little boy and girl. The Savior went about saving *individuals*. Even the poor woman who was caught in sin and dragged and thrown at the feet of the Savior was precious in his sight. Her accusers said to Jesus, thinking they could ensnare him:

. . . Master, this woman was taken in adultery, in the very act. Now Moses in the law commanded us, that such should be stoned: but what sayest thou? (John 8:4, 5.)

His sublime answer was: ". . . he that is without sin among you, let him first cast a stone at her." (John 8:7) And then he wrote something on the ground with his finger, the only line that he ever wrote according to the record, and nobody knows what it was. But while he wrote, those who judged her drew away one by one. Then to the poor woman who was still bowed in the dust, he said,

. . . Woman, where are those thine accusers? hath no man condemned thee?

She said, No man, Lord. And Jesus said unto her, Neither do I condemn thee: go, and sin no more. (John 8:10, 11.)

Each Individual Is Precious

Each individual is precious in the sight of our Father in heaven, and his beloved Son desires that each be saved and exalted by obedience to the principles of the gospel. And when women and men will say, "I do not believe in the Church," they are saying that they do not believe in the happiness and joy of this present life and do not have an assurance of the eternal life to come.

A love of the gospel is our most precious possession. It can be lost by sin. We can be unhappy by violating the principles of the gospel, or we can keep our testimonies and be happy and joyous no matter what happens to us in the world.

Wicked men threw Paul and Silas into jail in Macedonia, but at midnight when the prisoners had their hands in stocks parallel with their feet, they sang hymns of praise to our Father in heaven because they had the testimony of the gospel in their hearts. (See Acts 16:19-26.)

Salvation and peace, contentment of the human family, not only in the home but also in community life, will come through obedience to the principles of the gospel of Jesus Christ. We cannot be true to ourselves and to our loved ones and our associates without being determined to live more in accordance with those divine principles. I mean in daily life, in our speech, in our self-control, in home associations, with business associates, in political fields. We cannot be true to ourselves, to our loved ones, and to our associates without feeling a determination to know more about the great truths of the gospel. The spirit within bears testimony that truth exists in this old world, and the spirit feeds upon that truth.

We Need Not Worry

We cannot truly believe that we are the children of God and that God exists, without believing in the final inevitable triumph of the truth of the gospel of Jesus Christ. If we do believe that, we shall have less worry about the destruction of the world and the present civilization, because God has established his Church never to be thrown down nor given to another people. And as God lives, and his people

147

are true to him and to one another, we need not worry about the ultimate triumph of truth.

If you have that testimony on your side, you can pass through the dark valley of slander, misrepresentation, and abuse, undaunted as though you wore a magic suit of mail that no bullet could enter, no arrow could pierce. You can hold your head high, toss it fearlessly and defiantly, look every man calmly and unflinchingly in the eye as though you were a victorious king, returning at the head of legions, with banners waving and lances glistening and bugles filling the air with music. You can feel the great expansive world of more health surging through you as the quickened blood courses through the body of him who is gladly, gloriously proud of physical health. You will know that all will come out right in the end; that it must come; that all must flee before the great white light of truth, as the darkness slinks away into nothingness in the presence of the sunburst.

So with truth as our guide, our companion, our ally, our inspiration, we may tingle with the consciousness of our kinship with the Infinite, and all the petty trials, sorrows, and sufferings of this life will fade away as temporary, harmless visions seen in a dream.

That is our privilege through God's blessing and guidance, if we possess the greatest gift in life, a testimony of the truth of the gospel of Jesus Christ, and apply in daily activity the spiritual blessings and privileges of his gospel.

Chapter Twenty-seven

Law of Compensation, of Retribution Constantly Operative

"There is a law, irrevocably decreed
in heaven before the foundations
of this world, upon which all
blessings are predicated—and
when we obtain any blessing from
God, it is by obedience to that
law upon which it is predicated."

THE remarkable saying above
declares the existence of a law as eternal as creation itself.
The word "irrevocable" indicates that this law will always
exist. In other words, it is an eternal edict to the effect that
any blessing obtained from God must come as the result
of obedience to the law upon which the blessing is predicated. This declaration was made by the Prophet Joseph
Smith.

In the world today there is a great need for more
practical religion—a need for making obedience to social
laws and moral order, potent factors in our daily affairs and
conduct.

To influence men to do this is the purpose of true religion. It is not alone sufficient to come together in con-
ferences and other meetings to awaken a union between the
soul and the divine spirit; we must also foster honorable

149

relationships toward our fellowmen. The first is essential; the second is of equal importance.

It is true, also, that spiritual growth comes only through obedience to spiritual laws. One of our leading thinkers, referring to the present great accomplishments in material things, writes as follows: "Life abundant, beauteous, laughing life, has been our age-long labor's end. What other conceivable worth has the mastery of the material world, the exploitation of the resources of nature, and the creation of wealth except as a basis for the release of the life of the spirit?"

It is a self-evident fact that law is constantly operative in the universe around us. You may turn to the old almanac and determine the very second at which the sun will set on any day in the year. You may determine almost to the very second when the sun will rise in the morning. You can learn when the moon's phases occur. All around in everyday observation, we discover operation of law in the world about us.

Just as plainly evident is the fact that law is operative in our bodily functions. Unless we conform to the laws of health, our bodies will suffer impairment. It is simply a recognition of the operation of law as it relates to the health and vitality of the body.

Every student knows that unless he conforms to certain intellectual laws at school he is not going to succeed. He may deceive the teacher and cheat in examinations, and receive subsequently the 100-percent mark; but deep down in the student's soul he knows he has not received the credit which he would have merited had he, through honest effort, gained a knowledge of the questions.

You may cheat your fellowmen and apparently for awhile succeed, but nature is never deceived. She credits and debits according to merit; for here in this old world the law of retribution is just as constant as the law of compensation.

The Immutable Law of Retribution

The same condition exists in the moral world. You cannot violate a moral principle without suffering the consequences. The world may not know of the violation but there are two beings who do know it. One is God, and one is he who perpetrates the deed. In that connection Charles Kingsley has aptly said:

The more I know intimately the lives of other men, to say nothing of my own, the more obvious is it to me that the wicked do not flourish nor is the righteous punished. The ledger of the Almighty is strictly kept and every one of us has the balance of his operations paid over to him at the end of every minute of his existence. The absolute justice of the system of things is as clear to me as any scientific fact. The gravitation of sin to sorrow is as certain as that of the earth to the sun; and more so, for experimental truth of that fact is within the reach of all, nay, is before us all in our lives, daily if we have the eyes to see it.

That sets forth clearly the importance of making obedience to the moral and social law the guiding principle of life. Look about you and see examples just as impressive, just as obvious as the examples referred to in the movements of the planets, or the development of the physical muscles, or of success in the intellectual world.

If law is operative in the physical, intellectual, and moral world; it is also operative in the spiritual world. Jesus Christ, our Redeemer, has given us laws—fundamental and eternal—by obedience to which we might enjoy abundant life, might keep the spirit free, and gain complete mastery over all things physical. It is the purpose of life to subdue matter that we might realize the ideal. I like to think of life's ideal as the ever-ready response of the spirit to the guiding influence of the Holy Ghost.

Laws for Abundant Living

What are these laws? The first is " . . . Love the Lord thy God with all thy heart, and with all thy soul, and with

all thy mind. And the second is like unto it, Thou shalt love
thy neighbour as thyself." (Matthew 22:37, 39.)

But how can a man love God if he does not believe in
him? No man can know of the existence of a Supreme Being
unless his spirit is in harmony with God's spirit.

> . . . Walk in the Spirit, and ye shall not fulfil the lust of the flesh.
> . . . The fruit of the Spirit is love, joy, peace, longsuffering, gentleness,
> goodness, faith. . . . If we live in the Spirit, let us also walk in the
> Spirit. (Galatians 5:16, 22, 25.)

That is not only a simple law; it is a divine promise; it
is a guiding principle for the freedom of the spirit. If you do
the will of the Father, you shall know; but if you refuse to
do it, you cannot know.

Then Jesus adds: "If ye love me, keep my commandments." (John 14:15.) These commandments are many, but
they all apply to our relations with our fellowman. Deal
honestly with him in political struggles. Do not berate a
brother. Do not cover his reputation with that which might
injure him in the minds of those who love him.

Religion in practical life is what is going to react upon
the freedom of the soul and contribute to its freedom. If you
would have the spirit free; if you would have happiness in
your homes, in your individual lives, when you are alone, or
in the crowd; if you would have less contention and strife in
all your associations—you should apply the principles of the
gospel of Jesus Christ in your daily lives. What if a man does
revile you? Do not retaliate. A man is happier when he can
reach that standard.

The Church of Jesus Christ of Latter-day Saints is
established to bring about good will among fellowmen and
to lead all to Christ. Members of the Church carry the obligation of exemplifying in their daily lives the principles of the
gospel. It is our duty to try to exemplify the spirit of the
Christ. The principles we believe in must be exemplified in

our daily lives if we would please God and accomplish his purposes.

Let us

. . . add to [our] faith virtue; and to virtue knowledge; and to knowledge temperance; and to temperance patience; and to patience godliness; and to godliness brotherly kindness; and to brotherly kindness charity. (2 Peter 1:5-7.)

Chapter Twenty-eight

The
Divine
Church

O<small>N</small> A<small>PRIL</small> 6, 1830, a group of men and women, in obedience to a commandment of God, were assembled in the house of Mr. Peter Whitmer, Sen., for the purpose of organizing the Church.

It was just a group of friendly neighbors, unknown to anyone beyond the countryside in which they followed their daily vocations. A good picture of the moral and economic atmosphere of the neighborhood may be surmised from the following introduction of one of the citizens: Joseph Knight, Sen. " 'owned a farm, a grist mill and carding machine. He was not rich, yet he possessed enough of this world's goods to secure to himself and family, not only the necessaries, but also the comforts of life. . . . ' He 'was . . . a sober, honest man, generally respected and beloved by his neighbors and acquaintances. He did not belong to any religious sect, but was a believer in the Universalian doctrine.' The business in which Joseph Knight, Sen., engaged, made it necessary at times for him to hire men, and the Prophet Joseph was occasionally employed by him. To the Knight family, . . . the young Prophet related many of the things God had revealed respecting the Book of Mormon, then as yet, to come forth."[1]

---

[1]Documentary History of the Church, Vol. 1, p. 47.

154

Of such ordinary, rural men and women was the group composed who assembled in Peter Whitmer's house in Fayette, Seneca County, New York, over a century ago.

Means of communication were primitive—seven years before the telegraph would be known. The only light in the house after dark would be furnished by candle, perhaps by kerosene lamp. The electric light globe would not be known for forty years. Sixty years—almost a lifetime—before the automobile would be used! And the airplane existed only in the realm of imagination. Yet one year before the organization of the Church, under the inspiration of the Lord, Joseph Smith had written:

". . . a marvelous work is about to come forth among the children of men." (D.&C. 4:1.)

There is no evidence that such a statement had ever before been made by an obscure lad, and if it had, it would have passed into obscurity with the boastful pretensions or imaginations of its author. Just as the anticipated, foolish aspirations of "Darius Green and his flying machine,"—I am not sure whether I am right on that, but that is as I remember it as a boy—who spoke disdainfully of the man who had made "wings of wax" that would not stand "sunshine and hard whacks," and who boastfully said: "I shall make mine of leather, or something or other."

I mention that merely to emphasize the fact that a Church to become a "marvelous work and a wonder" must contain those elements of truth which find lodgment in the human mind, which in honesty recognizes and loves truth wherever or whenever it is found.

It is true that over a century ago, when men heard that a young man claimed that God had revealed himself, they mocked him, and in doubt turned away from him just as in the beginning of the Christian Era wise and able men in Athens turned away from a lonely little brown-eyed man who challenged much of their philosophy as false and their worship of images as gross error, yet the fact remained that he was the only man in that great city of intellectuals who knew by actual experience that a man may pass through the portals of death and live—the only man in Athens who could clearly sense the difference between the formality of idolatry and the heartfelt worship of the only true and living God. By the Epicureans and Stoics with whom he had conversed and argued, Paul had been called a "babbler," a "setterforth of strange gods";

> And they took him, and brought him unto Areopagus, saying, May we know what this new doctrine, whereof thou speakest is?
>
> For thou bringest certain strange things to our ears: we would know therefore what these things mean. (Acts 17:19-20.)
>
> Then Paul stood in the midst of Mars' hill, and said, Ye men of Athens, I perceive that in all things ye are too superstitious.
>
> For as I passed by, and beheld your devotions, I found an altar with this inscription, TO THE UNKNOWN GOD, Whom therefore ye ignorantly worship, him declare I unto you. (Acts 17:22-23.)

Today, as then, too many men and women have other gods to which they give more thought than to the resurrected Lord—the god of pleasure, the god of wealth, the god of indulgence, the god of political power, the god of popularity, the god of race superiority— as varied and numerous as were the gods in ancient Athens and Rome.

Thoughts that most frequently occupy the mind determine a man's course of action. It is therefore a blessing to the world that there are occasions such as this, which, as warning semaphores, say to mankind: *In your mad rush for pleasure, wealth, and fame, pause and think what is of most value in life.*

What fundamental truths, what eternal principles, if any, were associated with that little group which assembled over one hundred years ago?

The first was Man's Relationship to Deity. For the first time in eighteen hundred years, God had revealed himself as a Personal Being. The relationship of Father and Son had been established by the divine introduction: "This is My Beloved Son. Hear Him!" (Joseph Smith 2:17.)

Those who were baptized into the Church that day in April 1830 *believed in the existence of a Personal God; that his reality and that of his Son Jesus Christ constitute the eternal foundation upon which this Church is built.*

Commenting upon this eternally existent, creative power of God, Dr. Charles A. Dinsmore of Yale University, in *Christianity and Modern Thought,* aptly says:

> Religion, standing on the known experience of the race, makes one bold and glorious affirmation. She asserts that this power that makes for truth, for beauty, and for goodness is not less personal than we. This leap of faith is justified because *God cannot be less than the greatest of his works,* the *Cause* must be adequate to the effect. When, therefore, we call God personal, we have interpreted him by the loftiest symbol we have. He may be infinitely more. He cannot be less. When we call God a Spirit, we use the clearest lens we have to look at the Everlasting. As Herbert Spencer has well said: *"The choice is not between a personal God and something lower, but between a personal God and something higher."*

"My Lord and my God" was not merely a spontaneous, meaningless exclamation of Thomas when he beheld his Risen Lord. The Being before him was his God. Once we accept Christ as divine, it is easy to visualize his Father as being just as personal as he; for Christ said, " . . . he that hath seen me hath seen the Father. . . . " (John 14:9.)

How boastful, how unfounded, is the brazen declaration of communism that "there is no God," and that "Religion (the church) is but an opiate!"

Faith in the existence of an Intelligent Creator was the first element that contributed to the perpetuity of the Church, *the everlasting foundation upon which the Church is built.*

The second cornerstone is the Divine Sonship of Jesus Christ. The gospel teaches that Christ is the Son of God, the Redeemer of the world. No true follower is satisfied to accept

157

him merely as a great teacher, a great reformer, or even as the One Perfect Man. The Man of Galilee is not figuratively, but *literally* the Son of the Living God.

A *third principle* which contributes to the stability of the Church and which impressed not only that little group, but millions since, that a great and marvelous work was about to come forth, *is the immortality of the human soul.*

Jesus passed through all the experiences of mortality just as you and I. He knew happiness. He experienced pain. He rejoiced as well as sorrowed with others. He knew friendship. He experienced also the sadness that comes through traitors and false accusers. He died a mortal death even as every other mortal. As his spirit lived after death, so shall yours and mine.

A *fourth element* which contributed to the perpetuity of that little group was the *Cherished Hope for the Brotherhood of Man.* One of the two great general principles to which all others are subsidiary is this: " . . . love thy neighbour as thyself," (Matt. 19:19) and correlated with it, the promise: "Inasmuch as ye have done it unto the least of these my brethren, ye have done it unto me." (Matt. 25:40.)

The gospel bids the strong bear the burdens of the weak, and to use the advantages given them by their larger opportunities in the interest of the common good that the whole level of humanity may be lifted, and the path of spiritual attainment opened to the weakest and most unlearned as well as to the strong and intelligent.

The Savior condemned hypocrisy and praised sincerity of purpose. He taught that if the heart be pure, actions will be in accord therewith. Social sins—lying, stealing, dishonest dealings, adultery, and the like—are first committed in thought.

> Sow a thought, reap an act,
> Sow an act, reap a habit,
> Sow a habit, reap a character,
> Sow a character, reap an eternal destiny.
>
> E. D. Boardman

Jesus taught that an unsullied character is the noblest aim in life. No man can sincerely resolve to apply to his daily life the teachings of Jesus of Nazareth without sensing a change in his own nature. The phrase, "born again," has a deeper significance than many people attach to it. This *changed feeling* may be indescribable, *but it is real.* Happy the person who has truly sensed the uplifting, transforming power that comes from this nearness to the Savior, this kinship to the Living Christ.

Resistance is necessary along with obtaining a sense of the real divinity. There should be developed also the *power of self-mastery.* Someone has said that when God makes the prophet, he does not unmake the man. I believe that, though being "born anew," and being entitled to new life, new vigor, new blessings, yet the old weaknesses may still remain. The adversary stands by, ever eager and ready to attack and strike us at our weakest point.

Take, for example, the incident of Jesus on the Mount of Temptation. After he had passed through the ordinance of baptism to fulfill all righteousness, after he had received the commendation of the Father and the testimony from on high that he is the Beloved Son in whom the Father is well pleased, the tempter was there ready to thwart, if possible, his divine mission. At his weakest moment, as Satan thought, when his body was famished by long fasting, the Evil One presented himself saying, " . . . If thou be the Son of God, command that these stones be made bread." (Matt. 4:3.) Though his body was weak, his spirit was strong, as he answered: " . . . It is written, Man shall not live by bread alone, but by every word that proceedeth out of the mouth of God." (Matt. 4:4.)

With unwavering strength, Jesus withstood the tempter's taunts and promises that followed, and triumphantly demanded, " . . . *Get thee hence, Satan: for it is written, Thou shalt worship the Lord thy God, and him only shalt thou serve.*" (Matt. 4:10.)

159

So it is with each of us in our daily resisting of the tempter. He will make his appeal to what may be our weakest point of resistance. His strongest strain will be on the weakest link in the chain that binds our character. It may come in the form of yielding to habit, tendency, or passion which we have indulged for years. It may be a desire for the old pipe or the cigarette which we determined, if we were sincere, to put aside when we entered the waters of baptism. And when that longing comes, after we are in the Church or kingdom, in that moment when temptation comes, we may say to ourselves, "Though I intend to throw it aside, I will take it only once more—this once will not count." That is the moment of resistance when we should say, as Christ, "Get thee behind me."

This power of self-control in regard to our bodily longings, satisfying the passions, applies to every member of the Church of Christ. In some way, the Evil One will attack us; some way he can weaken us. In some way, he will bring before us that which will weaken our souls and will tend to thwart the true development of the spirit within, the strengthening and growth of the spirit, which time cannot kill, which is as enduring as the Eternal Father of the spirit. And the things which will tend to dwarf this spirit or to hinder its growth are things which members of the Church are called upon to resist.

In 1830, the Church was officially organized with six members. It was unknown, and, I repeat, would be known only to the extent that it contained and radiated those eternal principles which harmonize with the eternity of its Author, and only thus could it become a great and marvelous work.

Today there are branches of the Church in many parts of the world. As the effulgent light of a glorious sun gladdens the surface of the earth by day, so the light of truth is entering into the hearts of many honest men and women throughout the world.

The marvelous progress that has been made in transportation and communication makes it possible for the promulgation of the truths of the restored gospel to be made known to the children of men everywhere on the face of the globe. It is possible for millions in America, Europe, Asia, Africa, and the islands of the sea not only to hear, but in many instances to see what you are doing as members for the gospel of truth.

To all members, and to our Father's children everywhere, we declare in all sincerity that God lives! As sure as the light of the sun shines upon everything on the physical earth, so the radiance that emanates from the Creator brightens every soul that comes into the world of humanity, for it is in him that we "live and move and have our being." All of us, therefore, should make him the center of our lives.

Jesus Christ his Beloved Son also lives and stands at the head of the kingdom of God on earth. Through him the eternal plan of the gospel has been given to man and restored in its fullness to the Prophet Joseph Smith. Through obedience to the principles of the gospel, we may become partakers of his divine Spirit, as Peter of old, after two and a half years of association with the Redeemer, testified. (See 2 Peter 1:4.)

In the words of President John Taylor:

> Go, ye messengers of glory;
> Run, ye legates of the skies;
> Go and tell the pleasing story
> That a glorious angel flies;
>
> Go, to all the gospel carry;
> Let the joyful news abound;
> Go till every nation hear you,
> Jew and Gentile greet the sound.
> Let the gospel echo all the earth around.

Chapter Twenty-nine

The Church—
A Worldwide
Institution

THE mission of The Church of
Jesus Christ of Latter-day Saints may be considered in two
great aspects: (1) the proclamation to the world of the
restoration of the gospel of Jesus Christ—the declaration to
all mankind that God the Father and his Son Jesus Christ
appeared in this dispensation to the Prophet Joseph Smith;
(2) the other great purpose of the Church is to translate
truth into a better social order or, in other words, to make
our religion effective in the individual lives of men and in
improving social conditions.

It is the first great purpose to which I wish to call
attention.

On a momentous occasion two thousand years ago,
eleven men assembled near a mountain in Galilee—eleven
humble, obscure men who had been chosen and ordained
apostles of the Lord Jesus Christ. According to appointment,
these men met the resurrected Christ, who made what to
them must have been a startling declaration. They had been
with their Master fewer than three years and had been
expressly enjoined by him to go not in the way of the Gentiles, to enter no city of the Samaritans, but to go rather to the
lost sheep of the house of Israel. (Matt. 10:6.) At this meeting, however, as his final parting instructions, he opened

162

their eyes to the universality of the gospel by giving them this divine commission:

"Go ye therefore, and teach all nations, baptizing them in the name of the Father and of the Son, and of the Holy Ghost.
Teaching them to observe all things whatsoever I have commanded you: and, lo, I am with you alway, even unto the end of the world. (Matt. 28:19-20.)

In the restricted experience of these eleven disciples, the idea of preaching Christ and his saving doctrine to any but members of their own race germinated very slowly. Indeed, the Savior of men found it necessary to give another direct revelation to Peter, the chief apostle, before he fully realized that the Gentiles "should hear the word of the gospel, and believe." (Acts 15:7.)

However, as the light of truth dawned in their hearts, these earnest followers set about to give the gospel to the world—

twelve simple men, with only the wind to bear them over the seas, with only a few pence in their pockets, and a shining faith in their hearts. They fell far short of their ideal, their words were twisted and mocked, and false temples were built over their bones, in praise of a Christ they would have rejected. And yet, by the light of their inspiration many of the world's loveliest things were created, and many of the world's finest minds inspired.[1]

The followers of the Redeemer were reviled, persecuted, and martyred, but they continued to testify to the truth of their risen Lord.

Three hundred years passed, and Christianity became the dominant religion of the most powerful nation in the world, and the persecuted became the persecutors. Pride and worldiness supplanted humility and faith. The church became corrupt. Doctrines of men supplanted the commandments of God; spiritual darkness enshrouded the nations of the world.

----
[1] Beverly Nichols, *The Fool Hath Said* (New York: Doubleday, 1936).

Later, courageous, God-fearing men began to protest against the evil practices of a corrupt clergy. The dawn of a spiritual awakening appeared, but none either claimed or received divine authority to re-establish the Church.

Roger Williams, pastor of the oldest Baptist Church in America, resigned his position because, said he,

There is no regularly constituted church on earth, nor any person authorized to administer any church ordinance; nor can there be until new apostles are sent by the Great Head of the Church, for whose coming I am seeking.[2]

We know that that authority came early in the nineteenth century by the personal appearance of the risen Lord. Again, was given the divine injunction for authorized servants to be sent forth to the East and to the West, to the North and to the South that

every man might speak in the name of God the Lord, even the Savior of the world; That faith also might increase in the earth; That mine everlasting covenant might be established; That the fulness of my gospel might be proclaimed by the weak and the simple unto the ends of the world, and before kings and rulers. (D.&C. 1:20-23.)

In Section Four of the Doctrine and Covenants, the Prophet Joseph Smith received a revelation that

Behold, a marvelous work is about to come forth among the children of men.

Therefore, O ye that embark in the service of God, see that ye serve him with all your heart, might, mind and strength, that ye may stand blameless before God at the last day. (D.&C. 4:1-2.)

When this revelation was given to the Prophet Joseph, he was only 23 years of age. The Book of Mormon was not yet published; no man had been ordained to the priesthood. The Church was not organized; yet the statement was made and written without qualification that "a marvelous work [was] about to come forth among the children of men."

---

[2]Roger Williams, *Picturesque America*, p. 502.

Another significant feature of this revelation, and of others given about the same period, is the naming of essential qualifications of those who were to participate in the bringing about of this marvelous work. These qualifications were *not the possession of wealth, not social distinction, not political preferment, not military achievement, not nobility of birth;* but *a desire to serve God with all your "heart, might, mind and strength"—* spiritual qualities that contribute to *nobility of soul.* I repeat: No popularity, no wealth, no theological training in church government—yet "a marvelous work [was] about to come forth among the children of men."

Manifestly, some higher power was operating to bring about this marvelous work other than through mere human and material means.

The same charge that was given by the risen Lord to his authorized disciples more than nineteen hundred years ago has been given by direct revelation to his authorized servants today.

Though the Church is still young and has had to struggle through persecution, mobocracy, drivings, poverty, misrepresentation by egotists, uninformed preachers, apostates, and by a prejudiced public sentiment, it is moving steadily forward toward its worldwide destiny. Almost immediately after the organization of the Church, the proclamation of the restored gospel began. The Church was scarcely seven years old before the scope of missionary work had included the United States, Canada, and the British Isles.

Since that humble beginning in 1830, 75 missions, including one in Italy that has just recently been organized, have been established throughout the world. Our missionaries, each paying individually, or with the aid of his parents, his or her own expenses, are now declaring to a troubled world that the message heralded at the birth of Jesus— "peace on earth, good will toward men"— may become a reality here and now by obedience to the principles of the gospel.

They are instructed that they go out as representatives of the Church, as representatives of their families, and most important, as representatives of the Lord Jesus Christ, whose servants they are. They are instructed that a representative of any organization, economic or religious, must possess at least one outstanding quality, and that is *trustworthiness*.

These missionaries go out in the spirit of love, seeking nothing from any nation to which they are sent—no personal acclaim, no monetary acquisition.

What is the outstanding message that they have to give Christian, as well as non-Christian, countries? There must surely be something distinctive to justify their presence in all parts of the world.

First, they are to declare the divinity of the mission of the Lord Jesus Christ, the Son of God, the Redeemer and Savior of mankind. They declare with Peter of old that "there is none other name under heaven given among men, whereby we must be saved." (Acts 4:12.)

The second distinctive message is the restoration of his gospel by the appearance of God the Father and his Son Jesus Christ to the Prophet Joseph Smith, and that divine authority through the priesthood has been given to represent Deity in establishing Christ's Church upon the earth. Thus, they are fulfilling to the best of their ability the injunction to preach the gospel to every creature, baptizing them in the name of the Father, and of the Son, and of the Holy Ghost, teaching them to observe all things whatsoever the Lord has commanded.

True Christianity is love in action. There is no better way to manifest love for God than to show an unselfish love for our fellowmen. This is the spirit of missionary work. Our hearts respond with the poet:

> O Brother Man! fold to thy heart thy brother;
> Where pity dwells, the peace of God is there;

To worship rightly is to love each other,
Each smile a hymn, each kindly deed a prayer.[3]

This, then, is a worldwide Church, organized preparatory to the establishment of the kingdom of God on earth. God has given us the power of whispering across space, of transmitting our thoughts within minutes from one end of the earth to another. Geographical conditions or distances are just the same, but modern means of transportation have made practically all nations neighbors.

The Church is using these modern means through its Information Service and broadcasting facilities to disseminate the Gospel throughout the world.

May God bless you men of the priesthood. God bless our missionaries and brethren everywhere for their willingness to consecrate their time, their means, and their ability to the advancement of the kingdom of God.

I bear you my testimony that Joseph Smith was a prophet of God, and when I say this, it means that I know that Jesus lives, that he is our Redeemer, and that this is his Church. We are merely his representatives. When we accept that, then the reality of God the Father, the Father of our spirits, is easy to accept.

With all my heart I bless you, and pray that peace and love and kindness will abide not only in your hearts but in your homes, that your wives, our wives, and our children, may have memories sweet of a home in which God would be pleased to dwell.

---

[3]John Greenleaf Whittier, "Worship."

Chapter Thirty

Church
Organized by
Divine Edict

THE Church, which was designated by the Lord as "a marvelous work and a wonder," had its beginning as an official organization in a room in Peter Whitmer, Junior's home, on Tuesday, April 6, 1830 — one hundred thirty-seven years ago! Six men comprised the membership. None of these laid any claim either to learning or leadership. They were respectable citizens, but, outside of their own immediate neighborhood, were unknown. Judging from all human experience, what these men would do on that humble occasion would give the world but little if any concern. None of that little group had fame, wealth, influential patronage, or even local popularity.

However, one man among them had set forth a most remarkable claim; viz., that he had received several divine communications, as a result of which a book purporting to be a record of the ancient inhabitants of America had already been published, and further that he had been commanded by the Lord to organize a Church, which should be designated in honor of its Founder *the Church of Jesus Christ.*

The Church of Christ

Two facts associated with that first meeting are very significant — first, that the Church was not patterned after any other then in existence, but was organized by a divine edict which did away with "all old covenants" and established "a new and everlasting covenant"; (D.&C. 22:1) and, second, that it was organized "according to the order of the Church as recorded in the New Testament."[1]

Thus, humbly but most significantly, was opened the first scene in the Great Church Drama which eventually is to affect not only the present generation of men, but the whole human family. A humble beginning, yes; but the claim that the Church was organized and its doctrines approved by divine revelation was the most astounding declaration made to the world since the days of the Savior.

From a scholastic standpoint, Joseph Smith was unlearned and wholly untrained in the ministry as accepted by the world; yet something made him bold in his declarations against the false doctrines pertaining to infant baptism, predestination, etc., which were being preached by the ministers of his day.

There were those who hated Jesus when he walked as a man on the shores of Galilee, and there were others who felt as Thomas did when he said: "Let us also go that we may die with him." (John 11:16.)

Likewise, there were those who scorned Joseph Smith and scoffed at his teachings when he declared that he had received a revelation from the Lord. There were others who loved him and felt as Willard Richards, who said, "Brother Joseph, you did not ask me to cross the river with you — you did not ask me to come to Carthage — you did not ask me to come to jail with you — and do you think I would forsake you now? But I will tell you what I will do; if you are condemned to be hung for treason, I will be hung in your stead, and you shall go free."[2]

There is something great about a man who can so impress other able, sincere men that they are ready to die with

---

[1]*DHC*, Vol. 1, p. 79.
[2]*DHC*, Vol. 6, p. 616.

him or for him. As with the Savior, so it will be with Joseph Smith, God's chosen servant — he will grow in greatness and honor as the centuries pass.

Joseph Smith was not only a great man, but he was an inspired servant of the Lord. Indeed, his greatness consists in divine inspiration.

Charles A. Ellwood, author of *Man's Social Destiny,* printed in 1929, wrote that —

> . . . the religion of the future cannot be based upon historical Christianity, but must, in order to avoid misunderstanding, go back to the teachings of Christ, as recorded in the Gospels.

Said the Prophet Joseph one hundred years previously:

"The Church of Jesus Christ was organized in accordance with the order of the Church as recorded in the New Testament."[3]

Nobody can study critically and intelligently the restored gospel of Jesus Christ without being deeply impressed with the harmony of the teachings with those given by the Lord and Savior himself when he was on the earth with his disciples. Consider, for example, the Prophet's revelation concerning the Creator — God as an intelligent Being, one who is, as Jesus taught, "our Father in Heaven." Applying the words of a distinguished writer, Charles A. Dinsmore of Yale, Joseph Smith makes "one bold and glorious affirmation. He asserts that this Power that makes for truth, for beauty, and for goodness is not less personal than we." Dr. Dinsmore continues: "This leap of faith is justified, because God cannot be less than the greatest of his works, the Cause must be adequate to the Effect. When, therefore, we call God personal, we have interpreted him by the loftiest symbol we have. He may be infinitely more. He cannot be less. When we call God a Spirit, we use the clearest lens we have to look at the Infinite. As Herbert Spencer has well said: 'The

---

[3]*DHC,* Vol. 1, p. 79.

choice is not between a personal God and something lower, but between a personal God and something higher.' "

Joseph Smith's doctrine that Jesus Christ is the only Begotten of the Father, the Savior of the world, is identical with the teachings of Jesus himself to his apostles.

So also is his doctrine of the persistence of personality after death.

On these three fundamentals of religion, there can be little or no doubt about the harmony of the teachings of the restored church with those of the Savior — the doctrine of God; the doctrine of sin and salvation; and, the doctrine of immortality.

The same harmony is found in the teachings of other principles of the gospel such as faith, repentance, baptism, laying on of hands for the gift of the Holy Ghost, ordination to the priesthood, his teachings on "knowledge, temperance, godliness, brotherly kindness, charity," etc.

But I think the greatest evidence of Joseph Smith's inspiration is found in the organization of the Church itself. As already stated, the original members of the Church were practically unknown; they were financially poor, and had no political nor social standing, yet, for over one hundred years this organization has survived financial panics, social upheavals, and religious turmoil, and today stands as a means of supplying the highest needs of mankind as it conforms to the best concepts of men who understand government and who are seeking social betterment. Truly, from the standpoint of efficiency and progress, The Church of Jesus Christ of Latter-day Saints has that form of government which will best contribute to the peace and happiness of mankind.

"How knoweth this man letters, having never learned?" (John 7:15) questioned the Jews as they marveled at the wisdom of Jesus. So may we repeat the question regarding Joseph Smith as we consider his outstanding accomplishments during the brief span of fourteen years between the organization of the Church and his martyrdom; as we contemplate the perfect harmony of the restored gospel with that of the primitive Church established by Jesus and his apostles; as we note his penetrating insight into principles and doctrines; and as we see the incomparable plan and efficiency of the Church established by the inspiration of the Christ whose name it bears — the answer to the question "Whence this man's wisdom?" is given in the stirring stanza:

> Praise to the man who communed with Jehovah!
> Jesus anointed that Prophet and Seer.
> Blessed to open the last dispensation,
> Kings shall extol him, and nations revere.
>
> William W. Phelps

Chapter Thirty-one

Determining
Your Own
Future

If thy whole body therefore
be full of light, having no part
dark, the whole shall be full of
light, as when the bright shining
of a candle doth give thee light.
(Luke 11:36.)

WHAT company do you keep
when you are alone? What is your dominating train of
thought? This to a great degree will shape your character.

About forty years ago, in a sculptural yard in Milan,
Italy, there stood a magnificent, now famous, statue of David
of Old. Around it were shapeless, irregular blocks of granite
from which a student sculptor was choosing a suitable speci-
man from which to carve something he had in mind. Visitors
paid little or no attention to him as they stood in admiration
before the heroic statue carved over 400 years ago by Michel-
angelo. That statue stands today in an unfinished state in a
museum at Florence, Italy.

If, on that occasion, you had been among those tourists,
and a master artist had placed in your hands a chisel and
hammer, would you have taken one of those unchiseled
blocks and attempted to carve a human image out of it? You
would probably have refused, saying: "I am not a sculptor;
I cannot do it."

173

Yet each one of you this very hour is carving character —shaping a soul. Is it going to be defaced, or will it be something admirable and noble?

You are the person who has to decide, whether you'll do it or toss it aside.

Yours is the responsibility! No one else can carve it for you. Parents may guide; teachers may help; companions may and will assist, but every young man and young woman has the responsibility of carving his or her own character.

Your tools are ideals. The thought in your mind at this moment is contributing, however infinitesimally, almost imperceptibly, to the shaping of your soul, even to the lineaments of your countenance.

Thoughts Impress

True, it is the dominant and recurring ideals that affect us most; but even passing and idle thoughts leave their impression. Trees that can withstand the hurricane, sometimes yield to destroying pests that can scarcely be seen except with the aid of a microscope. Likewise, the greatest foes of the individual are not always the glaring evils of humanity, but subtle influences of thought and of continual association with companions.

Ideals are stimulants to progress. Without them mankind would become dormant. Through ideals, *confidence*, and *aspirations* men may move upward toward the higher and better life. Selfish or evil thoughts debase the soul. More strongly than the neglect of rituals in worship, Jesus condemned the fostering of wrong ideals, motives, and feelings. He decried the fatal effects of hatred and jealousy in the mind more vehemently than he did the acts that hate and jealousy prompt. Contrariwise, he taught that if evil passions are banished, and kindly thoughts take their place, man becomes incapable of commiting overt acts. Modern physiology and psychology confirm the wisdom of his teachings. Evil passions destroy a man's physical vigor and efficiency. They pervert his mental perception and render him incapable of resisting the temptation to commit acts of violence. They undermine his moral health. By insidious stages they transform the man who cherishes them into a criminal. On the other hand, if they are banished, and wholesome, kindly thoughts and emotions take their place, the man is incapable of crime.

Right Acts

Right thought and feelings if consistently kept in the forefront, inevitably lead to right acts. Fundamental in our Savior's teachings lies this truth:

A *good tree bringeth forth good fruit; but a corrupt tree bringeth forth evil fruit.*" (Matt. 7:17.)

In some of our canyons one can observe the various formations that record part of the creation of the earth. In many places the strata are as distinct and readable as are the leaves in a book. In Ogden Canyon, Utah, for example, there are first conglomerate and rubble, then the solid strata of gneiss, followed by layers of limestone and slate. Just so, there are strata in human society, as varied and broken as are the physical strata in the crust of the earth. *What a man continually thinks about, the ideals he cherishes, determine the realm or realms to which he belongs; determine his place in the scale of manhood.*

Thoughts are the seeds of acts, and precede them. Mere compliance to law, without a corresponding inward desire, will avail but little. Indeed, such outward actions and pretending phrases may disclose hypocrisy. There is eternally operative in the moral world a law of compensation and retribution—compensation commensurate with conformity to law; retribution in actual degree to the extent of disobedience.

A Deeper Sense

In this regard, I use the word "law" in a deeper sense than a rule or dictum prescribed by authority for human action. It means rather "a uniform order of sequence" as operative and unvarying as the law of the inclined plane, or of the law of falling bodies.

No man can disobey moral law without paying the penalty. No sin, however secret, can escape retribution.

True, you may lie and not be detected; you may violate virtue without its being known by any who would scandalize you; yet you cannot escape the judgment that follows transgression.

The lie is lodged in the recesses of your mind, an impairment of your character that will be reflected sometime, somehow in your countenance or bearing. Your moral turpitude, through only you and your accomplice may ever know it, will canker your soul.

As definitely and surely as the weaver shapes his flowers and figures out of the warp and woof of his loom, so every moment the shuttle of thought moves back and forth forming character. Thoughts lift your soul heavenward, or drag you toward hell. It was said of John Keats that his face was the face of one who had seen a vision. *So long had his inner eye been fixed upon beauty, so long had* he loved that "vision splendid," so long had he lived with it, that not only did his soul take on the loveliness of what he contemplated, but the very lines of the poet's face were chiseled into beauty by those sculptors called "thoughts" and "ideals."

Careful observers have noticed that old persons who have lived long together, 'midst sunshine and 'midst cloudy weather, come at length to look as nearly alike as do brother and sister. Emerson explains this likeness by saying that long thinking the same thoughts and loving the same objects mold similarity into the features.

Merit Self-Respect

To have the approval of your conscience when you are alone with your thoughts is like being in the company of true and loving friends. To merit your own self-respect gives strength of character.

The handsomest youth and the most beautiful maiden may mar their beauty by a morose, cross-tempered disposition, or by nursing dissatisfaction in the soul.

Notwithstanding the complexity of human society, we can encompass all purposes by three great important ones:

(1) *Personal Pleasures and Gratification of Appetites and Passions,*

(2) *Material Gain*

(3) *Spiritual Attainment*

First, is it your purpose to have *pleasure* in life, and are you going to have that satisfaction at any cost? I would ask you to pause before deciding, and look at those who have spent their lives in the world of personal indulgence. Pleasure as the uppermost aim eventually brings disappointment, be it the seeking of a new sensation, the satisfying of an appetite, or the gratifying of passion.

> You seize the flow'r, its bloom is shed;
> Pleasures are like poppies spread,
> Or like the snow falls in the river,
> A moment white—then melts for ever;
> Or like the Borealis race,
> That flit ere you can point their place;
> Or like the Rainbow's lovely form
> Vanishing amid the storm
> Robert Burns—"Tom O'Shanter"

Quotes Wagner

On this point, may I quote Charles Wagner in his book, "The Simple Life," wherein he says:

"Here is the secret of the unrest, the madness, of our contemporaries; having condemned their will to the service of their appetites, they suffer the penalty. They are delivered up to violent passions which devour their flesh, crush their bones, suck their blood, and cannot be sated. This is not a lofty moral denunciation. I have been listening to what life says; and have recorded, as I have heard them, some of the truths that resound in every square.

177

"Has drunkenness, inventive as it is of new drinks, found the means of quenching thirst? Not at all! It might rather be called the art of making thirst inextinguishable. Frank libertinage, does it deaden the senses? No!—it envenoms it, converts natural desire into a morbid obsession, and makes it the dominant passion. Let your needs rule you, pamper them—you will see them multiply like insects in the sun. The more you give them, the more they demand. He is senseless, who seeks for happiness in material prosperity alone.

"Our needs in place of servants that they should be, have become a turbulent and seditious crowd, a legion of tyrants in miniature. A man enslaved in his needs may best be compared to a bear with a ring in its nose, that is led about and made to dance at will. The likeness is not flattering, but you will grant that it is true."

Worldly Gain

Second, is it your purpose to get worldly gain? You may obtain it! You may win in this world almost anything for which you strive. If you work for wealth, you can get it; but before you make it an end in itself, take a look at those who have desired wealth for its sake alone. Gold does not corrupt men. It is the motive of acquiring that gold that impairs or shrivels the soul. It is the purpose one has in acquiring it.

Wordsworth's comment is applicable:

> The world is too much with us; late and soon,
> Getting and spending, we lay waste our powers;
> Little we see in Nature that is ours;
> We have given our hearts away, a sordid boon!

Third, if not pleasure or indulgence; if not worldly gain; what, then, may be cherished as a dominant ideal?

Service to Others

We are told that service to others is service to God. That is the antithesis of pure nature. Nature's law is the survival of the fittest. God's law is—use your personal power and possessions for the advancement and happiness of others. This is the highest ideal ever given!

There are some who say that such a religion is too idealistic—that a society dominated by enlightened altruism or the intelligent love of humanity is improbable, if not impossible. Since human history began it seems that the majority of the millions of the earth's inhabitants have sought first the law of indulgence and conquests rather than the ideals of toleration and human sympathy.

Let each one personally make the test—try it out in your life and note the result. If you seek pleasure for its own sake, when you find it, it may be a head of wheat that has been smitten by "smut"; *but seek to share joy with others, or to make somebody else happy, and you will find your own soul radiant with the joy you wished for another.*

This guiding, ever-present thought was expressed by Jesus when he said:

> Seek ye first the kingdom of God, and his righteousness; and all these things shall be added unto you. (Matthew 6:33.)

What a man is may largely be determined by his dominant quest. His success or failure, happiness or misery, depends upon what he seeks, upon what he chooses.

> So whatever it is you want to be,
> Remember, to fashion the choice you are free.
> Kindly or selfish or gentle or strong,
> Keeping the right way or taking the wrong.
> Careless of honor or guarding your pride,
> All these are questions which you must decide.
> Yours the selection, whichever you do;
> The thing men call character's all up to you.
>
> Guest

Young men and young women of the Church, may I admonish you to consider seriously Mormon's last affectionate wish for his son Moroni:

My son, be faithful in Christ, and may his sufferings and death, and the showing his body unto our fathers, and his mercy and long-suffering, and the hope of his glory and of eternal life, rest in your mind forever. (Moroni 9:25.)

Youth, Love, And Marriage

3

Chapter Thirty-two

Widening Horizons

How beautiful is youth!
How bright it gleams
With its illusions, aspirations,
    dreams!
Book of beginnings, story without
    end,
Each maid a heroine, each man
    a friend!

Longfellow

A s we consider together the subject, "The Road to Happiness Through Widening and Extending Horizons," I may not give to you what you are anticipating. I am not going to pretend to. All I ask is that I may express some thought which will call up in your minds nobler thoughts and feelings, that you may thereby profit more than by what I may have in mind.

First let us consider this thing, *happiness*. After all, it is the aim of life, is it not? We are not selfish when we say that. Latter-day Saints know that "men are that they might have joy." The word *joy* is very accurately chosen. I think the Prophet Joseph Smith makes a nice distinction when he refers to *happiness* as the purpose and design of existence and does not mention *pleasure*. On one occasion he said:

Happiness is the object and design of our existence and will be the end thereof if we pursue the path that leads to it; and this path is virtue, uprightness, faithfulness, holiness, and keeping all the commandments of God. But we cannot keep all the commandments without first knowing them, and we cannot expect to know all, or more than we now know, unless we comply with or keep those we have already received.

I submit that as sound philosophy, and there is something upbuilding about it. There is something encouraging. There is something optimistic. It implies that virtue, uprightness, faithfulness, holiness, and keeping the commandments of God lead to a happy life; that those who follow that path are not long-faced and sanctimonious, depriving themselves of the joys of existence. I believe that is worth thinking about while we are young. We all like to be happy. Youth is entitled to happiness, and we are untrue to youth if we deprive them of it. But let us ever keep in mind the fact that there is a distinction between happiness and mere pleasing sensation or pleasure.

Our theme suggests that the road to happiness lies through widening and extending horizons.

Horizon means something bounded by observation or experience. Geographically our horizon is bounded by the limits of our physical view, but those other horizons which we shall here contemplate are *within us*, limited only by the boundary of our imaginations. After all, it is these personal experiences and observations which contribute either to our joy or to our unhappiness.

You who have read Pope's "Essay on Criticism" will at once recall the very beautiful comparison he gives wherein he mentions that "Hills peep o'er hills and Alps on Alps arise":

> So pleas'd at first the tow'ring Alps to try,
> Mount o'er the vales, and seem to tread the sky,
> Th' eternal snows appear already past,
> And the first clouds and mountains seem the last;
> But, those attain'd, we tremble to survey
> The growing labors of the lengthen'd way,
> Th' increasing prospect tires our wand'ring eyes,
> Hills peep o'er hills and Alps on Alps arise!

A poetic expression of a common experience.

We have all been in the country and rejoiced as we started out on a picnic to climb the hills. As we got to the foot of the hill and climbed we could see what we thought was the top. That was our bounded horizon, and so we climbed over rocks and sagebrush, admiring a dainty flower here, an unusual shrub there, and ever and anon turning to view the scene below. We were surprised when we got to that first level which we thought was the top to find that it wasn't the top at all. There were hills still ahead of us; but as we turned, our view was much more impressive than it had been at the foot of the hill. And so with light hearts and aspiring eagerness we started to climb the next. One more climb, we thought, and we shall be at the top. Again we were surprised to see "hills peeping o'er hills," but again our horizon was more extended. How uniform the streets down in the old town! How the canyon assumes a new aspect, and the winding rivers wending toward it look like silver threads stretching across the valley. We can't stop now; another climb, and we continue until at length we reach the crest. It is just a daily experience of what Pope so beautifully has expressed: "Hills peep o'er hills and Alps on Alps arise."

Some of you have been in the Alps and scanned those wonderful peaks, and there you experienced hour after hour and perhaps day after day what it means to acquire more extended horizons.

Well, now we are going to climb introspectively.

The fifteen-hundred-dollar Pulitzer prize for the best symphony written in 1938 was won by a man who as a boy lived in the squalor of the slums. His music is a protest against such conditions. His name is Dante Fiorillo, and he is declared to be "the most talented and deserving composer of the year." As a boy he could see nothing but the dirty streets and the sunless tenements. The surroundings were repulsive to him, and to get away from them he would go for a walk until he reached another part of the town where streets were clean and where sunshine could be enjoyed.

There are too many of us content to dwell in the slums of the intellect and of the spirit. Too many of us seek for happiness in the sunless surrounding of indulgence. Unlike the young Dante Fiorillo, we hesitate to put forth the energy to walk out into the sunshine and find the clean streets and rejoice in the broader horizons of intellectual joys and spiritual ecstasies. "There are depths in man which go to the lowest hell, and heights which reach the highest heaven, for are not heaven and hell made out of him, everlasting miracle and mystery that he is?" says Carlyle.

And so I ask you, young men and women, to begin the climb now to the intellectual and spiritual hills that I believe will lead to happiness. You may not agree with me. Be that as it may, I believe the course that I shall point out is safe and sure. Let us remember, that:

> It's no in titles nor in rank;
> It's no in wealth like Lon'on bank,
> To purchase peace and rest;
> It's no in makin' muckle mair;
> It's no in books, it's no in lear,
> To make you truly blest;
>
> If happiness hae not her seat
> And centre in the breast,
> We may be wise, or rich, or great
> But never can be blest:
> Nae treasures, nor pleasures,
> Could make us happy lang;
> The heart ay's the part, aye,
> That makes us right or wrang.
>
> Robert Burns

With this basic truth in mind let's broaden our horizons and start climbing.

The first hill that we ascend I shall name *Soul Freedom.* There cannot be happiness without free agency. If the soul feels circumscribed, harassed, or enslaved by something or somebody, there cannot be true progress. That is why some of the nations today are wrong, and some day in the future will have to change their policy. God intends men to be free. One recent writer not in the Church very significantly wrote these words: "God is endeavoring to make men and women like himself. To do this he must first make them free." Let each remember:

You are the fellow that has to decide
Whether you'll do it or toss it aside.
You are the fellow who makes up your mind
Whether you'll lead or will linger behind.
Whether you'll try for the goal that's afar
Or just be contented to stay where you are.
Take it or leave it. Here's something to do!
Just think it over—It's all up to you!

What do you wish? To be known as a shirk,
Known as a good man who's willing to work,
Scorned as a loafer, or praised by your chief,
Rich man or poor man or beggar or thief?
Eager or earnest or dull through the day?
Honest or crooked? It's you who must say!
You must decide in the face of the test
Whether you'll shirk or give it your best.

Nobody here will compel you to rise;
No one will force you to open your eyes;
No one will answer for you yes or no,
Whether to stay there or whether to go;
Life is a game, but it's you who must say
Whether as cheat or as sportsman you'll play.
Fate may betray you, but you settle first
Whether to live to your best or your worst.

So, whatever it is you are wanting to be.
Remember, to fashion the choice you are free.
Kindly or selfish, or gentle or strong,
Keeping the right way or taking the wrong,
Careless of honor or guarding your pride,
All these are questions which you must decide,
Yours the selection, whichever you do;
The thing men call character's all up to you.

                                        Edgar A. Guest

187

With that decision we turn round on the hill *Soul Freedom* and see an extended view. Within us is a sense of strength and confidence. There is hope; there is exhilaration. We are independent and we can make the best of our lives.

But there is another hill ahead of us, and I think that hill is more rugged. There are more rocks. There are more stones rolling as we step along. We may slip occasionally. We may bruise our knees and scratch our hands because that is not an easy ascension. We approach the hill *Victory*.

As we climb it we get the consciousness of self-mastery, which is equal in importance to the consciousness of soul freedom. Look way down there, where the rays of intellect do not penetrate, where the sunshine of morality is seldom seen, and see how people grovel. Many—too many—either will not or cannot come out of the slums to reach this hill from which we broaden our horizon. As a result, their search for happiness is in vain. They grasp at the substance and it turns to ashes.

He who lives to eat, drink, sleep, dress, take his walk—in short, pamper himself all that he can—be it the courtier basking in the sun, the drunken laborer, the commoner serving his belly, the woman absorbed in her toilettes, the profligate of low estate or high, or simply the ordinary pleasure-lover, a "good fellow," but too obedient to material needs—that man or woman is on the downward way of desire, and the descent is fatal.

So writes Charles Wagner in *The Simple Life,* and what he says is true. He continues:

Those who follow it obey the same laws as a body on an inclined plane. Dupes of an illusion forever repeated, they think, "Just a few steps more, the last, toward the thing down there that we covet; then we will halt." But the velocity they gain sweeps them on, and the further they go the less they are able to resist it.

Here is the secret of the unrest, the madness, of many of our contemporaries; having condemned their will to the service of their appetites, they suffer the penalty. They are delivered up to violent passions which devour their flesh, crush their bones, suck their blood, and cannot be sated. This is not a lofty moral denunciation. I have been listening to what life says, and have recorded, as I have heard them, some of the truths that resound in every square.

Has drinking, inventive as it is of new drinks, found the means of quenching thirst? Not at all. It might rather be called the art of making thirst inextinguishable. Frank libertinage, does it deaden the sting of the senses? No—it envenoms it, converts natural desire into a morbid obsession and makes it the dominant passion. Let your needs rule you, pamper them—you will see them multiply like insects in the sun. The more you give them, the more they demand. It is senseless, who seeks for happiness in material prosperity alone.

Thank you, Charles Wagner, for that message. We are trying to live, to profit, to achieve the opposite on this hill of *Victory*. It is significant that it was on the Mount of Temptation that Christ gained the victory over the tempter and cried, "Get thee hence, Satan: for it is written, Thou shalt worship the Lord thy God, and him only shalt thou serve."

I think that second hill is important. Literature is full of confirmation. Remember that passage quoted so frequently:

> It is easy enough to be prudent when
>   Nothing tempts you to stray,
> When without or within no voice of sin
>   Is luring your soul away.
> But it's only a negative virtue until it is tried by fire;
> And the life that is worth the honor of earth
> Is the life that resists desire.
>
> By the cynic, the sad, the fallen,
>   Who had no strength for the strife,
> The world's highway is cumbered today;
>   They make up the item of life.
> But the virtue that conquers passion
> And the sorrow that hides in a smile,
> It is these that are worth the homage of earth
> For we find them but once in a while.
>   Ella Wheeler Wilcox

189

But we must climb. That next hill leads to a sweeter happiness in life. All our associations thus far have been with one another, boys and girls together. Those who made any of the low things their aim in life, of course, aren't ready to go on. They remain on the plane *Indulgence*, because the effort to ascend is too much, too great; but those of us who have been together, studying one another, finding out with whom we are congenial and who contributed the best in our lives, the boys who find the girls who inspire them to do their best and the girls who make the boys feel, "I want to succeed; I want to become worthy of you,"—those are the girls whose company you should seek. And, girls, those are the boys who are worthy of your companionship, of your love. They are not grovelers. Their aim isn't to experience merely sensation which any animal may know. Their dances and their parties and their socials and their music are all but a means to an end, and they look forward to the next ascent—the *Mount Industry*.

Here each one chooses his vocation. The hill is a hard one, but he has mastered some of those things in youth and he is ready now to overcome almost any difficulty. Of course, it will be hard to get an education. Of course, it will take application. Of course, he will have to deny himself some pleasures, but he has already mastered himself physically and he can master himself intellectually. He chooses a vocation and starts out with a view of building a home for that sweet girl who has inspired him. He seeks the supreme happiness that comes from contributing to the blessing of others, and to the strength of the nation. Together the couple are building on the hill of *Industry*. Building a home together, they share happiness. The husband is happiest when that sweet wife, his sweetheart, is happy; and she is happiest when he succeeds. They are both happiest when the children succeed. After all, in rearing and loving a family lies the supremest happiness. Anything else must take second place in value to those boys and girls who make happy our homes. This experience is found on the hill of *Industry*:

Let me but do my work from day to day,
In field or forest, at the desk or loom;
In roaring market place or tranquil room;
Let me but find it in my heart to say,
When vagrant wishes beckon me astray,
"This is my work; my blessing, not my doom,
Of all who live, I am the one by whom
This work can best be done in the right way."
Then shall I see it not too great nor small,
To suit my spirit and to prove my powers;
Then shall I cheerful greet the laboring hours,
And cheerful turn when the long shadows fall
At eventide, to play and love and rest,
Because I know for me my work is best.

"Alps" still rise as we approach the hill *Appreciation.* Perhaps we live in a cottage—only in a log cabin. We read about the millions that men pay for paintings from abroad, and on our wall hangs just a cutting from a calendar, but by this time we have learned to appreciate God's gifts and the most beautiful pictures in the world are ours for the looking.

We turn from that and view our broadened horizon, and we can bask together in the glorious sunset that is ours. It doesn't belong to any millionaire any more than it does to us. If our ears are attuned, we can hear the music of the birds and of the humming insects.

It may be that we can see tragedy, too, in this old world if we have eyes to see and ears to hear.

This life is good to us. Out of our little cabin, even between the chinks of the logs we can see the golden grain. We can hear the rippling stream. The Lord's gifts are free—

'Tis heaven alone that is given away,
'Tis only God may be had for the asking.

Appreciation cannot be obtained without climbing. It is not to be found in the slums of indulgence and lethargy and idleness and intemperance, drinking and smoking, and trying to get some physical stimulant for happiness. Think about it. You can't do it. You are never satisfied with it. You take your bottle of wine and then you want champagne, and you drink your champagne and it may be that you will be led to take drugs. Read the Book of Life and you will have ample evidence of the value and truth of the Word of Wisdom. Keep your eyes open and see life down there in the shadows, particularly from the high hill of *Industry* and *Appreciation*.

But let us continue our journey upward. Together hand in hand we climb the last hill and reach the top—the hill of *Success*.

As we begin this final ascent and behold our extended horizons, we are conscious of a conviction that true happiness is found in the parodoxical saying of the Savior, "He that loseth his life for my sake shall find it." Our lives are wrapped up with the lives of others, and we are happiest as we contribute to their happiness.

This principle is portrayed by Robert Browning in his immortal story of Paracelsus, who selfishly sought fame and glory by withdrawing from direct contact with his fellowmen. Old age overtook him before he realized his mistake, and before he learned the great lesson of life. When his friend Festus found him, after a separation of many years, Paracelsus, lying on a bed in a Greek conjurer's house, said:

I am happy, my foot is on the threshold of boundless life. I see the whole world and hurricane of life behind me. All my life passes by and I know its purpose, and to what end it has brought me, and whither I am going. I will tell you all the meaning of life.

Festus exclaimed: "My friend, tell it to the world."

Paracelsus: "There was a time when I was happy; the secret of life was in that happiness."

Festus: "When, when was that? All I hope that answer will decide."

Paracelsus: "When, but the time I vowed myself to man."

Festus: "Great God, thy judgments are inscrutable."

Paracelsus: "There is an answer to the passionate longings of the heart for fullness, and I knew it, and the answer is this: Live in all things outside yourself by love, and you will have joy. That is the life of God; it ought to be our life. In him it is accomplished and perfect; but in all created things it is a lesson learned slowly and through difficulty."

"Serve ye one another by love," writes the Apostle; and Jesus sums it up as follows:

Love the Lord thy God with all thy heart, and with all thy soul, and with all thy mind.

This is the first and great commandment.

And the second is like unto it, Thou shalt love thy neighbor as thyself.

On these two commandments hang all the law and the prophets.

There are those who declare such an ideal merely theoretical; they call it impractical! Why not try it? A test by application will prove its practicability. Let the nations of the world which are today descending the hills of progress and slipping down into the slums and gutters of animal indulgence, sneer at the ideals if they will; but as sure as God has given us the revelation of life, so shall we find happiness supreme as we climb the hill of *Service*.

God bless you young men and women as you travel the road of happiness through extended and broadened horizons. I believe these steps are sound: first, "Soul Freedom"; the second, "Victory" through self-mastery; the third, "Industry" and the home; the fourth, "Appreciation"; and the fifth, "Success"—willingness and ability to serve.

God help us as representatives of the Church, of our homes, and as men who hold the Priesthood of God, to set the proper example to the world and thus bring happiness to it.

Chapter Thirty-three

Youth and the
Five Faiths
which Concern Them

How beautiful is youth! How
  bright it gleams
With its illusions, aspirations,
  dreams!
Book of Beginnings, Story without
  End,
Each maid a heroine, and each
  man a friend!

Longfellow

As YOUTH passes into maturity some of the illusions and dreams to which the poet, Long-fellow, makes reference above fade in the light of stern reality. It is regrettable when this change of transfiguration inhibits or retards youthful aspirations. It is lamentable if, in the discarding of his illusions and dreams, the youth discards also facts and eternal truths.

Every progressively minded youth is at one time or another deeply concerned over five hopes or faiths, and his attitude toward life generally is influenced thereby. They are: God, science, government, human nature, and family.

Belief In God and In Immortality

In childhood, especially in the true Latter-day Saint home, God and immortality are accepted as being just as real as the lungs of the body, or as the heart, or the stomach, or the brain. Illustrative of this fact, the poet Wordsworth has written a very beautiful but simple poem entitled, "We Are Seven," the introductory stanza of which says:

> . . . a simple child
> That lightly draws its breath,
> And feels its life in every limb,
> What should it know of death?

Belief In Science

The Church concerns itself with its college students because not infrequently science shatters youthful concept and leaves students adrift on the sea of doubt. The thinking youth learns:

> Man has always lived by knowledge, and he can live in no other way and remain human. Knowledge is the basis of all his successful adjustments, except a few made upon the animal levels of instinct, emotion, or accident. An adequate knowledge means the elimination of error and success in making adjustments. It is, therefore, the great source of all mastery over nature; and we believe that in the future it will be the greatest means of controlling human nature and human relations.

The immature mind, hungering for truth and accepting such statements as absolute, is likely to place science above all other influences or forces and the scientific mind as the safest mind to follow. The student just emerging into maturity remembers the time when he was told and believed that God made it rain. Now science demonstrates that atmospheric conditions responding to natural laws cause rain and snow, dew, mist, and fog. Science can explain on natural principles lightning and thunder. The student once believed that God placed the rainbow in the sky. Now science explains how a raindrop, acting as a prism, separates the ray of light into its seven component parts.

Thus science "goes merrily stripping the universe of the mysteries which once were religion's 'stock in trade.'"

The Church concerns itself with a young man who, as his immature beliefs fall from him one by one, finds himself substituting science for religion, and the scientist for God.

Science, unsupported by the refining and restraining influence of religion, instead of contributing to progress and happiness, as the electric light, the automobile, the television and radio, and the airplane, might prove a "Frankenstein" by putting atomic submarines, jet airplanes, and the H bomb at the disposal of political gangsters and modern cavemen. Although atomic power opens up boundless opportunities, it also threatens mankind with limitless perils. As one thinker put it, "All depends upon whether we can match this flood of new material powers with an equal gain in spiritual forces."

Belief In Government

Youth in the United States have been taught to believe in a republican form of government. They have thrilled with the stories of American history that tell of the overthrow of autocracy and the subsequent Declaration of Independence; of that immortal document, The Constitution of the United States, which guarantees every citizen life, liberty, and the pursuit of happiness. After two world wars, the youth of today see democracy stifled in many parts of the world.

The Church is interested in college youth because it knows that it is God's will that every individual should be free, and that he should be able to worship God according to the dictates of his own conscience. Communist dictatorships are contrary to the Gospel plan.

Belief In Human Nature

The youth of our Church have been taught to believe that there is good in humanity; that the world has progressed because of people who cared but little for material rewards, who knew that moral self-denial is the only path for self-realization.

Dr. Ralph V. Chamberlain said in his tribute to his brother:

By sacrificing for our ideals we do not throw ourselves away, but achieve the higher sides of ourselves. Civilization has come from the struggles of men and women in the past who risked all for ideals, for spiritual values that they might become the common possession of the race. We who see the path today are unworthy if we do not take up the burden. The race goes down when it loses its sense of values, and the success of democracy depends upon the people's living in the understanding of the spirit the obligations of righteousness.

Today our youth see hysterical barbarisms of the dictator triumph over these high ideals, and his trust in human nature is shaken. The Church is interested in college students because it desires them to know that "human nature has produced and is producing today saints, artists, and scientists, as well as gangsters and imperial powers." Also that "there is a fund of generosity in human nature, and inventiveness in the human mind that may still save us. A faith in man himself and in the cooperative adventure of mankind requires courage today."

The Church desires its young men to realize that man has a right to be proud of himself as a living image of God and as belonging to the same race as the peerless Son of Man, Jesus Christ. Our belief in equality and brotherhood is a Christian heritage, and it fades out of the picture when Christian belief is forgotten. We have to treat everyone as sacrosanct and free. We have to educate a race to realize that no man is unwanted, that every soul is unique and has a life to live made up of momentous choices which will make or mar his own life, and the life of the community and the universe.

Belief In the Family

The Church concerns itself with college students because it believes that the low view of marriage that is gaining momentum throughout the world threatens civilization itself and is contrary to the mind and will of God.

To all really true men, as well as women, children are their most precious possessions; and man's most important obligation and duty is the making of a home and the proper rearing of children.

Marriage is a divine ordinance. It should not be entered into lightly nor terminated at pleasure. A clean body and uncontaminated blood are prerequisites to an ideal marriage. The domestic relations precede; and, in our present existence, are worth more than all other social ties. They give the first throb to the heart and unseal the deep foundation of its love. Home is the chief school of human virtue. Its responsibilities, joys, sorrows, smiles, tears, hopes, and solicitudes form the chief interests of human life.

The Church concerns itself with its college students because it wants them to become anchored in the truth. The gospel of Jesus Christ is the unfailing measuring rod of all theories, of all philosophies. To convince all its youth that true success and happiness lie along the path of conformity to the ideals and teachings of the gospel, the Church will bend every effort. God's existence, and his relationship to man, the relation of science to religion and to man's progress, the proper form of government, the worth of the individual in the sight of God, the family as the indispensable unit of society—all the perplexities of these ever-recurring questions in the minds of college students may be answered satisfactorily in the light of the restored gospel of Jesus Christ.

The Church is concerned with its youth because true religion is essential to the proper interpretation of current theories and philosophies, and proclaims that the gospel of Jesus Christ is the true philosophy of life.

Chapter Thirty-four

The Fleetness
and Responsibility
of Youth

No PARENT would ever do anything to lessen the sweetness of life in youth. No law has ever been passed to make youth less vigorous, less hopeful. There is no person living who has even had a thought, I hope, of depriving youth of the happiness due them.

Just a word to the youth of this Church. It will not be long until you will be carrying the responsibility of the men and women who are here with us today. Oh, how quickly the years pass! I thought of that not long ago when Sister McKay and I attended the baptism of our eight-year-old grandson. In one instant it recalled to me my own baptism as a boy. It answered a question that I heard asked by someone who was doubting the advisability of baptizing at eight years of age, stating, "The child knows nothing and does not understand it."

Baptism Symbolic of Purification

However, I was surprised to realize how many things I could remember of that baptism many years ago there on the banks of old Spring Creek in Huntsville, (Utah). I seemed to recall the willows that lined the bank of the creek. I could see again the old flour mill in the distance, and I recalled the people who were baptized. A sister from Denmark was one of them. I recalled Peter G. Geertsen who

199

had charge of the baptism. I could hear the words spoken. An eight-year-old boy knows a great deal. I recalled the significance of that baptism ordinance. Of course, I could not remember all that was said; but I do remember that I was instructed not to swear nor use bad words; that if I had spoken harshly to my mother, I was not to do it any more; that I was never to be disobedient.

These things are just as significant to adults who understand that baptism has a three-fold significance—a burial in water, not sprinkling, not water poured on the head. There is no symbolism in that.

There are three elements in which the human being may be buried: the air, which is our native element; the earth, which is our final resting place; and third, the element of water, symbolizing purification as well as burial. It is really more than a figure of speech. Therefore, when we are buried with Christ by baptism unto his death, just as Christ was raised from the dead by the glory of his Father, even so we should walk in the newness of life.

Our old life is buried. To profane the name of God is buried. Dishonest dealing with our fellowmen is buried. Desecration of holy things is buried. This is one thing which baptism means—we are *born again that we may walk in a newness of life!*

A Child Understands

Everyone does not understand this as we do. A child understands it as the initial ordinance to membership in the Church of Christ. It is the door through which he is to walk. He understands that baptism is in obedience to a command of God. Adults can hear the words of the Savior, ". . . Suffer it to be so now: for thus it becometh us to fulfil all righteousness. . . ." (Matt. 3:15.) This is truly significant!

I am not saying that an eight-year-old boy understands that. No, he does not; but he does understand the things significant to him in his boyhood. In part, he is obedient to his parents, particularly in responding to the instructions of the ward officers, in attending Primary, Sunday School, etc., and in telling the truth, a wonderful virtue in childhood.

Choose To Worship the Lord

The years pass quickly when you arrive in your teens. Looking forward, the future seems to be away off; but when you look backward, it seems a short time indeed. Young people must choose the old questions as given by Joshua thousands of years ago—it is still the question of today:

. . . Choose you this day whom ye will serve; whether the gods which your fathers served that were on the other side of the flood, or the gods of the Amorites, in whose land ye dwell: but as for me and my house, we will serve the Lord. (Joshua 24:15.)

Choose to worship the Lord! That is your choice, young folks, not in the way Joshua put it; but it is your decision now. Every day you have to make a choice—whether it will be for good or for evil.

I wonder whenever I meet young people how many are strong enough to choose the right way. There are some who think that to choose the religious way of life brings unhappiness. Hundreds of thousands, indeed millions of people think that to be religious is to deprive one of the joy of life. One of the most erroneous conclusions of the human mind is to think that to choose a religious life is to deprive one of happiness. There is a big difference between pleasure and joy and happiness. Any animal can enjoy pleasure; a cow, a horse, a lion, or a pig—they know nothing about happiness, about joy. It is surprising how many intelligent men and women choose pleasure instead of happiness or joy.

Religion for Youth

Many years ago one of our early patriots, Patrick Henry, in his old age said: "I have now disposed of all my property to my family.—There is one thing more I wish I could give them, and that is the Christian religion.—If they had that, and

I had not given them one shilling, they would have been rich, and if they had not that, and I had given them all the world, they would be poor."

Sir Humphrey Davy, a great English philosopher, a clear-thinking man who glimpsed the values of the Christian religion, said: "If I could choose what of all things would be at the same time the most delightful and useful to me, I should prefer a firm religious belief to every other blessing. . . ."

I would say to the young people, choose the right life, the religious life, if you please. Choose the happy way of life. It is not in indulgence, not in defiance of the laws of virtue—it is by obedience to the laws of virtue that you are happy. Learn that early in life, then three or four score years will soon pass, and you can look back without any regrets.

The Prodigal Son

Jesus has given us a wonderful example in the parable of the "Prodigal Son." It touches the heart of man. You will recall that the son of a wealthy man felt irked by his surroundings. He resented family restraint; and, in the second place, he was afflicted (and I use that word advisedly) with self-conceit. He thought he knew more how to handle his portion of the family wealth than did his father. Such self-conceit is an affliction of youth. Young men think they know more when they graduate from university than their parents will ever know. This Prodigal Son had a desire to get enjoyment out of life, and his self-conceit led him into it. He wished to be free, to indulge himself as he would; and so he went to his father and said, "Give me my portion." He knew he could spend it as he wanted to, and so the father gave him his portion of wealth.

The young man left the family. He had his pleasure. His would-be friends flocked around to share the expenditure of his wealth, and they all had a good time.

The Prodigal Son found that while his money lasted he had many friends; but, finally, when his money vanished, so did those friends. Then he found himself under the necessity of going to work. And the only work that he could find—the lowest place mentioned in the scriptures—was feeding hogs. He would eat of the husks thrown out to these beasts. There is a phrase used in that parable which is very significant. It is, *"when he came to himself."* The Prodigal Son said that the servants in his father's employ were better taken care of than he was. So he said, "I will arise and go to my father, and will say unto him, Father, I have sinned against heaven, and before thee, And am no more worthy to be called thy son: make me as one of thy hired servants." (Luke 15:18, 19.) And he went and asked his father's forgiveness.

"Learn Wisdom In Thy Youth"

Young people, that is a parable that Jesus gave! As in all his parables and sayings, it has a lesson of life. Are we wise enough in our teens to read it? That Prodigal Son had his good time. Any boy or girl can have a good time. No matter what father says, or how mother pleads, any boy or girl can have that kind of good time. She can sneak it; he can sneak it. Sin never was happiness. "Wickedness never was happiness"; we never find it to be so; it is a mirage. I remember reading in a young girl's letter the statement that her sweetheart who had proposed marriage had said to her: "The marriage ceremony is merely a form. Since we love each other, we may take all the liberties." A young man who will talk to his proposed wife in that manner is contemptible! He would deprive that sweet, young girl of that which is most precious in life. He was seeking joy that would not come. He crushed the rose from the hand; it wilted to dust. "Wickedness never was happiness." The man who intends to get something for nothing will probably pay for it in the penitentiary, if he assumes to live wrongfully. "In the sweat of thy face shalt thou eat bread" is an eternal law. Young folks should learn this in their teens. They should learn to put forth an effort to bring joy into their souls.

Youth, Keep Virtue

Young folks, if you would be happy, keep within the bounds of virtue, within the bounds of integrity; keep within the bounds of beauty of soul which has power even to transform your features.

You are the fellow who has to decide
Whether you'll do it or toss it aside.
You are the fellow who makes up your mind
Whether you'll lead or will linger behind.
Whether you'll try for the goal that's afar
Or just be contented to stay where you are.
Take it or leave it. Here's something to do!
Just think it over—It's all up to you!

So, whatever it is you are wanting to be,
Remember, to fashion the choice you are free
Kindly or selfish, or gentle or strong,
Keeping the right way or taking the wrong,
Careless of honor or guarding your pride,
All these are questions which you must decide.
Yours the selection, whichever you do;
The thing men call character's all up to you.
                                    Edgar A. Guest

Young people all over the world, I wish you could say just those things, because they are vital to the next few years for your happiness and your joy. I repeat, how quickly those dream years pass! What you do now determines your happiness throughout eternity. So, in the words of Charles Mac-Kay, the Scottish poet:

If I were a voice—a persuasive voice
That could travel the wide world through,
I would fly on the beams of the morning light,
And speak to men with a gentle might,
And tell them to be true.

Chapter Thirty-five

Reaching
Youth...
A Great Obligation

AN EMINENT statesman in the United States once wrote:

> If we work upon marble, it will perish. If we work upon brass, time will efface it. If we rear temples, they will crumble to dust. But if we work upon men's immortal minds, if we imbue them with high principles, with the just fear of God and love of their fellowmen, we engrave on those tablets something which no time can efface, and which will brighten and brighten to all eternity.
> —Daniel Webster

We are deeply perturbed in these days about great social questions. I believe one of the greatest obligations that now rests upon all of us is to determine how best to guide, protect, and educate properly, childhood and youth. There are phases of this problem which affect the happiness and peace of mind of every father and mother in the land. The question of child health and guidance goes to the very root of our national life. It is a great mission, the greatest in the world, to reach out after young people, to extend a hand to the child, following Jesus' injunction to Peter to bring the lambs into Christ's fold. Indeed, there is nothing greater.

Herbert Hoover, when President of the United States, expressed the importance of such a mission most impressively when he said:

These questions of child health and protection are a complicated problem, requiring much learning and much action. And we need have great concern over this matter. Let no one believe that these are questions which should not stir a nation; that they are below the dignity of statesmen or governments. If we could have but one generation of properly born, trained, educated, and healthy children, a thousand other problems of government would vanish. We would assure ourselves of healthier minds in more vigorous bodies to direct the energies of our nation to yet greater heights of achievement. Moreover, one good community nurse will save a dozen future policemen.[1]

Youth Must Feel Your Heart-touch

How may we reach these youth? In some of the organizations of the Church every boy and girl should be enrolled. His name or her name should appear on some record, if not on several records, throughout the Church; and some teacher or some officer has the obligation of coming in contact with that individual boy or girl. You are not going to bring back erring youth unless you first let them know that you are interested in them. Let them feel your heart-touch. Only the warm heart can kindle warmth in another. Wayward boys and girls are sometimes suspicious of people around them. Others get the idea that they are not wanted. The kind hand or the loving arm removes suspicion and awakens confidence. Your own experience bears ample evidence of the value of personal companionship.

We train by thoughts. There is no one great thing we can give a child which will determine his future, but there are many little things we can give. As a child grows physically by eating at regular intervals, so character is built by little things, by daily contacts, by an influence here, and a fact or truth there.

Dandy Resented Restraint

Up on our farm in Huntsville, I have had great pleasure in training horses. I shall never forget one well-bred colt I trained. We called him Dandy. He had a good disposition; a

---

[1]*White House Conference 1930* (The Century Company, New York, N. Y., 1931), p. 7.

clean, well-rounded eye. He was well-proportioned and, all in all, a choice equine possession. Under the saddle he was as willing, responsive, and cooperative as a horse could be. He and my dog Scotty were real companions. I liked the way Dandy would go up to something of which he was afraid. He had confidence that if he would do as I bade him he would not be injured.

But Dandy resented restraint. He was ill-contented when tied and would nibble at the tie-rope until he was free. He would not run away; he just wanted to be free. Thinking other horses felt the same, he would proceed to untie their ropes. He hated to be confined to the pasture, and if he could find a place in the fence where there was only smooth wire, he would paw the wire carefully with his feet until he could step over to freedom. More than once my neighbors were kind enough to put him back in the field. He even learned to push open the gate. Though his depredations were provoking and sometimes expensive, I admired his intelligence and ingenuity.

Dandy's Wanderlust Led To Tragedy

But his curiosity and desire to explore the neighborhood led him and me into trouble. Once, on the highway, he was hit by an automobile, resulting in a demolished machine, injury to the horse, and slight, though not serious injury to the driver. Recovering from that, and still impelled with a feeling of wanderlust, Dandy inspected the fence throughout the entire boundary. He found even the gates wired. So for a while we thought we had him secure in the pasture.

One day, however, somebody left the gate unwired. Detecting this, Dandy unlatched it, took Nig, his companion, and together they visited the neighbor's field. They went to an old house used for storage. Dandy's curiosity prompted him to push open the door. Just as he had surmised, there was a sack of grain inside. What a find! Yes, and what a tragedy! The grain was poison bait for rodents! In a few minutes Dandy and Nig were in spasmodic pain, and shortly both were dead.

Youth Must Be Guided

How like Dandy are many of our youth! They are not bad; they do not even intend to do wrong, but they are impulsive, full of life, full of curiosity, and long to do something. They, too, are restive under restraint; but if they are kept busy, guided carefully and rightly, they prove to be responsive and capable. If left to wander unguided, they all too frequently find themselves in the environment of temptation, and too often become entangled in the snares of evil.

To change men and nations, we must change and direct their way of thinking. "Train up a child in the way he should go. . . ." (Prob. 22:6.) That is our duty. The home is the most potent influence in this training. Sunday Schools, Mutual Improvement Associations, Primaries, Relief Societies are only supplemental. *No social, educational, or service group can effectively supplant the home as an effective force in making men out of boys, and women out of girls!*

No man, woman, or child is happy in doing wrong. Nature herself teaches us that our actions are bound within certain limits. But, as "Dandys," we want to break away from those limits and go to the dangers beyond them; and our young men and young women should sense that. Growth and happiness are found within certain restricted areas, beyond which lie dangerous and injurious indulgences. There is pleasure and health in eating; but pain and sickness in gormandizing. There is pleasure in moderate exercise; pain in excessive exertion. In all things, nature says, "Thus far shalt thou go and no farther."

Home Must Give Freedom and Restraint

The home is the best place in the world to teach the child self-restraint, to teach him that there is happiness in self-control, and that he must have respect for the rights of others.

Unhappiness in the child's life, as in the adult life, springs largely from nonconformity to natural and social laws. The home is the best place in which to develop obedience, which nature and society will later demand. The child should learn these rules of conformity during the ages from three to five; and if parents do not get control of the child during this period, they will find great difficulty in getting control later.

I feel that the *first* contribution of the home to the happiness of the child is to impress him with the fact that there are bounds beyond which he cannot go with safety. Do not push, drag, or confine—just let the small child be perfectly free to develop until he goes beyond the bounds of safety, then let him feel the gentle but firm hand of restraint. *Second,* teach him to be considerate of the rights of others. *Third,* teach him to feel that home is a place where confidences and consolations are exchanged. *Fourth,* have him cherish the thought that home is a haven of seclusion and rest from the worries and perplexities of life.

Times Call for Courageous Youth

It is the duty of parents and of the Church not only to teach, but also to demonstrate to young people that living a life of truth and moral purity brings joy and happiness, while violation of moral and social laws results only in dissatisfaction, sorrow, and, when carried to extreme, degradation.

Youth must be courageous in maintaining the ideals of the Church. These are times when they should keep their heads and not be swept from their mooring by every will-o'-wisp theory that is offered as a panacea of our present ills. The times call for courageous youth to hold aloft the moral standard. In that field we can find the truest moral courage. It is said that heroism is concentrated courage. Well, our greatest heroes are not always found on the battlefield. I think we find them also among our youth—young men and young women who, when put in social groups, will stand up fearlessly and denounce those things which we know sap the character, the very life energy of youth!

I appeal to youth to be courageous in maintaining the moral and spiritual values of the gospel of Jesus Christ. After all,

> For what is a man profited, if he shall gain the whole world, and lose his own soul? or what shall a man give in exchange for his soul. (Matt. 16:26.)

Chapter Thirty-six

As Youth Contemplates an Eternal Partnership

And again, verily I say unto you, that whoso forbiddeth to marry is not ordained of God, for marriage is ordained of God unto man. Wherefore, it is lawful that he should have one wife, and they twain shall be one flesh, and all this that the earth might answer the end of its creation.

(D.&C. 49:15, 16.)

I N GREEK MYTHOLOGY there is a story of *The Three Fates*. In Rome these fates were painted, presumably by Michaelangelo, as three old women who control the destiny of mortals. They are three sisters. *Clotha*, the youngest, holds the distaff of life. *Lachesis*, the second sister, spins the thread as the years come and go. *Atropos*, the third, stands by with large open shears ready to cut the thread of life. If she cuts it short, the infant dies. If she permits the thread to unwind a little more, life is cut off in youth. But ofttimes she permits the thread of life to lengthen to old age. The mythical story implies that we are all subject to those three fates.

Applying this myth to our modern age, one writer on eugenics says: Science, and the wide dissemination of knowledge, have given us three fundamental things which

211

determine our lives. These are heredity, environment, and self-effort, or what we make of ourselves by our own determination. These three modern fates should be kept in mind as we consider courtship and marriage.

What we are by heredity is determined; we cannot change it. We, who spring from families that have observed the gospel teachings, have inherited good qualities as well as good names. The least we can do is to transmit the same inheritance to our children. We are recreant to our obligation to society if we do not give to our progeny all the nobility bequeathed to us by our ancestors.

In our early youth, our environment is largely determined for us, but I wish to refer to the thought that in courtship and marriage we can modify, aye, can control to a very great extent, our environment. Morally speaking, we can carve the very atmosphere in which we live.

But the most important of these elements now is personal effort—that which we make of ourselves.

History and our own teachings tell us that marriage in some form or other has been man's fundamental association since time began. Marriage is ordained of God, and so marriage was instituted by divine edict. That was in the beginning; but man has prostituted it and practiced different forms of marriage, and different methods of obtaining mates. Among certain races, wives were obtained by theft; and among some tribes of nomadic peoples wives were and still are obtained by purchase. On one occasion Brother Hugh J. Cannon and I had an interesting experience in seeing an apt illustration of such bargaining. We were riding along the Nile River on the edge of the Sahara Desert, not far from the large pyramid *Cheops*. Our guide had promised that he would show us a glimpse of Bedouin life that would be interesting. We had been out along that desert trail less than an hour when his promise was fulfilled. We saw in the distance a caravan of probably four or five camels, headed by one carrying a beautifully colored canopy.

"What is that?" we asked Abdul.

"That," he said, "is a Bedouin wedding."

"Who rides in the canopy?"

"Nobody," he aswered, "that is for the bride."

"Are the people going to the wedding?"

"They are going for the bride," answered Abdul.

Then briefly he explained that the bride had been chosen by one of the bridegroom's relatives—a mother or a sister, or perhaps the father. Quite possibly the bridegroom had not even seen the bride. The bargain had been made at "so much." It had been arranged that when the bride left the parental roof, a part of that bargain money would be paid. The balance of it would be withheld for a reason I shall relate.

The bridegroom was at his home waiting for the bride, who would come to him veiled, half the dowry money, so Abdul explained, having been paid to the father. The bride entered, with her maids, the brilliantly colored canopy, and all went to the bridegroom's home. After due ceremony the bridegroom saw his bride for the first time. Then, our guide expiained, there would be two or three days of feasting, during which time the bridegroom could decide whether his bride would prove congenial and whether he would be happy with her.

We said, "Suppose she doesn't please him, then what would he do?"

Then Abdul gave his own experience: "Oh, go right on with the celebration and with the ceremonies, at the conclusion of which the bridegroom might (very considerately?) say: 'Perhaps it would be well for us to visit your parents again.' Together they return to her home. She knows why. Taking a witness with him, the disappointed bridegroom calls the girl's father into another room and says: 'Here is the rest of the money. Keep your girl' "—and that is all there is to it.

We asked: "Suppose the bride is dissatisfied with the bridegroom—what then?"

"If she leaves her husband, she must come back."

"Suppose she does not want to come back?"

"The law makes her come back," our guide replied.

Abdul confessed that he had made, unsuccessfully, three such attempts to secure a congenial companion, and had then given up discouraged.

Another form of securing a mate, and most common among civilized peoples, is by *common consent*. Even as late as when I was on my first mission in Scotland a couple who merely agreed to marry became husband and wife in a common-law marriage, which was recognized as a legal union. Later in history the marriage ceremony became sanctified by the Church, and even later than that it was legalized by the law of the land.

Thus we have throughout the various nations of the world in modified form various systems of marriage. I wish you to keep them in mind, and compare them with the scriptural text appearing at the beginning of the article—that *"marriage is ordained of God."* It is something not to be entered into lightly or terminated at pleasure or at the first difficulty that might arise as you journey down the highway of matrimony. If the world could realize that—just that one thought—we should not have in the United States today one out of every five marriages wrecked on the shoals of divorce.

No couple should enter into matrimony without careful observation and serious prayerful thought. Everyone desires to live happily in married life. It is the natural, it is the normal life. The stability of government, and the perpetuation of the race depend upon it. The happiness of mankind is not complete without congenial marriage. Let us then consider briefly some conditions which will contribute to the happiness of married life:

The first step is choosing the right companion. On the importance of this a noted divine gives the following ominous warning:

By the fate of Ahab, whose wife induced him to steal; by the fate of Macbeth, whose wife pushed him into massacre; by the fate of James Ferguson, the philosopher, whose wife entered the room while he was lecturing and wilfully upset his astronomical apparatus so that he turned to the audience and said, "Ladies and gentlemen, I have the misfortune to be married to this woman"; by the fate of Bulwer-Lytton, the novelist, whose wife's temper was so incompatible that he furnished her with a beautiful house near London and withdrew from her company, leaving her with a dozen dogs which she entertained as pets; by the fate of John Milton, who married a termagant after he was blind, and when someone called her a rose, the poet said: "I am no judge of flowers, but it may be so, for I feel the thorns daily": by the fate of all these—I warn you.

As I read that I was reminded of experiences that prompt me to say this to our girls:

By the fate of the girl who married a man unfit for marriage, who was warned, who did not heed the warning, and whom I met ten years later in sorrow; by the fate of the girl who married a brute, although she knew that three other women had had to leave him; and by the fate of the girl who married a disloyal—a rake; by the fate of the girl who married a drunkard—I warn you.

I know those are negative pictures, but it is well for us to keep our eyes open in courtship. That is one way in which we can "carve" our environment. Association is the element in which our hearts become warm. How important it is, then, that the companion of each be chosen wisely and prayerfully. The choosing of a companion determines our future happiness or unhappiness. It is a part of wisdom, therefore, to associate only with those from whose company you can select a life's partner with whom you will be congenial. If in such companionship you recognize negative characteristics in him who attracts you, try to let your judgment rule your heart. Don't fool yourselves, girls, by thinking that after you are married, a man will overcome evil habits or negative traits of character. Let him prove himself before marriage.

I know you are now asking: "What are the positive characteristics for which we should seek?"

Among the dominant characteristics a true lover should possess are: first, honesty; second, loyalty; third, chastity; and fourth, reverence.

Never marry a man who would deceive you, who would tell you a lie. I think it was Sir Walter Scott who said: "I will withdraw my hand from a man, were he my best friend, who would wrong a woman or tell a lie." These virtues which I have named are qualities which will appeal to your mind, to your observation, to your judgment.

The real guiding principle, however, is the divinest attribute of the soul—love.

Before I consider this virtue further, let me give you a word-picture of different kinds of wives as written by James Allen. He says:

Some women in marrying demand all, and give all. With good men they are happy. With base men they are brokenhearted.

Some women demand everything and give little. With weak men they are tyrants. With strong men they are divorced.

Some demand little, and give all. With congenial souls they are in Heaven. With uncongenial men, they are soon in their graves.

Some give little and demand little. These are heartless beings who bring neither the joy of life nor the peace of death.

In choosing a companion, it is necessary to study the disposition, the inheritance, and training of the one with whom you are contemplating making life's journey. You see how necessary it is to look for the characteristics of honesty, of loyalty, of chastity, and of reverence. But after having found them—"How then," you ask, "may you tell whether or not there is any consanguinity, that something which will make you at least congenial in each other's company?" "Is there," you ask, "some guide?" Though love is not always a true guide, especially if that love be not reciprocated, or is bestowed upon a surly creature or a brute, yet certainly there is no happiness without love. "Well," you may ask, "how may I know when I am in love?"

216

That is a very important question. A fellow student and I considered that query one night as we walked together. As boys of that age frequently do, we were talking about girls. Neither he nor I knew whether we were in love or not. Of course I had not then met my present sweetheart. That young man was the late Elder George Q. Morris of the Council of the Twelve. In answer to my question, "How may we know when we are in love?" he replied: "My mother once said that if you meet a girl in whose presence you feel a desire to achieve, who inspires you to do your best, and to make the most of yourself, such a young woman is worthy of your love and is awakening love in your heart."

I submit that, young men, as a true guide. In the presence of the girl you truly love you do not feel to grovel; in her presence you do not attempt to take advantage of her; in her presence you feel that you would like to be everything that a Master Man should become, for she will inspire you to that ideal. And I ask you young women to cherish that same guide. What does *he* inspire in you—to feel as Portia did when she loved? She was wealthy; she was beautiful; but for Bassanio she wished she were a thousand times more beautiful, ten thousand times more rich—that is what true love does. When a young man accompanies you after a meeting, or after a dance, and he shows an inclination to use you as a convenience, or as a means of gratification, then you may put it down that he is not prompted by love.

Under such circumstances, no matter how fascinated you may be, young woman, no matter how confident you may feel that you love him, let your judgment rule and you be master of your feelings. It may grieve you not to follow the inclination of your heart, but you had better be pained a little in your youth than to suffer pangs of torture later.

Courtship is a wonderful period. It should be a sacred one. That is the time in which you choose your mate. Young men, your success in life depends upon that choice. Choose prayerfully the one who inspires you to your best and always remember that no man injures the thing he loves.

Young men and women have just entered into that state of life when they are driven by heaven-bestowed passions—I say God-given passions. There are young men, who, recognizing this fact, say: "Having them, why cannot we gratify them?" And they receive justification for such gratification sometimes from modern psychologists—false leaders who say that repression is wrong; that indulgence is the natural course of life. Do not be misled. I repeat, you are at that period of life in which your physical nature manifests itself, but you must also remember that God has given you, in that same period of life, powers of reasoning; he has given you judgment, and these for a divine purpose. Let reason and judgment be your guide—your balance.

Did you ever stand by the side of a power engine—throbbing, throbbing, throwing out its power and disseminating heat? On those stationary engines, you will find balances. If it were not for them the whole building might be blown up. But as the heat intensifies, those balances are thrown farther out and out, so that the whole thing is under control. So you have your reason, your judgment, as balances to your passion, young men. Try not to lose these balances, or there may be an explosion that will wreck your life.

This brings me to another fact, equally if not more important than those already mentioned. It is this: The seeds of a happy married life are sown in youth. Happiness does not begin at the altar; it begins during the period of youth and courtship. These seeds of happiness are sown by your ability to master your driving passion. Chastity should be the dominant virtue among young people—the ideal which the world has not accepted, and which many in the world will not believe exists or is cherished in the hearts of youth. You young men who have been on missions well know how astonished some people were when you told of your pure life. Some of them said bluntly that they did not believe you. But it is true.

In the Latter-day Saint Church there is but one standard of morality. In the world many people protect their girls and daughters, irrespective of religion. They know what it means for young girls to be treated as slaves, as playthings, and they shield their own daughters from the ravages of men. But their boys are too often left free to prey upon helpless creatures who are not so protected.

Thus in the world you have the double standard, but in the Church of Christ there is but a single standard. It applies to the boys as well as to the girls. If you follow that standard—indeed, if you will listen to the promptings of your best self, your clearest judgment, the whispering of your own true heart, you will learn this lesson: That self-mastery during youth and the compliance with the single standard of morality is (1) the source of virile manhood; (2) the crown of beautiful womanhood; (3) the foundation of a happy home, and (4) the contributing factor to the strength and perpetuity of the race!

Shakespeare uttered an eternal truth when he had the old servant Adam say, as he pleaded to accompany his young master in the forest:

> Though I look old, yet I am strong and lusty;
> For in my youth I never did apply
> Hot and rebellious liquors in my blood;
> Nor did not with unbashful forehead woo
> The means of weakness and debility.
> Therefore my age is as a lusty winter,
> Frosty, but kindly.

Laxity in youth is a sight draft that must be paid in age. Twenty, thirty, forty years hence, you must pay it. Mastery, and chastity, are also seeds sown which will pay large dividends in years hence, and those years pass quickly—oh, so quickly. Self-control is not achieved without effort—

> It is easy enough to be virtuous
> When nothing tempts you to stray,
> When without or within no voice of sin
> Is luring your soul away.
> But it's only a negative virtue

219

Until it's tried by fire;
And the soul that is worth the honor of earth
Is the soul that resists desire.

By the cynic, the sad, the fallen
Who had no strength for the strife,
The world's highway is cumbered today;
They make up the items of life.
But the virtue that conquers passion,
And the sadness that hides in a smile,
It is these that are worthy the homage of earth,
And we find them but once in a while.
Ella Wheeler Wilcox

Young man, always remember when you take your girl out to a party that her father and mother trust her to you. She is their most precious possession. If they gave you in trust a thousand dollars, you would not think of misusing it or spending it. They are giving into your keeping something which cannot be priced in money, and you are base indeed if you become disloyal to that trust. May I give you a heart petal here? I remember my father's admonition when I started in my teens to court a young girl: "David, you treat that young lady as you would have any young boy treat your sister." Young men, follow that advice and you will go through life with your conscience clear, and later in life you can say truthfully that with all your mistakes, you have never wronged a woman or told a lie.

Oh, I know that there are many people who look askance at such ideals. But I am speaking now of happiness, real happiness—not only to you as youth, to you as husband, or to you as a wife, but to the strength and happiness of unborn children. You have inherited strength and beauty and pure blood. What right have you, because of selfishness or a lack of restraint, to pollute that stream of life and shackle some innocent, unborn babe?

Marriage is for a higher purpose than for mere physical gratification. It has as its divine purpose the rearing of a family. Only by consummating this ideal can true and lasting happiness come. I fully realize what economic difficulties you are facing—the problem of getting your education, your meager income, and the seeming impossibility you are facing of rearing a family. But, I repeat, that family responsibility is the dominant purpose of marriage. Young man, if the girl with whom you are in love lives in a home of comparative luxury, and you hesitate to propose to her because you cannot offer her luxuries to which she has become accustomed, I suggest that a frank and open presentation to her of your problem might reveal the fact that you are misjudging her. You might discover that she will willingly share your poverty and help build your home. If you enter into homebuilding with a spirit of love and sacrifice, some day you will say as Henry Ward Beecher said: "We have a lovely home; it is fairly well-furnished, and we have a good income, but I would like to live again those first two years when we rented one room in an attic and struggled together to make a picnic of our life."

And now a word about the eternity of the marriage covenant. Some people question that too. But let's look at the principle of it. Will you name for me in your minds the most divine attribute of the human soul? It isn't sympathy. And girls, be careful not to be misled by sympathy. True, sympathy is next to love, but it is not love. Love is the most divine attribute of the human soul, and if you accept the immortality of the soul, that is, if you believe that personality persists after death, then, you must believe that love also lives. Isn't that sound? And I ask you this: Whom shall we love when we recognize those personalities in the next world?

True, we are admonished to love everybody. Yes, we should love everybody now; but you and I know that we love those whom we know best. I love her whom I have seen sacrifice her life for the little loved ones—her by whose side I have sat and together prayed and yearned over our little darlings. I shall love my mother who I know offered her life that I might have being. When we meet these personalities in the eternal realm, we shall recognize them, and know

221

them because of these experiences in this life. And that union of loving hearts will be perpetuated after life. That is why we are married—sealed—for time and eternity. It isn't just a mere dogma of the Church—it is a truth fundamental to the life and happiness of all humanity. It is the part of wisdom to choose the House of the Lord in which to plight your love and to consecrate your vows.

Let me conclude by giving you a glimpse of the significance of such a marriage. The bridegroom kneeling at the altar has in his heart the dearest possession that a husband can cherish—the assurance that she who places her hand in his, in confidence, in marriage, is as pure as a sunbeam—as spotless as the snow newly fallen from the heavens. He has the assurance that in her purity and sweetness she typifies divine motherhood. Now, young man, you tell me whether that assurance, that complete faith and confidence, is not worth everything else in the world.

And equally sublime is the assurance the young girl has that the man whom she loves, to whom she gives herself in marriage, comes to her with that same purity and strength of character which she brings to him. Such a union will indeed be a marriage ordained of God for the glory of His creation.

This is your heritage, youth, as you contemplate an eternal partnership, and I pray that you may realize it and find the true joy and happiness of such a cherished ideal.

Chapter Thirty-seven

Conservation
and Training
of Youth

As THE YEARS come and go, I experience an ever-increasing wonderment for life itself and a deep sense of appreciation for the opportunities and blessings it affords.

Six Guardians of My Youth

First, I am grateful for the wise and careful guardianship and training of noble parents—guardianship and training— two qualities of parenthood wisely and discreetly applied during the extremely active, somewhat reckless days of youth —a guardianship which kept me from turning to paths that would have opened to an entirely different kind of life! Every year increases my appreciation and love for an ever watchful, precious mother, and a noble father.

Second, I am grateful for nine brothers and sisters, four of whom still survive, who made up a home environment— now a cherished memory—which, as an influence in character building, was second only to the ever kind and discreet parental family guidance.

Third, I am grateful for the sacrifices made to permit us children to enter the field of education.

Through that opportunity I met my life's companion, who has ever been an inspiration, the mother and wise

223

guardian of our seven children and the heart and center of a second lovely home.

Fourth, I am grateful for my many friends. He is truly blessed who has experienced the peace and richness of soul that springs from true and loyal friendship. I love my friends and true associates as one of the most priceless possessions of life.

Fifth, I am grateful for citizenship in this great land where the constitution guarantees freedom. I denounce any ideology, any attempt of man to change the fundamental principles of this great American republic.

Sixth, I am grateful most of all for the gospel, the true philosophy of a happy life, which sanctifies and makes operative all other blessings.

Our Dearest Possessions

We hear much about the necessity of conservation. We have been admonished to conserve our resources. Economy and thrift are fundamentals in the social organization and in the teachings of this Church. Conservation and care are in keeping with the example which Jesus gave his disciples. You remember on one occasion he fed the multitude, after which he said, ". . . Gather up the fragments that remain, that nothing be lost." (John 6:12.)

Conservation of material things is most commendable and pleasing to God, but the greatest conservation mankind can engage in is the conservation of youth, the conservation of manhood and the protection of womanhood; and I appeal to the Latter-day Saints to give more thought to the protection, to the consideration, of the dearest possession you have— your sons and daughters.

The day after Christ gave the lesson of economy in taking care of things of the earth, he said to some of the same multitude who gathered around him in Capernaum:

. . . Ye seek me, not because ye saw the miracles, but because ye did eat of the loaves, and were filled.

Labour not for the meat which perisheth, but for that meat which endureth unto everlasting life, which the Son of man shall give unto you. . . . (John 6:26-27.)

And they said, in substance, "What is that, Master? Where shall we get this?"

And he said, ". . . This is the work of God, that ye believe on him whom he hath sent." (John 6:28-29.)

Faith in Christ is one of the principles we should teach our boys and girls. The Prophet Joseph Smith, through revelation, received the admonition, and he has given it to the world; and it is now a standing law in the Church that it is the duty of fathers and mothers to teach to their children the principles of life and salvation based upon faith in the Lord Jesus Christ.

The First Institution Ordained by God

I praise God for the instructions he has given his people concerning the sacredness, sanctity, and permanence of the family relationship. Let us impress these instructions upon our children. First, let us teach them that the proper place to begin the family relationship is in the house of God, kneeling at his sacred altar worthily. This means that the young man is just as pure and sweet in his life, and that he has been during his teens and early manhood, as she whose hand he holds in his, and who gives to him a life of purity and virtue, worthy of motherhood, worthy of one who in the holy office of motherhood joins with the Creator in bringing to the earth eternal souls.

We are not conserving that which will perish in time when we protect and guide eternal spirits. The little babe comes to the home as an eternal part of it, when the father and mother plight each other's troth for time and all eternity. *Let us teach the youth, then, that the marriage relationship is one of the most sacred obligations known to man or that man can make. Teach them that the family is the first institution ordained of God and instituted among men. If every couple sensed the sacredness of this obligation, there would be fewer homes broken up by disagreements that lead to divorces.*

The safety, the perpetuity of our government, or of any republican form of government, depends upon the safety and permanency of the home. Herein we get a glimpse of a great truth in which this people may be the saviors, in a way, of this great nation. Home is the place where the perpetuation of the principles of liberty, as well as instructions in the gospel of Jesus Christ, should be given to children. When the home breaks up, the children begin to wander off into sin. Then the law must reach out to bring them back and try to teach them principles of service and of true government; but, oh, how helpless the state when the home has failed!

Between the Hours of Sunset and Retiring

The inspiration of God is seen in requiring the Latter-day Saints to keep their homes intact and to teach their children the principles of the gospel of Jesus Christ. I do not mean by that that we should make such teaching purely formal. I mean that the Gospel of Jesus Christ should radiate in every home, that prayer night and morning should be offered up in sincerity; that the children daily should realize that we desire in our home the presence of God. *If we can invite the Savior there, we may know that the angels will be not only willing but also eager to protect our boys and girls.*

I believe that in most homes boys and girls are taught to pray before retiring for the night. I believe, however, that too generally, the morning prayers are neglected. When we come to think of it, though, it is during the waking hours that our boys and girls need the protection of God, and the guidance of his Holy Spirit, more even than when they are asleep. The dangers surrounding them today are the dangers that come to them out in society, out in the darkness of the night, when they are away from parental influence. *I plead with you parents of the Church to know where your boys and girls are at night, between the hour of sunset and the hour of retiring. I plead with you to know where they are during the day. Keep your minds upon them. Let your thoughts go with them. Labor not so much for that which will perish, but for that which endures eternally, for the lives which God has given you to protect in this world, that the sin of their failing, the sin of their degradation may not rest upon your shoulders.*

Live to Get Your Children's Love

Homes are made permanent through love. Oh, then, let love abound! *If you feel that you have not the love of your children, live to get it. Though you neglect some of the cattle, though you fall short in some material matters, study and work and pray to hold your children's love.*

Loyalty is another element of the permanent home. The loyalty you afterwards want them to show to the priesthood of God should be manifest in the home—*love, loyalty, virtue. Cherish these principles as you cherish and treasure your life.*

Set children the proper example. Latter-day Saints, keep the commandments of God. Teach your children the commandments. The auxiliary associations are doing much to help us. The Church in all its organizations is putting forth an effort to make ideal men in ideal communities; but, after all, the responsibility of making those ideal men and women, those ideal boys and girls, rests with the parents, and next with the older brothers and sisters. The responsibility is with the family, God's unit in the social fabric of humanity. We shall never get away from it.

God help us to conserve the powers of our boys and girls. God help us to implant in their hearts the principles of life and salvation. May they have an undying testimony of the truth of the gospel of Jesus Christ—for it is true. The principles of the Gospel of Jesus Christ are the principles of eternal life. God help us to instill this into the hearts of the young and keep them free and unspotted from association with those who would deprive them of the ideals of purity!

Chapter Thirty-eight

Courtship
and
Marriage

In the forty-ninth section of the Doctrine and Covenants, verse 15, the Lord clearly sets forth the significance of marriage: "And again, verily I say unto you . . . marriage is ordained of God unto man." It is, therefore, not a ceremony to be entered into lightly, to be terminated at pleasure, nor a union to be dissolved at the first difficulty that might arise.

To members of the Restored Church, marriage is a divine ordinance; and, when directed by intelligent parenthood, is the surest and safest means for the improvement of mankind.

When Jesus referred to marriage, he associated with it the lofty command: "What therefore God hath joined together, let no man put asunder." (Mark 10:9.)

It has been truly said that the strength of a nation, especially of a republican nation, is in the intelligent, well-ordered homes of its people. In no other group in the world should there be more contented, more happy homes than in The Church of Jesus Christ of Latter-day Saints.

We must never lose sight of the fundamental fact that home is the basis of civilization, and that members of the Church have the obligation to build ideal homes and to rear exemplary families. With this obligation in mind, I should like to name five conditions contributing to a successful marriage.

To the young people of the Church, particularly, I should like to say first that a happy home begins not at the marriage altar, but during the brilliant, fiery days of youth.

The first contributing factor to a happy home is the sublime virtue of loyalty, one of the noblest attributes of the human soul. Loyalty means being faithful and true. It means fidelity to parents, fidelity to duty, fidelity to a cause or principle, fidelity to love. Disloyalty to parents during teen age is often a source of sorrow and sometimes tragedy in married life.

A successful marriage begins when you are accepting invitations in your teen-age years to attend social parties. It begins with the manner in which you say goodnight to your companion.

Maintaining an unsullied reputation during courtship contributes to a solid foundation upon which to build a happy home.

A second important factor is choosing a congenial companion.

The problem of choosing a proper, congenial mate is very vital. During the period of courtship young people should mingle with one another and become acquainted with one another's dispositions. The young girl inclined to music who learns to play an instrument, or who sings, is more likely to find a good mate than one who sits at home refusing to go out in society.

The boy who participates in athletics is more likely to find a congenial mate than one who sits by the television or radio. In other words, associations are conducive to happy marriages because young folk become acquainted with one another and have more opportunity for choice.

Let me sound a note of warning against "going steady" too young. It is true that a young girl finds in it a sense of present security so far as dates to public functions and social parties are concerned, and it may be the determining of a final union; but "going steady" too early in life is fraught with handicaps with which hopeful, fiery youth should not be subjected.

In the first place, young people are very susceptible— quick to "fall in love"; and, being immature in judgment, may not distinguish between fascination or passion and true admiration or genuine love.

In the second place, "going steady" limits, if not excludes, girls and boys from having the opportunity of becoming acquainted with one another. For example, dancing with the same partner during an entire evening goes against the social spirit of the ballroom.

But the worst of early choosing to "go steady" is that it gives to the young man a sense of familiarity or ownership; and to the young girl, a feeling of belonging, a rapturous state to be consummated rightly only by marriage vows. But marriage, when experienced by unbridled, daring youth, becomes like fruit plucked before it is ripe—something unsavory, uncontributive to matrimonial joy.

Ever be mindful that, following childhood, a youth has other obligations besides choosing a mate or having a "good time." He must determine first of all what kind of character he will develop; he must decide what his trade or profession will be; and, if and when he chooses a wife, how he will support her and the children.

"Going steady" may so enchant the couple that these other associated obligations may be given too little consideration.

The third ideal I name as contributive to the happy marriage begins when you kneel at the altar, each covenanting to be true to the other. A man who gives his word, if he be honorable, is bound more than when he signs a contract because his word is his bond, and so is that contract of marriage, and particularly when the couple kneels in the house of the Lord, signifying that each is worthy of the other.

230

The young girl knows that he to whom she gives herself is just as worthy of fatherhood as she of motherhood, and she is justified in thinking so. Each is free from any memory of the boy who "had his fling." It is a glorious feeling to know that each is only for the other.

Marriage offers an opportunity to share in the love and care of children, the paramount purpose of marriage. If we do not put the proper value on parenthood, we are not emotionally nor socially ready for marriage.

Marriage is a relationship that cannot survive selfishness, impatience, domination, inequality, and lack of respect. Marriage is a relationship that thrives on acceptance, equality, sharing, giving, helping, doing one's part, learning, and laughing together.

Violation of the marriage vows proves the violator to be one who cannot be trusted, and "to be trusted is a greater compliment than to be loved."

A fourth factor is self-control in the home. During courtship, keep your eyes wide open; but, after marriage, keep them half shut. A wise mate learns to control the tongue. Do not speak the complaining, unkind word; just walk outdoors.

Under the heading of self control, indulgence in tobacco and failure to master appetites for intoxicants have been a source of unhappiness in otherwise happy homes; and have changed into tragedy many an otherwise useful life.

A fifth contributing factor to a happy marriage is courtesy. During courtship each is pleased to anticipate the wishes of the other; and, within the bounds of propriety, to take joy in granting those wishes. Too many couples look upon the covenant at the marriage altar as the end of courtship. It should be the beginning of an eternal courtship. Let us not forget that during the burdens of home life—and they come—that tender words of appreciation, courteous acts, are even more appreciated than during those sweet days and months of courtship.

It is well to keep in mind that love can be starved to death as literally as the body that receives no sustenance.

Love feeds upon kindness and courtesy. It is significant that the first sentence of what is now known throughout the Christian world as the *Psalm of Love,* is, "Love suffereth long, and is kind." The wedding ring gives no man the right to be cruel or inconsiderate; and no woman has the right to be slovenly, cross, or disagreeable.

In the home blessed with children, children seeing father courteous to mother, and mother to father, partake themselves of that attribute, just as they breathe the air of the home; and thus become refined and cultured children, for the essence of true culture is consideration for others.

Nothing is more becoming in a great man than courtesy and forbearance. Be punctual with your wife and with your children. If duties detain you, do not hesitate to apologize and explain. Punctuality and consideration after marriage are important factors of a congenial home.

Let me give you a glimpse of the significance of an ideal marriage ceremony: The bridegroom kneeling at the altar has in his heart the dearest possession that a husband can cherish— the assurance that she who places her hand in his in confidence is as pure as a sunbeam, as spotless as the newly fallen snow. He has the assurance that in her purity and sweetness she typifies divine motherhood. That assurance, that complete faith and confidence, is worth everything else in the world.

And equally sublime is the assurance the young girl has that the man whom she loves, to whom she gives herself in marriage, comes to her with that same purity and strength of character which she brings to him. Such a union will indeed be a marriage ordained of God for the glory of his creation.

This is your heritage, youth, as you contemplate an eternal partnership. May you realize it and find the true joy and happiness of such a cherished ideal!

Chapter Thirty-nine

The Importance of Courtship and Significance of Temple Marriage

. . . Whoso forbiddeth to marry
is not ordained of God, for
marriage is ordained of God unto
man. Wherefore, it is lawful that
he should have one wife, and
they twain shall be one flesh, and
all this that the earth might
answer the end of its creation.
(D.&C. 49:15-16.)

By DIRECT REVELATION, in this passage is stated in a few words the true purpose of marriage. It is to bear children and rear a family.

I have but one thought in my heart for the young people of the Church, and that is that they be happy. I know of no other place than the home where true happiness can be found in this life. It is possible to make home a bit of heaven; indeed, I picture heaven to be a continuation of the ideal home.

I could not find the little maid content
So out I rushed, and sought her far and wide;
But not where pleasure each new fancy tried,
Heading the maze of rioting merriment,
Nor where, with restless eyes and bow half bent,
Love in the brake of sweetbriar smiled and sighed,

Nor yet where Fame towered, crowned and glorified,
Found I her face, nor wheresoe'er I went.
So somewhat back I crawled, like wounded bird,
    When lo! Content sat spinning at my door;
    And when I asked her where she was before—
"Here all the time," she said; "I never stirred;
    Too eager in thy search, you passed me o'er,
And, though I called, you neither saw nor heard."
                                    Alfred Austin.

Yes, truly, the "maid content" is in the ideal home. Thinking men generally have come to that conclusion. Scientists today say that civilization is to be measured at different stages largely by the development of the home.

In early youth, our environment is largely determined for us, but in courtship and marriage we can modify, yes, even control to a very great extent, our environment. Morally speaking, we can carve the very atmosphere in which we live. But the most important of these elements is personal effort—that which we make of ourselves.

History, and our own teachings, tell us that marriage in some form or other has been man's fundamental association since time began. We know from revelation that marriage is ordained of God and was instituted by divine edict. That was in the beginning, but man has prostituted it and practiced different forms of marriage and different methods of obtaining mates. Among certain races, wives were obtained by theft; and among some tribes of nomadic peoples, wives were and still are obtained by purchase. Another form of securing a mate, most common among civilized peoples, is by common consent. When I was on my first mission in Scotland a couple who merely agreed to marry became husband and wife in a common-law marriage, which was recognized as a legal union. Later in history the marriage ceremony became sanctified by the various churches, and even later than that it was legalized by the law of the land.

Thus we have throughout various nations of the world in modified form various systems of marriage. I wish you to keep them in mind, and compare them with the scriptural text appearing at the beginning of this article that "*marriage is ordained of God.*" It is something not to be entered into lightly nor terminated at pleasure or at the first difficulty that might arise as we journey down the highway of matrimony. If the world could realize that—just that one thought —we should not have the broken homes and the resultant unhappiness and misery.

Marriage and Happiness Controls Government

No couple should enter into matrimony without careful observation and serious, prayerful thought. Everyone desires to live happily in married life. It is the natural, the normal life. The stability of government and the perpetuation of the race depend upon happiness in marriage. The happiness of mankind is not complete without congenial marriage.

It is well for young people to keep their eyes open in courtship. That is one way in which we can "carve" our environment. Association is the element in which our hearts become warm. How important it is, then, that the companion of each be chosen wisely and prayerfully. The choosing of a companion determines our future happiness or unhappiness. It is a part of wisdom, therefore, to associate only with those from whose company you can select a life's partner with whom you will be congenial. If, in such companionship you recognize negative characteristics in him who attracts you, try to let your judgment rule your heart. Do not fool yourselves, girls, by thinking that after you are married a man will overcome evil habits or negative traits of character. Let him prove himself before marriage.

I know you are now asking: "What are the positive characteristics for which we should seek?"

True Lover's Characteristics

Among the dominant characteristics a true lover should possess are: first, *Honesty;* second, *Loyalty;* third, *Chastity;* and, fourth, *Reverence.*

235

Never marry a man who would deceive you or who would tell you a lie. I think it was Sir Walter Scott who said: "I will withdraw my hand from a man, were he my best friend, who would wrong a woman or tell a lie."

These virtues which I have named are qualities which will appeal to your mind, to your observation, to your judgment. The real guiding principle, however, is the divinest attribute of the soul—*Love.*

Before I consider this virtue further, let me give you a word-picture of different kinds of wives as written by James Allen. He says:

> Some women in marrying demand all and give all.
>> With good men they are happy;
>> With base men they are brokenhearted.
>
> Some demand everything and give little.
>> With weak men they are tyrants;
>> With strong men they are divorced.
>
> Some demand little and give all.
>> With congenial souls they are in heaven;
>> With uncongenial they are soon in their graves.
>
> Some give little and demand little.
>> They are the heartless—they bring neither
>> The joy of life nor the peace of death.

In choosing a companion, it is necessary to study the disposition, the inheritance, and training of the one with whom you are contemplating making life's journey. You see how necessary it is to look for the characteristics of honesty, loyalty, chastity, and reverence. But after having found them—"How then," you ask, "may you tell whether or not there is a consanguinity, that something which will make you at least congenial in each other's company?" Though love is not always a true guide, especially if that love be not reciprocated, or is bestowed upon a surly creature, or a bruite, yet certainly there is no happiness without love. "Well," you may ask, "how may I know when I am in love?"

Am I In Love?

This is a very important question. A fellow student and I considered that query one night as we walked together. As young men of that age frequently do, we were talking about girls. Neither he nor I knew whether we were in love or not. In answer to my question, "How may we know when we are in love?" That young man, who later became a member of the Council of the Twelve, said, "My mother once said that if you meet a girl in whose presence you feel a desire to achieve; who inspires you to do your best, and to make the most of yourself, such a young woman is worthy of your love, and is awakening love in your heart."

I submit that, young men, as a true guide. In the presence of the girl you truly love you do not feel to grovel; in her presence you do not attempt to take advantage of her; in her presence you feel that you would like to be everything that a true man should become, for she will inspire you to that ideal. And I ask you young women to cherish that same guide. What does he inspire in you—to feel as Portia did when she loved? She was wealthy; she was beautiful; but for Bassanio she wished she were a thousand times more beautiful, ten thousand times more rich—that is what true love does! When a young man accompanies you after a meeting, or after a dance, and he shows an inclination to use you as a convenience, or as a means of gratification, then you may know he is not prompted by love.

Let Judgment Rule

Under such circumstances, no matter how fascinated you may be, young woman, no matter how confident you may feel that you love him, let your judgment rule and you be master of your feelings. It may grieve you not to follow the inclination of your heart, but you had better be pained a little in your youth than to suffer pangs of torture later.

Courtship is a wonderful period. It should be a sacred one. That is the time in which you choose your mate. Young men, your success in life depends upon that choice! Choose prayerfully the one who inspires you to do your best, and always remember that no man injures the thing he loves. In the world there is the double standard of morality, but in The Church of Jesus Christ of Latter-day Saints there is but a single standard. It applies to the boys as well as to the girls. If you follow that standard, and, indeed, if you will listen to the promptings of your best self, your clearest judgment, the whisperings of your own true heart, you will learn this lesson: *That self-mastery during youth, and compliance with the single standard of morality is (1) the source of virile manhood; (2) the crown of beautiful womanhood; (3) the foundation of a happy home, and (4) the contributing factor to the strength and perpetuity of the race!*

Temple Marriage

And now a word about the eternity of the marriage covenant: Let us look at the principle of it. Name in your own minds the most divine attribute of the human soul. It is not sympathy. And girls, be careful not to be misled by sympathy. True, sympathy is next to love, but it is not love.

Love is the most divine attribute of the human soul; and if you accept the immortality of the soul, that is, if you believe that personality persists after death, then you must believe that love also persists after death. Is that not sound? And I ask you this: Whom shall we love when we recognize those personalities in the next world?

True, we are admonished to love everybody. Yes, we should love everybody now; but you and I know that we love most those whom we know best. I shall love my wife, my children, mother and father, brothers and sisters, and shall recognize them and know them beyond the veil because of the experiences we have shared in this life. And the union of loving hearts will be perpetuated after life. That is why we are married—sealed in the temple for time and all eternity. This is not just a mere dogma of the Church—it is a truth fundamental to the life and happiness of all humanity. It is the part of wisdom to choose the house of the Lord in which to plight your love and to consecrate your vows.

Significance of Marriage

Let me give you a glimpse of the significance of such a marriage. The bridegroom kneeling at the altar has in his heart the dearest possession that a husband can cherish—the assurance that she who places her hand in his, in confidence, in marriage, is as pure as a sunbeam—as spotless as the snow newly fallen from the heavens. He has the assurance that in her purity and sweetness she typifies divine motherhood. Now, young man, you tell me whether that assurance, that complete faith and confidence, is not worth everything else in the world.

Equally sublime is the assurance the young girl has that the man whom she loves, to whom she gives herself in marriage, comes to her with that same purity and strength of character which she brings to him. Such a union will indeed be a marriage ordained of God for the glory of his creation.

This is your heritage, youth of the Church, as you contemplate an eternal partnership.

Chapter Forty

Temples Erected
for the
Blessing of the People

THE eternity of the marriage covenant has its base in the eternal truth of the immortality of the soul. Great thinkers generally recognize Jesus as the greatest philosopher and greatest teacher who ever walked the earth. He accepted the immortality of the soul without question.

To members of the Church, he is God made manifest in the flesh. He lived before he came, He accepted the hereafter as you accept your sleep tonight or the sunshine tomorrow. He said: "In my Father's house are many mansions: if it were not so, I would have told you. . . ." (John 14:2.) He did not argue it. To him it was an accepted fact. Upon the eternal truth of immortality rests the value, the importance of marriage in the temple.

Temples are erected for the blessing of the people through the covenants they make. Everybody who enters the temple will make certain covenants or take upon himself certain responsibilities.

One great purpose carried out by those who come into the temple is the sealing of man and wife in the sacred bonds of matrimony. That purpose is based upon the fact that man and woman truly love each other. That means that a couple coming to the altar should be sure that there is love in each heart.

Let us ever remember that love is the divinest attribute of the human soul. God himself is love. Our hearts are really one with him in that eternal home; and so when a couple kneels at the altar and receives the privilege and blessing of that eternal sealing, they should be sure that love is binding those two hearts that will now be bound by the holy power of the priesthood for time and all eternity. With that should go the feeling, the realization, that love must be fed; otherwise that binding, that sealing power, that covenant which is made, may not last forever. Love must be nourished; love can be starved to death just as literally as the body can be starved without daily sustenance. There is no one great protestation that anybody can make that will be sufficient to keep that love alive always.

There are certain obligations taken by those who make covenants at the altar, and those obligations must be manifest after they go out of the temple. One is *kindness.* There should be no unkindness manifest in the homes occupied by couples who leave the house of God.

In one of the great epistles that Paul wrote, now known throughout the Christian world as the "Psalm of Love" (see 1 Corinthians 13), there are some statements, the first of which is, "Love suffereth long and is kind." The word *suffereth* includes patience, tolerance, and consideration. We can visualize homes in The Church of Jesus Christ in the great majority of which there is kindness on both parts because there is love there, a binding love which will not be separated by death. Love suffereth long, and is always kind and gentle.

Men of the Church should remember, and women of the Church should realize that kindness will foster love, and it should be a reciprocal act. There are men of courtesy, men who think of and give special thought to their wives, and wives who consider their husbands. Paul, in the same epistle,

241

says, "Love seeketh not her own" but the welfare and happiness of others. Another line in that same epistle says, "Love believeth all things." If that love is fed daily and monthly and yearly throughout a lifetime, the husband's attention will not be drawn to somebody else, because there is trust in that binding power of the priesthood. Neither will the wife seek attraction or indulgence in any other way, because love trusts, "believeth all things;" and there must be foundation and cause for that trust which the husband has in the wife, and the trust which the wife has in her husband.

It is a glorious thing to be sealed for time and eternity to one whom you love. If your spirit lives after death, as it does, then that attribute of love will persist also, just as sympathy, just as reverence, and every other virtue that you have will persist.

Love Is Eternal

If love then is as eternal as the spirit, and you love that girl whom you take to the altar, do you not want to have her for time and eternity? To that question there is only one answer. And if death comes to separate you and you look upon that sweetheart as living in the world beyond, do you not have that same love for her that you had here? Whom would you like to meet when you go the the Other Side? I asked that of some critics one time; and a woman answered, "Why, we should love everybody." Yes, we should love everybody here also, but I love my wife by whose side I have sat at night watching a little, sick child. I love those children for whom we have worked and struggled and who have reciprocated that love; and if earthly things are typical of heavenly things, when I shall meet those loved ones over There, I shall think more of them than of persons whom I have never met or known.

Temple Marriage Is Appealing

Temple marriage is basically appealing; it is scientifically sound, and any young man who takes his sweetheart to a temple should go there with the understanding that their union is to be just as eternal as the love that has brought them to the altar. There is no question about it.

Before you get married in the temple, it is required that you have lived a clean life. You have the assurance, young lady, that the man whom you are about to marry is bringing to you a clean body. Each of us has the assurance that the source of life is unpolluted. Young men and young women who would live the happiest lives would do well to prepare themselves to be worthy of that form of marriage which God has ordained—the union of a man and woman worthy to have their marriage consummated in the temple of the Most High. There, as true lovers kneel to plight their troth, each may cherish the assurance of the following:

First, that their married course begins in purity. The children who come to bless the union are guaranteed a royal birth so far as inheriting a clean body is concerned.

Second, that their religious views are the same. The difficulty of rearing children properly is aggravated when father and mother have divergent views regarding doctrine and Church affiliation.

Third, that their vows are made with the idea of an eternal union, not to be broken by petty misunderstanding or difficulties.

Fourth, that a covenant made in God's presence, and sealed by the Holy Priesthood, is more binding than any other bond.

Fifth, that a marriage thus commenced is as eternal as love, the most divine attribute of the human soul.

Sixth, that the family unit will remain unbroken throughout eternity.

God bless our boys and girls that they may keep their lives unpolluted; that they may go in prayer to God and ask him to guide them in choosing their mates; and when chosen, that they will so live that they can enter the house of God, and if he were present and asked them about their lives, they could answer him honestly, "Yes, we are clean."

A marriage begun on that basis will bring happiness, the sweetest joy known in this life or throughout eternity. I know it! God bless our young people that they may have that consummation and joy!

Chapter Forty-one

Sacredness
of the
Marriage Covenant

Whoso forbiddeth to marry is not ordained of God unto man. Wherefore, it is lawful that he should have one wife, and they twain shall be one flesh, and all this that the earth might answer the end of its creation.
(D.&C. 49:15-16.)

THE text that I read to you that marriage is ordained of God is a modern revelation found in the Doctrine and Covenants. In that passage we have set forth in a few words the true purpose of marriage—to bear children, to rear a family. I know of no other place where happiness abides more surely than in the home, do you? It is possible to make home a bit of heaven. Indeed, I picture heaven as a continuation of the ideal home. Some man has said: "Home filled with contentment is one of the highest hopes of this life." He is not far from it.

Historically we are told about practices of different forms of marriage among early peoples and races. Most of them are united in the conclusion that the family stands forth as the highest form of associated life. It is the natural unit of all future civic development, for in the home we find content.

"There is something wrong," said one man, "with our present-day marriages." The fault, he thinks, lies in the fact that men marry without any thought of fatherhood. They choose their mates from the "pin-up" girls rather than ask the question, "Will she be a good mother to my children?" and she, looking for a hero instead of thinking "Will he make a good husband and father?"

This author continues:

One current fundamental thing becomes plain: Nobody teaches fatherhood in America. And yet it is the basic reason for the very existence of males! . . . To take the place of fatherhood and, to some extent, of motherhood also—our society has invented endless forms of child appeasement: radio programs and comic books, movies and kindergartens and summer camps—parent substitutes of every possible sort. . . .

If the home is the foundation of the nation and of society, which it is, we as a people had better begin making real homes and real families. It has become increasingly popular to regard young-sters as a bore and to seize every possible means to escape their company. Children raised by such couples will inevitably be bored by everything in marriage except pleasure. *But the good life is not a pleasure hunt. If we want to be happy, we must pursue happiness, not pleasure. And the measure of a happy person is his ability to be tough with himself and tender with others.*

If we are to give marriages their proper start, we must change the ideas and values of those who are to marry. The question of the young man must not be: Who's the cutest number I know? The young woman must not ask: Who will treat me like a bride forever? The question most likely to yield the right lifetime answer is this:

Is she the best mother I can find for my children? He the best father?

Or phrase it: Would I want to be her child? His?

Such is the expression of one who senses the responsibility of the home as a place in which to rear children. That is the point I am asking, and if we keep that in mind—not look upon marriage as a means of selfish indulgence—we are going to save many misunderstandings, for father and mother lose themselves in the lives of the little babes that come.

In the lives of little children they find content and true happiness.

Evils of Divorce

Here, to young folk particularly, and to all of you, and to the nation, I should like to say a word about divorce because there are too many who are wrecking their lives upon the shoals of broken homes. I used to think that the man was entirely to blame. I grew to manhood thinking there was no unfaithful woman. My mother was my ideal, my sisters, and my wife. And for all marital troubles in life I blamed the man. I am deeply sorry that during my schooldays I had to change that ideal. Here are some of the usual causes for divorce: infidelity on the part of one or the other, habitual drunkenness, physical cruelty or violence, union of an innocent girl with a reprobate. I mention these as conditions which seem to justify in some cases, a separation. If we could remove them, I would say there never should be a divorce. It is Christ's ideal that home and marriage should be perpetual—eternal. To the Pharisee's question, "Is it lawful for a man to put away his wife?" the Savior answered:

Have ye not read, that he which made them at the beginning made them male and female.

And said, For this cause shall a man leave father and mother, and shall cleave to his wife: and they twain shall be one flesh.

Wherefore they are no more twain, but one flesh. What therefore, God hath joined together, let not man put asunder.

(Matt. 19:3-6.)

Marriage is a sacred relationship entered into for purposes that are well recognized. It is claimed by some observers that our present modern marriages tend to frustrate these purposes. "Modern living conditions," writes one, "contribute to these frustrations.

"Formerly a married woman had a home to care for, often several children. Today, in many parts of our country, a married woman continues either to follow her vocation or to spend her time seeking new stimulations—no children to care for—no house to clean—no meals to cook. Under such conditions her leisure-time activities become her all-absorbing interests—interests which often lead her away from her husband rather than to him."

Here is a paragraph from a letter I received only last week:

The first year of our marriage seemed to go very well, but after our baby was born, it seemed like things started going on the rocks. My husband seemed to resent the attention I paid to the baby. When the baby was cross, instead of trying to make things easier for me by helping me with what I was doing so I could go and take care of the baby, or care for the baby himself, he would lose his temper, yell at the baby, shake the baby basket and scare the child.

Dangerous Reefs

After reading that, I rode to Ogden and entered a business store. An old friend came up and said, "I should like to ask you a question. My daughter is having trouble with her husband. They have three children, three boys. He has fallen in love with an 18-year-old girl."

"Were they married in the temple?" said I.

"Yes."

"Well, if I were you I would see that girl's parents and tell them the danger that the girl is in. She and your daughter's husband are standing on a precipice."

I will not relate the entire circumstance, but I am going to say this: that that condition with that couple is one in which a husband has an opportunity to prove himself either a man or a monkey; one in which he proves whether his character is that of a lion or a rat.

A married man's trifling with a young girl's affections, a flippant attitude toward marriage, the ill-advised suggestion of "companionate marriage," the base, diabolical theory of "free sex experiment," and the ready-made divorce courts are dangerous reefs upon which many a family bark is wrecked.

An ever-decreasing birth rate, and an increasing divorce rate are ominous signs threatening the stability of the American home, and the perpetuity of our present form of constitutional government. An editorial in a weekly magazine, published in the capital of our nation, says:

Since 1890 the United States of America's national birthrate has dropped from 32.9 per 1,000 population to 19.6 per 1,000 population in 1945.

In those same years, the national average for divorces jumped from 6.2 per 100 marriages to 31.0 per 100 marriages.

Birthrate Drops

Now statistics are rather dry and I am not going to bore you with them, but will say that "A falling birth rate plus a rising divorce rate speak ill for one's faith in the future. Hence it speaks ill for the nation's future."

"Our state rests upon our homes," said ex-President Taft on one occasion. "And if we cannot keep our homes from this constant demoralizing breaking up, we had better go out of the business of government entirely."

In some of the States of the Union, it is almost as easy to get a divorce as it is to get married. As a result of this laxity, one out of every five marriages ends either in divorce or annulment. And in one book I find that that is reduced now to one out of three.

I have here comparisons from 1923 to the present. They show that the tendency has increased in divorce and decreased in birth. Now there is something wrong in a community when conditions of this kind exist. One contributor to a current magazine says:

We are concerned with the whole community, with you and me and the stake we all have in the preservation of marriage, home, and family as an American way of life.

Promiscuity, sociologists agree, is the greatest foe of marriage.

Promiscuity, especially among young people, remains the major source of venereal infections.

Well, that is the condition of the world, but we must remember that this is our country, and we are very much concerned, for we love it. It is a land choice above all other lands. Young people are proud to call it their own. Today, however, I am talking to young people, I hope, who look upon their virtue as being as sacred as life itself. If you want to have a happy home, ever keep in mind the fact that you are going to lay the foundation for it in your teens before you even choose your mate. I know that there is spreading among the young people in high schools and other places the feeling that we parents are rather old-fashioned, and that it is out of date to keep ourselves clean and wholesome morally.

There are some things which never grow old-fashioned. The sweetness of a baby is one. The virtue and chastity of manhood is another. Youth is the time to lay the foundation for our homes. I know there are those who tell you that suppression is wrong, but I assure you that self-mastery, not indulgence, is the virtue that contributes to the virility of manhood and to the beauty of womanhood.

Chastity a Crown

In your studies, you students, keep yourselves free from the tendencies that will arouse your physical passions, and you will have increased intellectual energy. You know, as every man and woman knows, that chastity is the crown of beautiful womanhood, and when you seek the girl of your choice, you want a woman of virtue. Chastity is the foundation of a happy home. Remember that in youth things might come which would make a heavy heart but not so heavy as the memory that in youth you proved a traitor to your future wife or husband.

Shakespeare was right when he put in the mouth of Adam, the old faithful servant in *As You Like It*, when he pleaded to go out into the woods with his young master— you will remember he was pleading to go out into the woods

250

with Orlando, and Orlando thought he was too old to endure the hardships, etc., but the faithful old servant said:

> Though I look old, yet I am strong and lusty;
> For in my youth I never did apply
> Hot and rebellious liquors in my blood,
> Nor did not with unbashful forehead woo
> The means of weakness and debility;
> Therefore my age is as a lusty winter,
> Frosty, but kindly.

Youth of the Church, God bless you. You are nearing the marriageable age, some of you have reached it already. May you so prepare yourselves to be worthy of that form of marriage which God has ordained—the union of a man and a woman worthy to have their marriage consummated in the temple of the Most High. There, as true lovers kneel to plight their troth, each may cherish the assurances summarized as follows:

1. That your marriage begins in purity. You know who sits by your side or kneels there at the altar is as worthy of motherhood as the purest of virgins. Man with red blood— what does that mean to you? You are recreant if you cannot give her that same assurance, that he to whom she is giving her life is just as worthy of fatherhood as she of motherhood.

2. You know that your religious views are the same. The difficulty of rearing children properly is aggravated when father and mother have divergent views regarding doctrine and church affiliation.

A Sacred Covenant

3. You know that your vows are made with an ideal of an eternal union, not to be broken by misunderstanding or difficulties. There are too many who, as with the young man to whom I have already made reference, forget the value of a vow, the sacredness of a covenant, and let their affections go astray. That young man had no right to let his affections go to an 18-year-old girl. He had solemnly vowed that he

251

would be true to the girl who became the mother of three fine boys. I do not hesitate to call him a rat.

4. They know that a covenant made in God's presence and sealed by the Holy Priesthood is more binding than any other bond.

5. They know that if children come to bless the union they are guaranteed a royal birth, a clean, unpolluted body, to which every unborn baby is entitled.

6. A marriage thus commenced is as eternal as love, the divinest attribute of the human soul, and you who question temple marriage as possibly a mere dogma of the Church, let me ask you to name the divinest, most precious virtue known to man. I have named it. It is love. Let me ask you another question. Do you believe in the persistence of personality after death, the immortality of the soul, a fundamental doctrine of Christianity? In our Church, more than fundamental, a truth revealed. If you do, then you have to answer that love will characterize that personality over there as here. Whom will you love over there?

I asked that of a woman north of Australia on a boat one day. She said, "Why we should love everybody."

"Yes," I said, "we should love everybody, but I find that I love my wife, who has been an inspiration to me, by whose side I have sat when our loved ones have been ill. I love my mother. I find I love these children. I love my dearest friends. I think that those heavenly feelings will be over there just the same as they are here. I love everybody, but I shall cherish and I shall love my dear ones."

7. Finally, they know that the family unit will remain unbroken throughout eternity.

Such is temple marriage. Is it not worthwhile? As I glimpsed how the training in Scout work, training in Beehive work, in speech, in drama, in the dance, in music, and every phase of our efforts contributes to the preparing of a young couple to be worthy to enter the house of God and build a happy home. Do you know of anything higher and nobler? I do not.

Will you then, my young folks, look forward to such a marriage and the building of a happy home? To make it such, each must lose himself or herself for the good of others, and for the welfare of your family. Home may be a heaven on earth, as many of us have already found it!

Chapter Forty-two

Responsibility and Mission of the Youth of the Church

ABIDE YE IN THE LIBERTY wherewith ye are made free, . . . and the truth shall make you free." (D.&C. 88:86; John 8:32.) Fundamental in that "truth" is the free agency given to us—the right to think and act as we wish—a God-given blessing as precious as life itself, without which we should not be able to progress nor to be happy.

I should like to say that emphasis upon "liberty" is most timely at present, not only in the United States, but throughout the world. Two great ideologies are now being heralded before the nations of the world: One is that the individual is a vassal of the state. He or she must do what the state demands. That is not liberty. The other is that the individual is independent, an individual entity; and the state exists for the good of that individual, and to protect that individual in his or her liberties.

This contrast was empasized sometime ago in Washington. A senator met a representative from Russia, and during the conversation, while the senator held the Russian's hand, the senator from the United States said, "We pray." The Communist answered, "We do not pray."

"There," said the senator, "is one of the paramount differences between the democratic state and the autocratic,

254

domineering Russian policy—belief in God, our ideal; denial of the existence of God, theirs."

Let me remind you—"Abide ye in the liberty wherewith ye are made free."

Now let us emphasize the other element: "Entangle not yourselves in sin." (D.&C. 88:86.) Yours the selection, you have the right, you do as you please, and nobody will deprive you of that privilege. But let us consider this.

When the announcement was made of man's conquering Mount Everest, the world's highest known peak, the world was greatly stirred. One more epoch of courage and endurance man had added to his list of achievements over nature. For nearly half a century man had attempted to accomplish this seemingly-impossible feat. At last, as a mighty colossus, man stood astride the hitherto unconquered Mount Everest.

Now man has conquered the air, the ocean. He has overcome distance. He now speeds through space. *He is master of everything except himself.*

It is a great achievement to stand atop Mount Everest. The queen of England knighted the British subject and his companion who achieved it. I was very much interested when we received the announcement of that thrilling conquest; of the difficulties encountered. Here are some of them:

Treacherous glaciers and icefalls guard the top of Everest. Freezing wind blasts are likely to hurl rocks and chunks of ice at a climber. In 1924, two Britons were seen to pass the 28,200-foot level, and then were enveloped in a wind-whipped cloud of snow. They were never seen again.

For centuries man has desired to conquer nature. Now he has accomplished that feat, but the unconquered spirit of man yearns for other unchartered realms. Plans are now well on the way for a landing on the moon, and even a trip to Mars does not seem to be an impossibility.

But this "conquering" has not been done without effort and without loss of life. The Mount Everest expedition that succeeded May 29, 1953, was directed by Colonel H. J. C. Hunt of the King's Royal Rifle Corps. He did not make the final climb, but two of his men did. One was Edward P. Hillary, 34-year-old New Zealander, who kept bees for a living. His companion was Bhutia Tensing, 39-year-old Sherpa guide. "The Hunt Expedition was elaborately organized. It left Katmandu, Nepal on March 10, with 362 porters, 20 Sherpa guides, and 10,000 pounds of baggage. Eight advance camps were spotted up the mountain slopes, with the last shelter at 28,000 feet. The men carried new lightweight oxygen apparatus, radios to pick up weather reports from India, and special mortars to blast away dangerous overhanging ice."

At last they succeeded. I repeat, man has conquered everything but his own animal nature.

"Entangle not yourselves in sin." Young men and women, my first thought is that you realize the responsibility that comes with that "free agency," and to realize that what you think today, and what you do today will largely determine what your great nation will be, for it has been truly said that "the destiny of any nation at any given time depends on the opinions of its young men under five and twenty." (Goethe.)

Never before in history was our country in greater need of young men who cherish the higher life in preference to the sordid, the selfish and the obscene. What your opinions are today regarding life and its objectives will determine what your country will be tomorrow. This is pertinent.

What about spiritual power and the power of judgment, discretion, and self-control? Unless there is development of character equal to the expansion of physical forces, there is trouble ahead.

It has been said that the purpose of life may be summed up in one sentence: "To subdue matter that we might realize the ideal."

Self-mastery—mastery over temper in the home; mastery over quick speech, hasty condemnation, controlling the tongue, and thus saving heartaches, injured feelings; mastery over the appetite, controlling an appetite which is God-given, but keeping it within bounds—there is no gourmandizing or injuring the body, weakening it; mastery over the passions, that too, a God-given gift. But how many millions prostitute it because they lack self-control?

Young people, you can be in this world, but not of the world! You have entered into that state of life when you are driven by heavenly-bestowed passions. There are some young men who, recognizing this fact, say, "Well, having these passions, why cannot we gratify them?" And they receive justification sometimes from some modern psychologists, false teachers and leaders who say that repression is wrong; that indulgence is the natural course of life. But I say, do not be misled!

I repeat, young people, you are in that period of life in which your physical nature manifests itself, but you must also remember that God has given you, in that same period of your life, power of reasoning; he has given you the power of judgment, discretion, and self-control, and these for a divine purpose. Let reason and judgment be your guide, your balance.

This brings me to another fact equally, if not more, important than those already mentioned. The seeds of a happy married life are sown in youth. Happiness does not begin at the altar; it begins during the period of youth and courtship. These seeds of happiness are sown by your ability to master your driving passion. Chastity should be the dominant virtue among young people—the ideal which the world has not accepted, and which many in the world will not believe exists or is cherished in the hearts of youth. You young men and you young women who have been on missions well know how astonished some people were when you told of your pure life. Some of them said bluntly that they did not believe you. But it is true.

In our Church there is but one standard of morality. In

the world many people protect their girls and daughters, irrespective of religion. They know what it means for young girls to be treated as slaves or playthings, and they shield their own daughters from the ravages of men. But their boys are too often left free to prey upon helpless creatures who are not so protected.

Thus, in the world you find a double standard, but in the Church of Christ there is but a single standard. It applies to the boys as well as the girls.

It is virility and faith which we must exercise in The Church of Jesus Christ of Latter-day Saints if we are to counteract the dangerous conditions in the world today. The communist leaders blatantly declare that they deny Christ and the gospel and Christian principles, and their satellite nations instruct their youth not to believe in these truths—and they constitute millions. Add to that the possibility of professing Christians, too many of whom acknowledge Christain and classical heritage, but do not believe in it. Do you see what humanity is facing?

Our responsibility is to declare Jesus Christ and him crucified, and to set such examples of faith and works in the Church world-wide, that millions of honest souls who are seeking to know the truth will find in the Church what the Christians found in the Church in the days of the early Apostles. That is the responsibility I declare to our young people today, and it is a responsibility which rests upon every member of the Church of Jesus Christ in all the world. Ours is the responsibility, not merely to acknowledge the reality of those testimonies, but to believe in them, and to make that word of faith a reality that will influence men everywhere.

God give our young people the power to protect their liberty by being true to the free agency he has given them, and give them strength to master themselves and set an example to the whole world!

Success In The Home 4

Chapter Forty-three

Motherhood: The Mightiest of All Forces in Human Society

A beautiful, modest, gracious woman is creation's masterpiece. When a woman adds to these virtues, as guiding stars in her life, righteousness and godliness, and an irresistable impulse and desire to make others happy, no one will question if she be classed among those who are the truly great.

Womanhood should be intelligent and pure, because it is the living life-fountain from which flows the stream of humanity. She who would pollute that stream by tobacco, poisonous drugs, or by germs that would shackle the unborn, is untrue to her sex and an enemy to the strength and perpetuity of the race.

When one contemplates what the Creator expects and receives from his most precious creation, one is thoroughly convinced that woman has his divine trust and favor.

The poet Tennyson's statement, "The Mother Makes Us Most," has now become, at least throughout Western civilization, a truism.

> Sow a thought, reap an act,
> Sow an act, reap a habit,
> Sow a habit, reap a character,
> Sow a character, reap an eternal destiny.
> Thackeray

"Not only individuals, but nations, are of such stuff as thoughts are made of."

Mothers Sow Seeds

Mothers sow the seeds in childhood that determine to a great extent life's harvests in adulthood. A mother who instils into the souls of her children respect for one another and love for motherhood and fatherhood, renders a great service to the Church and to humanity in general. Children from such homes go out into the world as good citizens—citizens who will render the service which their parents have rendered, to fight the battles which their fathers and mothers have fought.

We talk about the greatest thing in the world, but it is difficult to decide what the greatest profession is. Teachers claim that it is teaching; doctors say medical science is the greatest profession. The noblest calling, then, must be one in which the attribute of love will manifest itself not for self, but for others. It must be that calling which most nearly emulates true motherhood, the mightiest of all forces in human society. Indeed, if motherhood were not a "distinct and individual creation," we could pause here and have all true men agree that it is the noblest, purest calling in life; and that which makes motherhood so is the Christlike element of giving her life for another. "A father may turn his back on his child; brothers and sisters may become inveterate enemies; husbands may desert their wives, and wives their husbands. But a mother's love endures through all. . . ." (Washington Irving.)

Motherhood Divine

The element, then, that makes true motherhood divine must also permeate that call or vocation which may be distinguished by the term "noblest." The most worthy calling in life, therefore, is that in which man can best serve his fellowman. It is not preaching; it is not teaching; it is not medicine; it is not engineering, nor any other vocation common among men. Each of these, though offering opportunities for service, may be followed by men actuated by the most selfish and sordid motives.

The noblest aim in life is to strive to make other lives better and happier. Browning sounded the keynote in "Paracelsus" when he said: "There is an answer to the passionate longings of the heart for fullness, and I knew it, and the answer is this: Live in all things outside yourself by love, and you will have joy. That is the life of God; it ought to be our life. In him it is accomplished and perfect; but in all created things it is a lesson learned slowly and through difficulty." That is a mother's love!

Mothers Overcome Self-love

The sweetness, as well as the greatness, of motherhood lies in the overcoming of self-love by mother for her children. By nature, the true mother is self-sacrificing. She is ever giving something of her life to make another happier or better.

Motherhood is the one thing in all the world which most truly exemplifes the God-given virtues of creating and sacrificing. Though it carries the woman close to the brink of death, motherhood also leads her into the very realm of the fountains of life, and makes her co-partner with the Creator in bestowing upon eternal spirits mortal life.

All through the years of babyhood, childhood, and youth, yes, even after her girls themselves become mothers and her sons become fathers, the mother tenderly, lovingly sacrifices for them her time, her comfort, her pleasures, her needed rest and recreation, and, if necessary, health and life itself. No language can express the power and beauty and heroism of a mother's love.

Mothers Ask Nothing

For all this consecrated devotion, she asks nothing in return. If her love is reciprocated, she is content; but if not, and her wayward child with poisoned feelings turns heedlessly from her, she still loves on, giving in yearning and solici-

263

tude far more than the recreant deserves. No, she asks nothing in return; nothing for the roses she has transplanted from her own cheeks to those of her darling; nothing for the hours of vigilance during days and nights of sickness; nothing for the thousand self-denials and sacrifices that had to be made in order that children in their "teens" might receive proper schooling and "appear well" with their companions; nothing for the heartaches caused by thoughtless word or act of wayward youth.

No, for all this and a thousand other things incident to motherhood, mother asks nothing; but she *deserves* much. For kindness, she deserves kindness; for tenderness, she should be given tenderness; for self-sacrifice, a little self-denial on the part of the children; for love, she should in return receive love.

It is an unfortunate phase of human nature that it is always inclined to undervalue its present blessings, that of mother and father's presence being no exception.

Mother's Love Undervalued

It is most fitting, therefore, that our attention should be called to the fact that we are prone not only to undervalue mother's presence and love, but in consequence of this unconscious indifference, to neglect to express the appreciation and love we do feel for her. This is one purpose of Mother's Day.

The older I grow, the more deeply grateful I am for the life and influence of a perfect mother. Among my most precious soul-treasures is the memory of Mother's prayers by the bedside, of her affectionate touch as she tucked the bed clothes around my brother and me and gave each a loving, goodnight kiss. We were too young and roguish then to appreciate fully such devotion, but not too young to know that Mother loved us.

It was this realization of Mother's love, with a loyalty to the precepts of an exemplary father, which more than once during fiery youth turned my steps from the precipice of temptation.

> My mother! God bless you!
> Your purity of soul,
> Your faith, your tenderness,
> Your watchful care,
> Your supreme patience,
> Your companionship and trust,
> Your loyalty to the Right,
> Your help and inspiration to Father,
> Your unselfish devotion to us children—
> These and every other virtue that
>   contribute to ideal motherhood,
> I associate with you, My Mother!
>   President David O. McKay.

Chapter Forty-four

Woman's Influence

They say that man is mighty,
He governs land and sea;
He wields a mighty scepter
O'er lesser powers that be;
But a mightier power and stronger
Man from his throne has hurled;
And the hand that rocks the cradle
Is the hand that rules the world.[1]

I believe in the potency of woman's influence. I believe with Tennyson that it is "the woman who makes us most." It truly has been said that:

Into the hands of every individual is given a marvelous power for good or for evil, the silent, unconscious, unseen influence of his life. This is simply the constant radiation of what a man really is, not what he pretends to be. Every man, by his mere living, is radiating sympathy, or sorrow, or morbidness, or cynicism, or happiness, or hope, or any of a hundred other qualities. Life is a state of constant radiation and absorption; to exist is to radiate; to exist is to be the recipient of radiations.

. . . Man cannot escape for one moment from this radiation of his character, this constantly weakening or strengthening of others. He cannot evade the responsibility by saying it is an unconscious influence. He can select the qualities that he will permit to be radiated. He can cultivate sweetness, calmness, trust, generosity, truth, justice, loyalty, nobility—make them vitally active in his character—and by these qualities he will constantly affect the world.[2]

---

[1]"What Rules the World," by William Ross Wallace.
[2]William George Jordan, *Majesty of Calmness* (Fleming H. Revell Company, Westwood, New Jersey), pp. 20, 22, 23.

Of the responsibility of women in wielding their influence, Ruskin writes:

There is not a war in the world, no, nor an injustice, but you women are answerable for it; not in that you have provoked, but in that you have not hindered.

Do you remember reading in "Marmion" how the young woman who accompanied him in his wars, dressed as a page, buckled on his armor? Commenting on that custom, Ruskin says:

The buckling on of the knight's armor by his lady's hand was not a mere caprice of romantic fashion. It is the type of an eternal truth that the soul's armor is never well set to the heart unless a woman's hand has braced it, and it is only when she braces it loosely, that the honor of manhood fails.

Home Is the Center of Woman's Power

At the turn of the century, in 1901, there was distributed throughout the Church, with the approval of the general presidency and general board of the Relief Society, a book entitled *Woman,* one paragraph of which is so applicable and true today that I quote it:

As for woman, wherever she goes and whatever her mission— for travel or for service—her native instincts draw her homewards.

She may have unusual power and be distinguished for versatility; she may have artistic ability and attain distinction on the stage or in the studio; she may make bargains behind the counter or "be mighty in ledger and great upon Change"; she may serve as shopgirl, toil as fieldhand or in factory, be a typist, ticket agent; . . . she may skillfully wield the pen and prove a very magician in journalism and in the nobler literatures; she may possess great persuasive power in the pulpit or on the platform; she may display diplomatic ability in the lobby or cabinet; she may fill the professor's chair or preside over college or university; she may, like Joan of Arc, be the heroine of many a battlefield, or, like Victoria, reign with "all the royal makings of a queen"—*but wherever a woman is, or whatever a woman does, she is at her best, her divinest best, at home! There is the center of her power. Amiel says, "Woman is the salvation or destruction of the family. She carries its destiny in the folds of her mantle.*"[3]

Four Requirements of Motherhood

It is wonderful what a responsibility each wife and mother carries. A successful wife and mother is responsible, *First*, for the physical welfare of her children. *Second*, she must have the qualities of a teacher. She should be, indeed is expected to be, not only a disciplinarian but one who wisely guides her children in their quest for truth and knowledge. In this she becomes a confidant—she warns—she protects. *Third*, she must be a business woman. *Fourth*, upon her, even more than upon the father, depends the child's guidance in spirituality.

After a lecture by Francis Wayland Parker, a great Chicago educator, a woman asked:

"How early can I begin the education of my child?"

"When will your child be born?" asked the educator.

"Born?" she gasped. "Why, he is already five years old."

"My goodness, woman," he cried, "don't stand here talking to me—hurry home; already you have lost the best five years."

I believe that that is absolutely true. If mothers would get control of their children throughout childhood and youth, they should get control of the child before he is five years of age. That is fundamental, and it can be done in kindness and love.

The world has a right to expect that a person or an organization will live up to his or its pretentions, and a married woman who refuses to assume the responsibilities of motherhood, or who, having children, neglects them for pleasure or social prestige, is recreant to the highest calling and privilege of womankind. It is the mother who inculates in the lives of children a nobility of soul that leads them instinctively to love the beautiful, the genuine, the virtuous, and, as instinc-

---

[3]John H. Vincent, *Woman*, The King-Richardson Company, Springfield, Massachusetts, 1902; p. 656.

tively, to turn from the ugly, the spurious, and the vile. Home is the center from which woman rules the world. It is there she teaches her child self-restraint, develops in him the confidence and strength that spring from self-control. It is there the child learns respect for the rights of others. It is in a well-directed home that men and women first develop a consciousness that true happiness lies in conforming one's life to the laws of nature and to the rules of social conduct.

Home Influence Is Ever Constant

The inspiration of God is seen in requiring the Latter-day Saints to keep their homes intact, and to teach their children the principles of the gospel of Jesus Christ. Every child is, to a great degree, what he is because of the ever-constant influence of home environment and the careful or neglectful training of the mother. Parents should make it obvious, both by actions and conversation, that they are seriously interested in religious things and believe in them themselves—faith in God, in the divine mission of Jesus Christ, and in the restoration of the gospel. Our religion should also take the form of honesty in our dealings with our family, our neighbors, and all with whom we come in contact.

I first received my unwavering faith in the existence of God in the home of my childhood when Father and Mother invariably called their children around them in the morning and at night and invoked God's blessing upon the household and upon mankind. There was a sincerity in that good patriarch's voice that left an undying impression upon our souls, and Mother's prayers were equally impressive. Every father, every mother, should see to it that in all sincerity the child is impressed with the reality of the existence of God, and with the reality that God will guide and protect his children. You carry that responsibility.

Prayer Combats Evil

No matter what they may be without, are your homes pure within? Are morning prayers offered regularly, or do the things of this world take you away from your homes and make you deprive yourself of morning prayers with the children? "Woe to that home where the mother abandons her holy mission or neglects the divine instruction, influence, and example while she bows, a devotee at the shrine of social pleasure; or neglects the essential duties in her own household."

Wherever possible, we should exert an influence, silent it may be, active it should be, to eliminate from our homes and our communities evil elements that are constantly disintegrating society—the liquor problem with its drunkenness, poverty, and misery—the harmful effects of cigarette smoking —immorality with all its attendant evils. See to it as individuals that we do not by our own acts contribute to their existence. The dangers surrounding our boys and girls today are the dangers that come to them out in society, out in the darkness of the night, when they are away from the parental influence. I plead with you to know where your boys and girls are at night; to know where they are during the day. Keep your minds upon them. Let your thoughts go with them.

Yes, the woman wields a mighty influence! Let that influence be felt even more potently throughout the Church and our communities in the protection of our homes from the impurities that are now sweeping the nation. The Lord bless every mother, every woman, that she may be wise and strong in teaching our boys and girls in maintaining ethical standards and in being exemplary examples to young people in all the world!

Chapter Forty-five

True
Manhood
and Womanhood

The world wants men—true men
Who cannot be bought or sold;
Men who will scorn to violate truth
Genuine gold.

THERE is nothing in life so admirable as true manhood; there is nothing so sacred as true womanhood. Manhood! Oh, what that means—to be a man, to be worthy of the tribute that Antony gave to Brutus, when he said:

> This was the noblest Roman of them all: . . .
> His life was gentle; and the elements
> So mixt in him that Nature might stand up
> And say to all the world, "This was a man!"[1]

"Man," says Shakespeare, "is the beauty of the world, the paragon of animals." We delight in associating with true men; it is good to be in their presence. An honest man is the noblest work of God. "He is the living light-fountain," says Carlyle, "which it is good and pleasant to be near." I often think it is easy to be honest; and to be honest means that we are in harmony with divine law, that we are in keeping with the noblest work of God.

---

[1]Shakespeare, William, *Julius Caesar*, Act V, Scene V.

The dishonest man brings only misery into the world. Look what Judas brought upon himself by not being true! He associated with his Lord and heard the divine truths from his Master's lips. It may be that once he felt in his heart the truth, but he let outside influences come upon him. He let his appetite for greed lead him into dishonesty.

Following that prompting, he opposed the work of the Master, found fault with conditions around him. Six days before the passover, Mary, out of the great love in her heart, anointed Jesus with costly oils. Who was it that found fault? Not the honest man in whose heart was the truth; but Judas. And even in his faultfinding, you detect the lie: "Why was not this ointment sold for three hundred pence, and given to the poor?" (John 12:5.)

What a dissembler! What a hypocrite! He did not want the money for the poor, "but," says one of his companions, "because he was a thief, and had the bag. . . ." (John 12:6.) He sat at meat with his Lord, near his Master's side, there in the presence of the Divine Man, pretending to be one with him—not only in friendship, but in discipleship; not only that, but a disciple in whom had been placed trust. There at the table eating bread by the side of the Master, he was still untrue and had already bargained to betray his Lord into the hands of his enemies. Later he passed out from Christ's presence into outer darkness.

God pity the man who so leaves the light! Pity Judas that night, when he left the radiance of that room, the company, the discipleship and divine presence of the Lord, and passed into the darkness to give expression not to his better self, but to the dishonesty within him, responding to the appeals of a morbid appetite of a dishonest soul.

Compare his life with that of James, the brother of the Lord, or even James, the brother of John. We do not know much about them, but they were both true men. James, who wrote the Epistle, was true under all conditions. He was a Jew, born with the prejudices of the Jews against the Gentiles. Yet, when the light came to his soul that Christ's truths were for all the world, his old traditions were swept aside; and he stood there in the face of his countrymen and declared the truth, which God had revealed to him, that the gospel was for all.

Follow that man from there on in his just acts, the few we know, and see how he commanded the respect even of his enemies. Why? Because he was true to his Lord: he was true to that which he knew to be right. When he had occasion, a few years before his death, to rebuke dishonesty, to call the attention of the people to evils that existed, and admonish them to be true to the gospel of Christ, he speaks such words as these:

> But let him ask in faith, nothing wavering. For he that wavereth is like a wave of the sea driven with the wind and tossed.
> For let not that man think that he shall receive anything of the Lord.
> A double minded man is unstable in all his ways.
> If any man among you seem to be religious, and bridleth not his tongue, but deceiveth his own heart, this man's religion is vain.
> (James 1:6-8, 26.)

Then again:

> Out of the same mouth proceedeth blessing and cursing. My brethren, these things out not so to be.
> Doth a fountain send forth at the same place sweet water and bitter?
> Can the fig tree, my brethren, bear olive berries? either a vine, figs? so can no fountain both yield salt water and fresh.
> Who is a wise man and endued with knowledge among you? let him shew out of a good conversation his works with meekness of wisdom.
> But if ye have bitter envying and strife in your hearts, glory not, and lie not against the truth. (James 3:10-14.)

The man who is true to his manhood will not lie against the truth. We are told that we can crucify the Lord afresh. If that be true, we can *betray* the Lord afresh. There is that within every man which is divine, a divinity within every man's soul. It cannot die. God renews it, inspires it, works to keep it alive. The man who will be true to the divine within is true to his Lord, and is true to his fellowmen. The man who betrays that, the man who is untrue to that which he knows to be right, is wavering, is weakening. God pity him; he may go so far that he will step out of the light, out of that divine presence, and woe be unto him when he does; God help him!

Probably the most audacious experiment in creation was man's endowment with freedom of choice. No other creature on earth has such freedom. Everything else in the universe, animate or inanimate, follows a pattern to which it is bound and from which it cannot escape. Only man is free to control himself or run uncontrolled, to pray or to curse, to become a saint or to be a sinner. As we regard ourselves in this light, the conviction dawns that God in us is aiming at the production of superior beings, creatures of such high order that we may be both worthy and capable of cooperation with God in the unfinished work of creation. "For creation waits with eager longing for the revealing of the sons of God; for creation was subjected to futility" yet "will be set free from its bondage to decay. . . ." (Romans 8:19-21.)[2]

We have declared to the world that we have the gospel of Christ; that we stand against dishonesty and all manner of vice and crime. Shall we take the charge, or shall we waver and be driven by the wind and tossed? Shall we forsake the cause of justice, truth, and honesty, in order to please men, or because we desire to give "eye service" or "lip service" rather than "heart service" because of some political power that is brought to bear upon us? No! We will stand true to ourselves, true to the divine within us, true to that truth which we have received. Let us be true today; let us act. Let us, as James of old, be true to the death. As he stood there on the pinnacle of the temple, and the men, looking upon him then as a just man, said: "Where is the gate of Christ?" he bore his testimony of the Lord Jesus. Even then, historians tell us, they said: "We can't believe him, even though he is

---

[2]Taken from the article, "Freedom's Foundation," by Carlton Williams.

just; . . . ." and they hurled him down and beat him to death. James's death is inspiring; Judas' death is *death*—death in its gloomiest form!

All men who have moved the world have been men who would stand true to their conscience—not only James, not only Paul, Peter, and all those ancient apostles, but all other great men in history. I admire Luther. I cannot help but feel better when I read his words to the assembly at the Diet of Worms—all the Catholic church opposing him, and all the powers of the land staring him in the face, yet he said: "Confute me by proof of Scripture or by sound argument. I cannot recant otherwise. It is not safe for a man to do aught against his conscience. Here stand I; I cannot do otherwise; God assist me."

It was Joseph Smith who, after having a testimony of the Lord Jesus in his bosom, declared to the men who said. "It is from the devil"—ministers who had had influence with him before, whom he respected as at least attempting to teach the word of God—". . . For I had seen a vision; I knew it, and I knew that God knew it. . . ." (Joseph Smith 2:25.) He was true to his testimony to the last. When he was going to his death, he declared to all the world: ". . . I have a conscience void of offense toward God, and towards all men. . . ." (D. &C. 135:4.) Why? Because he had been true to the light that had come to him. He was a man possessing divine manhood, for true manhood is divine.

It is for us to say whether we shall be Judases or the Jameses; whether we shall be true to the divine within us.

God bless us all, that we may, above all, be true to the divine within us; be men, true men; be noble women, true to motherhood, true to wifehood, true to God.

Chapter Forty-Six

Safeguards
Against the
Delinquency of Youth

"I charge thee," wrote Paul to Timothy, "before God, and the Lord Jesus Christ . . . Teach the word; be instant in season, out of season; reprove, rebuke, exhort with all long-suffering." (2 Tim. 4:1-2.)

In the same letter he prophetically declared "that in the last days perilous times shall come. For men shall be lovers of their own selves . . . lovers of pleasures more than lovers of God: Having a form of godliness, but denying the power thereof." (2 Tim. 3:1-2, 4-5.)

It is in the spirit of Paul's charge and prophecy that I approach the subject of safeguards against delinquency of youth. In naming these safeguards, I have nothing new to offer. You have heard them mentioned frequently, but I think, as with the gospel principles, it is fitting that we be active in season and out of season, that we reprove, rebuke, exhort, admonish, with all long-suffering as we contemplate the rising crime wave, and bring home to each of us, if possible, the realization that greater diligence is needed.

Few will question the fact that we are living in perilous times; that many people have lost their moorings and are being ". . . tossed to and fro . . . with every wind of doctrine, by the sleight of men, and cunning craftiness, whereby they lie in wait to deceive." (Eph. 4:14.)

Among the glaring evils of our day are two which seem to be most detrimental, and which must be curbed if we would preserve true Christian ideals. These are: *first,* an *increasing tendency to dishonor the marriage vow*; and, *second,* the *mounting juvenile delinquency.* Careful study discloses a close relationship between these two unwholesome social conditions.

As evidence of the first, we need only to glance at the number of divorces in the country at large. Recent statistics disclose that *one out of every four marriages* is separated by the ever-grinding divorce mill.

But it is the *ever-increasing crime wave* to which I desire to call attention this morning. Children are being corrupted by it; youth are caught in its whirlpool, and are being contaminated overwhelmingly by it.

J. Edgar Hoover, director of the Federal Bureau of Investigation, who is probably our nation's leading authority on crime, made the following alarming report at a dinner held in his honor in Chicago, Illinois on November 24, 1964:

To every man and every nation there comes a time when decisions must be made about grave problems. Further delay in seeking solutions can bring disaster. That time has come for the United States.

The moment has arrived when we must face realistically the startling fact that since 1958 crime in this country *has increased five times faster than our population growth!* Serious crimes— murder, forcible rape, robbery, burglary, aggravated assault, automobile theft—have mounted steadily since the end of World War II. In 1951, these crimes for the first time topped the one-million mark, and *more than two and one-quarter million serious crimes* were reported during 1963.

Even more ominous is the fact that this terrifying spiral in crime has come about through a growing wave of youthful criminality across the nation. Last year for the fifteenth consecutive year, crimes involving our young people increased over the previous year. For all serious crimes committed in the United States in 1963, youthful offenders were responsible for *72 per cent of the total arrests for these crimes! The cost of our crime has now reached the staggering sum of twenty-seven billion dollars a year!*

What a grim and unhappy commentary on the moral climate of this great nation! The moral strength of our nation has decreased alarmingly. We must return to the teachings of God if we are to cure this sickness. These shocking statistics, *together with the public's apparent indifference to them*, are indicative of the false morality we are tolerating today. It is a false code which is based on the worship of things of man's own creation. It is as imperfect and feeble as man himself! However captivating to the senses, this type of moral climate cannot give the support nor the strength which is so vital to our national survival. This breakdown in our moral standards can only render us impotent as a people and as a nation.

In calling attention to these conditions, I would not have you think that our young people generally do not merit our confidence. It is *the few, not the many*, of whom we now speak.

When, a few years ago, a little four-year-old lad wandered into the Bad Lands of North Dakota, the whole countryside was aroused and organized for the rescue. They gave no thought, however, to the hundreds of four-year-olds who were safe in their mothers' keeping. A train wreck or an airplane disaster shocks us to attention, awakens sympathy and a demand for more safeguards, while to the hundreds of trains and airplanes carrying millions to safety, we give scarcely a passing thought.

So while we solicitously call attention to the tragedies in the stream of human life, let us not be unmindful of the much greater group who move steadily and successfully along, avoiding the sandbars and rapids of sinful indulgence and spiritual decay, whose noble lives confirm and increase confidence in the growing generation. As we seek the lost sheep, let us be appreciative of the "ninety and nine" that are safe in the fold.

But no matter how firm our confidence in the majority of the young, *we must not close our eyes to the fact that the number of delinquents and youthful criminals is ominously increasing*. In the interest of the moral atmosphere of our communities, the welfare of the state, the perpetuity of our democratic form of government, we must search for the causes of this upswing in crime, and, if possible, remove them and apply the proper remedies.

One important cause of the increase in child delinquency is a let down in home ideals. A growing desire for economic independence, or a too eager willingness to improve financial circumstances, has influenced too many of our mothers to neglect the greatest of all responsibilities—the rearing of a family. Director Hoover makes the definite statement that

In the background of these youth offenders lies the story of shocking neglect. Boys and girls are being deprived of the care and guidance necessary to the proper foundation of their characters. Their lawlessness had its roots in every instance in broken homes where mothers and fathers, because of their neglect, misunderstanding, or irresponsibility had failed in their primary obligations. More often than not, God was unknown, or, more important, was unwelcome in their homes.

On the other hand, in nearly every instance the youthful offender would have been a strong, upright citizen had he been given a chance. If his pent-up energies and desires had been directed along wholesome channels; if his problems—the problems that made him a problem child—had been solved by patient and attentive parents, he would have proved to be an influence for good in his community.

You may think me extreme, but I am going to say that a married woman who refuses to assume the responsibilities of motherhood, or who, having children, neglects them for pleasure or social prestige, is recreant to the highest calling and privilege of womankind. The father, who because of business or political or social responsibilities, fails to share with his wife the responsibilities of rearing his sons and daughters, is untrue to his marital obligations, is a negative element in what might and should be a joyous home atmosphere, and is a possible contributor to discord and delinquency.

There are three fundamental things to which every child is entitled: (1) *a respected name*, (2) *a sense of security*, (3) *opportunities for development.*

The family gives to the child his name and standing in the community. A child wants his family to be as good as those of his friends. He wants to be able to point with pride to his father, and to feel an inspiration always as he thinks of his mother. It is a mother's duty so to live that her children will associate with her everything that is beautiful, sweet, and pure. In the words of former President of the United States, Herbert Hoover:

> After we have determined every scientific fact, after we have erected every public safeguard, after we have constructed every edifice for education or training or hospitalization or play, yet all these things are but a tithe of the physical, moral, and spiritual gifts which motherhood gives and home confers. None of these things carry that affection, that devotion of soul, which is the great endowment from mothers.

And the father should so live that the child, emulating his example, will be a good citizen, and, in the Church, a true Latter-day Saint.

A child has a right to feel that in his home he has a place of refuge, a place of protection from the dangers and evils of the outside world. Family unity and integrity are necessary to supply this need.

The home is the best place in the world to teach the highest ideal in the social and political life of man; namely, perfect liberty of action so long as you do not trespass upon the rights and privileges of another.

The great need of the American home today is more religion. Parents should make it obvious both by their actions and their conversation that they are seriously interested in the fruits of true religion. Example of parents should emphasize the need of honesty in our dealings with our family, our neighbors, and all with whom we come in contact; of kindness to our employees, of fair play to our employers, or good measure to our customers.

The Lord places the responsibility directly where it belongs, wherein he says that it is the duty of parents to teach their children the principles of the gospel and to walk uprightly before the Lord, and if they do not so teach, the sin be upon the heads of the parents.

Next to the home as a safeguard to delinquency, the Church should be a dominant force. Recently I was pleased to note a recent Gallup Poll published in a late edition of the New York Herald Tribune, which revealed that in 1964 at least *45 per cent of the entire adult population* of the nation attended church in one typical week, and that although the percentage dropped four points since the peak year of 1958, it is still so high that it completely eclipses the *5 per cent and 7 per cent in some of the other leading countries.* It is interesting that although men are reputedly not very religious, 40 per cent of the entire male adult population of the United States attends church each Sunday. Forty-nine per cent of the women attend regularly. This means that 49,500,000 adult men and women attend church services in the United States. But what of the other 55 per cent of men and women who do not attend church, and what of the children who come from the homes of these men and women? Their indifference towards church should tend only to spur us to more earnest and diligent activity.

Where there is an indifference toward Christian churches, we shall have to place next to the home, not the church, but the public school as the most influential factor in lessening delinquency.

I believe with all my heart that the most paramount objective of the public school system from kindergarten to the university should be character-building and the evolving of true, loyal citizens of the republic. The teaching of the three "R's," of the arts and sciences, even the delving into research work, should be but a means to the development of true manhood and noble womanhood.

True education is awakening a love for truth, a just sense of duty, opening the eyes of the soul to the great purpose and end of life. It is not teaching the individual to love the good for personal sake; it is to teach him to love the good for the sake of the good itself; to be virtuous in action because he is so in heart; to love God and serve him supremely, not from fear but from delight in his perfect character.

Upon the teacher rests much of the responsibility of lifting society to this hgh level. Ralph Waldo Emerson, reputedly the wisest American, said, "Character is higher than intellect. A great soul will be fit to live as well as to think."

Another safeguard against delinquency of youth is the moral atmosphere of the leaders of the nation, town, and community. This is determined by the ideals and actions of adults, and particularly of civic officers and those who are entrusted to enforce the law.

If we are sincere in our desire to reduce the delinquency among youth, let us look to ourselves as members of the community and as leaders and officials in civic circles. A nation that has conquered great material difficulties, and harnessed the physical powers, must have some more effective means of combatting the cynicism of its youth—the cynicism born of widely flaunted dishonesty of those in high places, insincerity of leadership, and gaudy pageantry of crime.

Yes, we are living in perilous times, but let us hope that they may be to the present generation as the fiery furnace that consumes the dross but purifies the gold.

A clean man is a national asset. A pure woman is the incarnation of true national glory. A citizen who loves justice and hates evil is better than a battleship. The strength of any community consists of and exists in the men who are pure, clean, upright and straightforward, ready for the right and sensitive to every approach of evil. Let such ideals be the standard of citizenship.

Let us here and now express gratitude for The Church of Jesus Christ of Latter-day Saints, with its priesthood quorums and auxiliary organizations especially organized to combat the evils of crime and juvenile delinquency. It was established by divine revelation of God the Father and his Son Jesus Christ.

Its glorious mission is to proclaim the birth of the restored gospel, to uplift society that people may mingle more amicably one with another; to create in our communities a wholesome environment in which our children may find strength to resist temptation, and encouragement to strive for cultural and spiritual attainment; to make ineffective the influence of designing men who would make profit out of their fellows, who are fallen so low as to be slaves to their appetites and passions—and who would fill their purses through the weaknesses of addicts of gambling, drunkenness, and vicious drugs. The gospel is a rational philosophy that teaches men how to attain happiness in this life, and exaltation in the life to come.

God help us to discharge our responsibilities to our youth by making an environment in our home, in school, in Church, and in our community that will be uplifting, wholesome and faith-inspiring!

Chapter Forty-seven

Harmony
in the
Home

. . . verily I say unto you, . . .
[that] marriage is ordained of
God unto man.
Wherefore, it is lawful that he
should have one wife, and they
twain shall be one flesh, and
all this that the earth might answer
the end of its creation.
(D.&C. 49:15-16.)

THAT passage from the Doctrine and Covenants indicates the message I have in mind to give—some helpful hints for happy homes.

Are we maintaining the high standards required of us in our homes? I feel constrained, therefore, at this opening session to make an appeal for more stability, more harmony and happiness in home life. It has been truly said that the strength of a nation, especially of a republican nation, is in the intelligent, well-ordered homes of the people. In no other group in the world should there be more contented, more happy homes than in The Church of Jesus Christ of Latter-day Saints.

Recently there appeared in a leading magazine the encouraging statement that American homes and family life are steadily strengthening. According to that article, the total population of our country has doubled since 1900. The number of families has tripled. This growth in family life is shown by the rapid increase in home ownership.

Loyalty as Contributing Factor

Recently our attention has been called to conditions that seem to justify our admonishing the membership of the Church to keep their homes exemplary before the world.

To the young people of the Church, particularly, I should like to say first that a happy home begins not at the marriage altar, but during the brilliant, fiery days of youth. The first contributing factor to a happy home is the sublime virtue of loyalty, one of the noblest attributes of the human soul. Loyalty means being faithful and true. It means fidelity to parents, fidelity to duty, fidelity to a cause or principle, fidelity to love. Disloyalty to parents during teen-age is often a source of sorrow and sometimes tragedy in married life.

I have received several letters from young folk in their teens irked because of what they consider interference of parents. Young people in all the Church and all the nation should understand that both the Church and the state hold parents responsible for the conduct and protection of their children. The Church, you will recall, is very explicit in that.

. . . inasmuch as parents have children in Zion, or in any of her stakes which are organized, that teach them not to understand the doctrine of repentance, faith in Christ the Son of the Living God, and of baptism and the gift of the Holy Ghost by the laying on of the hands, when eight years old, the sin be upon the heads of the parents.

For this shall be a law unto the inhabitants of Zion, or in any of her stakes which are organized. (D.&C. 68:25-26.)

That is explicit, and parents, that is your responsibility!

Some of you would be surprised to know that the statute of the state requires explicitly that not only parents, but also any guardian who has charge of a child eighteen or under is held responsible for the protection of that child and for his moral teachings. Any guardian or parent that will do anything to injure the morals of the child is guilty of a misdemeanor and subject to imprisonment of not more, if I remember rightly, than six months, and a fine of not less than three hundred dollars, or both.

So, girls and boys, your parents, not only because of their love, but also by command of the Lord, and by legislative enactment of the state, are compelled to watch over you and guide you. And parents, once again, that is your responsibility. The effect of this guardianship will be shown by this illustration.

A New York City judge not long ago wrote to the New York *Times*, saying that in seventeen years that he had been on the bench not one Chinese-American teen-ager had been brought before him on a juvenile delinquency charge. The judged queried his colleagues, and they agreed that not one of the city's estimated 10,000 Chinese-American teen-agers, to their knowledge, (not one) had ever been hailed into court on a charge of depredation, narcotics, speeding, burglary, vandalism, stickup, purse snatching, or mugging accusations.

A check with San Francisco, where there is a large colony of Chinese-Americans, tells the same story.

P. H. Chang, Chinese Consul-General in New York City, was asked to comment on that. He said,

I have heard this story many times from many judges. I'll tell you why I think this is so. Filial piety is a cardinal virtue my people have brought over from the China that was once free. A Chinese child, no matter where he lives, is brought up to recognize that he cannot shame his parents. Before a Chinese child makes a move, he stops to think what the reaction of his parents will be. Will they be proud or will they be ashamed? Above all other things, the Chinese teen-ager is anxious to please his parents.

Most Chinese-Americans, no matter how wealthy or poor, maintain a strict family style home. Mealtime is a ceremonious affair which must be attended by every member of the family. Schooling, reverence for religion, and decorum plus reverence for the elders, are the prime movers in developing the child from infancy.

And the paper says, "The amazing record of the Chinese-American youngsters shows that it is in the home that the cure for juvenile delinquency will be found, and in no other place.[1]

So, young people, loyalty to parents, if not a direct contributing factor to a happy home, is at least a safeguard against hastily assuming and lightly esteeming the duties and responsibilities of marriage.

Loyalty To Self

Next to loyalty to parents, I should like to urge loyalty to self. Remember, if you would be happy, if you reach the goal of success in the distant future, your first duty is to be loyal to the best that is in you, not to the basest.

There is a saying in the Bible that "every idle word that men shall speak, they shall give account thereof in the day of judgment." (Matt. 12:36.) Psychology assures us that

We are spinning our own fates, good or evil, and never to be undone. Every smallest stroke of virtue or of vice leaves its never so little scar. The drunken Rip Van Winkle, in Jefferson's play, excuses himself for every fresh dereliction by saying, "I won't count this time."

Well, he may not count it, and a kind Heaven may not count it; but it is being counted none the less. Down among his nerve cells and fibres the molecules are counting it, registering and storing it up to be used against him when the next temptation comes. Nothing we ever do is, in strict scientific literalness, wiped out. Of course, this has its good side as well as its bad one. As we become permanent drunkards by so many separate drinks, so we become saints in the moral, and authorities and experts in the practical and scientific spheres, by so many separate acts and hours of work. Let no youth have any anxiety about the upshot of his education, whatever the line of it may be. If he keep faithfully busy each hour of the working day, he may safely leave the final result to itself. He can with perfect certainty count on waking up some fine morning, to find himself one of the competent ones of his generation, in whatever pursuit he may have singled out. Silently, between all the details of

[1]From an editorial in the *Saturday Evening Post* reprinted in the *Reader's Digest,* July 1955.

his business, the *power of judging* in all that class of matter will have built itself up within him as a possession that will never pass away. Young people should know this truth in advance. The ignorance of it has probably engendered more discouragement and faint-heartedness in youth embarking on arduous careers than all other causes put together.[2]

A good ideal for youth to build a happy home is this: Keep true to the best and never let an hour of indulgence scar your life for eternity.

Loyalty To Your Future Companion

Next under that heading of loyalty, I urge *loyalty to your future companion*. When harmony, mutual consideration, and trust pass out of the home, hell enters in. A memory of a simple indulgence in youth sometimes opens hell's door. Girls, choose a husband who has respect for womanhood! Young man, choose a girl who, in her teens, has virtue and strength enough to keep herself true to her future husband! Down the road of indulgence are too many good young girls, seeking vainly for happiness in the by-ways where people grovel but do not aspire. As a result their search for happiness is in vain. They grasp at what seems substance to find only ashes.

If you would have a happy marriage, keep your reputation as well as your character unsullied.

It is a common saying throughout the world that young men may sow their wild oats, but young women should be chaperoned. In general, this is pretty well carried out, but in the Church we have but one single standard, and it is just as important for young men to keep themselves chaste as it is for young women. No matter what the opportunity, no matter what the temptation, let the young man know that to find happiness he must hold sacred his true manhood. Marriage is a failure when manhood is a failure. Let him know that to gain moral strength he must learn to resist temptation, learn to say with Christ, "Get thee hence, Satan: for it is

_____

[2]William James, *Psychology* (Henry Holt, 1892) p. 150.

written, Thou shalt worship the Lord thy God, and him only shalt thou serve." (Matt. 4:10.) Then he is happy; there is peace instead of turbulency in his soul.

Continued Courtship

Next to loyalty as contributive to a happy home, I should like to urge *continued courtship,* and apply this to grown people. Too many couples have come to the altar of marriage looking upon the marriage ceremony as the end of courtship instead of the beginning of an eternal courtship. Let us not forget that during the burdens of home life—and they come—that tender words of appreciation, courteous acts are even more appreciated than during those sweet days and months of courtship. It is after the ceremony and during the trials that daily arise in the home that a word of "thank you," or "pardon me," "if you please," on the part of husband or wife contributes to that love which brought you to the altar. It is well to keep in mind that love can be starved to death as literally as the body that receives no sustenance. Love feeds upon kindness and courtesy. It is significant that the first sentence of what is now known throughout the Christian world as the Psalm of Love, is, "Love suffereth long, and is kind." The wedding ring gives no man the right to be cruel or inconsiderate, and no woman the right to be solvenly, cross, or disagreeable.

Self-Control

The next contributing factor to your happy marriage I would name is *self-control.* Little things happen that annoy you, and you speak quickly, sharply, loudly, and wound the other's heart. I know of no virtue that helps to contribute to the happiness and peace of the home more than that great quality of self-control in speech. Refrain from saying the sharp word that comes to your mind at once if you are wounded or if you see something in the other which offends you. It is said that during courtship we should keep our eyes wide open, but after marriage keep them half-shut.

What I mean may be illustrated by a young woman who said to her husband, "I know that my cooking isn't good; I hate it as much as you do, but do you find me sitting around griping about it?" This griping after marriage is what makes it unpleasant. I recall the words of Will Carleton:

> Boys flying kites haul in their white-winged birds—
> You can't do that when you're flying words. . . .
> Thoughts unexpressed may sometimes fall back dead,
> But God himself can't kill them when they're said.

Children In the Home

Marriage offers an opportunity to share in the love and care of children, and that is the true purpose of marriage. One writer truly says: "Without children, or without believing that children are important, marriage is incomplete and unfulfilled. Children take time, trouble, and more patience than we usually have. They interfere with freedom, good times, and luxury, but children are the real purpose and reason behind marriage. If we do not put the proper value on parenthood, we are not emotionally or socially ready for marriage.

"Marriage is a relationship that cannot survive selfishness, impatience, domineering, inequality, and lack of respect. Marriage is a relationship that thrives on acceptance, equality, sharing, giving, helping, doing one's part, learning together, enjoying humor," and a home is full of humor with children.

The more you keep in company with your wife, the happier you are. Business takes you away from home. She is there alone. Do not let companionship with other women divide your affection, and that applies to woman as well as to man. At one time I thought that it did not; that man was wholly to blame for the unrest, the disagreements and sorrows that are occurring too frequently, but I have had to modify my opinion. Companionship is the means of perpetuating that love which brought about your union.

In conclusion, for the proper solution of the great problems of marriage we may turn with safety to Jesus, our Guide. He declared, as I read in the beginning, that marriage is ordained of God and that only under the most exceptional conditions should it be set aside. In the teachings of the Church of Jesus Christ, the family assumes supreme importance in the development of the individual and of society. "Happy and thrice happy are they who enjoy an uninterrupted union, and whose love, unbroken by any complaints, shall not dissolve until the last day."

It will not dissolve when sealed by the authority of the Holy Priesthood throughout all eternity. The marriage ceremony, when thus sealed, produces happiness and joy unsurpassed by any other experience in the world. "What therefore God hath joined together, let not man put asunder."

> Home's not merely four square walls,
> Though with pictures hung and gilded;
> Home is where affection calls,
> Filled with shrines the heart has builded!
>
> Home's not merely roof and room—
> It needs something to endear it;
> Home is where the heart can bloom,
> Where there's some kind [heart] to cheer it!
>
> What is home with none to meet,
> None to welcome, none to greet us?
> Home is sweet—and only sweet—
> Where there's one we love to meet us.
>   Charles Swain

To the Church, not only to young people, but also to married people, I plead for more contented homes brought about through love, faithfulness, loyalty, self-control, and obedience to the principles of marriage as set for us by revelation to the members of the restored Church of Jesus Christ.

Chapter Forty-eight

Man's
Greatest
Trust

THE GOSPEL OF PEACE should find its most fruitful effects in the homes of Church members. Flowers in our gardens require good soil and favorable climate. So children, to be healthy and happy, should have a favorable mental and emotional atmosphere in the home.

It is inconsistent for us to proclaim peace if we have not peace in our own lives and homes.

The greatest trust that can come to a man and woman is to have placed in their keeping the life of a little child. If a man who is entrusted with other people's funds defaults, whether he be a bank, municipal, or state official, he usually is apprehended and sent to prison. If a person entrusted with a government secret discloses that secret and betrays his country, he is called a traitor. What must the Lord think, then, of parents who, through their own negligence or willful desire to indulge their selfishness, fail properly to rear their children, and thereby prove untrue to the greatest trust that has been given to human beings? In reply the Lord has said: ". . . the sin be upon the heads of the parents." (D.&C. 68:25.)

The happiest homes in the world should be found among members of the Church. I am sufficiently old-fashioned to think that the home is still the foundation of the state, especially of a republic. Do not forget it! And the state has no right to take children and attempt to train them and substitute for mother's protection and prayerful guidance. Statistics on broken homes, with resultant divorces, should alert all citizens, and particularly members of the Church to greater activity in preserving harmony in home circles. Let us begin at once as parents to maintain the kind of influence or home atmosphere that will contribute to the normal, moral development of the children and eliminate from the home those elements which cause discord and strife.

Quareling Contributes To Delinquency

Fathers and mothers sometimes by unwise conduct unwittingly influence their children toward delinquency. Among these unwise acts, I mention first, disagreeing or quarreling on the part of parents in the presence of children. Sometimes such quarrels arise out of an attempt to correct or to discipline a child. One parent criticizes, the other objects; and the good influence of the home, so far as the child is concerned, is nullified. A child of such parents can never say truthfully in afterlife what John Ruskin writes of his memory of home:

I never heard my father's or mother's voice once raised in any question with each other; nor saw an angry or even slightly hurt or offended glance in the eyes of either. . . . I never saw a moment's trouble or disorder in any household matter.

Courtesy Begets Courtesy

Courtesy is a wonderful virtue, and it should be shown in the home. A husband may greatly contribute to peace and harmony in the home by showing a high sense of regard and courtesy to his wife. Courtesy is saying, "thank you," "if you please," "pardon me." Many people have forgotten those terms in the home. Children hearing them will themselves become courteous to Mother and to Father, and to each other. The home is the place to teach the virtues of society. Husbands should remember the covenants they have made with their wives. They should not permit their affections to be led away from the mother of their children. Mothers should not forget that they owe something to their children and to their husbands. They should keep themselves neat and attractive. They, too, can refrain from finding fault and can contribute to the happiness and contentment of the home, the sweetest place on earth. Home is about as near heaven as you will ever get here on earth.

There is no use terminating marriage just because of a few misunderstandings. Guard against misunderstandings by curbing your tongue. Those who hold the priesthood should control their tongues as well as their actions. Do not say the thing that comes to your mind when things go wrong and by a quick-tempered remark wound her who has given her life to you. Control your temper! Yes, you may see weaknesses; women see them in their husbands, too. Women control their tongues, I think, more frequently than the men. Let us reverence womanhood.

Vulgarity and Profanity Are Weakening

Another unwise condition stems from those parents who pollute the home atmosphere with vulgarity and profanity. I use the term "vulgarity" in the sense used by David Starr Jordan, who wrote:

> To be vulgar is to do that which is not the best of its kind to do. It is to do poor things in poor ways, and to be satisfied with that. Vulgarity weakens the mind, and thus brings all other weakness in its train. It is vulgar to like poor music . . . to find amusement in trashy novels, to enjoy vulgar theatres, to find pleasure in cheap jokes, to tolerate courseness and looseness in any of its myriad forms.

Parents are particularly untrue to their trust who will use profane words in the home. Profanity is a national vice. Parents pollute their home when they use it. The people of our nation would stand on a higher moral plane if they would cease to profane, which George Washington said, ". . . is a vice so mean and low, without any temptation, that every person of sense and character detests and despises it."

Vulgarity and profanity among the young are often, though not always, the result of the presence of those evils in the home.

To quarreling of parents before children, to lack of courtesy in the home, to vulgarity, and to the condemnatory use of profanity, there may be added a fourth contributing factor to parental delinquency, and that is the nonconformity in the homes to Church standards.

Remember, fellow parents, that children are quick to detect insincerity; and they resent in their feelings false pretension. Parents, of all people on earth, should be honest with their children. Keep your promises to them and speak the truth always. Children are more influenced by *sermons you act* than by *sermons you preach*. It is the consistent parent who gains the trust of his child. When children feel that you reciprocate their trust, they will not violate your confidence nor bring dishonor to your name.

Parents Must Live Truth

The parent must live truth, or the child will not live it. The child will startle you with his quickness in puncturing the bubble of your pretended knowledge, in instinctively piercing the heart of sophistry without being conscious of process, in relentlessly enumerating your unfulfilled promises, in detecting with the justice of a court of equity a technicality of speech that is virtually a lie. He will justify his own lapses from truth by appeal to some white lie told to a visitor in the home, unknown to be overheard by little ones whose mental powers we ever underestimate in theory, though we may overpraise in words.

If truth be the rock-foundation of the child's character, as a fact, not as a theory, the future of that child is as fully assured as it is possible for human prevision to guarantee.

There are parents who fail to teach obedience to their children. If the home does not develop obedience, society

---

[1]William George Jordan, *The Power of Truth.*

will demand it and get it. It is, therefore, better for the home with its kindness, sympathy, and understanding to train the child to obey, rather than callously to leave him to the brutal and unsympathetic discipline that society will impose if the home has not already fulfilled this obligation.

The best time for a child to learn obedience is between the ages of two and four. It is then that the child should learn that there are limits to his actions, that there are certain bounds beyond which he cannot pass with impunity. This conformity to home conditions can be easily obtained with kindness, but with firmness. "Train up a child in the way he should go: and when he is old, he will not depart from it." (Prov. 22:6.) In this old adage, the word "train" has great significance. There are parents who say: "We shall let our children grow to manhood and womanhood, and then choose for themselves." In taking this attitude parents fail in discharging parental responsibility. Parents and teachers are God's fellow workers. The Father of all mankind expects parents, as his representatives, to assist him in shaping and guiding human lives and immortal souls. That is the greatest assignment which the Lord can bestow upon man.

The Most Effective Way To Teach Religion

The most effective way to teach religion in the home is not by preaching, but by living. If you would teach faith in God, show faith in him yourself; if you would teach prayer, pray yourself. Would you have them temperate? Then you yourself refrain from intemperance. If you would have your child live a life of virtue, of self-control, of good report, then set him a worthy example in all these things. A child brought up under such home environment will be fortified for the doubts, questions, and yearnings that will stir his soul when the real period of religious awakening comes at 12 or 14 years years of age. It is then that he needs positive teaching regarding God and truth and his relations with others. Activity in the Church is a good safeguard during youth. Continual absence from Church makes continual absence easy. Other interests in life make the growing youth indifferent to religion. Success makes him think that religion is not essential to his happiness. "It is a law of life that *use* gives strength; a capacity *unused* weakens and dies. It is as true of religious instincts as of any other. One need not be a sinner to lose God; he need only forget him."

Responsibility of Parents

With respect to the responsibility of parents teaching religion to their children, the Lord is very explicit:

And again, inasmuch as parents have children in Zion, or in any of her stakes which are organized, that teach them not to understand the doctrine of repentance, faith in Christ the Son of the living God, and of baptism and the gift of the Holy Ghost by the laying on of hands, when eight years old, the sin be upon the heads of the parents.

For this shall be a law unto the inhabitants of Zion, or in any of her stakes which are organized.

And their children shall be baptized for the remission of their sins when eight years old, and receive the laying on of the hands.

And they shall also teach their children to pray and to walk uprightly before the Lord. (D.&C. 68:25-28.)

Let us strive to have fewer broken homes, and in our homes to have harmony and peace. From such homes will go men and women motivated with a desire to build, not to destroy.

Chapter Forty-nine

The Home
and
the Church

Оυτ οf the homes of America
go the future citizens of America, and what those American
homes are will largely determine what our citizenry will be
in the future. Indeed, Victor Hugo said: "The future of any
country may be largely determined by the attitude of its
young men between the ages of 18 and 21." Well, before
those boys reach that age, their characters are pretty well
established. One of our leading statesmen, Herbert Hoover,
writing on this very subject a number of years ago, said:

After we have determined every scientific fact, after we have
erected every public safeguard, after we have constructed every
edifice for education or training or hospitalization, or play, yet all
these things are but a tithe of the physical, moral, and spiritual gifts
which motherhood gives and home confers.

None of these things carry that affection, that devotion
of soul, which is the great endowment from mothers.

No man nor child is happy in doing wrong. Nature
herself teaches us that our actions are bound within certain
limits. Growth and happiness are found within certain restricted areas, beyond which lie painful inhibitions. There
is pleasure and health in eating, but pain and sickness in
gormandizing; there is pleasure in moderate exercise, pain
in excessive exertion.

298

The home is the best place in the world to teach the child his responsibilities, to give him happiness in self-control and respect for the rights of others. Unhappiness in the child's life, as in the adult's life, springs largely from nonconformity to natural and social laws. The home is the best place in which to develop obedience, which nature and society will later demand. Some mothers foolishly overlook that and let children do as they please. That is all right within certain limits.

Let the child do certain things just as he pleases, so long as he does not interfere with the rights of a little brother or sister; and then the parent has the right to curtail him. A person's individuality is best safeguarded and developed through conformity with social conventions. If he has learned the rules of the game, he may hope to modify them; and until he has learned them, his attempts at modification will be amateurish. If these rules are never learned, then personal individuality is cramped and happiness constricted.

It is my opinion—and my opinion is confirmed by experience—that the best time for a child to learn these rules of conformity is between the ages of three and four. If a mother does not get control of her child during these ages, she will find great difficulty in getting control later. I do not mean getting control by cruelty, nor by foolish threats, but merely by letting the child know that he is part of a community in the home; and that the other children have their rights and each child must respect those rights. There is the beginning of democracy, and it is in the home.

Home Contributes To Happiness

It is easy to understand, then, how the home contributes to the happiness of the child. First, by teaching obedience; second, by teaching him to be considerate of the rights of others; third, by being a place where confidence and consolations are exchanged; and, fourth, by being a place which serves as a haven of seclusion and rest from the worries and perplexities of life. Such a home is possible. There are thousands of such homes in the Church. From those homes go the future citizens of America. Upon every Latter-day Saint rests the responsibility of developing just such a home.

It is the duty of the Church to teach religion. The home should also do it; but the Bible has been taken not only out of the schools, largely it has been taken out of our homes as well. There is quite a laxity in teaching religion in the homes. Family prayers are being neglected.

Parents, if you do not do anything else, kneel down in the morning with your children. I know your mornings are usually busy, getting the children off to school and Father off to work; but have some time when you can kneel and invite God into your home. Prayer is a potent force. You will hear some men reason that prayer is only what you think. Well, if it were just what you think, even that would benefit you. Prayer is a potent force, and into the homes of America we need to invite God, for this is a Christian nation.

Patrick Henry was right when he said, "I have now disposed of all my property to my family. There is one thing more I wish I could give them, and that is the Christian religion. If they had that, and I had not given them one shilling they would have been rich; and if they had not that, and I had given them all the world, they would be poor."

Sunday Schools Foster Religion

The function of the Sunday School is to foster religion— to give religious education. To inculcate moral and religious ideals in the lives of children was the dominant motive in the mind of Robert Raikes of Gloucester, England, when he first established the Sunday School, and also in the mind of Richard Ballantyne when he organized that school in the little log house on First West and Third South in Salt Lake City.

Today we have thousands of officers and teachers—every one of whom gives his or her services gratuitously—devoting 52 Sundays every year, and hours of study during each week for the betterment of children and youth: training them to have virtue; habituating them to industry, activity, and spirituality; making them consider every vice as shameful and unmanly; firing them with ambition to be useful; making them disdain to be destitute of any useful knowledge; and leading them into the joy of the Christ-life into the friendship of God and the guidance of his Holy Spirit.

There is not a home in the Church, not an individual, that may not and should not come within the radiance of one or more of these teachers. The influence of each Sunday School upon the boys and girls, and upon the community, depends first upon the character, preparation, and devotion of the officers and teachers. No teacher who smokes a cigarette can conscientiously and effectively teach children to refrain from the use of tobacco. A teacher has no rght to set an unworthy example to those children who trust him. "What you are," says Emerson, "thunders so loud in my ears, I cannot hear what you say."

Choose Spiritual Life

In both the home and in the Church, with all its auxiliaries and priesthood quorums, there is but one ideal, and that is to inculcate high ideals. The mission of the whole Church is to lift our young people, and the older ones, above the animal plane into the realm of spirituality. I think that is the whole mission of life. The Savior has given us the example. He rose above all things physical and temporal and lived in the spirit, and it is our duty to approach that ideal.

Let us choose the spiritual life. Let us conquer the animal in us. The Christ-life beckons. Christ is our Lord, our Savior, our Guide, our Light. He has restored his Church with all its opportunities for spiritual development. Let us be more determined to make beautiful homes, to be kinder husbands, more thoughtful wives, more exemplary parents to our children; determined that in our homes we are going to have just a little taste of heaven here on this earth. And may there come into our homes the true spirit of Christ, our Redeemer, whose reality, whose inspiring guidance I know to be real!

Chapter Fifty

Two Paramount
Obligations of
Members of the Church

THERE ARE two great functions of the Church: *first,* the putting in order of our homes, and keeping them in order; and, *second,* the proclaiming of the divinity of the mission of our Lord and Savior, Jesus Christ.

"For what is a man profited," said the Savior, "if he shall gain the whole world, and lose his own soul? or what shall a man give in exchange for his soul?" (Matt. 16:26.)

The first recorded question of the Savior after his baptism in the river Jordan was, "What seekest thou?" In the text I have just quoted, he again refers to the dominant incentive prompting man's actions in daily life. If a man seeks wealth, worldly honors, pleasures, and all that riches and honor can bestow, but neglects and leaves undeveloped the eternal riches of his soul, what is he profited?

Seeking First the Kingdom

Thus does the Lord emphasize in a simple though majestic comparison the relative value of material and spiritual possessions.

On another occasion, in the Sermon on the Mount, he admonished his hearers to seek ". . . first the kingdom of God, and his righteousness; and all these things shall be added unto you." (Matt. 6:33.) Seeking to establish the kingdom of God and to foster his righteousness should be the paramount purpose of life. I think none will deny that.

Leading statesmen, clear-thinking educators, in public addresses and in magazine articles, frequently refer to what they declare is an apparent spiritual poverty of the present age; and they cite the need for higher moral and ethical standards.

Religion In Education

Professor William J. Russell, instructor in the Memorial High School at Pelham, New York, says:

Courses required of all students in our public schools should include all the important areas of study that directly or indirectly provide the student with opportunities for spiritual growth and religious inspiration.

From such study, it is reasonable to expect that our students will better understand how vital has been the role of religion at critical moments in history, how important spiritual insights and religious faith can be in the lives of men and women, how closely related are true human greatness and such qualities as honesty, integrity, humility, generosity, compassion. We may expect in our students more idealism and less cynicism, more wholesome courage and faith in the future and less pessimism and foreboding and fear.

We may hope for increased tolerance of . . . religious differences, increased respect for those of opposite political views or of lower social and economic levels, increased awareness of the basic and inviolable dignity of the individual man or woman. We may contribute to the development of a more sensitive social conscience, a greater sense of responsibility for the less fortunate in our society. We may even, perhaps, without knowing it, bring a boy or girl closer to God.[1]

I cite that because of the opportunities which may be utilized in our public schools. Many men of clear vision and sound judgment call for a rededication of schools and homes to moral and spiritual values.

---

[1]Professor William J. Russell in the March, 1953, issue of *Think,* p. 5.

Our Greatest Obligation

Our most precious possession is the youth of the land, and to instruct them to walk uprightly and to become worthy citizens in the kingdom of God is our greatest obligation.

Religious freedom and the separation of the church and state are clearly set forth in the first amendment to the Constitution of the United States, and no governmental agency can have any supervision, control, nor jurisdiction over religion. Though our public schools may emphasize moral, ethical, and spiritual values as essential elements in the public school program, they cannot favor any particular religion or religious system. The teaching of religion is, therefore, definitely a responsibility of the home and the Church.

In discharging this responsibility, members of the Church should ever keep in mind two paramount obligations: (1) to put and to keep their homes in order; and (2) to proclaim the divinity of Jesus Christ and the essentiality of his teachings to the salvation of the human family.

Rebuild and Purify the Home

If, upon examination, one finds that termites are undermining the foundation of his house, he should lose no time in having experts make a thorough examination and exterminate the destructive insects. He should have the weakened materials removed and the foundation strengthened and, if necessary, rebuilt.

Well, more important than the building of our house is the rebuilding and purifying of our home.

"Our home joys," says Johann Pestalozzi, Swiss educator and reformer, "are the most delightful earth affords, and the joy of parents in their children is the most holy joy of humanity. It makes their hearts pure and good; it lifts them up to their Father in heaven."

Foster High Ideals, Avoid Slander

You know and I know that such joys are within the

305

reach of most men and women if high ideals of marriage and home be properly fostered and cherished.

But there are destructive termites in homes, as well as in houses; and some of these are backbiting, evil-speaking, faultfinding on the part either of parents or of children. Slander is poison to the soul. "Slanderers are like flies, that pass all over a man's good parts to light only on his sores." In the ideal home, there is no slanderous gossip about school teachers, about public officials or Church officials. I am more grateful now, as the years have come and gone, to my father, who with hands lifted, emphatically said, "Now, no faultfinding about your teacher or anybody else."

Deterrents To Happiness

Quarreling and profaning also are evils that lower the standards of the ideal home. I cannot imagine a father or mother profaning in the presence of children or ever letting profane words pass their lips.

Another deterrent to happiness in the home is the refusal to bear the full responsibility of motherhood and fatherhood. Members of the Church who are healthy and normal should not be guilty of restricting the number of children in the home, especially when such action is prompted by a desire for a good time, or for personal gain, or to keep up with the neighbors, or by a false impression that one or two children in a family can be better educated. These are excuses which members of the Church should not harbor, for they are unjustified.

The question of size of families, I know, brings up many problems—the question of woman's career, the false cry of "quality, not quantity," which one writer rightly says should read "extinction, not preservation," or the matter-of-fact question of daily living and getting on in the world.

The True Purpose of Marriage

With the high ideal of marriage as revealed to the Prophet Joseph Smith, members of the Church should have

306

but one goal; and that is to keep in mind the fact that marriage, the foundation of society, is "ordained of God" for the building of permanent homes in which children may be properly reared and taught the principles of the gospel.

The following, I am sure, will strike a responsive chord in the hearts of the majority of parents in the Church:

> Every period of human life is wonderful; the irresponsible age of childhood, the thrilling years of adolescence and courtship, the productive, fighting, burden-bearing era of parenthood; but the most wonderful time of life comes when the father and mother become chums of their grown-up, successful sons and daughters, and can begin to enjoy their children's children. Youth is confined with restrictions, limitations, schedules, and dominations; adolescence is full of mysteries, longings, and defeats; early fatherhood is absorbed in struggles and in the solution of problems; extreme old age is shadowed by eternal mysteries; but middle age and normal old age, if life has been rightly and fully lived, are filled with the thrills, not merely of success, but of companionship with children and grandchildren. . . . Each age has satisfactions which can be known only by experience. . . . When a young man and woman of the right biological type marry in the early twenties and are prepared to earn a living and support and rear a family, they have started in the normal cycle of life. They are likely to give society fewer problems of crime, immorality, divorce, or poverty than are their unmarried companions. They will have children and rear them while they are strong, enjoy them when they are grown-up and successful, depend upon them in weakness, and profit by the finest type of old-age insurance ever invented by man or God, an insurance which pays its annuities in material goods when necessary, but which mainly pays in the rich joys of love and fellowship. . . . The crowning joys of human experience will come in middle age and onward, through the companionship, love, and honor of children and grandchildren.
>
> R. J. Sprague

All members of the Church should set their homes in order so that they may enjoy the true happiness of harmonious family life.

Proclaim the Mission of Christ

As already stated, the second paramount obligation is to

proclaim the divine mission of Jesus Christ. Nineteen hundred years ago, a valiant defender of that cause said:

This is the stone which was set at nought of you builders, which is become the head of the corner.

Neither is there salvation in any other: for there is none other name under heaven given among men, whereby we must be saved.
(Acts 4:11, 12.)

The man who thus declared Jesus to be the one and only safe leader and guide in the world was an ordinary fisherman who lived nearly two thousand years ago. He was thoroughly a man of action, though somewhat impetuous. He was fairly prosperous, possessed qualities of leadership; and, above all, he was honest.

Circumstances drew Peter into close relationship with Jesus of Nazareth. For nearly three years this hardheaded fisherman accompanied Jesus almost constantly. He became intimately acquainted with the Master. Jesus' philosophy of life became Peter's philosophy. Not suddenly, but gradually, through careful, critical observation and inward experience, Peter arrived at a firm and sublime conviction, expressed clearly and unhesitatingly when he declared before his accusers, the leaders of the Jewish Sanhedrin, ". . . there is none other name under heaven given among men, whereby we must be saved."

The Church stands with Peter, with Paul, with James, and with all other apostles who accepted the resurrection not only as being literally true, but as being also the consummation of Christ's divine mission upon the earth. To the unimpeachable evidence of the ancient apostles to the resurrection of our Lord, we add the sublime declaration of the Prophet Joseph Smith: "And now, after the many testimonies which have been given of him, this is the testimony, last of all, which we give of him: That he lives!" (D.&C. 76:22.)

Greater Resolution

The responsibility of preaching the Gospel rests upon us.

Let me urge more diligence in living the principles of the gospel. We may preach, we may write and publish books; but the most effective way of preaching the gospel to the peoples of the world is by example.

Let us have greater resolution to defend one another in righteous living, to defend the Church, not to speak against our neighbors, nor against authorities of the Church, local, stake, or general. Let us avoid evil-speaking. Let us avoid slander and gossip. These are poisons to the soul to those who indulge. Evil-speaking injures the reviler more than the reviled.

May peace be in our hearts, and peace and harmony be in our homes. Happy homes give to their inmates a taste of heaven on earth. Acceptance of the divinity of Christ's mission and compliance with the principles of his gospel give assurance of immortality and eternal life.

Chapter Fifty-one

The
Power of
Choice

I am reminded of the passage from the Doctrine and Covenants, "Retire to thy bed early . . . arise early." Sometimes as boys Thomas E. and I did not retire early. The next morning father would stand at the door upstairs and say, "Come boys, it's time to get up," and we would turn over, hoping for a few more winks; but he would stand there, and say, "Come boys, those who dance must pay the fiddler." Oh, those happy days of youth!

But there came with these thoughts appreciation of parenthood. It is a wonderful thing to have an inheritance, though it carries great responsibility, and I share with you appreciation for my birthright. You have yours, and it is your responsibility to bring honor to that heritage. Every young man and every young woman carries this responsibility. You have it this morning.

Every boy and girl in the past has had it; each age carries with it the responsibility to choose the right—to choose the truth. I do not know of any other church in the world in which that appreciation could be so manifestly expressed, and in which the responsibility of discharging that inheritance is greater than in The Church of Jesus Christ of Latter-day Saints. Each member has the responsibility of making a choice. That choice will affect his future and the future of others, and will reflect credit or discredit upon those to whom each is responsible.

In Days of Paul

They had that responsibility in the days of Paul when he sent his first letter back to the little branch of Thessalonica. He had been driven away from there; the Jews did not like his teaching, and he had gone to the Gentiles. He had left the little branch of Phillipi in Europe. Thessalonica was not many miles away in our measurement today, and they were rather distracted. He sent Timotheus (Timothy) back with a letter, in an effort to encourage them and to find out just how true they were to the ideals of the Church.

Among other things he said in that Epistle, "Prove all things; hold fast that which is good." (1 Thess. 5:21.) One thing to which they were admonished to hold fast was the reality of Christ's death and resurrection, particularly his resurrection. Some of them were thinking that Christ's second coming was near, but Paul told them that nobody knows the hour or day when it will come. However, the *reality of Christ and his literal resurrection was one of the truths mentioned in that first epistle.*

Mission Emphasized

Christ's resurrection being real, you have the greatest truth in all the world, and you have the responsibility of upholding it because today there are those who declare this declaration to be false. They reject the spiritual influence of Christ. They reject his mission, his message, his reality now as our Savior.

You will come in contact with those opposing influences. Marx for example declared that there is no God; that Jesus is not a reality. Well, if you know anything about Marx's life, you do not want to follow him. Anybody who can even glimpse the suffering of his sweet wife as his children starved to death cannot have much respect for the philosophy of Marx. Engel supported him when he could. Lenin who

311

followed him declared the same falsehood; so did Stalin and Khrushchev. Such falsehoods are extant and sincere students and other members of the Church should be able to refute them.

I was impressed recently with a statement in *Dr. Zhivago*, the novel that took the Nobel prize as you know, although its author Boris Pasternack had to reject it. Referring to history he said,

> No single man makes history. History cannot be seen, just as one cannot see grass growing. Wars and revolutions, kings and Robespierres are history's organic agents, its yeast. But revolutions are made by fanatical men of action with one-track minds, geniuses in their ability to confine themselves to a limited field. They overturn the old order in a few hours or days. The whole upheaval takes a few weeks, or at most years, but the fanatical spirit that inspires the upheaval is worshipped for decades thereafter for centuries.

Communism Is Wrong

Now we know that communism is wrong; it has been tried before and failed. Some of us have hoped that it would break of itself as error always does, but over 40 years have passed and it still exists. Its atheistic spirit however is abroad, and the feeling that life is just an animal existence after all, and young people are going to be influenced by it. You have to make a choice. Either Christ is a realty, and communism is wrong; or Christ is a theory and communism is right. Well, we know that communism is wrong, absolutely. If we do not know it we can find it out, for every person, every child of God, may know for himself or herself that it is wrong, and that Jesus Christ is the Son of the living God; that he is directing today his gospel, the means of happiness and salvation to the human family. *I say every person may know it, but he must find out for himself. The trouble is that every person is not brave enough or strong enough to live the life that will bring that testimony.*

> If any man will do his will, he shall know of the doctrine, whether it be of God, or whether I speak of myself. (John 7:17.)

Every day each one has the power of choice to make. Every day each one makes his decision.

Each one may know for himself the reality of the existence of God, the reality of his Beloved Son's life, death, and service for humanity, no matter what these fanatical leader may tell us, and they are working even in our own midst.

Proof Of Truth

A philosopher was once asked to tell how a reported fact may be proved to be true. The person who asked for the information wanted to apply those points to prove the reality of Christ. And whoever this man was gave five marks which will prove the truth of any alleged fact. Let us consider those five marks.

First, he said that the event or incident should be of such a nature as would appeal to the physical senses. If I remember rightly he said that it should be a *sensible fact*. By that, he means it must be something which might be discerned by the eye, the ear, the nose, taste, or touch. *Second*, there should be witnesses to the claim of the alleged fact. *Third*, the witnesses should be reputable (that is, they must be honorable, trustworthy witnesses, men and women whose testimonies can be relied upon.) *Fourth*, there should be monuments or memorials to that alleged fact, and *fifth*, those monuments or memorials should date back to or near the event itself.

It is because of reputable witnesses and memorials that many have accepted the reality of Jesus of Nazareth. Men saw him, talked to him, and what he did appealed to their physical senses. Peter, James and John and other apostles had personal contact with him and so testified. Luke probably did not, but these other men did and they testified of his existence and of his teachings. Luke believed their testimonies. Mark, when but a teen-age boy, undoubtedly saw the Savior and later devoted his life to preaching the gospel.

313

I think he was the man who entered the Garden of Gethsemane with but a sheet around him. I shall not take time to tell you why I think so. But we do know that his mother was in the church and that they held meetings in her house, according to Luke.

First—The Event Should Appeal to the Physical Senses

Let us apply that test to the Book of Mormon: *First,* the plates were a physical substance. They could be seen and handled; they appealed to the physical senses. The claim that they existed, that they were found in a certain place and delivered to Joseph Smith, could all be verified by sight or feeling, two physical senses at least.

There Should Be Witnesses

Second, there were witnesses to that fact. Those witnesses lifted and felt the tangible plates. This is what they said,

Be it known unto all nations, kindreds, tongues, and people, unto whom this work shall come: That we, through the grace of God the Father, and our Lord Jesus Christ, have seen the plates which contain this record (keep analyzing that. Why would they tell a thing like that if it were not true?) which is a record of the people of Nephi, and also of the Lamanites, their brethren, and also of the people of Jared, who came from the tower of which hath been spoken. And we also know that they have been translated by the gift and power of God, for his voice hath declared it unto us; wherefore we know of a surety that the work is true. And we also testify that we have seen the engravings which are upon the plates; (the details) and they have been shown unto us by the power of God, and not of man. And we declare with words of soberness, that an angel of God came down from heaven, and he brought and laid before our eyes, that we beheld and saw the plates, and the engravings thereon; and we know that it is by the grace of God the Father, and our Lord Jesus Christ, that we beheld and bear record that these things are true. And it is marvelous in our eyes. * * *

Oliver Cowdery
David Whitmer
Martin Harris[1]

---

[1]Testimony of The Three Witnesses, *Book of Mormon.*

Third—The Reliability of Witnesses

Now the third mark is the reliability of those witnesses. Perhaps they were deceived; maybe they were deceivers. Did they tell the truth, or was their some collusion or deception? Let us just for a moment consider briefly the character of each of these men. Oliver Cowdery was one, a young schoolteacher. He signed his name to his testimony under oath, for God commanded him to do it. That is more sacred than putting your hand on your Bible and swearing to tell the truth.

In the course of events Oliver Cowdery did not sustain the Prophet in certain Church procedures and fell out of harmony with his leader and was excommunicated from the Church. Had there been collusion in his testimony then would have been the time to confess and proclaim it and by so doing expose any chicanery or fraud. This he did not do.

Following his Church excommunication, Oliver Cowdery practiced law. During the 10 years he was away from the Church he maintained that his testimony was true. For example, on one occasion an opposing lawyer in court accused him of having signed his name to a document stating that an angel appeared to him and showed him the plates from which the Book of Mormon was translated. Oliver Cowdery replied, "May it please your honor and gentlemen of the jury, this I say: I saw the angel and heard his voice— How can I deny it? It happened in the daytime when the sun was shining bright in the firmament; not in the night when I was asleep. That glorious messenger from heaven, dressed in white, standing above the ground, in a glory I have never seen anything to compare with—the sun insignificant in comparison—and this personage told us that if we denied that testimony there is no forgiveness in this life nor in the world to come. Now how can I deny it—I dare not; I will not!"

He came back into the Church later, and said, "I don't

ask for any position; I was wrong," and he was baptized and re-entered the Church.

David Whitmer was excommunicated because he was out of harmony. Did he ever deny his testimony? There is one encyclopedia which falsely states that he did. You students will probably pick that up and read it. As ample evidence that he maintained the truth to the last, I am going to give you the evidence of one whom I knew personally, Elder James H. Moyle, who is the father of the late President Henry D. Moyle. Several months before Elder James H. Moyle's death, Sister McKay and I were guests at a party given by Henry D. Moyle whose father, during the evening, addressed the company and gave us directly his experience with David Whitmer. The following in substance is the testimony we heard:

From my boyhood I had read the Book of Mormon, and during my study of the same, found it nothing but that which is virtuous, pure and ennobling . . . a great and wonderful history of a pre-historic people who lived on this continent in former ages. I was always interested in utilizing such opportunities as were given me to demonstrate its divinity, to know whether or not I might be deceived, and whether my parents, grandparents, and friends were likewise deceived. Therefore, on my way home from school in 1885, I took advantage of the opportunity to visit David Whitmer, another of the Three Witnesses, then an old grayhaired man, bowed in years and expecting almost any time the summons to call him thence to his eternal reward.

As I left the train in the little village of Richmond, Missouri, I inquired of those whom I met: "What kind of man is David Whitmer?" From all I received the same response, that he was a good citizen, an honest man, and that he was highly respected in the community. I went to his humble home, for it was a humble home, and I told him of my origin, my belief, and as a young man starting out in life I wanted to know from him, older than my grandfather, what he knew about the Book of Mormon, and what about the testimony he had published to the world concerning it.

He told me in all solemnity of his advanced years, that the

testimony he had given to the world, and which was published in the Book of Mormon was true, and that he had never deviated or departed in any particular from that testimony, and that nothing in the world could separate him from that sacred message that was delivered to him.

I still wondered if it was not possible that he could have been deceived. I wondered if there were not something in the psychological operation which some offer as the cause of these miracluous declarations and by which he could have been deceived—although there were three witnesses present besides the Prophet Joseph Smith who saw and heard the same mighty and solemn truths; so I induced him to relate to me, under such cross-examination as I was able to interpose, every detail of what took place.

He described minutely the spot in the woods, the large log that separated him from the angel, and that he saw the plates from which the Book of Mormon was translated, and that he handled them, and that he did hear the voice of God declare that the plates were correctly translated. I asked him if there was any possibility for him to have been deceived, and that it was all a mistake, but he said: "No." I asked him, then, why he had left the Church. He said he had not, that the Church left him. (Now that is a condition.)

He said that his faith in the fundamental principles of the gospel, which had been revealed prior to the year 1835, had never been changed; and that he was still devoted to them, and believed in them just as much as he ever did, and was trying to live those principles and exemplify them in his life. He said he knew Joseph Smith was a prophet of God, and that through him had been restored the gospel of Jesus Christ in these latter-days. To me this was a wonderful testimony.[2]

I had a personal friend, Charles C. Richards, who was on the Sunday School Board in Weber Stake who graduated from law school, and who personally called with his father, Franklin D. Richards, upon David Whitmer just as Brother Moyle had. I shall read just a part of this account:

When father explained to him the object of our visit he received us very cordially. He was, apparently, sound and well preserved physically, and in excellent spirits. He was alert mentally, and possessed a wonderful recollection of the sacred events in regard to

---

[2]Elder James H. Moyle, March 22, 1908.

which we were interviewing him. Mr. Whitmer was then eighty years of age, my father was sixteen years younger, and I was a youngster of twenty-five. My father did most of the visiting with Mr. Whitmer, while I sat quietly listening to them discuss the important events that transpired at Nauvoo; and, when I thought it would be permissible for him to do so, I said that we would appreciate being told, if Mr. Whitmer felt like telling us, some of the incidents connected with the vision he had at the time the plates were shown to him and to the other witnesses. Mr. Whitmer turned his large, kind, but penetrating eyes upon me and, in a very pleasant and considerate, but firm and steady voice said, "Read the printed testimony of the three witnesses which you will find on one of the front pages of the Book of Mormon, and I say to you that every word of it is true."

Martin Harris did not come West with the Church. I think he was excommunicated before the exodus when so many of the Twelve were misled during those political days. But he did come West later, joined the Church, and spoke in the Salt Lake Tabernacle. My father and mother were present on that occasion. Mother told us what he had said and how he looked. And she heard his testimony in the Salt Lake Tabernacle that his testimony in the Book of Mormon is true.

There we have the physical fact; we have testimonies, witnesses to the fact; we have the reliability of those witnesses.

Fourth—Monuments or Memorials

The Book of Mormon itself is a monument, and it dates from 1829 right from the house which stood nearby when I heard myself from Justice Sawyer in 1935 testify that he was a boy when Oliver Cowdery carried the Book of Mormon manuscript to that printing house and back.

Fifth—Monuments or Memorials Should Date Back to or Near Event Itself

It was my privilege to be in attendance at the dedication of the Hill Cumorah Monument at Palmyra in 1935. At that dedication, an old gentleman—a Justice Sawyer—gave an extemporaneous speech of his very impressions of Joseph Smith at that place.

I remember his saying, "I met two young men who were preaching the gospel. They were gentlemen, but people ridiculed their claims. One of the young men said to me, 'If you had lived through the days of the Savior, you probably would have ridiculed his claim.' " Justice Sawyer then said: "I began to think that probably he was right."

Justice Sawyer remembered the building in which the Book of Mormon was printed. The following inscription is on the building: "Here is where the first Book of Mormon was printed."

Thus reason when properly applied leads us to reject the atheistic philosophy of communism and accept the spirituality and lofty teachings of Christianity—but,

> Dim as the borrow'd beams of moon and stars
> To lonely, weary, wandering travelers,
> Is reason to the soul; and as on high
> Those rolling fires discover but the sky,
> Not light us here, so Reason's glimmering ray
> Was lent, not to assure our doubtful way,
> But lead us upward to a better day.
> And as those nightly tapers disappear,
> When day's bright lord ascends our hemisphere,
> So pale grows Reason at Religion's sight,
> So dies and so dissolves in supernatural light.
> In this wild maze their vain endeavors end:
> How can the less the greater comprehend?
> Or finite Reason reach Infinity?
> For what could fathom God were more than He."
> —John Dryden
> (From "The Poetical Works of John Dryden,
> 1883 edition; J. B. Lippincott Publishing Co.,
> Philadelphia, Penn. Page 155.)

There are those in this history-making period, who say there are no heavenly beings. I read you some of their names. Times are changing just as imperceptibly as the grass and the trees are changing all nature. You do not see it; you are hardly conscious of it, but so history is in the making.

Time To Choose

Now is the time to choose. *"Choose ye this day, whom ye will serve"* has been an obligation since the days of Joshua. Do not doubt the existence of spiritual elements. You cannot! So live by choosing your life this day that you may be susceptible to those divine influences. I testify to you that they are real. Men who reject them do so because they prefer to live their selfish, indulgent life of the animal-like existence, on the animal plane. Thinking men are recognizing that this is the time in this great historical change that is taking place when the human spirit should respond to that *Something* out *Beyond.*They do not know what it is. They hesitate about giving God a real existence, but the Savior is God manifest in the flesh. He is our God, our leader, our Savior. He appeared to the Prophet Joseph and to these witnesses I have mentioned through the spirit, and you have the record right within your lifetime of the reality of those appearances.

Young man, (says John P. Altgeld) life is before you. Two voices are calling you— one coming out from the swamps of selfishness and force, where success means death; and the other from the hilltops of justice and progress, where even failure brings glory.

Two lights are seen in your horizon—one the fast fading marsh light of power, and the other the slowly rising sun of human brotherhood. Two ways lie open for you—one leading to an even lower and lower plain, where are heard the cries of despair and the curses of the poor, where manhood shrivels and possession rots down the possessor; and the other leading to the highlands of the morning, where are heard the glad shouts of humanity and where honest effort is rewarded with immortality.

Youth hold fast to that which is true. Have in your heart, when you have to make a choice, the spirit and courage of Peter who, after fewer than three years' contact with the Son of Man in the Flesh, wrote that he knew what it was to be in harmony with the divine spirit. Later, when he was accused of having performed a miracle, he was demanded to tell by what power he had healed the lame man. He stood facing members of the Sanhedrin who themselves had put the Christ to death. They said to him, "If you bear your testimony no longer in Jesus' name we will let you go." Peter answered: "Whether it be right in the sight of God to hearken unto you more than unto God, judge ye. For we (John was with him) cannot but speak the things which we have seen and heard. Be it known unto you all, and to all the people of Israel, that by the name of Jesus Christ of Nazareth whom ye crucified, whom God raised from the dead, even by him doth this man stand here before you whole. For there is none other name under the heaven given among men, whereby we must be saved." (Read Acts 4:10-21.)

God help us as younger men, older men; help us as members of The Church of Jesus Christ, to be true to that testimony and proclaim it to all the world, especially to those who ridicule his name.

Inspired Teaching

5

Chapter Fifty-two

The
Teacher

I<small>N</small> Section 88 of the Doctrine and Covenants, we find the following commandment:

And I give unto you a commandment that you shall teach one another the doctrine of the kingdom.

Teach ye diligently and my grace shall attend you, that you may be instructed more perfectly in theory, in principle, in doctrine, in the law of the gospel, in all things that pertain unto the kingdom of God, that are expedient for you to understand;

Of things both in heaven and in the earth, and under the earth; things which have been, things which are, things which must shortly come to pass; things which are at home, things which are abroad; the wars and the perplexities of the nations, and the judgments which are on the land; and a knowledge also of countries and of kingdoms —

That ye may be prepared in all things when I shall send you again to magnify the calling whereunto I have called you, and the mission with which I have commissioned you. (D.&C. 88:77-80.)

Can you get in all literature a more comprehensive statement of the field into which teachers must enter for the purpose of being prepared to teach the word of God than in that revelation?

In a thoughtful work entitled *The Religion Worth Having,* Thomas Nixon Carver once gave several sociological marks of what he considered the true church. Among other things I find this comparison:

Everyone is familiar with the intense struggle for existence that is carried on among the trees of the forest. It is asserted that the struggle is so intense and the issue of life and death is so sharply drawn among the young pines of a thicket, that the cutting of an inch from the top of one of them will doom it to ultimate extinction. Even that slight difference puts it at a disadvantage, and it never regains what was lost, but falls farther and farther behind and eventually is killed by its less unfortunate rivals.

Now let us imagine, that these trees were conscious beings and capable of having a religion. Let us suppose further that one set of trees possessed a religion which stimulated growth and helped them in the struggle for soil and light, while another possessed a religion which retarded growth and hindered in the struggle, is there any doubt as to which of these religions would ultimately dominate the forest? Those trees which happen to possess the religion which helped them would survive, and those which happen to possess the kind of religion which hinders them would perish, and their religion would perish with them.

The issue of life and death is never so sharply drawn among human beings as among the trees of the forest, but in the long run the result appears to be very much the same; . . . if that be true, it will follow that the religion which best fits men for the struggle with the forces of the world, which enables them to survive in this struggle, will eventually be left in possession of the world.

I am grateful for membership in a Church whose religion fits men for the struggle with the forces of the world and which enables them to survive in this struggle. One of these acting forces is the responsibility of teaching and the opportunity afforded in this Church for so many to share this responsibility.

There are others, also; for example, much might be said about the accomplishments of the Church in enabling men to win dominion over the forces of nature; in other words, efficiency in helping supply the material needs of mankind. Though this phase of our religion is glorious to contemplate and will establish in the minds of thinking men the superiority of this divine organization, I shall merely mention it as one of the many commendable features which help to fit us in the struggle with nature's forces.

Neither shall I dwell upon the social efficiency except to suggest that anyone who will give thought to it, and examine the divine organization and the opportunity that we have for influencing for good our young people as social beings, will be convinced of the efficacy and superiority of the Church in this regard.

But I should like now particularly to draw attention to the teaching force of the Church.

Martin Luther once said:

Count it one of the highest virtues upon earth to educate faithfully the children of others which so few, and scarcely any, do their own.

The obligation of teaching is placed by the Church first upon the parents, and the responsibility thereof has been placed upon them by divine command. But besides parents there are tens of thousands of men and women, and of boys and girls, who have accepted the responsibility of teaching. In the priesthood quorums alone the number runs into many thousands. And if we add mothers and fathers and young men and young women in the Relief Society, the Sunday Schools, the Mutual Improvement Associations, the Primary, and the seminaries, we have an army of teachers who have the privilege and responsibility of exercising what Luther calls "one of the highest virtues upon earth."

Now in furnishing opportunity for so many to get the development that comes to the true teacher, think what the Church is doing to help this army of teachers as individuals to become strong in the battle against the forces of the world!

First, it places upon them the obligation of teaching their fellow men by example; and there is no better safeguard placed upon an honest man or a sincere woman.

Second, it develops the divine attribute of *love for others.* Jesus said to one of his Apostles, "Simon, son of Jonas, lovest thou me more than these? . . . Yea, Lord; thou knowest that I love thee . . . Feed my lambs." (John 21:15.) Love should precede the responsibility of feeding those lambs. And these tens of thousands of teachers must have in their hearts the love of teaching, the love of their fellowmen, and a willingness to accept this responsibility with the divine attribute of love.

Then there is a *third* requirement; namely, *purity of life.* I cannot imagine one who has soiled himself teaching successfully purity to boys. I cannot imagine one who has doubt in his mind about the existence of God teaching impressively this existence of a Deity to young boys and girls. He cannot do it. If he acts the hypocrite and attempts so to teach, what he is will speak louder than what he says—and that is the danger of having doubting men as teachers of your children. The poison sinks in, and unconsciously they become sick in spirit, because of the poison which the person in whom they have confidence has insidiously instilled into their souls. The thought of teachers attempting to teach youth faith in God, when they haven't it, is irreconcilable with consistency, if not indeed unthinkable. So the third qualification is purity of life and faith in the gospel of Jesus Christ.

Finally, it gives them an opportunity to serve their fellowmen, and therein magnify the calling which has come to them, and indeed prove that they are real disicples of Christ. "Inasmuch as ye have done it unto one of the least of these my brethren, ye have done it unto me." (Matt. 25:40.) Thus the divine principle of service is instilled in their hearts.

I ask you to think of the effect upon society, if every worthy teacher, everyone, will succeed in influencing only one other to love, to have that same purity of life, and that same desire to serve his fellow men as he has!

I once observed a young girl in her teens put forth a special effort to speak to the little boy who was by my side. I could see that she wanted to recognize that boy, and that he was glad when he saw her to return her salutation. After we passed her I said, "Who is she?"

"She is my teacher," he answered.

"What is her name?"

"I do not know what her name is, but, oh, she is a dandy!"

He used an incorrect word, but the significance he gave to the word I knew, and the expression on his face I read, and in my heart I thanked the young girl for the influence she had over that boy. Only in her teens, but what that girl will say to him in his class he will accept as gospel truth; what she does in her life he will emulate; and that young girl (with untold tens of thousands of other teachers) carries the responsibility, in a measure, of molding that boy's character.

Oh, how mighty is the responsibility of a teacher!

God help our teachers to feel the responsibility that comes to them, and to remember that responsibility is not measured alone by what they say, but by what they do, and by the opportunities that have come to them to know good from evil.

Chapter Fifty-three

Responsibilities
and Opportunities
of Religious Teachers

Teaching is the noblest profession in the world. Upon the proper education of youth depend the permanency and purity of home and the safety and perpetuity of the nation. The parent gives the child an opportunity to live; the teacher enables the child to live well. That parent who gives life and teaches his child to live abundantly is the true parent-teacher. Today the customs and demands of society are such that the responsibility of training the child to live well is largely, and in many, too many instances, shifted entirely from the parent to the teacher. In the ideal state, the teacher would be but the parent's ally, training the mind and encouraging worthy habits, and fostering noble traits of character inculcated by wise parental teaching and example; but in reality, the teacher, instead of being merely an ally, must become the foster parent in training the child in the art of living. If that were all, his responsibility would be great enough. But it is not all. Often he faces even the greater task of overcoming the false teaching and the vicious training of unwise, irresponsible parents. In the light of such self-evident facts, is it not apparent to every thinking mind that the *noblest* of all noble professions is that of *teaching*, and that upon the effectiveness of that teaching hangs the destiny of nations?

"All who have meditated on the art of governing mankind," says Aristotle, "have been convinced that the fate of empires depends upon the education of youth."

The general objectives in our public schools should be to assist the individual in the proper development of his physical, intellectual, and spiritual nature, that he may become of value to his country and of service to his fellowman. This objective can be accomplished only on the basis of true education.

True Education

True education—what is it?

It is awakening a love for truth; giving a just sense of duty; opening the eyes of the soul to the great purpose and end of life. It is not so much giving words, as thoughts; or mere maxims, as living principles. It is teaching to be honest, not because "honesty is the best policy"; but because it is right. It is teaching the individual to love the good, for the sake of the good; to be virtuous in action, because one is so in heart; to love and serve God supremely, not from fear, but from delight in His perfect character.[1]

No one can successfully controvert the fact that upon the teacher rests much of the responsibility of lifting society to this high ideal.

There is a renowned painting depicting Christ as a youth standing before learned men in the temple. In that picture the artist has combined physical strength, intellectual fire, moral beauty, and spiritual fervor. There is an ideal for every boy and girl!

I ask you, fellow teachers, to take the artist's brush and canvas and try to reproduce that picture of perfect youth! You hesitate! You say you have neither the skill nor the training? Very well; and yet every person who enters the profession of teaching assumes the responsibility not of attempting to put on canvas an ideal picture of youth, but of cooperating with every youth under his tuition to make out of a living, breathing soul a perfect character.

------

[1] Dr. Robert Maynard Hutchins, the American educator.

Teach Positively

The responsibility of the teacher, however, does not end in his duty to teach truth positively. He enters the realm of what-not-to-do, as well as the realm of what-to-do. In the garden of the human soul, as well as in the fields of human endeavor, there are thorns and thistles as well as flowers and useful plants.

Thrice worthy of condemnation is he who would crush in a boy's mind a flower of truth, and sow in its stead the seed of error. Touching on this point, the greatest of all Teachers has said:

"But whoso shall offend one of these little ones which believe in me,"—that is, cause one of them to stumble—"it were better for him that a millstone were hanged about his neck, and that he were drowned in the depth of the sea." (Matt. 18:6.)

Those who enter the teaching profession with no sincere purpose of perfecting the individual, with no view of bettering the race; who think their duty done when they give a few dry facts in history, literature, science, and art, and draw their monthly remuneration therefor, are but stumbling blocks to national progress. And those who, trusted by parents to be guides and inspirers of children, will daily inculcate pernicious and rebellious thoughts in the minds of youth, who will actually teach young men and women to look with impunity upon immorality, surely merit, if any offenders merit, the condemnation to which the Great Teacher refers.

Wise parents and leading educators in the nation should realize that good citizenship can be obtained only through character development. They should recognize, with Emerson, that "Character is higher than intellect. . . . A great soul will be fit to live as well as to think."

If teachers are truly sincere in their desire to make character the true aim in education, they will *manifest that sincerity in daily action;* they will be what they expect their pupils to become. Otherwise, their teaching becomes hollow and meaningless. Their words and precepts are but as "sounding brass and a tinkling cymbal."

To live an upright life, to conform to high ethical standards, is the responsibility and duty of every teacher in the land. Greater even than this is the responsibility of the religious teacher. The religious teacher's profession is higher than that of the teacher in the common school; for, in addition to his belief in the efficacy of ethical and moral precepts, the religious teacher assumes the responsibility of leading youth into the realm of spirituality. His duty, comporting with his pretension and profession, is to open the eyes of the blind that they may know God. Oh, it is wonderful to find "tongues in trees, books in the running brooks, sermons in stones, and good in everything."[2] It is a glorious achievement to lead a lonely, hungering soul out of the maze of temporal, sensual materiality into the realm of spirituality.

The True Educator

Leading youth to know God, to have faith in his laws, to have confidence in him, and to find solace and peace in his love—this is the greatest privilege, the most sublime opportunity offered the true educator.

Fifteen miles from Vernal, Uintah County, Utah, stands a hill over which people walked and rode at intervals for years without seeing anything unusual about it. They noticed two great rocks uniform in size, but to men bent upon pioneer duties, they were only rocks. One day a man from the Carnegie Institute walked over that same hill. The nature of the rocks suggested to him they probably belonged to the Jurassic period of the world's history. He knew that in these strata are sometimes found fossils of huge animals that once roamed over parts of the earth. What were only common rocks to the farmer, the cattleman, and the pioneer, were to the trained

---

[2]William Shakespeare, *As You Like It.*

mind of the scientist fossilized remains of two vertebrae of a gigantic creature that has been extinct for centuries. In the course of a short time this discoverer had a force of men carefully uncovering these fossilized remains, and the people of the surrounding valley looked on with interest and amazement as a dinosaur sixty-five feet long and thirty-five feet high was disclosed to view. Following indications as he perceived them, this educator in the realm of science, by great effort and expense, unearthed one of the finest specimens ever discovered. Others have since been unearthed, one of which is on display in the University of Utah. Still others are lying in their original positions in the quarry.

Thus do men go through life, catching occasional glimpses of a higher, spiritual world; but unfortunately, they remain satisfied with but a glimpse and refuse to put forth the effort required to uncover the beauties and glories of that spiritual realm. They sense it blindly. Crowded by temporal demands, some there are who lose sight of even the indications of the beauties and glories of that spiritual realm. The game of life is fascinating; and when men enter it, they enter to win. To win becomes the sole aim of life. Some merchants, for example, wish to succeed, no matter what it costs, sometimes even without honor itself. The politician (not the statesman) enters the political world to satisfy his ambition regardless of serving the community or his country. Thus, men lose sight of the high things of life; worldly things crush the spiritual light within the soul. Some follow the will-o'-the-wisp of indulgence in passion. Dupes of an illusion, they soon begin to grovel.

Lead the Child

The most cherished opportunities of the religious teacher should be to lead the child to see through the trouble and turmoil of a physical world that "in all his dispensations God is at work for our good. *In prosperity* he tries our gratitude; *in mediocrity,* our contentment; *in misfortune,* our submission; *in darkness,* our faith; *under temptation,* our steadfast-ness; and *at all times,* our obedience and trust in him."[3]

To summarize: The choosing of the great profession of teaching involves to a greater or lesser extent the responsi-bility of parenthood and that of the highest leadership among men. It means a life endeavor to know the truth, and a constant, sincere desire to lead others to obtain this same knowledge. It means an exemplary life, for virtuous actions are but the result of a virtuous heart. The teacher's responsi-bility is also that of a watchman, and from his tower he warns fiery, brilliant youth of the realm of wasteful indulgence, and points to the higher realm of self-mastery and true service.

All this should be every teacher's responsibility, but the religious teacher's responsibility is even greater—*it is his duty and privilege to lead his pupils over moral and ethical hills to the glorious heights of spiritual reality where the spirit of man may receive the illumination and inspiration of God's Holy Spirit, by the light of which every youth may obtain the realization of what Robert A. Millikan, the American physi-cist, says is the most important thing in the world: "The consciousness of the reality of moral and spiritual values."*

The responsibility and opportunity of the religious teacher is summarized in the ninety-third section of the Doctrine and Covenants:

> I give unto you these sayings that you may understand and know how to worship, and know what you worship, that you may come unto the Father in my name, and in due time receive his fulness.
>
> For if you keep my commandments you shall receive of his ful-ness, and be glorified in me as I am in the Father. . . . (D.&C. 93:19, 20.)

God bless our teachers, and spare them to live that God might be their Light and their Guide as they reach out and say to the youth and to all the land—come, follow me, as I lead the way to Christ!

---

[3]John Jay, former Chief Justice of the U. S. Supreme Court.

Chapter Fifty-four

Guidance of a Human Soul -- The Teacher's Greatest Responsibility

---

THE most important responsibility that can come to a man or woman, not only in the Church, but also in life, is the responsibility of training and teaching children and youth, and in that training to avoid leaving any impression that might misdirect or injure any one of those boys or girls.

Standing in front of our old home in Huntsville are several stately poplars. One, when a sapling, had its bark injured. The scar remains in that stately old tree to this day, though over half a century has passed since the scar was made. Such is the effect of early impressions upon childhood. Of what inexpressible importance is the calling of a teacher who produces impressions which only death can obliterate, and mingles with the "cradle dream what shall be read in eternity!"

Train up a child in the way he should go; and when he is old, he will not depart from it. (Proverbs 22:6.)

"Train" means to form by instruction, discipline, drill— to establish good habits by teaching or discipline. To initiate or instruct. Training in ways selected for him, in the way he should go, and habitually walk therein.

Discipline in the Classroom

I believe that discipline in the classroom, which implies *self-control*, and which connotes *consideration for others*, is the most important part of teaching. Note these two elements.

The best lesson a child can learn is self-control, and to feel his relationship to others to the extent that he must have respect for their feelings. Self-denial is so important and self-control such a valuable quality in human nature, that one man has said truly that the worst education that teaches self-denial is better than the best which teaches everything else and not that. Therefore, let us consider the importance of order and discipline in the classroom, with these two great elements in mind.

Education begins with life. Before we are aware, the foundations of character are laid; and subsequent teaching avails but little to remove or alter them. Daniel Webster, who gained his education through the self-sacrifice of his father and mother, in the height of his influence in our great country, said:

> Educate your children in self-control, to the habit of holding passion and prejudice and evil tendencies subject to an upright and reasoning will, and you have done much to abolish misery from their future lives and crimes from society.
>
> Knowledge does not comprise all which is contained in the larger term of education. The feelings are to be disciplined; the passions are to be restrained; true and worthy motives are to be instilled; and pure morality inculcated under all circumstances. All this is comprised in education.

Associated with this thought of self-mastery and self-control is the word *self-abnegation*—"a rare virtue," says Holmes, "that good men preach, but good women practice."

Three Sources of Disorder

What are the sources of disorder in a classroom? Disorderly conduct should not be permitted in any class in the Church or in any class in public schools.

A disorderly environment, one in which disrespect is shown to the teacher and to fellow pupils, is one that will stifle the most important qualities in character.

What are the sources of this disorder? I name (1) *the presence of a hoodlum.* What is a hoodlum? He is a spoiled brat. And a brat is an ill-mannered, annoying child. (2) *Lack of interest.* (3) *An unprepared teacher.* How shall we eliminate these three sources of disorder?

First, regarding the child who probably comes from a home that has neglected to teach him the importance of self-control: Parents have failed to impress upon him the need of consideration for other members of the family, the first consideration of parental care. There is a phrase that has just come into use which probably we could use, and that is a word they call *empathy,* not sympathy, but *empathy,* which means an imaginative projection of one's own consciousness into another being; or better, the ability to appreciate another person's feelings.

It may be wise before condemning this disorderly boy—strangely enough, you very seldom have a defiant girl—to understand what his home life is. You can get acquainted with the conditions. You may have to appeal to the parents later. But before condemning the child too much, just try to put yourself in his place and find out just what is motivating him. Perhaps he has been permitted to develop in the home a selfishness, a desire to be recognized in the home.

I think you will find, if you go into that home, that his parents seek to make him the center of it when visitors come. He is the one who must be noticed, and they have developed in him a desire to be the center of attraction. He is the one to whom visitors must listen. In the home perhaps that child really has been taught not to control himself, but to do everything to make himself the center of attraction.

An Example To Teach the Hoodlum

That might help you, and perhaps aid you in influencing

him, not by force, but by giving, in a surprising way some morning, a lesson to show how he should consider others. You might change the lesson and give the story entirely for his benefit. Suppose he is building up the thought that he is going to do as he pleases; that he is not going to serve others nor have any consideration for them. It may be that you can approach him by telling the story of Sidney Carton, one of the characters in Charles Dickens' *A Tale of Two Cities*. Sidney Carton was a brilliant lawyer, but he was dissolute; he had little if any concern for others. He cared for himself alone. No, there was one for whom he cared, and that was a sweet woman with whom he had fallen in love years before. He spent his life indulging in his own interests, taking everything he could get for himself, never thinking of the welfare of others. Finally, when he sat in the presence of a 78-year-old man, Sidney realized that he had wasted his life. He said to his old friend:

"Yours is a long life to look back upon, sir."

"Yes, I am 78 years," said the old gentleman.

"You have been useful all your life, steadily and constantly occupied, trusted, respected, and looked up to."

"Oh, I have been a man of business ever since I have been a man. Indeed, I may say that I was a man of business when a boy."

Sidney said: "See what place you fill at 78. How many people will miss you when you leave it empty!"

"Oh," said Mr. Lorry, "I'm only a solitary old bachelor. There is nobody to weep for me."

"How can you say that? Wouldn't she weep for you?"—referring to the one girl Sidney had loved. "Wouldn't her child?"

"Yes, yes, thank God. I didn't quite mean what I said."

"Ah, it is a thing to thank God for," said Sidney. And then he pictured himself in these words: "If you could say with truth to your own solitary heart tonight, 'I have secured to myself the love and attachment, the gratitude, or respect of no human creature; I have won myself a tender place in no regard; I have done nothing good or serviceable to be remembered by.' If you could say that, your 78 years would be 78 curses, would they not?"

"You say truly, Mr. Carton. I think they would be."

339

If you have the attention of that disturbing boy by that time, perhaps you could close by saying: When Sidney Carton offered his own life for the husband of the girl he loved, there was an enlightening halo in his face, which seemed to say, as Charles Dickens puts it: "This is the happiest moment of my life. I am doing something that has made my life worthwhile."

If you fail to reach him that day, you can make an appeal to class loyalty. "Let's make our class the best in the entire stake. Let's have our class the most quiet class in our Sunday School. Let's have our record the best in the stake so that I may report to our stake president that our class has no disturbing influence."

I think you may be able to appeal to that spoiled boy. You can make him the leader, probably—a leader in class loyalty. If that fails, then you can make an appeal to the parents, and you can say: "If his misconduct continues, we shall have to put him off the roll." That is the extreme action. Any teacher can dismiss a boy; you should exhaust all your other sources before you come to that. But order we *must* have!—it is necessary for soul growth, and if one boy refuses, or if two boys refuse to produce that element, then they must leave. Better one boy starve than an entire class be slowly poisoned.

The Second Cause for disturbance is *lack of interest.* That can be increased probably by having a social. Invite them to your home. I have noticed through the years when I have met classes of Sunday School children, how proud the children are to say, "This is our class—see, these two are our teachers." They came together; the children know of the interest of the teachers. You can have them in your home. You can gain their confidence that way.

Third: We can overcome that disorder by the teacher's preparation. I know of nothing so important. Once you have their confidence, then what you say is a guiding influence in their lives. Your life itself, your personal appearance, your presentation of your lesson, emphasizing a definite truth in the lessons prescribed by the general board—all contribute to guiding their lives. I suggest that you make your own outline of the lessons, so that you will have it in mind, so you can emphasize some truth that will be applicable to the boys and girls you teach.

True Teaching Demands Personality

But remember in the presentation of your lessons, yes, and in the preparation for presentation, *that no matter how well prepared you may be, those children's interest will depend upon the personality which you place in that lesson. There is no teaching of morality without personality.* Note the parables of Jesus. Many of them refer to plants, to the field and the soil, fishermen, and so on; but most of them will introduce personalities. The life of Jesus is the life of a personality. He did not write a line, except with his finger in the sand, and no one knows what he wrote; but his life, which he gave for our salvation, our eternal exaltation, is still living. It is the impressive, the inspiring element throughout the Gospels—his life! Introduce personalities. Have an illustrative story. The children will follow you as you give it.

The Greater Power Which Every Teacher Needs

With these three things in mind, I believe that we can eliminate from our classes the disorder that is causing you so much worry and concern.

But there is one more thing most important, and that is that you cannot do these things of your own skill, of your own ability, no matter how much training you have had, nor how much study you put into your lesson. There is a greater power which every teacher needs, which he must have, and that power comes from above. I know from experience of the efficacy of prayer. As a child I thought I would have to kneel always before I could say a prayer, and there is virtue in kneeling. You cannot imagine offering a prayer if you take the position of a pugilist; position of the body has something to do with prayer. We kneel. One man said: "If you are going to pray, go into the room and kneel in the center, and just think for a minute or two of what God has done for you and what your needs are, without saying anything." I think this is a good idea.

There is never a moment in life when you cannot pray. If you are studying as a student, you can offer a silent prayer, for "Prayer is the soul's sincere desire, uttered or unexpressed."

Every Sunday School teacher—I think every teacher in the world—should offer a prayer before he meets his students. The teacher, sensing his responsibility, should realize his dependence upon a greater power.

Teachers have the greatest responsibility of anyone in the world—the guidance of a human soul! As I stated in the beginning, a scar might remain throughout life, but so will the virtues remain throughout life and all eternity.

Freedom And Liberty 6

Chapter Fifty-five

Ours
Is a
Rich Heritage

J ULY is usually a hot month, but it is a glorious month. On two days in that month, in Utah, we have opportunity to pay tribute to the founders of the nation and to the founders of Utah. It is well that we do so.

On the Fourth of July, we join in celebrating the signing of the Declaration of Independence. How glorious it would be on that day in every home in the United States of America, in each heart in every home, if not in words, the inhabitants of this country would say: "I pledge allegiance to the flag of the United States of America and to the Republic for which it stands, one nation under God, indivisible with liberty and justice for all."

I believe that in the hearts of the majority of the inhabitants of this great country that feeling of loyalty persists.

If we would make the world better, let us foster a keener appreciation of the freedom and liberty guaranteed by the government of the United States, as framed by the founders of this nation. There are some self-proclaimed progressives who cry that such old-time adherence is out-of-date. But there are some fundamental principles of this Republic which, like eternal truths, never get out-of-date; and which are applicable at all times to liberty-loving peoples. Such are the underlying principles of the Constitution, a document framed by patriotic, freedom-loving men, who we declare were inspired by the Lord.

Members of the Church should have nothing to do with secret combinations and groups antagonistic to the constitutional law of the land, which the Lord ". . . suffered to be established"; and which

> . . . should be maintaind for the rights and protection of all flesh, according to just and holy principles;
>
> That every man may act in doctrine and principle pertaining to futurity, according to the moral agency which I have given unto him, that every man may be accountable for his own sins in the day of judgment.
>
> Therefore, it is not right that any man should be in bondage one to another.
>
> And for this purpose have I established the Constitution of this land, by the hands of wise men whom I raised up unto this very purpose, and redeemed the land by the shedding of blood. (D.&C. 101: 77-80.)

Of course, there are errors in government which some would correct; certainly there are manifest injustices and inequalities, and there always will be such in any government in the management of which enter the frailties of human nature. If you want changes, go to the polls on election day, express yourself as an American citizen, and thank the Lord for the privilege that is yours to have a say as to who shall serve you in public office.

Next to being one in worshiping God, there is nothing in this world upon which the Church should be more united than in upholding and defending the Constitution of the United States.

It was faith that braved Columbus to sail on and on into the unknown horizon until he discovered a new land. It is *faith in God as a Loving Father*—who through inspiration and revelation, guides those who seek him in sincerity. It was in *defense of liberty to worship God as conscience dictates* that impelled the Mormon Pioneers to establish settlements in a forbidding, defiant western desert. They believed in the Fatherhood of God, the brotherhood of man, the divineness of nature, and the eternal verities of honor, duty, and self-renunciation.

Notwithstanding the warnings of the desolation of the country, and the plea to go on to more productive climes, there was that assurance in President Brigham Young's mind which had greater influence upon him than the trapper's experience of unproductivity and of monthly frosts, and more influential than the glowing description of the California coast. Greater than human judgment, towering above man's experience, was the great leader's trust in God.

As President Young and the main body of the pioneers came out of Emigration Canyon into the valley of the Great Salt Lake 116 years ago, they gazed upon a barren landscape so uninviting and desolate that one of the three women in the company, out of sheer disappointment and hopelessness, broke down and wept. Truly to her and to others of the company, it must have seemed impossible that in such a desolate place could be fulfilled the prophecy of their first great leader, Joseph Smith, that the Saints "would become a mighty people in the midst of the Rocky Mountains." And yet, in our day, that prophecy has become a reality.

When they arrived in the valley, to quote the words of President Young, they "prayed over the land, and dedicated it and the water, air, and everything pertaining to them unto the Lord, and the smiles of heaven rested upon the land and it became productive, . . . There never has been a land, from the days of Adam until now, that has been blessed more than this land has been blessed by our Father in heaven; and it will still be blessed more and more, if we are faithful and humble, and thankful to God for the wheat and the corn, the oats, the fruit, the vegetables, the cattle, and everything He bestows upon us, and try to use them for the building up his kingdom on earth."

The noblest ideal of those honored pioneers, and the noblest ideal in the Church today, is the ideal of service.

Each day before they started out on the trail, *they had their prayers* either in the wagon or around the circle. Every family in every wagon had its prayers. *The second thing* which they had to do was to see that their muskets were properly loaded. The driver would carry his musket across his knees with the firelock ready; those who walked at the side of their teams carried the musket on the arm, in preparation for any eventuality. And *the third instruction* was, "Let every man be as considerate and as interested in his neighbor's cattle as in his own."

Service—*rendering service to each other.* They helped one another in adversity, shared with the hungry the last loaf of bread, gave of their time and means for the upbuilding of the community, and on not a few occasions offered their lives for the truth. Thus they exemplified in their teachings the two great commandments: ". . . Thou shalt love the Lord thy God with all thy heart, with all thy might, mind, and strength; . . . [and] . . . Thou shalt love thy neighbor as thyself. . . ." (D.&C. 59:5,6.)

Truly, our pioneers cherished two great ideals which, I think, are the most worthwhile ideals, for they represent all that we can take back to God when we leave; and that time will surely come.

First is *the character* that is developed by adherence to these principles; and that is in harmony with the greatest of the revelations given, and given only through the Prophet Joseph:

> For behold, this is my work and my glory—to bring to pass the immortality and eternal life of man. (Moses 1:39.)

And how else may that become so except by approaching as best we can the character of the one perfect Being who ever walked the earth, Christ, our Redeemer.

The *second is the service you have rendered mankind.* ". . . Inasmuch as ye have done it unto one of the least of these my brethren, ye have done it unto me." (Matt. 25:40.)

348

The best way to honor the memory of our intrepid pioneers on the twenty-fourth of July, and on every other day of our lives, is not merely by words but by emulating their deeds. If we do that, we will obey the principles of the gospel of Jesus Christ, as restored in this dispensation.

Ours is a rich heritage. The wealth inherited must neither be buried nor squandered, but should be handed down to posterity with a tenfold increase.

May we ever emulate the virtues and spiritual aspirations of our pioneer fathers!

Chapter Fifty-six

The Founding of an American Republic

As we celebrate the birth of the Declaration of Independence on July 4, 1776, let us catch the spirit of that morning and awaken appreciation for the blessings and privileges that are ours if we remain loyal and true to the Constitution of the United States as established by our Founding Fathers. Compared to other nations, we are still just a young nation. But what has happened during that period of nearly two hundred years? We are a nation now leading all others. Uncounted billions of dollars have been poured out to protect the world against dictatorship and slavery, and gigantic burdens have been borne successfully by America.

It is almost 200 years since those 56 men sat in the Old State House at Philadelphia, determining whether they should break away from the mother country and the tyranny of George the Third. I do not know who wrote the poem, "Independence Bell," but its lines give the spirit of the momentous occasion that morning. I used to study it in school.

INDEPENDENCE BELL

There was a tumult in the city
In the quaint old Quaker town,
And the streets were rife with people

Pacing restless up and down—
People gathering at the corners,
Where they whispered each to each,
And the sweat stood on their temples
With the earnestness of speech.

As the bleak Atlantic currents
Lash the wild Newfoundland shore,
So they beat against the State House,
So they surged against the door;
And the mingling of their voices
Made the harmony profound,
Till the quiet street of Chestnut
Was all turbulent with sound.

"Will they do it?" "Dare they do it?"
"Who is speaking?" "What's the news?"
"What of Adams?" "What of Sherman?"
"Oh, God grant they won't refuse!"
"Make some way there!" "Let me nearer!"
"I am stifling!" "Stifle then!
When a nation's life's at hazard,
We've no time to think of men!"

So they surged against the State House
While all solemnly inside,
Sat the Continental Congress,
Truth and reason for their guide.
O'er a simple scroll debating,
Which, though simple it might be,
Yet should shake the cliffs of England
With the thunders of the free.

Far aloft in that high steeple
Sat the bellman, old and gray,
He was weary of the tyrant
And his iron-sceptered sway;
So he sat with one hand ready
On the clapper of the bell,
When his eye should catch the signal,
The long-expected news to tell.

See! See! The dense crowd quivers
Through all its lengthy line,
As the boy beside the portal

Hastens forth to give the sign!
With his little hands uplifted,
Breezes dallying in his hair,
Hark! with deep, clear intonation,
Breaks his young voice on the air.

Hushed the people's swelling murmur,
Wilst the boy cries joyously;
"Ring!" he shouts, "Ring! Grandpa,
Ring! Oh, ring for Liberty!"
Quickly at the given signal
The old bellman lifts his hand,
Forth he sends the good news, making
Iron music through the land.

How they shouted! What rejoicing!
How the old bell shook the air,
Till the clang of freedom ruffled
The calmly gliding Delaware!
How the bonfires and the torches
Lighted up the night's repose,
And from the flames, like fables Phoenix,
Our glorious liberty arose.

That old State House bell is silent,
Hushed is now its clamorous tongue;
But the spirit it awakened
Still is living—ever young!
And when we greet the smiling sunlight
On the fourth of each July,
We shall ne'er forget the bellman
Who, betwixt the earth and sky,
Rang out, loudly, "Independence;
Which please God, shall never die!"

Fifty-six men signed that document, the Declaration of Independence! They were all educated, well-trained, but common, loyal, ordinary men. Their average age was only 44, and that included Benjamin Franklin who was 70 years of age. Some were in their fifties. Others, however, were just young men.

This is what they signed: "And for the support of this Declaration, *with a firm reliance on the protection of divine*

Providence, we mutually *pledge* to each other *our Lives, our Fortunes,* and *our Sacred Honor.*"

That gives the spirit of that occasion in the old Philadelphia town in the year 1776!

Independence Gained

The Revolutionary War was fought; and the colonists gained their independence from the despot, George the Third. I say George the Third because there were many Englishmen who were in sympathy with the American colonies. William Pitt, a member of Parliament, was one of them. You will remember reading in school about Pitt's reply to Walpole when they were discussing the rebellion of the American colonies. Walpole made an accusation against Pitt, accusing him of being a young man and said that Parliament should not listen to him. As I remember, Pitt arose and said: "Of the irretrievable crime of being a young man, I shall neither palliate nor deny." And then he said, "Were I an American, as I am an Englishman, I would never lay down my arms. Never! Never! Never!"

After the Revolutionary War was over and nine years after the Declaration of Independence was signed, the Founding Fathers met in the same Old State Hall to frame the Constitution of the United States.

The French historian, Francois Pierre Guillaume Guizot, while visiting in the United States, asked James Russell Lowell, "How long will the American Republic endure?" Lowell's answer was: "As long as the ideas of the men who founded it continue dominant."

And what were those ideas? Two fundamental principles were: *Freedom from Dictatorship* and *Freedom of the Individual!* This goes right back to our free agency, which is as precious as life itself.

The rebellion against that dictatorship of George the Third had begun hundreds of years before that meeting in the Old State Hall, when freedom-loving men in England brought King John to Runnymeade and made him sign that great document which gave to them the right of trial by jury by their peers and took away the right from the kings to say: "This man's head or that man's head shall come off!" Men had been imprisoned and beheaded without fair trial because of a whim or because of the king's fear of being overthrown.

Man Defies Compulsion

There is something in human nature that rebels against dominance and compulsion. In our day, we have witnessed one of the greatest uprisings against just such dictatorship that the world has ever known. I refer to those loyal Hungarians who rose up against the tyranny of oppression! I do not suppose there has ever been such an uprising—not since the Declaration of Independence, at any rate—of a people. They used their bare hands; and children, youths, and adults rose up against tyranny and won—until the communist gangsters turned on them and killed them by the hundreds; and hundreds of others were shipped off to Siberia. This is in your time and mine! Do we realize it? Do we realize what it means to have a knock come at the door at night, and to be afraid because it is the police, then to hear a voice commanding: "Open the door!"? One woman who was alone got such a command; and, scantily dressed, was rushed, not down in the elevator, but down four flights of stairs, put in a black wagon with guards on each side, and carried off to prison. She was innocent; but the door closed behind her, and that was the beginning of a nine-year prison sentence. This is a frequent happening in dictator countries in this the twentieth century!

That is the kind of treatment the spirit of man rebels against; that is why we had the Declaration of Independence; that is why we had the Constitution of the United States drawn up by men who were inspired; and that is why we have the Bill of Rights, granting protection to each individual. The government was established to protect the individual; the individual is not a part of the State, nor should he be used as part of the State. The government is set up to protect him in his rights.

Constitution Is Greatest Writing

What other fundamental prompted these men when they framed the Constitution—"the greatest instrument," said one man, "ever written by the hands of man"? I name it as *Faith in God*, next to free agency, or correlative with free agency. As an illustration, during the critical time when the representatives of the colonies were trying to frame the Con- stitution in that Old State Hall, Benjamin Franklin, the old- est man present, arose and stated his faith in an overruling Providence and in the power of prayer, and then said:

> I have lived, sir, a long time, and the longer I live, the more con- vincing proofs I see of this truth: That God governs in the affairs of men. And if a sparrow cannot fall to the ground without His notice is it probable that an empire can rise without His aid?
>
> We have been assured, sir, in the sacred writings, that "Except the Lord build the house, they labour in vain that build it." I firmly believe this; and I also believe that without His concurring aid we shall succeed in this political building no better than the builders of Babel. . . .
>
> I therefore beg leave to move that henceforth prayers imploring the assistance of Heaven, and its blessings on our deliberations, be held in this Assembly every morning before we proceed to business, and that one or more of the clergy of this city be requested to officiate in that service.

It is difficult to learn from history whether that was ever carried out. They did not have any money to pay for prayers, and John Quincy Adams implies that they did not have prayers there. Another man says they did. However, the point I wish to make is that Benjamin Franklin empha- sized that faith in God is a fundamental principle of the Constitution of the United States. I should also like to refer to a remark made by George Washington, who following the establishment of the Constitution and the acceptance of it by the 13 Colonies, wrote this:

Of all the dispositions of habits which lead to political prosperity, religion and morality are indispensable supports.

He stated that neither prosperity nor reputation nor life itself is secure when people are not sincerely religious.

Actuated by these two fundamental and eternal principles—the free agency of the individual and faith in an overruling Providence—those 56 men who signed the Declaration of Independence, those who drew up the Constitution of the United States nine years later, gave to the world a concept of government which, if applied, will strike from the arms of downtrodden humanity the shackles of tyranny, and give hope, ambition, and freedom to the teeming millions throughout the world.

All Americans should be on guard against the scheming of those who would take from us the freedom so dearly bought. Edward F. Hutton gives us this warning:

Why do our people possess more autos, more radios, more washing machines, more of so many things, than the people of any other country? After all, we are plain, ordinary human beings. Why then do we have many more of God's blessings? One impelling reason I think lies in the simple fact that we have believed in the rights of man and have lived under a government of laws as distinguished from a government of men. We have enjoyed the safeguards of the Constitution and Bill of Rights, whose word, until recently, we believed was immutable and inalienable. The protection, the confidence, the assurance provided by the Bill of Rights opened up the faucets of human ambition and let loose an avalanche of new incentives. Men were free to inquire, to reject, to choose, to risk, to create!

Till twenty years ago, the Bill of Rights, generator of the genius of America, was taken for granted. For two decades now it has been under attack . . . by those who assert, though without proof, that they can improve upon our system of government. The plan seems to be to impose upon the people political control of the daily activities. Under Communism you lose your liberties immediately and perhaps your life. Under Socialism, you lose your liberties a little more slowly but just as surely.

Today the Bill of Rights is in jeopardy. If it could speak, I believe it would have this to say: I am your Bill of Rights. Don't take me for granted. As man brought me to life, I can be slain by men, and will be slain unless you, the plain people of America, organize to defend me.

I am freedom of religion, freedom of speech, freedom of the press, freedom of assembly. I am the privacy and sanctity of your home. I am your guarantee of trial by jury, and I am the custodian who guards your property rights. I am your signed lease to spiritual, mental, and physical freedom.

My existence depends on how vigilantly you watch those who administer your government. Put every law proposed in Washington into the crucible of my ten commandments. Your question must always be: "Not what does a law give me, but what does it take away from me?"

We, the plain, humble, God-fearing people, made this republic what it is. Let us unite our voice in defense of the Constitution and Bill of Rights.[1]

I love the Stars and Stripes! I love the people who make this country great, and I believe in their loyalty. In its leadership is the greatest responsibility that ever came to a nation. We pray to God to guide our president and congress. I know that they and we do not want war, but there are things that are worse than death—*one is to be deprived of our liberty!*

God help us as a people to be true to the Stars and Stripes which stands for individual freedom, the free agency of man, for faith in God, and for service to our country and to our fellowmen!

----

[1] Edward F. Hutton, *Pathfinder Magazine*, June 27, 1951.

Chapter Fifty-seven

An Enduring Civilization Must Be Built Upon Integrity

IF one of you students in geometry were requested to demonstrate that the square on the hypotenuse of a right angle triangle is equal to the sum of the square of the other two sides, you could prove the proposition in a few minutes. You students in chemistry can perform a chemical experiment, the results of which are plainly apparent to all, in the brief time of a class period. But to prove that "righteousness exalteth a nation, and that sin is a reproach to any people" may take centuries, yet the latter is just as inevitably demonstrable as your proposition in geometry or your chemical experiment. Two principal factors contribute to the "righteousness" of a people: (1) sterling integrity in the citizenry and in officials who are above corrupting influences; and (2) the fundamental ideals for which the nation stands.

Each year on the 22nd of February, we honor the Father of our Country. In his boyhood and youth, George Washington, as hundreds of other British subjects, living in a new world, found himself free to choose whatever mode of life seemed most desirable. He and others in the new world found few if any restraints in their getting a livelihood by any legitimate means they chose. They were conscious of an individualism, and independence of spirit. Their souls were their own. Thus almost unconsciously, but inevitably the colonists imbibed the spirit of individual freedom. When, therefore, they perceived an attempt to deprive them of this inherent right and privilege, they could, in keeping with their own honor, do nothing else but resist.

Washington loved the peace and the tranquil joys of his Mt. Vernon estate; but duty called him into the turmoil of public life. From youth he grew up to be a man of peace; yet he was given the appellation of "First in War." He was not so brilliant in intellect as others of his brilliant contemporaries; "he had no pretensions to that vivacity which fascinates or to that wit which dazzles, and frequently imposes on the understanding"; yet, in the words of General Henry Lee who knew him intimately, and who loved him almost to adoration: "When our monuments shall be done away; when nations now existing shall be no more; when even our young and far-spreading empire shall have perished; still will our Washington's glory unfaded shine, and die not, until love of virtue cease on earth, and earth itself sinks into chaos."

Why did this peace-loving, even-tempered man take to war, and win undying fame as a general?

Wherein lies the secret of his greatness?

Two Conflicting Ideologies

To answer these questions intelligently, it will be well for us to recognize in humanity's struggle to achive happiness two conflicting ideologies:

One,—Government by Force; the other—Government by Popular Consent.

The first is the law of the jungle; the second, the law of mutual consideration. The first, is the application of selfishness; the second, an attempt to apply Christ's law of "love your neighbor as yourself."

Illustration of the First

Some of you on a quiet summer evening in the past have sat on benches provided for spectators at the feeding grounds of the Grand Canyon of the Yellowstone. As trucks withdrew after unloading the garbage, you saw a dozen or more black bears scold, scratch, and struggle for the food thus provided. Then a proud grizzly appeared on the scene. As he approached with the air of a conqueror, the black bears scampered, leaving to him and his grizzly associates all the spoils of the garbage feast. Might was conqueror, the weak subdued and frightened.

That is the law of the jungle.

Illustration of the Law of Helpfulness

A few years ago, after years of intensive research, laborious labor, and extreme self-denial, Pierre and Madame Curie discovered a new element in the universe. There came a moment in their lives when they faced the question whether they should use their discovery for their own aggrandizement or whether they should give it gratuitously for the benefit of mankind. Said Pierre one Sunday morning to Madame Curie: "We have a choice between two solutions. We can describe the results of our research without reserve, including the processes of purification. . . ."

Marie made a mechanical gesture of approval and murmured:

"Yes, naturally."

"Or else," Pierre went on, "we can consider ourselves to be the proprietors, the 'inventors' of radium. In this case it would be necessary, before publishing exactly how you worked to treat pitchblende, to patent the technique and assure ourselves in that way of rights over the manufacture of radium throughout the world."

Marie reflected a few seconds, then said:

"It is impossible. It would be contrary to the scientific spirit."

"I think so, too," replied Pierre, "but I do not want this decision to be taken lightly. Our life is hard—and it threatens to be hard forever. We have a daughter; perhaps we may have other children. For them, and for us, this patent would represent a great deal of money, a fortune. It would be comfort made certain, and the suppression of drudgery . . ."

"And," as his face lighted up, "we could have a fine laboratory, too."

Marie's gaze grew fixed. She steadily considered this idea of gain, of material compensation. Almost at once she rejected it.

"Physicists always publish their researches completely. If our discovery has a commercial future, that is an accident by which we must not profit. And radium is going to be of use in treating disease. . . . It seems to me impossible to take advantage of that."

Twenty years later Madame Curie said: "Pierre Curie decided to take no material profit from our discovery. In consequence we took out no patent and we have published the results of our research without reserve, as well as the processes of preparation of radium. Moreover, we gave interested persons all the information they requested." Then, realizing how slow true progress is, she said:

"No one of us can do much, yet each of us perhaps can catch some gleam of knowledge, which modest and insufficient of itself, may add to man's dream of truth. It is by these small candles that we see before us little by little the dim outlines of that great plan which shapes the universe, and I am among those who think that for this reason science is ever hopeful, and with its great spiritual strength will in time cleanse this world of its evils, its ignorance, its poverty, diseases, war, and heartaches."

That illustrates the ideal of mutual helpfulness.

Evidence of Political Chicanery

Recently a gentleman well informed with regard to the international conflict now raging gave me a glimpse behind the curtain where diplomats use nations as chess players use their pawns. From his point of view there had been duplicity, chicanery, double-crossing on the part of men who held in their hands the destiny of nations.

"What!" I exclaimed, "is there no integrity among the leaders of these mighty nations?" If not, then our civilization is doomed, for the law of retribution is as eternally active as the law of compensation. It is as true now as always that "righteousness exalteth a nation, and sin is a reproach to any people." There is but one bright hope shining through the dark clouds of this global war: That it will crush wicked principles, and make more potent righteous ideals.

Washington believed in giving every man a fair chance.

Why, then, did this lover of peace become a warrior? Because George the Third was a tyrant, an enemy to truths, which to the Colonists were self-evident: "That all men are created equal, that they are endowed by their Creator with inalienable rights. Among these are life, liberty, and the pursuit of happiness."

And for this same ideal—liberty and free agency of man— the Allies are struggling today against the spirit of despotism and the jungle rule.

The Secret of Washington's Greatness

Now we may answer the second question—Wherein is the secret of Washington's greatness?

It was Washington's character more than his brilliancy of intellect that made him the choice of all as their natural leader when the thirteen original colonies decided to sever their connection with the mother country. As one in eulogy to the father of our country truly said: "When he appeared among the eloquent orators, the ingenious thinkers, the vehement patriots of the Revolution, his modesty and temperate profession could not conceal his superiority; he at once, by the very nature of his character, was felt to be their leader."

1. Traits of Character Exemplified in Washington's life

If, in search of the secret of his greatness, we were to analyze Washington's character, I would name as one outstanding virtue—An unassumed modesty.

Though others united in choosing him as the one best fitted for the position to which he was called, he never felt himself as being indispensable. In his letter of acceptance as the commander-in-chief, he said:

> If any event should happen unfavorable to my reputation, I beg it may be remembered by every gentleman in the room that I this day declare with the utmost sincerity I do not think myself equal to the command I am honored with.

With a total absence of arrogance he accepted the calling and the appointment as an opportunity to serve his country. He would accept no pecuniary consideration. He refused any compensation, saying that he would keep an exact account of his expenses, which the government no doubt would discharge, and that was all he desired.

2. A second Outstanding Quality Was an Unwavering Strength To Do What He Thought Was Right

Says his dear friend, Major General Henry Lee:

> Commencing his administration, what heart has not charmed with the recollection of the pure and wise principles announced by himself as the basis of his political life? He best understood the indissoluble union between virtue and happiness, between duty and advantage, between the genuine maxims of an honest and magnanimous policy, and the sordid rewards of public prosperity and individual felicity.

3. A Third Virtue Contributive to His Greatness Was Moral Uprightness

Said one in eulogy:

> His morality was built up in warring with outward temptations and inward passions. Every grace of his conscience was a trophy of toil and struggle. He had no moral opinions which hardened experience and sturdy discipline had not vitalized into moral sentiments, and

363

organized into moral powers. These powers fixed and seated in the inmost heart of his character, were mighty and far-sighted forces which made his intelligence moral, and his morality intelligent, and which no sorcery of the selfish passions could overcome or deceive.

4. He Had A Sense of Responsibility to Others

He gave forty-five years of his life to his country, asking nothing in return but the privilege of enjoying his home in peace at Mt. Vernon.

5. He Possessed Calmness in Storms and Fearlessness Under Insults, Slander, and Misrepresentation

December 17, 1777 Washington's Army was in winter quarters at Valley Forge, about twenty-two miles from Philadelphia. He had fewer than ten thousand men, three hundred of whom deserted to the British. The soldiers were thinly clad, and some half naked; others with no clothing but tattered blankets wrapped around them. So many were sick as the result of privations, and so many were without coats, blankets, hats, or shoes, that one wonders how the army held together at all.

Under this stress of critical, desperate condition, it must have seemed to Washington that he was abandoned not only by Congress, then in session at York, but also by most of his friends as well. John Adams had turned against him. So also had Richard Henry Lee. General Gates insulted him by sending reports direct to Congress instead of to Washington, his superior officer.

As carrions hover around a dying creature, so in Washington's dire calamity came men to seek to crush him—men who formed what has been called the "Conway Cabal," a contemptible attempt to dishonor Washington, and to supplant him by a self-asserting, arrogant schemer. Falsehoods most damnable appeared in print. Lies fell like froth from unclean mouths.

In the midst of all this, Washington's imperturbable conduct makes his character shine in immortal glory.

> As some tall cliff, that lifts its awful form
> Swells from the vale, and midway leaves the storm,
> Though round its breast the rolling clouds are spread,
> Eternal sunshine settles on its head.

Washington's generosity was shown also, for in after years he never let the memory of this plot influence him in his relation with the men who had taken part in it.

Only Justifications for War

Washington took up the sword in defense of the only two principles that justify war.

(1) Justifiable resistance to attempts to dominate and deprive others of their free agency.

(2) Loyalty to one's country.

Man's free agency is fundamental to progress. An attempt to rob him of his free agency caused contention even in heaven.

In that rebellion Lucifer said in substance: By the law of force I will compel the human family to subscribe to the eternal plan, but give me thine honor and power. To deprive an intelligent human being of his free agency is to commit the crime of the ages.

Impelling motives of this arch-enemy to liberty were pride, ambition, a sense of superiority, a will to dominate his fellows, and to be exalted above them, and a determination to deprive human beings of their freedom to speak and to act as their reason and judgment would dictate.

So fundamental in man's eternal progress is his inherent right to choose that the Lord would defend it even at the price of war. Without freedom of thought, freedom of choice, freedom of action within lawful bounds man cannot progress. The Lord recognized this, and also the fact that it would take man thousands of years to make earth habitable for self-governing individuals. Throughout the ages advanced souls have yearned for a society in which liberty and justice prevail. Men have sought for it, fought for it, have died for it.

Ancient free-men prized it, slaves longed for it, the Magna Charta demanded it, the Constitution of the United States declared it.

"This love of liberty which God has planted in us," said Abraham Lincoln, "constitutes the bulwark of our liberty and independence. It is not our frowning battlements, our bristling seacoasts, our army, and our navy. Our defense is in the spirit which prizes liberty as the heritage of all men, in all lands, everywhere. Destroy this spirit, and we have planted the seeds of despotism at our very doors."

Loyalty to Government

A second obligation that impelled Washington, and that impels us to become participants in the world-war is loyalty to the government. The Doctrine and Covenants states that

We believe that governments were instituted of God for the benefit of man; and that He holds men accountable for their acts in relation to them, both in making laws and administering them, for the good and safety of society.

We believe that no government can exist in peace, except such laws are framed and held inviolate as will secure to each individual the free exercise of conscience, the right and control of property, and the protection of life. (D. & C. 134:1-2.)

Responsibility of State to Protect Its Citizens

The greatest responsibility of the state is to guard the lives, and to protect the property and rights of its citizens; and if the state is obligated to protect its citizens from lawlessness within its boundaries, it is equally obligated to protect them from lawless encroachment from without—whether the attacking criminals be individuals or nations.

We are informed by competent authority that over twenty years ago the government of the United States entered into agreement with Japan to maintain peace in the Pacific Ocean, and "keep honorable hands off China." "Before the year was over," writes Mark J. Gayn, in an article "Prelude to Treachery," "the ablest men on the Japanese Naval General

Staff went to work blue-printing war on the United States and Britain."

As I have said on another accasion, from such treachery the state is in duty bound to protect itself, and its only effective means of doing so under present world conditions is by armed force. As a Church we believe that all men are justified in defending themselves, their friends, and property, and the government from the unlawful assaults and encroachments of all persons in times of exigency, where immediate appeal cannot be made to laws, and relief afforded.

Duty To Combat Evil

Even though we sense the hellish origin of war, even though we feel confident that war will never end war, yet, under existing conditions, we find ourselves as a body committed to combat this evil thing. With other loyal citizens we serve our country as bearers of arms, rather than to stand aloof to enjoy a freedom for which others have fought and died.

Aillied Soldiers Fighting for an Eternal Principle

My purpose in emphasizing this theme today is to give encouragment to young men now engaged in armed conflict and to reassure them that they are fighting for an eternal principle fundamental to human progress and peace.

Again I say, God bless them and others now registered awaiting the call to duty, and those serving in defense! To each of you we send a message of confidence and trust. Many of you before entering upon your military duties were authorized messengers of peace. Others of you also hold the Priesthood. To all we say, in your personal habits let the same ideals guide you as soldiers in the army as guided you as missionaries. What the Lord said to you then is applicable to you now:

Wherefore gird up your loins, and take upon you my whole armor, that ye may be able to withstand the evil day, having done all, that ye may be able to stand.

Stand, therefore, having your loins girt about with truth, having on the breastplate of righteousness, and your feet shod with the preparation of the gospel of peace. . . . (D. & C. 27:15-16)

Keep yourselves morally clean. Being soldiers or sailors is not justification for indulgence in vulgarity, intemperance, or immorality. Others may be impelled to do these things because of the beastliness of war, but you who hold the priesthood cannot so indulge with impunity. For your own sweet lives, and for others who believe in you, keep yourselves unpolluted. As you do, your comrades will respect you, your officers will admire you, your loved ones will forever trust you.

Conclusion

America was a great land before Columbus discovered her island outposts; great when the Indian tribes roamed from the Bering Sea to the Gulf. It was a great land when Governor Dinwoodey sent George Washington, only 21 years of age, on the perilous expedition into the Ohio Valley.

Today America is even more glorious than ever! No observer can travel from the sun-kissed beaches of the Pacific to the wooded hills and power-producing rivers of New England without being thrilled by the greatness of these United States − − the painted deserts of the West, flower-carpeted in springtime, and holding hidden beauty and entrancing interest in every season; the inspiring monuments of the Rockies, harboring snows as reservoirs for crops in valleys below; the colorful canyons, painted only by the Creator Himself; the fertile food-producing valley of the Mississippi; the mighty forest of the Northwest; the navigable rivers; the climate, varying to suit all needs and conditions—all these and a thousand other equally glorious and productive features bear witness to the age-old declaration that this is a "land choice above all other lands," and inspire every patriot to say: "This is my own, my native land." Millions of Americans today declare with Winthrop: "Our country, to be cherished in all our hearts, to be defended by all our hands."

Today, yielding to the demands of the greatest economic era since the dawn of her creation, America is demonstrating the vastness of her resources and the extent of her natural possibilities as never before. Well may we sing:

> I love thy rocks and rills,
> Thy woods and templed hills;
> My heart with rapture thrills;
> Like that above.

This country is not only the choicest of all lands, but the preserver of true liberty, and the hope of civilized man!

However, a country may be ever so great and fruitful, yet a nation subsisting upon it be impotent and decadent. As Lyman Abbot has truly said:

> The greatness of a nation is measured not by its fruitful acres, but by the men who cultivate those acres; not by great forests, but by the men who use those forests; not by its mines, but by the men who work them.

God has made America beautiful; men must make and keep the nation great.

> And if it so be that they shall serve him according to the commandments which he hath given, it shall be a land of liberty unto them; wherefore, they shall never be brought down into captivity; for if iniquity shall abound cursed shall be the land for their sakes, but unto the righteous it shall be blessed forever. (2 Nephi 1:7.)

Chapter Fifty-eight

Free
Agency--
A Divine Gift

Remember, my brethren. . . .
ye are free; ye are permitted
to act for yourselves; for behold,
God hath given unto you a knowledge and he hath made you free.
(Book of Mormon)

NEXT to the bestowal of life
itself, the right to direct that life is God's greatest gift to
man. Among the immediate obligations and duties resting
upon members of the Church today, and one of the most
urgent and pressing for attention and action of all liberty-
loving people, is the preservation of individual liberty. Freedom of choice is more to be treasured than any possession
earth can give. It is inherent in the spirit of man. It is
a divine gift to every normal being. Whether born in abject
poverty, or shackled at birth by inherited riches, everyone
has this most precious of all life's endowments—the gift of
free agency; man's inherited and inalienable right.

Free agency is the impelling source of the soul's progress.
It is the purpose of the Lord that man become like him. In
order for man to achieve this it was necessary for the Creator
first to make him free. "Personal liberty," says Bulwer Lytton,
"is the paramount essential to human dignity and human
happiness."

The poet summarizes the value of this principle as follows:

> Know this, that every soul is free
> To choose his life and what he'll be,
> For this eternal truth is given
> That God will force no man to heaven.
>
> He'll call, persuade, direct aright—
> And bless with wisdom, love and light—
> In nameless ways be good and kind
> But never force the human mind.
>
> Freedom and reason make us men;
> Take these away, what are we then?
> Mere animals and just as well
> The beasts may think of heaven or hell.
> —William C. Gregg

Man Responsible For His Acts

With free agency there comes responsibility. If man is to be rewarded for righteousness and punished for evil, then common justice demands that he be given the power of independent action. A knowledge of good and evil is essential to man's progress on earth. If he were coerced to do right at all times, or were helplessly enticed to commit sin, he would merit neither a blessing for the first nor punishment for the second.

Wherefore, the Lord God gave unto man that he should act for himself. Wherefore, man could not act for himself save it should be that he was enticed by the one or the other.

. . . Wherefore men are free according to the flesh; and all things are given to them which are expedient unto man. And they are free to choose liberty and eternal life, through the great mediation of all men, or to choose captivity and death, according to the captivity and power of the devil; for he seeketh that all men might be miserable like unto himself. (2 Nephi 2:16, 27.)

Thus we see that man's responsibility is correspondingly operative with his free agency. Actions in harmony with divine law, and the laws of nature will bring happiness, and those in

371

opposition to divine truth, misery. Man is responsible not only for every deed, but for every idle word and thought. Said the Savior:

Every idle word that men shall speak, they shall give account thereof in the day of judgment. (Matt. 12:36.)

As a boy I questioned that truth when I first heard it expressed by my father. I remember saying to myself, "Not even the Lord knows what I am thinking now." I was very much surprised, therefore, when, later as a student in the university, I read the following in William James' psychology about the effect of thought and action on human character. I quote it for the young people particularly:

Spinning Our Own Fates

We are spinning our own fates good or evil, and never to be un- done. Every smallest stroke of virtue or of vice leaves its never so little scar. The drunken Rip Van Winkle, in Jefferson's play, excuses himself for every fresh dereliction by saying, "I won't count this time." Well! he may not count it, and a kind Heaven may not count it; but it is being counted none the less. Down among his nerve-cells and fibres the molecules are counting it, registering and storing it up to be used against him when the next temptation comes. Nothing we ever do is, in strict scientific literalness, wiped out. Of course this has its good side as well as its bad one. As we become permanent drunkards by so many separate drinks, so we become saints in the moral, and authorities and experts in the practical and scientific spheres, by so many separate acts and hours of work. Let no youth have any anxiety about the upshot of his education, whatever the line of it may be: If he keep faithfully busy each hour of the working day, he may safely leave the final result to itself. He can with perfect cer- tainty count on waking up some fine morning to find himself one of the competent ones of his generation, in whatever pursuit he may have singled out. Silently, between all the details of his business, the power of judging in all that class of matter will have built itself up within him as a possession that will never pass away. Young people should know this truth in advance. The ignorance of it has probably engen- dered more discouragement and faint-heartedness in youths embark- ing on arduous careers than all other causes put together.[1]

---

[1]William James, *Psychology* (Henry Hall & Co., N. Y., 1892) p. 150.

Responsibility Associated with Personal Influence

There is another responsibility correlated and even co-existent with free agency, which is too infrequently emphasized, and that is the effect not only of a person's actions, but of his thoughts upon others. Man radiates what he is, and that radiation affects to a greater or less degree every person who comes within that radiation.

Of the power of this personal influence William George Jordan impressively writes:

> Into the hands of every individal is given a marvelous power for good or evil—the silent, unconscious, unseen influence of his life. This is simply the constant radiation of what man really is, not what he pretends to be. Every man, by his mere living, is radiating sympathy, or sorrow, or morbidness, or cynicism, or happiness, or hope, or any of a hundred other qualities. Life is a state of constant radiation and absorption: to exist is to radiate; to exist is to be the recipient of radiation.

> Man cannot escape for one moment from this radiation of his character, this constantly weakening or strengthening of others. He cannot evade the responsibility by saying it is an unconscious influence. He can select the qualities that he will permit to be radiated. He can cultivate sweetness, calmness, trust, generosity, truth, justice, loyalty, nobility—make them vitally active in his character—and by these qualities he will constantly affect the world.

Freedom of Will Taught by Jesus

Freedom of the will and the responsibility associated with it are fundamental aspects of Jesus' teachings. Throughout his ministry he emphasized the worth of the individual, and exemplified what is now expressed in modern revelation as the work and glory of God—"To bring to pass the immortality and eternal life of man." Only through the divine gift of soul freedom is such progress possible.

Force of the Evil One

Force, on the other hand, emanates from Lucifer himself. Even in man's pre-existent state, Satan sought power to compel the human family to do his will by suggesting that the free agency of man be inoperative. If his plan had been accepted, human beings would have become mere puppets in the hands of a dictator, and the purpose of man's coming to earth would have been frustrated. Satan's proposed system of government, therefore, was rejected and the principle of free agency established in its place.

Force rules in the world today; consequently, our government must keep armies abroad, build navies and air squadrons, create atom bombs to protect itself from threatened aggression of a nation which seems to listen to no other appeal but compulsion.

Individual Freedom Threatened

Individual freedom is threatened by international rivalries, inter-racial animosities and false political ideals. Unwise legislation, too often prompted by political expediency, is periodically being enacted that seductively undermines man's right of free agency, robs him of his rightful liberties, and makes him but a cog in the crushing wheel of a regimentation, which, if persisted in, will end in dictatorship.

The Magna Charta, signed by King John at Runnymeade June 15, 1215, was an expression of freedom-loving men against a usurping king. It was a guarantee of civil and personal liberty. These guarantees later found fuller and more complete expression in the Constitution of the United States. Today, seven hundred years later, consider what is happening in Great Britain! With nationalization of industries, planned economy, control of all productive power, including persons and property, that country of liberty-loving people is on the verge of a totalitarian state as dictatorial as that which the feudal barons and the people wrested from King John. People are bargaining their liberty for a chimera of equality and security, not realizing that the more power you give the central government, the more you curtail your individual freedom.

Governments are the *servants*, not the *masters* of the people. All who love the Constitution of the United States can vow with Thomas Jefferson, who, when he was President, said:

I have sworn upon the altar of God eternal hostility against every form of tyranny over the mind of man. To preserve our independence, we must not let our rulers load us with perpetual debt. We must take our choice between economy and liberty, or profusion and servitude. If we run into such debts, we must be taxed in our meat and drink, in our necessities and in our comforts, in our labors and in our amusements.

If we can prevent the government from wasting the labors of the people under pretense of caring for them, they will be happy. The same prudence which in private life would forbid our paying our money for unexplained projects, forbids it in the disposition of public money. We are endeavoring to reduce the government to the practice of rigid economy to avoid burdening the people and arming the magistrate with a patronage of money which might be used to corrupt the principles of our government.

Leaders in our Government today would do well to follow this teaching and example of Thomas Jefferson.

Freedom of the Churches

This principle of free agency and the right of each individual to be free not only to think but to act within bounds that grant to everyone else the same privilege, are sometimes violated even by churches that claim to teach the doctrine of Jesus Christ. The attitude of any organization toward this principle of freedom is a pretty good index to its nearness to the teachings of Christ or to those of the evil one. For example, I read recently the statement of a leading clergyman who claimed the divine right of his church, wherever it was in power, to prohibit any other church from promulgating its doctrine. . . . And, "if religious minorities actually exist, they shall have only a defacto existence without opportunity to spread their beliefs."

He who thus tramples under foot one of God's greatest gifts to man, who would deny another the right to think and worship as he pleases, propagates error, and makes his own church in that regard as far as he represents it a propagator of evil.

Contrast this unchristian-like stand with the statement of the Prophet Joseph Smith:

We claim the privilege of worshiping Almighty God according to the dictates of our own conscience, and allow all men the same privilege, let them worship how, where, or what they may. (Eleventh Article of Faith.)

And, again, in one of the greatest revelations on government ever given, we read the following:

That the rights of the Priesthood are inseparably connected with the powers of heaven, and that the powers of heaven cannot be controlled nor handled only upon the principles of righteousness.

That they may be conferred upon us, it is true; but when we undertake to cover our sins, or to gratify our pride, our vain ambition, or to exercise control or dominion or compulsion upon the souls of the children of men, in any degree of unrighteousness, behold, the heavens withdraw themselves; the Spirit of the Lord is grieved; and when it is withdrawn, Amen to the priesthood or the authority of that man.

Influence By Persuasion

No power or influence can or ought to be maintained by virtue of the priesthood, only by persuasion, by long-suffering, by gentleness and meekness, and by love unfeigned;

By kindness, and pure knowledge; which shall greatly enlarge the soul without hypocrisy, and without guile—

Reproving betimes with sharpness, when moved upon by the Holy Ghost; and then showing forth afterwards an increase of love toward him whom thou hast reproved, lest he esteem thee to be his enemy;

That he may know that thy faithfulness is stronger than the cords of death.

Let thy bowels also be full of charity towards all men, and to the household of faith, and let virtue garnish thy thoughts unceasingly; then shall thy confidence wax strong in the presence of God; and the doctrine of the priesthood shall distill upon thy soul as the dews from heaven.

The Holy Ghost shall be thy constant companion, and thy scepter an unchanging scepter of righteousness and truth; and thy dominion shall be an everlasting dominion, and without compulsory means it shall flow unto thee forever and ever. (D.&C. 121:36-37; 41-46.)

If you can find more sublime thoughts anywhere in literature than expressed in that great revelation, please let me know where they are.

In conclusion, I repeat that *no greater immediate responsibility rests upon members of the Church, upon all citizens of this Republic and of neighboring Republics, than to protect the freedom vouchsafed by the Constitution of the United States.*

Let us by exercising our privileges under the Constitution—

(1) Preserve our right to worship God according to the dictates of our conscience,

(2) Preserve the right to work when and where we choose. No free man should be compelled to pay tribute in order to realize this God-given privilege. Read in the Doctrine and Covenants this statement:

It is not right that any man should be in bondage one to another. (D.&C. 101:79.)

(3) Feel free to plant and to reap without the handicap of bureaucratic interference.

(4) Devote our time, means, and life if necessary, to hold inviolate those laws which will secure to each individual the free exercise of conscience, the right and control of property, and the protection of life.

To sum up the whole question: In these days of uncertainty and unrest, liberty-loving people's greatest responsibility and paramount duty is to preserve and proclaim the freedom of the individual, his relationship to Deity, and the necessity of obedience to the principles of the gospel of

Jesus Christ—only thus will mankind find peace and happiness.

> If ye continue in my word, then are ye my disciples indeed:
> And ye shall know the truth and the truth shall make you free.
> (John 8:31-32.)

May God enlighten our minds to comprehend our responsibility, to proclaim the truth and maintain freedom throughout the world.

Chapter Fifty-nine

"Be of Good Courage and He Shall Strengthen Your Heart"

THE Creator, who gave man life, planted in his heart the seed of liberty. Free agency, as life, is a gift from God. "Do you wish to be free? Then above all things love God, love your neighbor, love one another, love the common weal; then you will have true liberty." (Savonarola.)

Knowing that they would be deprived of this inalienable right, untold thousands have fled East Germany during the past several years seeking freedom from the domination of Communism.

The Torch of Liberty

In contrast to the barbaric state-rule of the Communist, from which these peole have fled, I call your attention to the freedom-loving spirit of America. On Bedloe's Island in New York Harbor stands the Statue of Liberty—a gift of the French people to the American people. Israel Zangwill, in "The Melting Pot," gives the words spoken by David, the Russian emigrant Jew, as follows:

All my life America was waiting, beckoning, shining—the place where God would wipe away tears from off all faces. To think that the same great torch of Liberty which threw its light across all the seas and lands into my little garret in Russia is shining also for all those other weeping millions of Europe, shining wherever men hunger and are oppressed. . . , when I look at our Statue of Liberty, I just seem to hear the voice of America crying: "Come unto me, all ye who are weary and heavy laden, and I will give you rest."

There is a significant reference in the Apocalypse to a "war in heaven." (See Rev. 12:7.) It is not only significant, but also seemingly contradictory, for we think of heaven as a celestial abode of bliss, an impossible condition where war and contention could exist. The passage is significant, inasmuch as it sets forth the fact that there is freedom of choice and of action in the spirit world. This contention in heaven arose over the desire of Satan ". . . to destroy the agency of man, which I, the Lord God, had given him. . . ." (Moses 4:3.)

Freedom of thought, freedom of speech, freedom of action within boundaries that do not infringe upon the liberty of others are man's inherent right, granted him by his Creator— divine gifts essential to human dignity.

"Therefore, cheer up your hearts," admonished an ancient prophet in the Book of Mormon, "and remember that ye are free to act for yourselves. . . ." (2 Nephi 10:23.)

Abraham Lincoln said:

This love of liberty which God has planted in us constitutes the bulwark of our liberty and independence. It is not our frowning battlements, our bristling seacoasts, our army, and our navy. Our defense is in the spirit which prizes liberty as the heritage of all men, in all lands, everywhere. Destroy this spirit, and we have planted the seed of despotism at our very doors.

The Rights of Men

The opposite of freedom is bondage, servility, restraint— conditions that inhibit mentality, stifle the spirit, and crush manhood. To coerce, to compel, to bring into servitude is Satan's plan for the human family.

Throughout the history of the world man has contended even to death to free himself from bondage and usurpation, or to retain the freedom he already possessed. This is particu-

380

larly true in regard to the right to worship. Attempts to control the consciences of men have always resulted in conflict. To decide one's own relationship to the Creator and to his creations is the natural and inalienable right of all.

Equally fundamental and important to man's happiness and progress is the right of personal security, the right of personal liberty, the right of private property. The right of personal security consists in the enjoyment of life, limbs, body, health, and reputation. Life, being the immediate gift of God, is a right inherent by nature in every individual. Likewise, man has a natural inherent right to his limbs. His personal liberty consists in the right of changing his situation or habitation according to will. The right of property consists in the free use, enjoyment, and disposal of all acquisitions, without control or diminution save by the laws of the land. The right of private property is sacred and inviolable. If any part of these inalienable individual possessions should be required by the state, it should be given only with the consent of the people.

Christianity's Ultimate Purpose

The ultimate purpose of Christianity in the world is to develop an honorable, upright individual in an ideal society known as the Kingdom of God.

Nearly two thousand years have passed, and the world is still a long way from the realization of either achievement. Indeed, today Christianity itself, and its handmaiden, Democracy, are on trial before the world tribunal. Conditions in this war-torn world seem to bear witness that men are forever learning, but never coming to a knowledge of the truth.

True Christianity, as expressed in the divine law, " . . . love the Lord thy God with all thy heart, and with all thy soul, and with all thy mind . . . and . . . thy neighbour as thyself" (Matt. 22:37, 39), has never yet been accepted and practiced by the nations of the world, yet the spirit of

381

Christ has, like leaven in the lump, been influencing society toward the realization of freedom, justice, and better harmony in human relations.

In the world today, however, the spirit of paganism has again asserted itself and seems to be all but triumphant in its effort to overthrow the few Christian ideals that civilized peoples have absorbed.

If our Western civilization emerges from existing situations safely, it will be only through a deeper appreciation of the social ethics of Jesus than it has yet shown. And our danger is increased rather than diminished by the fancied security in which our masses live.

Merely an appreciation of the social ethics of Jesus, however, is not sufficient. Men's hearts must be changed. Instead of selfishness, men must be willing to dedicate their ability, their possessions—if necessary, their lives, their fortunes, and their sacred honor—for the alleviation of the ills of mankind. Hate must be supplanted by sympathy and forbearance. *Force and compulsion will never establish the ideal society. This can come only by a transformation within the individual soul—a life brought into harmony with the divine will. We must be "born again."*

Nuclear War Hovering

Today, as we see hovering over the nations of the earth the ever-darkening clouds of nuclear war, we are prone to think that righteousness among man is waning. In our own beloved country, "a land choice above all other lands," we are grieved and shocked when the Supreme Court renders a decision ruling that it is unconstitutional for the Federal Government or any state to require "a belief in the existence of God" as a qualification for public office; also, we experience apprehension when we know that enemies to our republican form of government are becoming more blatant; when we see political demagogues seemingly more successful, drunkenness and immorality flauntingly defiant—seeing these conditions we wonder whether mankind is growing better or worse. In private life, disappointments, adversity, sickness, and sorrow make us discouraged and sometimes despondent.

Still I am confident that truth will yet prevail, and in that confidence say with the Psalmist: "Be of good courage, and he shall strengthen your heart, all ye that hope in the Lord." (Psalm 31:24.)

We may take courage in what I believe is a fact, that in the hearts of more millions of honest men and women than ever before war is abhorrent. War has lost its false glamour and boasted glory. Such an attitude at least keeps alive our hope for the dawning of that day when "nation shall not lift up sword against nation, neither shall they learn war any more." (Isaiah 2:4.)

How utterly foolish men are to quarrel, fight, and cause misery, destruction, and death when the gifts of a divine and loving Father are all around us for the asking—are already in our possession if we would but recognize them.

Accept Jesus as the Redeemer of the World

The peace and happiness of mankind lie in the acceptance of Jesus Christ as the Redeemer of the world, our Saviour. The principles of the restored gospel as revealed to the Prophet Joseph Smith are the surest, safest guide to mortal man. Christ is the light to humanity. In that light man sees his way clearly. When it is rejected, the soul of man stumbles in darkness. No person, no group, no nation can achieve true success without following him who said: "I am the light of the world: he that followeth me shall not walk in darkness, but shall have the light of life." (John 8:12.)

It is a sad thing when individuals and nations extinguish that light—when Christ and his gospel are supplanted by the law of the jungle and the strength of the sword. The chief tragedy in the world at the present time is its disbelief in God's goodness, and its lack of faith in the teachings and doctrines of the gospel.

Life Is Beautiful to Believers

To all who believe in a living, personal God and his divine truth, life can be so delightful and beautiful. As a matter of fact, it is glorious just to be alive. Joy, even ecstasy, can be experienced in the consciousness of existence. There is supreme satisfaction in sensing one's individual entity and in realizing that that entity is part of God's great creative plan. There are none so poor, none so rich, sick, or maimed who may not be conscious of this relationship.

I know that for not a few of us the true joy of living is overcast by trials, failures, worries, and perplexities incident to making a living and attempting to achieve success. Tear-bedimmed eyes are often blind to the beauties that surround us. Life sometimes seems a parched and barren desert, when, as a matter of fact, there is comfort, even happiness within our grasp if we could or would but reach for it.

The Lord has given us life, and with it free agency; and eternal life is his greatest gift to man.

Be true and loyal to the restored gospel of Jesus Christ. "Be of good courage, and he shall strengthen your heart, all ye that hope in the Lord."

Chapter Sixty

Only Man
Is Free
To Choose

"FREEDOM of choice is probably the most audacious experiment in creation—man's endowment with freedom of choice. No other creature on earth has such freedom. Everything else in the universe, animate or inanimate, follows a pattern to which it is bound and from which it cannot escape. Only man is free to control himself or run uncontrolled, to pray or to curse, to become a saint or a sinner.

"As we regard ourselves in this light, the conviction dawns that God in us is aiming at the production of superior beings, creatures of such high order that we may be both worthy and capable of cooperation with God in the unfinished work of creation."[1]

For, as the Apostle Paul says:

For the earnest expectation of the creature waiteth for the manifestation of the sons of God. For the creature was made subject to vanity, not willingly, but by reason of him who hath subjected the same in hope. Because the creature itself also shall be delivered from the bondage of corruption into the glorious liberty of the children of God. (Romans 8:19-21.)

There are four fundamental institutions that contribute

---
[1]From *The Freeman*, July, 1962.

to our success and happiness: first, *the home;* second, *the Church;* third, *the school;* fourth, *the government.*

In the home we give our children their physical life, but we should also give them their spiritual enlightenment. Home training should be supplemented by the Church; and besides that supplementary teaching, the Church should instill faith in the hearts of the children who come from those homes. That is the duty of the Church. That is why we build church edifices—the only reason. In blessing those children, we give glory to God. That is the only way we can honor him. Oh, I know we can kneel down and, in words, praise the Lord, but his work and his glory is "to bring to pass the immortality and eternal life of man."

The third factor is the school, the duty of which is to instill in children patriotism and loyalty to the government and society. I think the real purpose of the school is to develop character! Educators say it is to teach the three "R's," science, social science, etc. That is why schools are maintained; but the main purpose (and I wish it were instilled in the heart of every teacher throughout this great country) is to develop character, loyalty to God, to the government; loyalty to the home, and loyalty to the individual himself. "Character is higher than intellect. . . . A great soul will be fit to live as well as to think." (Emerson.)

Fourth is the government, the duty of which is to protect these other three in the fulfillment of their mission, not to dictate, but to protect and guide. The value or mission of our government is to give freedom to these other institutions and to the individual.

On one occasion Jesus said to those Jews who believed in him:

. . . If ye continue in my word, then are ye my disciples indeed; and ye shall know the truth, and the truth shall make you free. (John 8:31-32.)

You will note that Jesus at that time spoke to those who

believed in him; and yet in the following paragraph in the Bible, we find someone in the group who challenged him, saying:

. . . We be Abraham's seed, and were never in bondage to any man: how sayest thou, Ye shall be made free?

Jesus answered them, Verily, verily, I say unto you, Whosoever committeth sin is the servant of sin. And the servant abideth not in the house for ever: but the Son abideth ever. If the Son therefore shall make you free, ye shall be free indeed. (John 8:33-36.)

In the Doctrine and Covenants, the Lord comments on this subject in these words—on the same theme, pertaining to the Constitution of the United States of America:

And that law of the land which is constitutional, supporting that principle of freedom in maintaining rights and privileges, belongs to all mankind, and is justifiable before me. Therefore, I, the Lord, justify you, and your brethren of my church, in befriending that law which is the constitutional law of the land.

I, the Lord God, make you free, therefore ye are free indeed; and the law also maketh you free. Nevertheless, when the wicked rule the people mourn. (D.&C. 98:5-6, 8-9.)

Most Precious Possession

Freedom is the most precious possession of life, next to life itself. All human beings crave it, even dictators, for themselves. Today there are two contending forces battling for the souls of men, battling for their minds, struggling for their support and adherence.

Here in the United States we have a guarantee of liberty, part of which is contained in Article One of the Bill of Rights. Note it:

Congress shall make no law respecting an establishment of religion, or prohibiting the free exercise thereof; or abridging the freedom of speech, or the press; or the right of the people peaceably to assemble, and to petition the government for a redress of grievances.

We should be grateful for our Founding Fathers, for Washington and Lincoln, and for our boys and other great men who have fought and died for our freedom. We should feel grateful that we are not hampered nor hindered in any way by a government that would presume to tell us how to worship, what to worship, or how to build. I wonder how many of us kneel down and thank the Lord for that freedom vouch-safed to us by the Constitution of the United States, a step towards the liberty, the freedom mentioned by the Savior when he said, "If ye continue in my word . . . ye shall know the truth, and the truth shall make you free."

Very seldom do we think of our God-given privileges to exercise the freedom which dates back to the Constitution, even to the Declaration of Independence.

Most Wonderful Work

William E. Gladstone, having read the Constitution one hundred years after it had been in force, said:

> The American Constitution is, so far as I can see, the most wonderful work ever struck off at a given time by the brain and purpose of men. It has had a century of trial, under the pressure of exigencies caused by an expansion unexampled in point of rapidity and range; and its exemption from formal change, though not entire, has certainly proved the sagacity of the constructors and the stubborn strength of the fabric.

To the average American, says one writer, "there are certain principles of government, which, until quite recently, were generally accepted without question. These include the proposition that the people are sovereign, that the government and its administrators are servants of the people, and not their masters; that the government can exercise no powers except those expressly conferred upon it by the Constitution, and that the rights of an individual are greater than the demands of a thousand who would deprive him of any basic right. These words should have the deepest meaning for every man, woman, and child in this land. To all American citizens who seek their benefits for themselves, these words must be recognized as a solemn obligation from which there can be no relief. The government, I say, must protect citizens in the pursuit of their lawful industry. It must see that none takes by force from them the property that they own, and do everything else that is necessary to preserve the welfare of all its citizens, great and small."

Are We Grateful?

Do we feel to thank God for the freedom we have here in this country? The government should protect the individual and his property. There are many people in the world today who are denied these privileges. Here in the United States we have the promise of life, liberty, and the pursuit of happiness, and the protection of the government in our individual affairs. We should guard these freedoms with our lives if necessary. Members of the Church should keep in mind what Jesus said to those Jews who believed in him: "If ye follow me (that is, continue in my word), ye shall know the truth, and the truth shall make you free."

Choose You This Day

Associated with this is the great principle of choice. Joshua addressed the people who were entering the promised land: ". . . Choose you this day whom ye will serve . . . but as for me and my house, we will serve the Lord." (Joshua 24:15.) That was said approximately 3,500 years ago.

There is one living thing in the world today that was alive at that time—a mighty, magnificent tree in Yosemite Park, California. It is gnarled and aged and bears the marks of a mighty struggle with the ravages of time. As Sister McKay and I stood and looked at it several years ago, I took my hat off reverently. That old thing was a sapling when the pyramids were built. It is alive today, and its worst enemy is man, from whom it is guarded and fenced. Every other living thing—vegetable and animal—has crumbled to dust, but the principle enunciated by the leader Joshua stands unchanged, unmodified, as active and potent in man's life to-

389

day as it was 40 centuries ago—it is the divine privilege, the mighty responsibility of making a choice—"Choose you this day whom ye will serve!" Associated with that in the Bible is another passage,

> . . . Be strong and of a good courage; be not afraid, neither be thou dismayed; for the Lord thy God is with thee withersoever thou goest. (Joshua 1:9.)

Strength and courage are virtues essential to success in all ages. Neither time nor eternity can limit or modify their effectiveness. The right to make a choice is God-given, just as is free agency. Once the choice is made, strength and courage are required to keep it.

The promised land is before us. We, too, must choose, as Joshua told the children of Israel; and if we would be free and happy in the home, in the Church, in school, and in the government, we should choose the way of Christ. His is a simple plan, glorious and divine; and the base of it is the foundation we find in the two principles—freedom to think and choose, and to act without restraint or dictation from government or any group, so long as we do not deprive another of that same privilege.

Jesus said to those of the Twelve, "If ye continue in my word . . . ye shall know the truth, and the truth shall make you free." The gospel of Jesus Christ is the perfect law of freedom. We do not wish to supplant any government, but we wish to have this truth in our homes, in our hearts; and it should be taught to our children as the best and most glorious thing in all the world. I know it is! We should ever keep the gospel of Jesus Christ sacred in our hearts.

Chapter Sixty-one

All Nations and All Peoples Should "Acknowledge the Providence of God"

E<small>VERY</small> person radiates to a great degree what he is; indeed, to live is to radiate. To a certain degree so does an important building. Every home, for example, has a particular radiation—a peculiar something created by those who live in it. So does every church, particularly every famous edifice. For example, call to mind the great pyramid of Khufu, which connotes the efforts of millions of persons building a tomb for a great king. Again, when the Taj Mahal is mentioned we have an entirely different connotation—we think of the most beautiful monument in the world to love. When we think of the 365 mosques in Cairo, we have a different connotation—each mosque standing for the peculiar worship of the Mohammedans and calling to mind the thousands going for their ablutions at midday.

Our temples and Church edifices should forever radiate the truth expressed by Peter on a very important occasion when he faced those who had arrested him: ". . . For there is none other name under heaven given among men, whereby we must be saved." (Acts 4:12.) That message is the sacrifice, the life, the resurrection, of our beloved Savior and the gospel which he gave.

In December, 1945, when the United Nations was being organized, Senator Henry Cabot Lodge, Jr., United States

Ambassador to the United Nations, in a letter to all delegations composing that body suggested that—"God should be openly and audibly invoked at the United Nations in accordance with any one of the religious faiths which are represented there."

That suggestion said, in effect: "As we sit here as the chosen representatives of sixty nations with the avowed purpose of establishing and of maintaining peace in the world, let us acknowledge the existence of a Supreme Being, and invoke his divine guidance as we seek the noblest accomplishment of all times—peace on earth, good will among men."

Just after that resolution was introduced in the United Nations, January 31, 1946, Russia formally announced its rejection of the United States' proposal, saying: "Due regard is given to the lofty motives" which inspire Senator Lodge, but "Russia considers that such a proposal is unnecessary," ignoring the scriptural admonition:

> . . . Thou shalt remember the Lord thy God; for it is he that giveth thee power to get wealth, that he may establish his covenant. . . .
> And it shall be, if thou do at all forget the Lord thy God, and walk after other gods, and serve them, and worship them, I testify against you this day that ye shall surely perish. Deut. 8:18-19.)

America Founded on Faith In God

In the first proclamation of a Thanksgiving day in this country, signed by George Washington on October 3, 1789, the element of divine faith is emphasized. In that proclamation Washington said:

> Whereas it is the duty of all nations to acknowledge the providence of Almighty God, to obey his will, to be grateful for his benefits, and humbly to implore his protection, aid and favor: And whereas both Houses of Congress have, by their joint Committee, requested me "to recommend to the people of the United States a day of public thanksgiving and prayer to be observed by acknowledging with grateful hearts the many and signal favors of Almighty God, especially by affording them an opportunity peaceably to establish a form of gov-

ernment for their safety and happiness"; Now, therefore, I do recommend and assign Thursday, the 26th day of November next, to be devoted by the people of these States to the service of that great and glorious Being, who is the Beneficent Author of all the good that was, that is, or that will be; that we may then all unite in rendering unto him our sincere and humble thanks for his kind care and protection of the people of this country. . . .[1]

Our government was founded on faith in a Supreme Being as evidenced by the Mayflower Compact, the Declaration of Independence, by George Washington and Benjamin Franklin in the Constitutional Convention, and by a hundred other incidents prior to, during, and following the birth of this Republic. Said the Father of our country: "We have raised a standard to which the good and wise can repair; the event is in the hands of God."

Constitutional Convention Invokes Prayer

Benjamin Franklin, recognizing the apparent inability of the Convention to solve the perplexing problems confronting it, stated his faith in an overruling Providence, and his assurance that God will answer prayers, as follows:

I have lived a long time, and the longer I live the more convincing proof I see of this truth: that God governs in the affairs of men, and if a sparrow cannot fall to the ground without His notice, is it probable that an empire can rise without His aid?

We have been assured, Sir, in the sacred writings, that "except the Lord build the house, they labour in vain that build it." I firmly believe this, and I also believe that without His concurring aid we shall succeed in this political building no better than the builders of Babel. We shall be divided by our little partial, local interests; our projects will be confounded, and we ourselves shall become a byword down to future ages. And, what is worse, mankind may hereafter, from this unfortunate instance, despair of establishing governments by human wisdom, and leave it to change, war, and conquest.

I, therefore, beg leave to move that henceforth prayers imploring the assistance of heaven, and its blessing on our deliberations, be held in this assembly every morning before we proceed to business,

---

[1]James D. Richardson, *Compilation of the Messages and Papers of the Presidents,* Vol. 1 (Bureau of National Literature, 1896, Washington, D. C.) p. 56.

and that one or more of the clergy of this city be requested to officiate in that service.[2]

Lincoln Relied on Providence

Abraham Lincoln, the greatest Emancipator, was born on February 12, 1809. This is how he felt about reliance on God—the great war of the rebellion was on: "My faith is greater than yours," Lincoln once said to ex-Senator James F. Wilson of Iowa and others; "I not only believe that Providence is not unmindful of the struggle in which this nation is engaged, that if we do not do right, God, will let us go our own way to ruin; and that if we do right, he will lead us safely out of this wilderness, crown our arms with victory and restore our disservered Union, as you have expressed your belief; *but I also believe he will compel us to do right, in order that he may do these things, not so much because we desire them as that they accord with his plans of dealing with this nation, in the midst of which he means to establish justice. I think that he means that we shall do more than we have yet done in the furtherance of his plans and he will open the way for our doing it. I have felt his hand upon me in great trials and submitted to his guidance, and I trust that as he shall farther open the way, I will be ready to walk therein, relying on his help and trusting in his goodness and wisdom.*"[3]

You see now what I have in mind when I say that our houses of worship should stand as a testimony of the reality of our Father in heaven and the divine mission of his Only Begotten who rendered sacrifice for us, and gave the plan of salvation by obedience to which the children of our Father may come back into his presence.

Hans Christian Anderson said: "Time is so fleeting that if we do not remember God in our youth, age may find us incapable of thinking about him."

---

[2]Nannie McCormick Coleman, *The Constitution and Its Framers*, p. 338.

[3]John Wesley Hill, *Abraham Lincoln, Man of God* (G. P. Putnam's Sons, 4th Edition, New York, N. Y., 1927) p. 129.

We cannot be too diligent in God's service if we consider that time is precious, short, passing, uncertain, irrevocable when gone, and that for which we must be responsible.

None Other Name

The message of every converted member of this Church is: ". . . There is none other name under heaven given among men, whereby we must be saved." (Acts 4:12.)

There are skeptics who say we have had nearly two thousands years of Christianity and it has brought us only hatreds, wars, man's inhumanity to man, manifested in thousands of ways. My answer to that is, Christianity has never yet been fully tried. What is really essential is faith in him as a divine being, as our Lord and Savior. It is such faith as the Apostle Peter had when he declared: ". . . Thou art the Christ, the Son of the living God." (Matt. 16:16.) It is such faith as that borne by Paul as he stood a prisoner before Agrippa. It is such faith that enabled the doubting Thomas to say: "My Lord and my God." (John 20:28.) It is that unwavering faith which brought forth that glorious vision of the Prophet Joseph Smith as follows:

And now, after the many testimonies which have been given of him, this is the testimony, last of all, which we give of him: That he lives!

For we saw him, even on the right hand of God; and we heard the voice bearing record that he is the Only Begotten of the Father—

That by him, and through him, and of him, the worlds are and were created, and the inhabitants thereof are begotten sons and daughters unto God. (D.&C. 76:22-24.)

Those who have such faith in their hearts accept him as the way, the truth and the light.

Chapter Sixty-two

The Cause
of
Human Liberty

MAN'S greatest endowment in mortal life is the power of choice—the divine gift of free agency. No true character was ever developed without a sense of soul freedom. If a man feels circumscribed, harassed, or enslaved by something or somebody, he is shackled. That is one fundamental reason why any 'ism" or system of government that would enslave or take away man's right to choose must be defeated. God intends man to be free. Among the immediate obligations and duties resting upon members of the Church, and one of the most urgent and pressing for attention and action of all liberty-loving people, is the preservation of individual liberty. Freedom of choice is more to be treasured than any possession earth can give. It is inherent in the spirit of man. It is a divine gift to every normal being. Whether born in abject poverty or shackled at birth by inherited riches, everyone has this most precious of all life's endowments—the gift of free agency, man's inherited and inalienable right. It is the impelling source of the soul's progress. The Lord has told us:

Behold, here is the agency of man, and here is the condemnation of man; because that which was from the beginning is plainly manifest unto them, and they receive not the light. (D.&C. 93:31.)

The documents and statements of our great statesmen who had to do with the founding of this nation show the reliance and firm faith they placed in God.

The Church has always maintained that the Constitution is a sacred document. The Lord revealed to the Prophet Joseph Smith:

Therefore, it is not right that any man should be in bondage one to another.

And for this purpose have I established the Constitution of this land, by the hands of wise men whom I raised up unto this very purpose, and redeemed the land by the shedding of blood. (D.&C. 101:79-80.)

On one occasion the Prophet proclaimed:

. . . The Constitution of the United States is a glorious standard; it is founded in the wisdom of God. It is a heavenly banner; it is to all those who are privileged with the sweets of its liberty, like the cooling shades and refreshing waters of a great rock in a thirsty and weary land. It is like a great tree under whose branches men from every clime can be shielded from the burning rays of the sun.[1]

And then, in the dedicatory prayer of the Kirtland Temple, the Prophet said:

Have mercy, O Lord, upon all the nations of the earth; have mercy upon the rulers of our land; may those principles, which were so honorably and nobly defended, namely, the Constitution of our land, by our fathers, be established forever. (D.&C. 109:54.)

There exists an eternal law that each human soul shall shape its own destiny. No one individual can make happiness or salvation for another. It has been said that "even God could not make men like himself without making them free."

Men may choose the right or they may choose the wrong; they may walk in darkness or they may walk in the light; and, mind you, God has not left his children without the light. He has given them in the various dispensations of the world the light of the gospel wherein they could walk and

---

[1]*DHC*, Vol. 3, p. 304.

not stumble; wherein they could find that peace and happiness which, as a loving Father, he desires his children should enjoy. But the Lord does not take from them their free agency.

The Prophet Lehi, in speaking to his son, Jacob, bears testimony to that truth in unmistakable terms. He says:

Wherefore, the Lord God gave unto man that he should act for himself. Wherefore, man could not act for himself save it should be that he was enticed by one or the other. (2 Nephi 2:16.)

Wherefore, men are free according to the flesh; and all things are given unto them which are expedient unto man. And they are free to choose liberty and eternal life, through the great mediation of all men, or to choose captivity and death, according to the captivity and power of the devil; for he seeketh that all men might be miserable like unto himself. (2 Nephi 2:27.)

I do not know that there was ever a time in the history of mankind when the evil one seemed so determined to strike at this fundamental virtue of free agency. But thank heaven, there is innate in man a feeling that will rebel against tyranny. It has been manifested by liberty-loving men throughout the ages.

With free agency there comes responsibility. If a man is to be rewarded for righteousness and punished for evil, then common justice demands that he be given the power of independent action. A knowledge of good and evil is essential to man's progress on earth. If he were coerced to do right at all times, or were helplessly enticed to commit sin, he would merit neither a blessing for the first nor punishment for the second. Thus we see that man's responsibility is correspondingly operative with his free agency. Freedom of the will and the responsibility associated with it are fundamental aspects of Jesus' teachings. Throughout his ministry he emphasized the worth of the individual and exemplified what is now expressed in modern revelation as the work and glory of God. Only through the divine gift of soul freedom is such progress possible.

We believe that governments were instituted of God for the benefit of man; and that he holds men accountable for their acts in relation to them, both in making laws and administering them, for the good and safety of society. (D.&C. 134:1.)

Conditions existing in our beloved country gave cause for real apprehension. David Lawrence, commentator, said in an editorial:

Is our written Constitution being abolished? . . . The present trend in the United States is apparently in the direction of an arbitrary use of power by the executive, legislative and judicial branches of the Federal Government in disregard of the provisions of the Constitution which have for 179 years been the law of the land.[2]

Just the other day I picked up one of our Church publications[3] and read a summary statement commenting upon the weakening of the moral strength and spiritual power of America, part of which I quote:

What has happened to our national morals?

An educator speaks out in favor of free love.

A man of God condones sexual excursions by unmarried adults.

Movies sell sex as a commercial commodity.

Book stores and cigar stands peddle pornography.

A high court labels yesterday's smut as today's literature. . . .

TV shows and TV commercials pour out a flood of sick, sadistic, and suggestive sex situations. . . .

Birth control counsel is urged for high school girls.

Look around you. These things are happening in your America. In the two decades since the end of World War II we have seen our national standards of morality lowered again and again. . . .

And—we have harvested a whirlwind. As our standards have lowered, our crime levels and social problems have increased.

Today, we have a higher percentage of our youth in jail . . . in reformatories . . . on probation and in trouble than ever before.

Study the statistics on illegitimate births . . . and broken marriages . . . on juvenile crimes . . . on school drop-outs . . . on sex deviation . . . on dope addiction . . . on high school marriages . . . and crimes of passion.

The figures are higher than ever. And going higher. . . .

---

[2]Copyrighted *U. S. News and World Report,* March 21, 1966, p. 119.

Our youngsters are no better and no worse than we were at the same age. Generally, they are wiser. But—they have more temptations than we had. They have more opportunities for getting into trouble.

We opened doors for them that were denied to us. We encouraged permissiveness. We indulged them. We granted maximum freedoms. And we asked for a minimum in respect . . . and in responsibility.

Rules and regulations that prevailed for generations as sane and sensible guides for personal conduct were reduced or removed. Or ignored.

Prayer was banned from the schoolroom and the traditional school books that taught moral precepts as well as reading were replaced with the inane banalities of "Dick and Jane."

No longer are our children encouraged to take pride in our nation's great and glorious past.

Heroes are down-graded. The role played by the United States in raising the hearts and hopes of all enslaved peoples for a century and a half is minimized. . . .[3]

Another editorial recently appearing in the *Church News* section of the *Deseret News* states:

Recent months have cast a shadow of gloom and despair over some parts of the United States as wholesale lawlessness has erupted into riots and mobbings.

It has reached a point in some cities where peace-loving people no longer feel safe on the streets, in public parks, or even on school grounds.

Some of the most regrettable blotches on the American scene have occurred among students at our public schools and colleges. . . .

Many students have felt because of a growing sense of mistaken freedom, that they must be against something or everything and that the best way to express this attitude is to join riots or strikes or indulge in their own peculiar brand of "sanctions." . . .

Ask many of these students why they participated in riots, and they frankly admit they do not know. "Everyone is doing it" is their most logical response. Is there any intelligence in that?

Too often it is to become part of the crowd, so they think. But frequently these so-called "crowds" are gangs led and inspired by

---

[3]Quoted in the *Deseret News*, February 26, 1966, p. 10-A; from the *San Francisco Examiner*, January 18, 1965, p. 32. Used by permission.

foreign elements trying to overthrow our government. Yet, many
follow them, thoughtlessly and foolishly, much to their subsequent
regret.

No one has the right to destroy another's property. No one has
a right to assault another individual.

Resorting to violence is the way of the jungle, not the path of
civilized and supposedly cultured persons.[4]

It is the insidious influences, as well as the blatant
heralding of ideas, that undermine century-tried principles
of peace, of justice, and of advancement toward the day of
universal brotherhood. We are grieved when we see or hear
men and women, some of whom even profess membership in
the Church, looking with favor upon the pernicious teachings of these groups, especially communism, which would
undermine our very way of life. These credulous, misguided
persons claim to be advocates of peace and accuse those
who oppose them as advocates of war. They should remember that all of us should ever keep in mind that there are
some eternal principles more precious than peace, dearer than
life itself.

Our revolutionary fathers sensed this, and their innermost
feelings were expressed in the words of Patrick Henry: "Is
life so dear, or peace so sweet, as to be purchased at the price
of chains and slavery?" There are in our midst influences,
the avowed object of which is to sow discord and contention among men with the view of undermining, weakening,
if not entirely destroying our constitutional form of government. Disintegration from within is often more dangerous
and more fatal than outward opposition.

Abraham Lincoln spoke for all who love their country
when he said:

Let every American, every lover of liberty, every well-wisher of
his prosperity, swear by the blood of the Revolution never to violate
in the least particular the laws of the country, *and never to tolerate
their violation by others.* As the patriots of Seventy-six did to the

---

[4]*Church News,* October 29, 1966.

support of the Declaration of Independence, so to the support of the Constitution and laws let every American pledge his life, his property, and his sacred honor. Let every man remember that to violate the law is to trample on the blood of his fathers and to tear the charter of his own and his children's liberty. Let reverence for the laws be breathed by every American mother to the lisping babe that prattles on her lap; let it be taught in schools, in seminaries, and in colleges; let it be written in primers, spelling books, and almanacs; let it be preached from pulpit, proclaimed in the legislative halls, and enforced in courts of justice. In short, let it become the political religion of the nation.[5]

Do not let the advocates of communism mislead you in their attempt to denounce capitalism. Fundamental in the belief and promulgation of communism is the denial of the existence of God, and the desire to substitute for this belief, confidence in the state. The state is not an organization to suppress people. The state should have no power but that which the people give it; and when the state becomes a director, a controller of the individual, it becomes despotism; and human nature has fought that since man was created, and man will continue to fight that false ideal.

President Woodrow Wilson's last written statement carried a warning to America and her people:

The sum of the whole matter is this, that our civilization cannot survive materially unless it be redeemed spiritually. It can be saved only by becoming permeated with the spirit of Christ and being made free and happy by the practices which spring out of that spirit. . . .[6]

The founders of this great Republic had faith in the economic and political welfare of this country because they had faith in God. Today it is not uncommon to note an apologetic attitude on the part of men when they refer to the need of God's governing in the affairs of men. Indeed, as I have already pointed out, success of communism depends

---

[5]Cited in Daniel L. Marsh, *The American Canon* (New York: Abingdon-Cokesbury Press, 1939) p. 78. Used by permission.
[6]Daniel L. Marsh, *The American Canon*, p. 83.

largely upon the substitution of belief in God by belief in the supremacy of the state.

But I say to you, preach in season and out of season belief in God the Eternal Father, in his Son Jesus Christ, and in the Holy Ghost. Proclaim that fundamental in this gospel plan is the sacredness of the individual; that God's work and glory is "to bring to pass the immortality and eternal life of man." (Moses 1:39.)

Jesus The Christ

7

Chapter Sixty-three

Christ:
The One
Perfect Guide

TRULY, the time has come, as perhaps never before, when men and women should counsel together and in wisdom determine how the world may be made a better place in which to live.

To achieve this desired end, the first and most important step is to choose as a leader one whose leadership is infallible, whose teachings when practiced have never failed. In the present tempestuous sea of uncertainty, the pilot must be one who through the storm can see the beacon in the harbor of peace.

The Church of Jesus Christ of Latter-day Saints proclaims that there is but one such guiding hand in the universe, but one unfailing light, and that is the light of Christ who said:

. . . I am come that they might have life, and that they might have it more abundantly. (John 10:10.)

An active, sincere faith in the basic teachings of Jesus of Nazareth is the greatest need of the world. Because many reject this truth, there is all the more reason why sincere believers should proclaim it.

A Promise and a Fact

The ultimate purpose of Christianity is to develop honorable, upright individuals in an ideal society known as the kingdom of God. No one, not even the unbeliever, can gainsay this as a most worthy goal. True, nearly two thousand years of trial have failed to bring about even an approach to the realization of either the perfecting of the individual or the establishing of an ideal society. Christianity, as summarized in the divine admonition, "Love the Lord thy God . . . and thy neighbour as thyself," has never yet really been accepted and practiced by the nations of the world. (See Luke 10:27.)

As the first essential to a better world, we declare with the Apostle Peter that ". . . there is none other name under heaven given among men, whereby we must be saved." (Acts 4:12.)

On one of the most solemn occasions of his entire ministry, Jesus said to his chosen Twelve:

> These things I have spoken unto you, that in me ye might have peace. In the world ye shall have tribulation; but be of good cheer; I have overcome the world. (John 16:33.)

These significant words contain both a promise and a statement of fact. The promise: *If men will hearken to his words they will find peace.* The fact: *In the world there is tribulation.* There is also an implication that each is dependent upon the attitude and actions of men themselves.

He came to redeem the world from sin. He came with love in his heart for every individual, with redemption and possibility for regeneration for all. By choosing him as our ideal, we create within ourselves a desire to be like him, to have fellowship with him. We perceive life as it should be and as it may be.

The Individual Is Supreme

Jesus always sought the welfare of the individual, and individuals grouped and laboring for the welfare of the whole in conformity with the principles of the Gospel constitute the kingdom of God. Jesus' regard for personality was supreme. "The ideal social state, which he described as the kingdom of God, is a commonwealth in which all men are united and governed by a commanding love both for God and for their neighbors."

The goal that Jesus Christ always set before his followers was the emancipation of men and women from greed, from anger, from jealousy, from hatred, from fear; and in their place he hoped to bring about a complete and normal development of the individual's divine powers through right thinking and unselfish, efficient service.

Peter, the chief apostle, the indefatigable Paul, the Prophet Joseph Smith, and other true followers of the Risen Lord recognized in him the Savior of the individual, for did he not say, "For behold, this is my work and my glory—to bring to pass the immortality and eternal life of man"? (Moses 1:39.)

A Glorious Relationship

Each one of us is the architect of his own fate, and he is unfortunate indeed who will try to build himself without the inspiration of God, without realizing that he grows from within, not from without.

Jesus proclaimed that men and women fail to live truly, and really amount to nothing, unless they have spirituality. The spiritual force underlies everything, and without it nothing worthwhile can be accomplished. Jesus taught that a man cannot be true to himself without being true to his fellowmen. Neither can a man be true to his fellowmen without being true to himself.

To all who believe in the living, personal Christ and his divine truth, life can be so delightful and beautiful. It is glorious just to be alive. Joy, even ecstasy, can be experienced in the consciousness of existence. There is supreme satisfaction in sensing one's individual entity and in realizing that that entity is part of God's creative plan. There are none so poor, none so rich, sick, or maimed, that they may not be conscious of this relationship.

He promised no material rewards, but he did promise perfected, divine manhood. And with that divine manhood comes the resultant true happiness.

Christ is the light of humanity. In that light man sees his way clearly; when it is rejected, the soul of man stumbles in darkness. It is a sad thing when individuals and nations extinguish that light—when Christ and his gospel are supplanted by the law of the jungle and the strength of the sword. The chief tragedy in the world at the present time is its disbelief in God's goodness and its lack of faith in the teachings and doctrines of the gospel.

Our Ideal

Jesus' teachings may be applied just as efficaciously to social groups and national problems as to individuals if men will only give them a trial. The spirit of the world is antagonistic to the establishment of peace. Peace can come to the world only through obedience to the gospel of Jesus Christ.

The gospel, the glad tidings of great joy, is the true guide to mankind; and that man or woman is happiest and most content who lives nearest to its teachings, which are the antitheses of hatred, persecution, tyranny, domination, injustice—actions which foster tribulation, destruction, and death throughout the world. What the sun in the heavenly blue is to the earth struggling to get free from winter's grip, so the gospel of Jesus Christ is to the sorrowing souls yearning for something higher and better than mankind has yet found on earth.

Members of the Church and all other people are under obligation to make the sinless Son of Man their ideal—the one perfect Being who ever walked the earth:

Sublimest example of nobility
Godlike in nature
Perfect in his love
Our Redeemer

Our Savior
The Only Begotten Son of our Eternal Father
The Light, the Life, the Way.

Our Heartfelt Convictions

Great minds in all ages who have contributed to the betterment of mankind have been inspired by noble ideals.

History is replete with men who, as Wordsworth expresses it, "By the vision splendid, were on their way attended."

J. A. Francis wrote a tribute to Christ as follows:

. . . When we try to sum up his influence, all the armies that ever marched, all the parliaments that ever sat, all the kings that ever reigned, are absolutely picayune in their influence on mankind, compared with that of this one solitary life.[1]

The highest of all ideals are the teachings and particularly the life of Jesus of Nazareth, and that man is most truly great who is most Christlike.

What you sincerely think in your heart of Christ will determine what you are, will largely determine what your acts will be. No person can study his divine personality, can accept his teachings, or follow his example, without becoming conscious of an uplifting and refining influence within himself. In fact, every individual may experience the operation of the most potent force that can affect humanity. Electricity lightens labor in the home, imprisons alike on a disc the warbling tones of the mockingbird and the convincing appeal of the orator. By the turn of the switch, it turns night into day. The possibilities of the force resulting from the breaking up of the atom seem to be limitless either for the destruction or the blessing of life. Other greater forces are already in use.

None, however, is so vital, so contributive to the peace and happiness of the human family as the surrendering of our selfish, animal-like natures to the life and teachings of our Lord and Savior, Jesus Christ.

---

[1]James Allen Francis, *The Real Jesus and Other Sermons* (Judson Press, Valley Forge, Pennsylvania, 1962) p. 123.

Chapter Sixty-four

Belief in Christ Essential to Man's Peace and Progress

And it came to pass, as the angels were gone away from them into heaven, the shepherds said one to another. Let us now go even unto Bethlehem, and see this thing which is come to pass, which the Lord hath made known unto us. (Luke 2:15.)

THIS confidence manifested by the shepherds is the belief and confidence the world must have before it will find its desired peace and progress. Belief in that glorious announcement and in the life and teachings of Jesus of Nazareth is essential to man's peace and progress.

I. What Constitutes Belief

I use "belief" in the sense of its true meaning—as *trust, confidence*—a belief that is expressed in action.

The Lord says in the Doctrine & Covenants: "He that receiveth my law and doeth it, the same is my disciple; and he that saith he receiveth it and doeth it not, the same is not my disciple."

"The thing a man does practically believe (and this is often enough without asserting it even to himself, much less to others); the thing a man does practically lay to heart,

412

and know for certain, concerning his vital relations to this mysterious universe, and his duty and destiny there, that is in all cases the primary thing for him, and creatively determines all the rest. This is his religion; or, it may be, his mere scepticism and *no-religion*: the manner it is in which he feels himself to be spiritually related to the Unseen World or No-World; and I say, if you tell me what that is, you tell me to a very great extent what the man is, what the kind of things he will do is."

All this is in keeping with Jesus' teachings. With him low ideals, wrong motives and improper feelings were more worthy of condemnation than the non-observance of rituals or the transgression of man-made laws. "He decried the fatal effects of hatred and jealousy in the mind of the individual more vehemently than he did the acts that hate and jealousy prompt." "A good tree bears good fruit, and evil tree, evil fruit," was the foundation of his moral and ethical teachings. "As a man thinketh in his heart so he is." If his thoughts are noble, so will be his acts. True religion is devotion to life's highest values.

2. Present World Conditions

Present world conditions indicate an absence of confidence and trust in Christ's doctrines. Spiritual growth has woefully trailed material progress. People with whom Jesus associated did not even dream of a railroad, an automobile, a steamboat. They would have thought a man demented if he had even mentioned an airplane, especially a modern air transport or bomber, or the radio. People in that day reaped their harvest with the sickle, and thrashed it with the flail. Today the combined harvester cuts, cleans, and sacks a score of acres of wheat a day. A man can speed along the highway at the rate of a mile a minute, or fly through the air at 600 miles or more per hour. He can eat breakfast in San Francisco and take his noon meal in New York, and in another few hours be with friends in London! Man has conquered the land, the ocean, the air. His slightest whisper may be heard in a moment on the opposite side of the globe!

Yet, notwithstanding all this advancement, mankind has witnessed two world wars in a quarter of a century! As a result of the first war seven million men were killed. Five million more dead of starvation and disease. Twice twelve million hearts flooded with woe. Twenty million wounded, five million of whom were maimed and crippled for life. Countless millions who suffered privations in the trenches, and in the lonely homes of the poor. Fifty billion dollars worth of material and property destroyed. One hundred billion dollars to provide for the cost of the war and interest.

Before World War Two, I said to an audience: It is inconceivable that intelligent men will foolishly take steps that will lead to another world conflagration. Inconceivable though it seemed, the facts are before us today (1942), and more millions of men are being killed, mangled, frozen to death, starved, and drowned.

A failure to apply Christ's gospel has brought this threatening destruction of civilization.

I want to appeal to the youth throughout the land to cherish a sincere, motivating belief in the divinity of the life and mission of the Babe of Bethlehem, and to accept his teachings as the only safe and sure guide for the peace and progress of the human family.

3. Opinions of Men Who Do Not Believe in Christ's Divinity

It is interesting to note that even those who reject as spurious the stories of the annunciation, of the miracles, and of the resurrection, have been forced to acknowledge a greatness in Christ, that can be attached to no other being on earth. With the exception of a few, such as Nietzsche who looks upon Christianity as "a most powerful instrument of racial degeneration," nearly all the critics after rejecting Christ's divinity, proclaim his mighty influence and his superiority to all other men.

Illustrative of this, let me refer to a paragraph or two from *The Great Galilean* by Keable:

"We do not know," he writes, "with anything approaching historical certainty of whom he (Jesus) was born, or when, or where; how long he lived, or how long he labored; and the sayings which are indubitably his are a mere handful." Yet this same writer concludes: "Christ stands for the highest development of man; and, try as we will, we cannot see any other intelligent mind than man's in universe. To the other forces that we dimly sense we cannot attribute personality, but to Christ we can and must. He is our God." True the author is referring to a traditional Christ more than to the historical Christ when he says this, but the two quotations illustrate the point I am making.

Again, Lewis Browne, author of *The Believing World,* says:

Almost two thousand years ago there was born in the Galilean village of Nazareth, a Jewish child to whom was given the name of Joshua, or Jesus. We do not know for certain how the early years of this child were spent.

Which is true.

The Gospels recount many legends concerning his conception, birth, and youth, but they are no more to be relied on than the suspiciously similar legends told many centuries earlier about Zoroaster.

Yet, of the efficiency of the Church of Christ, this same critic says:

It has made life liveable for countless millions of harried souls. It has taken rich and poor, learned and ignorant, white, red, yellow, and black—it has taken them all and tried to show them a way to salvation. To all in pain it has held out a balm; to all in distress it has offered peace. To every man without distinction it has said: "Jesus died for you!" To every human creature on earth it has said: "You too can be saved!" And therein lies Christianity's highest virtue. It has helped make the weak strong and the dejected happy. It has stilled the fear that howls in man's breast, and crushed the unrest that gnaws at his soul. In a word, it has worked—in a measure.

That is a remarkable admission when we realize that Christianity has in reality never yet been fully tried!

4. Testimonies of Ancient Disciples

What the world needs today is a belief in the hearts of many more millions of men as firm as that of Luke who wrote the account of the visitation of the shepherds and their chorus of angels.

I am going to give you some reasons for my thinking that we can take the testimony of this man and others concerning the Christ as unquestionable evidence of the divinity of the Christ. To make more convincing their testimonies with respect to time, I will refer to an instance that took place in the Hotel Utah, July 29, 1941. Mr. Gordon S. Rentschler, chairman of the board of the National City Bank, New York, was the honored guest at a luncheon given by Mr. Orval Adams. In his fitting address of appreciation, Mr. Rentschler made the following reference to a previous visit to Salt Lake City:

> One of my first experiences, 20 odd years ago—Orville Wright and I came here one day and four or five others. We went over to the Temple grounds. We were taken around by some man—we never learned his name. Here was an extraordinary individual telling the story (I think it was a noon time) Orville Wright and I came back to this hotel (the Utah), and Orville said: "You know, that fellow has got something that we are all missing, and that is the reason these fellows are a great people." We spent one of the most interesting hours I have ever spent in my life.

Testimony of Luke

Luke, who told us about the shepherds and the heavenly choir was a man of education. He was a Greek of Grecian culture. He was a physician. Though he was not an eyewitness of the Christ, he met many who were and then wrote two accounts which he dedicated either to a ruler or to a friend. In one of these he said: Christ "Had given commandments unto the apostles whom he had chosen: To whom also he shewed himself *alive after his passion by many infallible*

416

proofs." When Luke wrote that message he was just as convinced of the veracity and sincerity of the men whom he had interviewed as I was that Mr. Rentschler told the truth about his visit to the Temple Block 20 years before.

Of the value and effect of such nearness and intimacy, Mr. Nichols writes:

The authors of the epistles were within hailing distance, historically, of Christ, at any rate, when their ideas, which they afterwards transmitted to paper, were formed. The winds had hardly had time to efface the sacred print of his steps in the sands over which he walked. The rain had hardly had time to wash away, with its callous tears, the blood from the rotting wood of the deserted cross.

Yet, these men knew—I can't go on using the word "believe," which is far too vapid and colourless—that God had descended to earth in the shape of a certain man, that this man had met an obscure and clownish death, and that the grotesque mode of his dying had redeemed mankind from sin. They knew, moreover, that he had risen from the dead on the third day and ascended into heaven. It is no use saying that their minds were prepared for such legends because of the prophets, and because of the immemorial Jewish tradition that this sort of thing would happen, one day. Our minds might be prepared for all sorts of things which, if they happened, would be rejected for their sheer improbability. But these men's minds did not reject these things. They accepted them implicitly.

Testimony of Paul

One day in Corinth about 50 A.D. there was a little brown-eyed tent-maker patiently working with calloused hands at his chosen trade. With him were two young men— one of whom we know pretty well—Timotheus; of the other, Sylvanus, we know very little, and of him have no description. Paul, the tent-maker, alternating his work with dictation, is giving them a message to take back to the Thessalonians. Paul loved Timothy, and called him his own "son in the faith." Can you imagine any man who so loved a son telling him something which the tailor thought lacked authenticity, or which was not real? I cannot! I mention this instance because the tent-maker's words then sent to the Thessalonians are the oldest recorded testimony that we have of the Christ. When was it? Not earlier than 48 years after Christ, perhaps as late as 52 A.D. - — approximately fifteen years after the crucifixion! Many were then living who had walked with Jesus and talked with him. Only fifteen years! Hundreds of men still living who could testify of personal experiences with Jesus, the Christ!

Christ's Birth Not Heralded

There are some who defiantly ask: Why was the birth of Jesus revealed only to shepherds? Why did God not proclaim his advent to the whole world? Anything so important as to involve the salvation of the entire human family should be broadcasted. Why leave a truth of such import and magnitude so difficult to learn and to understand? I have heard the same questions and many more about the coming forth of the plates from which the Book of Mormon was translated. Why were they hidden? Why were they not put in the Smithsonian Institute for all of us to see and turn the pages so that we should know beyond a shadow of doubt that the story of the Book of Mormon is true? In reply to such queries Beverly Nicholes aptly writes:

Try to imagine what the world without doubt would be. Supposing he (Christ) had come only for an hour. Science would have perpetuated that hour for all time. We should be able to see him on the cinema, to hear his voice on the gramophone. We should be able to read in the newspapers a thousand reports of his lightest gesture. There would not be the faintest shadow of a reason why any man or woman in any country in the world should for one moment question the complete authenticity of the Christian legend.

What then?

Ask yourself that question. Really ask yourself. And gradually, if you shut your eyes and try to reason it all out, you will see a most tremendous paradox forming in your brain. The paradox is that the world, in the light of such a challenging revelation, would be a drab world, and that humanity would be infinitely the poorer. "What!" you may exclaim, "the world would be drab after Christ had shone

418

in glory over the streets, and after we have had actual photographs of his presence, and records of his voice? Drab, when we couldn't help believing, even if we tried?"

Yes, drab. But I do not think that word is quite strong enough. I think I should have said "dead."

Put it like this. If the Bible were as simple as, let us say, yesterday's issue of *The Times*, if we could personally consult the men who had written it, if we could go round the corner to a News Reel Theatre and see Christ raising Lazarus, if the whole thing were before our eyes. "What then?" I can only repeat we would also think that very drab. All merit would have been taken from faith, All glory from virtue. The man who did not do as Christ told him to do would be, quite frankly, a damned fool. And the man who *did* do as Christ told him to do would be no more admirable, and no more spiritually benefited, than the man who keeps within the speed limit and obeys the ordinary laws of the land.

In a world without doubt, Christ would descend, with a dull and sickening thud, to the level of a policeman. He would be, at best a sort of sublime magistrate.

If this revelation (of Christ) were to be of real value to man, in his climb upwards, it would be a veiled revelation, a revelation which forced men to do his part and to share in the sacrifice.

Man, the highest creation of God, has never got "something for nothing." Throughout every hour of history he has had to fight. No sooner does he appear to have won a triumph over Nature than he is reminded that he cannot rest and that he has a long way further to go. In times of peace, on fertile plains, in hot climates, men have waxed fat and prosperous, and a fever comes to slay them. In times of plenty, when the world is running with gold, and the granaries are full the men who should be friends stir up evil and fight, and the gold chokes them and the granaries are emptied. I often think that the last war may have been a supreme example of this sublime discipline. Men had been given power over the land and the sea and the air. In their hands were magic glasses which searched the secrets of the moon. They had learned to speak across continents, their voices carried more swiftly and clearly than the shout of a full-throated giant. They had imprisoned the song of the nightingale on a disk of shining wax, they had set up screens in the dark on which, like strange ghosts, their women danced and loved, mystically evoked by a film of celluloid. Man was a great magician, yes! Heaven, it seemed, was in his grasp, as a bubble is in the grasp of a child. And then, like a spoilt child, he shattered it. The wreckage is still strewn around him.

History is a record of struggle. Progress is a parable of pain. And every spiritual adventure which has advanced the soul of man, has been a leap in the dark.

Browne was right when he said this message to *you*. Christ's reality must be sensed by you, and by me and the reality of his philosophy must be mine and yours if we hope to advance spiritually and rise above the earth and the things which are akin to it.

With all my soul I believe with Peter, that impetuous apostle, that "there is none other name under heaven given among men, whereby we must be saved." In that day Christ was real to Peter; and he is just as real today.

The whole philosophy of the progress of man is associated with his divine coming. He is the Son of God, who took upon himself mortality even as you and I, yet divine even as you and I may become.

In the march of this spiritual progress there are certain necessary and definite steps, if we can only sense them.

A Sense of Freedom

The first step in spiritual strength is a consciousness of freedom. This is the principle which began when Christ accepted the appointment to his earthly mission. It is free agency and is fundamental to individual freedom. In the beginning the Lord asked for someone to go down on earth to redeem mankind. One responded saying: "Send me, and I will make all men do as I say, (the words are mine), but I want the glory." Another replied: "Here I am, send me and you may have the glory." He would give to each one the right of free agency. There is the beginning of soul progress. God desires to make men like himself but to do so he must first make them free. Yes, students, it is the sense of freedom. You may do as you please; accept or reject the highest and best in life: agree or disagree with the selfishness, enmity and antagonism of the world. Animal instincts permit you to crush your neighbor that you yourself might rise. Accept it, if you wish, or choose the higher and rougher road.

> Know this that every soul is free,
> To choose his course, and what he'll be;
> For this eternal truth is given,
> That God will force no man to Heaven.

Sense of Self-Mastery

The second is a sense of self-mastery. Before Jesus began his ministry, he proved himself capable of withstanding the tempter. He was tempted "like as we," yet never once did he yield, and finally declared: "Be of good cheer; I have overcome the world." You know that you cannot rise unless you overcome and conquer. Sneak around your examinations if you will, but in your hearts you will know you haven't conquered the difficulties of your subjects.

Don't yield to the appetites of the flesh with the thought to gain pleasure and happiness. If you do, you will find that the happiness you seek is a withered flower that crumbles in your grasp. You go and go and go until you can't get the desired sensation without destroying yourself physically.

> What though I conquer my enemies,
> And lay up store and pelf,
> I am a conquerer poor indeed,
> Till I subdue myself.

> What though I read and learn by heart
> Whole books while I am young,
> I am a linguist in disgrace,
> Who cannot guard my tongue.

> What though on campus I excell
> A champ in meet and fight,
> If trained, efficient still I can't
> Control an appetite.

> What though exemptions write my name
> High on the honor-roll,
> Electives, solids fail me if
> I learn no self control.

> What though I graduate and soar
> And life is good to me,
> My heart shall write me failure till
> I learn *SELF-MASTERY*.

A Sense of Obligation

The third step is a sense of obligation. As an aid in developing this spiritual virtue, Christ, as always, is the supreme example. Truly he gave his life for others. "The foxes have holes, the birds their nests, but the Son of Man has nowhere to lay his head." Thus sacrificing his own comforts and even his own needs he admonished all to "Love your enemies. Do good to them that curse you." "Inasmuch as ye do it unto the least of these ye do it unto me." "If you have aught against a brother, go to him"—a sublime principle, which if accepted and applied, would solve difficulties in communities, cities, and nations. But the Savior did not stop in admonishing the one who has ill-will; He went further. Note this: "If thou bring thy gift to the altar, and there rememberest that thy brother hath aught against thee, Leave there thy gift before the altar, and go thy way; first be reconciled to thy brother, and then come and offer thy gift."

When the nations accept and apply this principle, war will cease.

5. Consecration to Christ and the Right

Service to fellowmen makes easier the taking of the fourth step — — consecration to Christ and the right. When Jesus met the supreme crisis in the Garden of Gethsemane he said: "Father, not my will, but thine be done,"—an example of entire submission of self to the will of God. Weeks before this he had announced the same principle in the paradoxical saying, "He that findeth his life, shall lose it: and he that loseth his life for my sake shall find it." The verity of this principle in spiritual growth may be proved by every day experience. You may test it when you are studying lessons in school. If you will concentrate; that is, "lose yourself," in the study at hand, you will obtain the truth. In other words, you will "find yourself." It is true when you sit at the piano and play one of the inspiring Beethoven symphonies, if you become absorbed in the theme wholly unconscious of self, you will win your way into the hearts of your listeners, but if you fail to lose yourself, and think only of your own position and wonder whether you are pleasing your audience, you will certainly fail to the degree that you have tried to build yourself up. Man's highest spiritual achievement is to speak and act for the good of his fellowmen to the glory of God, and thus make of life a consecrated possession.

Conclusion

Christ is real; he lives! His life is real. He is the Son of God. The Babe of Bethlehem, The One Perfect Gentleman who ever lived—the Ideal Man whose character was supreme; our Brother, Our Savior, The "Anointed One."

God help us to believe in him with all our souls to make him real in our lives! Remember the ideals of his life as we associate his birth with Christmas time. It is not his birthday; we associate him with that day, and make the season glorious to the extent that we deny ourselves for the happiness of others.

Compliance with the principles of the gospel of Jesus Christ brings peace and happiness. Christ offers just these to this war-torn world.

May the reality of the Christ and the applicability of his teachings in this day to the happiness and progress of man be more fully realized than ever before.

Chapter Sixty-five

Christmas
and the
Spirit of Christ

|T IS OFTEN said that the happiest season of the year is Christmas time. I believe that is true because it is then that we have the Christmas spirit in our hearts, which is the spirit of Christ. I wish we might have that spirit every season of the year, every week in the year.

I love to attend Sunday School and be in the presence of children, to listen to their singing and speaking in praise of the Redeemer. It is music to hear little children speak the name of Jesus. There come to me the words of the Savior, ". . . Suffer the little children to come unto me, and forbid them not: for of such is the kingdom of God." (Mark 10:14.) It is glorious to hear them sing and speak of the first Christmas anthem, "Glory to God in the highest, and on earth peace, good will toward men." (Luke 2:14.)

Millions Celebrate His Birth

Millions and millions of people celebrate the birth of Christ. Looking at it from a natural standpoint, it is really wonderful, because we know so little about him. When we read about Abraham Lincoln, we can go through volumes and find out about his life, his characteristics, his temperament, his jocular nature, his moody nature. We can look at his photograph and judge him from his writings and his sayings. We can interpret them more intelligently as we look at his features, an iron frame.

If we study the life of Washington, we are helped in the same way. I often think, as I look at the portrait of Robert Burns, that his expression, as it has come down to us in portraits, is a help in interpreting his poetry. The same is true of Sir Walter Scott and other historical geniuses; but in the case of Jesus of Nazareth, we have no photograph.

There is no man who has ever lived since the days of those who walked with him who can form a correct conception of what he looked like, with the exception I shall note later. From a human standpoint, there is no photograph that will give us an exact likeness of his features. Artists have painted him as they thought he looked. The French artists have introduced French traits in his picture; the Italians, Italian features; and so on.

Not only have we not his portrait, but we have not his sayings in the original. We have his book; we have what the apostles remembered he said, but even that has not come to us in the language in which he spoke it. Even what we have is so little that it can be put in a vest pocket edition; and yet John tells us that if all he said and all he did were written, the world itself could scarcely contain the volumes. (See John 21:25.) In comparison to that, think how little we have, how little we know from a human standpoint.

The Greatest Influence

Yet, even from the human standpoint, no being has ever been on the earth that has wielded a thousandth part of the influence which this man of Nazareth wields throughout the world. Nearly two thousand years have gone, and he is still acknowledged as the one peerless person in the world.

Today his life is a more potent factor in influencing humanity than it has ever been before, notwithstanding the terrible conditions that exist in the world today. What is this influence? It is not just what he has written.

Thank heaven we do have a few of his words in the Bible, and that we have more of them in modern scripture, the Book of Mormon. But all told, this amounts to but little, even including the more glorious revelations, more direct words, in the Doctrine and Covenants. It is not just what he said, but rather *what he does to our spirits, how he influences our hearts and affects the very lives of men which makes him live.* It is through that power, by the operation of the Holy Ghost, that he influences the world, and gives men the power to bear testimony to his divinity. In that power, all men can read of his life and what he has done and can hear his voice through the whisperings of the Spirit. All men should do as he has done; that is the obligation that comes to us.

A Lesson In Humility

On one occasion when he was with the Twelve, he performed a sacred ceremony in which he taught them the lesson of humility. After he untied the towel from his waist, replaced the basin at the door, and took his place at the head of the assembly again, he said:

Ye call me Master and Lord: and ye say well; for so I am.

If I then, your Lord and Master, have washed your feet; ye also ought to wash one another's feet.

For I have given you an example, that ye should do as I have done to you. (John 13:13-15.)

There were three principles heralded to the world by the angel who came to the shepherds on that starry night and told them to:

. . . Fear not: For unto you is born this day in the city of David a Saviour, which is Christ the Lord. . . .

And suddenly there was with the angel a multitude of the heavenly host praising God, and saying,

Glory to God in the highest, and on earth peace, good will toword men. (Luke 2:10-11, 13-14.)

The first principle is a message to all people to give glory to God—and godliness was a trait that Jesus exemplified every day and every hour of his earthly existence here on earth.

Taught Principles of Godliness

When he taught the disciples how to pray, the simple and beautiful pattern which he gave to them and to the world contained that principle of godliness—". . . Our Father which art in heaven, hallowed be thy name." (Matt. 6:9.)

After he performed the miracle of feeding the five thousand, he saw how the people interpreted that power, desiring to make him king rather than to acknowledge the power of God. He dismissed them and retired to pray. Later that night, he joined his disciples. The people were surprised the next morning to find that Jesus was in Capernaum. They flocked around him again, asking him, no doubt, to give them something. They pretended to want to know his gospel, his teachings; but he turned, reading their hearts, and said: ". . . Ye seek me, not because ye saw the miracles, but because ye did eat of the loaves, and were filled." (John 6:26.) Sordid, temporal things dragging their minds down! He would lift them up to things which were heavenly. Then he gave them that memorable sermon on the bread of life, a synopsis of which is found in John, the eleventh chapter, when he performed the miracle of raising Lazarus from the dead.

Taught Principle of Peace

The second principle, "Peace on earth." Peace! Can you think of anything in life that is more acceptable than peace? Philosophers have given several purposes of life: many say it is happiness, others say that duty is the end purpose of life. I believe that those who place *peace* as the purpose come nearer to the real purpose.

When Jesus came forth from the tomb and appeared to his disciples, his first greeting was, ". . . Peace be unto you." (Luke 24:36.) Peace! You find it on his lips all the way through his life. Peace is exemption from individual turmoil, from family broils, from national difficultes. Peace refers to the individual just as much as it does to communities. That man is not at peace who is untrue to the whisperings of Christ, to the promptings of his conscience. He cannot be at peace when he is untrue to his better self; when he transgresses the law of righteousness, either in dealing with himself by indulging in passion or in appetite, yielding to the temptations of the flesh, or when he is unjust, transgressing the law of righteousness in dealing with his fellowmen.

Oh, if we could only have peace! And peace comes through obedience to the gospel of Jesus Christ; but the spirit of the flesh, the spirit of the world is antagonistic to the establishment of peace. Just think what it would mean today if only that spirit would penetrate the hearts of rulers of captive nations; if they could only have confidence in their fellowmen, and confidence in their God. I believe, when we read of the glorious message from that heavenly host which shall be to all people, that we ought to think just of that one word; *peace,* and the conditions that go to establish it. Happiness follows then—not mere pleasure—but happiness. Duty is a fundamental requirement in obtaining that peace. There is no peace in the violation of duty or in neglect of duty. It is the little things which constantly are being performed that produce peace; it is the little things which are neglected that destroy peace.

Taught Principle of Brotherliness

The third principle heralded by the heavenly host is good will toward men. We shall call it *brotherliness.* I cannot think of any other word that seems so expressive or that will give such an opportunity to emphasize good will toward men as brotherliness. All men, the poor, and even the sinner, were recipients of his kindness and his blessings.

Christ taught us to set our hearts not upon the things of this world, but upon God and godly things. And that is the obligation which comes to us—to preach and to live godly lives, to have reverence for our Father in heaven; to pray to him and to teach our children to have reverence and pray to him. Not only that, but we should teach them to honor and revere sacred things. Jesus not only had reverence for his Father, but he had reverence for those things which were God's. He denounced the men of his time who defaced or defamed sacred edifices. He cleansed the temple by driving the money changers away, and to those who sold the doves he said, ". . . Take these things hence; make not my Father's house an house of merchandise." (John 2:16.) Another time he said, ". . . ye have made it a den of thieves." (Matt. 21:13.) It was God's house.

In that beautiful Sermon on the Mount, to those who would swear by the heaven, and others who would swear by the earth to make an oath a sacred one, he said: ". . . Swear not at all; neither by heaven; for it is God's throne: Nor by the earth; for it is his footstool: . . ." (Matt. 5:34-35.)

There is the example; and I wish that we might follow it and impress it upon our children during these times. It is not uncommon, as we walk along the street, to hear young people, sometimes little children, profaning. They have not learned that lesson of godliness; or, if they have, the habits of their associates are such that the teachings of parents have gone unheeded. That is the second condition of peace, and the third is brotherly kindness. Thank Heaven for the Christmas spirit that brings us closer to each other in expression of that brotherhood.

Knowledge of the Redeemer

And so I say from a human standpoint it is surprising, since we know so little about the Redeemer, since so little is written about him, that his power is felt throughout the world as it is. However, from the divine standpoint, there is no surprise; and from the standpoint of the members of The Church of Jesus Christ of Latter-day Saints, we *do* know more about him. There was a boy in this dispensation who did know what he looks like, for he saw him: Joseph Smith, the

429

Prophet, saw the Redeemer with his Father, and he has given that testimony to the world and has recorded his messages for this generation, in this, the Dispensation of the Fullness of Times. What a mighty responsibility, then, rests upon us! Of all the Christian people throughout the civilized world, none carries the responsibility that a member of this Church carries today; and we must strive to follow the example of the Redeemer.

As we approach the New Year, I think it is most appropriate to repent and strive for something that is better; strive for something that is higher; introduce more godliness into our lives; establish peace first in our hearts; see that our families are at peace in the neighborhood; and use our influence as members of the Church in establishing peace in all the world. We can do this by that God-like, Christ-like principle of service. Every man, woman, and child in this Church has an opportunity to render that service to mankind.

May his peace and contentment abide in every home. May the cheer of Christmas time which springs from the true spirit of brotherhood, which is the spirit of Christ, be with us, and remain with us throughout the entire year.

Chapter Sixty-six

Christ
is the True Light
of Men's Lives

THERE IS JOY in Christmas which is unsurpassed by any other season or event in the year. With this celebration is associated the soul satisfaction that comes from losing self for the happiness of others. Because of this, though Christmas had no other virtue, each Yuletide should find the world a little better than the last, and men and women a little more inclined to strive to establish peace on earth.

Ever since man was placed on earth, peace has been among his noblest quests. Associated with it has been his desire for freedom—freedom to express what he thinks, freedom to choose his work without dictatorial compulsion, freedom to worship without molestation, freedom to own a home into which dictators or usurpers may not enter unbidden —indispensable conditions to the enjoyment of peace!

It is my conviction that millions of sincere people the world over are praying and striving for this consummation.

Church Members Loyal to Ideals and Teachings

The loyalty of the members of the Church to the ideals and teachings of the Man of Galilee has been evidenced by the response of tens of thousands to the message of the restored gospel as proclaimed by messengers at home and

431

abroad, by ready and willing response to "calls" and assignments, and by increased tithes and offerings.

All such efforts contribute to the joy and peace Christ came to establish.

But let us ever remember that the price of peace is eternal vigilance and constant righteous efforts. Forces of evil and misery are still rampant in the world and must be resisted. The powers of darkness have increased in accordance with the spread of the gospel. Whole nations are declaring atheism to be the law of the land. Atheism has become the greatest weapon Satan has to use, and its evil influence is bringing degradation to millions throughout the world. Even at this moment as the sun throws warm, genial rays on snow-capped summits and frost-covered valleys of this western land, the public press tells of increasing activity on the part of the evil one. Warlike activities and international misunderstandings prevent the establishing of peace and divert man's inventive genius from the paths of science, art, and literature, and apply it to human retardation and the holocausts of war.

Happiness and Peace Will Come

The rising sun can dispel the darkness of night, but it cannot banish the blackness of malice, hatred, bigotry, and selfishness from the hearts of humanity. Happiness and peace will come to earth only as the light of love and human compassion enter the souls of men.

It was for this purpose that Christ, the Son of Righteousness, "with healing in his wings" came in the meridian of time. Through him wickedness will be overcome; and hatred, enmity, strife, poverty, and war abolished. This will not be accomplished, however, with atomic bombs and battleshot; with submarines or poison gas, but with a slow but never-failing process of changing men's mental and spiritual attitudes. The ways and habits of the world depend upon the thoughts and soul-convictions of men and women. If, therefore, we would change the world, we must first change people's thoughts. Only to the extent that men *desire* peace and brotherhood can the world be made better. Only by adhering to sound principles can peace come, either to individuals or nations.

Christ Is the Savior

Christ is the true light of men's lives. He is the Son of God—the Savior of the world! His coming was heralded by heavenly hosts singing: "Glory to God in the highest, and on earth peace, good will toward men." (Luke 2:14.)

Thus was recorded the greatest and most momentous fact in the history of the world. In his taking upon himself mortality, Christ personified Deity; in his walks and teachings among men, he exemplified the true philosophy of being; in his death and resurrection, he opened the door to life and immortality.

Rejecting the tempter's scheme of coercion and self-glorification, the Savior established a plan that will regenerate men's souls. He knew that this regenerating force would be silent, almost imperceptible; slow in gaining momentum, and disappointing to all except only those who caught his vision; victorious only through his death, resurrection, and second coming.

With the announcement of the birth of the Savior by the heavenly hosts more than nineteen centuries ago, there was given a message which, if heeded, would unite peoples of all nations in a friendliness that would bring not suspicion and fear of the possibility of any atomic war, but confidence and resultant *peace.*

Many and swift are the changes that have come to the peoples of the world since the announcement of the angels, but the principles they gave remain changeless and ever applicable and essential to the happiness, salvation, and exaltation of the children of men. These principles as summarized are:

(1) Faith in God ("Glory to God in the Highest").
(2) Peace through brotherly love ("Peace on earth").
(3) Good will and fellowship ("Good will among men").

Christmas: Celebration of Jesus' Birth

No worry or anxiety over the choosing and giving of gifts; no enjoyment of holiday feasts; no decorations however modern or attractive; no social parties however jovial, should ever overshadow the fact that Christmas is the celebration of the birth of Jesus Christ who came to give life, light, and peace to all mankind, and who marked the way by which these eternal blessings may be obtained. Let us ever remember that ". . . God so loved the world, that he gave his only begotten Son, that whosoever believeth in him should not perish, but have everlasting life." (John 3:16.)

This love of our Father has been manifested ever since he gave free agency to man and was particularly made known during the earthly life of Jesus, by his teachings. To his disciples in that day, he said: "These things I have spoken unto you, that in me ye might have peace. In the world ye shall have tribulation: but be of good cheer; I have overcome the world." (John 16:33.)

"This Is My Beloved Son"

This love was again demonstrated eighteen hundred years later when the Father introduced the Savior to the young man, Joseph Smith, saying: *"This is My Beloved Son. Hear Him!"*

Under this divine authority, Jesus, the Babe of Bethlehem, who later established his gospel among men, who was crucified, resurrected, and who lives today, again established his Church that all mankind might hear his word and receive eternal blessings through obedience to the laws and ordinances of the gospel.

Therefore, let your gifts to one another carry with them a reminder of the Father's gift of his only begotten Son, who in turn gave to all the gift of the gospel. Let the pleasures of the Christmas season be subordinated to the true spiritual meaning of this greatest of all festivities—*The Birth of Our Lord and Savior Jesus Christ.*

. . . For there is none other name under heaven given among men, whereby we must be saved." (Acts 4:12.)

Chapter Sixty-seven

Three Guiding Principles Announced by the Angels at the Birth of Christ

And the angel said unto them,
Fear not: for, behold, I bring you
good tidings of great joy, which
shall be to all people.

For unto you is born this day in
the city of David a Saviour, which
is Christ the Lord. . . .

And suddenly there was with the
angel a multitude of the heavenly
host praising God, and saying,

Glory to God in the highest, and
on earth peace, good will toward
men. (Luke 2:10-11, 13-14.)

IN THIS announcement are im-
plied three guiding principles to the realization of the establishing of the kingdom of God.

First, is an *acknowledgment of the existence of Deity* to
whom we shall give glory and honor.

Second, is the *establishment of peace* through individual
righteousness.

Such a peace will result in the *third* principle—the
brotherhood of man.

Our faith in God springs from the heart: it is yours; it
is mine. It cannot be other than personal. ". . . He that

436

cometh to God must believe that he is, and that he is a rewarder of them that diligently seek him." (Hebrews 11:6.)

What does such a faith as that mean? The Lord becomes the center of our being, the guide to our thoughts and acts. With such a faith, men may know that over all there is our Father, "Lord of heaven and earth." With such a faith men may know this universe is not left to the guidance of an irrational and random chance, but, on the contrary, is ordered and controlled by divine intelligence and wisdom.

The Source of Peace on Earth

As faith in God, so peace on earth has its source in the heart of the individual; and it is this second principle, announced by the angels at the birth of the Christ child, that I should like to emphasize.

Jesus said the poor in spirit would possess the kingdom of God. Who are the poor in spirit? Those who, in deepest consciousness, realize their need of *spiritual possessions; those who yearn to be in harmony with God and his teachings.*

Again he said that it is the pure in heart who shall see God, and the peacemakers who shall be called the children of God.

There can be no happiness, no salvation, without peace in this life or in the hereafter. Christ exemplified that principle throughout his life. Everything that pertains to human happiness and salvation, Christ exemplified. He is the light and the life, the first example of salvation to the individual.

When Christ went to the Mount of Temptation from the banks of the Jordan, he was tempted by the evil one, who said unto him: "If thou be the Son of God, command that these stones be made bread"—an appeal to his appetite. "Man shall not live by bread alone, but by every word that proceedeth out of the mouth of God."

"If thou be the Son of God," again strong in his taunting, "cast thyself down: for it is written,"—he quotes scripture—"he shall give his angels charge concerning thee: and in their hands they shall bear thee up, lest at any time thou dash thy foot against a stone."

"It is written again," said the Savior, "Thou shalt not tempt the Lord thy God."

In the next temptation Satan is not taunting, but pleading: "All these things will I give thee,"—showing him the kingdoms of the world—"if thou wilt fall down and worship me."

That is a lesson of life. The tempter was foiled, taunting at first, strong in his assurance that he could tempt, but at last pleading, and finally banished. The Savior commanded him—"Get thee hence, Satan: for it is written, Thou shalt worship the Lord thy God, and him only shalt thou serve." And angels came and ministered to him. (See Matt. 4.)

Peace Comes from Within

Secondly, Christ taught that peace comes from within; not from without. He emphasized more than he did the outward ritual, that which is within the heart of man. One poet expressed it this way:

> Sow a thought, reap an act,
> Sow an act, reap a habit,
> Sow a habit, reap a character,
> Sow a character, reap an eternal
>   destiny.

What a man thinketh in his heart, so is he. That is emphasized throughout Christ's teachings. We are saved to the extent that we follow that teaching.

The third point I wish to emphasize is the power of what a man thinketh. Even before worship, Christ put the principle of reconciliation:

Therefore if thou bringest thy gift to the altar, and there rememberest that thy brother hath aught against thee; Leave there thy gift before the altar, and go thy way; first be reconciled to thy brother, and then come and offer thy gift. (Matt. 5:23-24.)

438

Harboring an evil thought injures the person who harbors it more than the man against whom he harbors it. Modern psychology emphasizes that truth. If we would have peace, we should banish our enmity for others. Bearing enmity in our hearts injures us and drives from our hearts that peace. If peoples and nations could just glimpse, and even attempt to apply that sublime principle, we would not have strife, riots, wars, and the killing of innocent men, women, and children. Just that one principle—if you have aught against your brother, go to him; arbitrate, and settle with him.

Christ Conquered Death

Jesus is our Savior, principally, of course, because he conquered death. Death could not touch him, and yet he took upon himself mortality. When he lived such a sinless life, he conquered death and cried out in his heart, as the Apostle Paul has stated it, "O death, where is thy sting? O grave, where is thy victory?" (1 Cor. 15:55.)

When a loved one is taken away by death, what do we want more than anything else? Is it not only the realization that death cannot touch that loved one when the spirit moves from its house of clay? Christ conquered death. Death is not victorious over the spirit of man. There is the source of true peace in this strife-torn, war-torn world today for fathers, mothers, wives, sisters, and loved ones. Furthermore, Christ not only redeemed us from death, and broke the bonds of death for mankind as the announcement said, "to all people," but he gave the gospel of Jesus Christ, by obedience to which men may be saved and exalted in the kingdom of the Father.

The enemies of liberty today are denying God. When any Communist comes around to say he has something better than what we have in the Constitution of the United States, I would ask you to remember just that one great truth which the Communists have rejected. They have thrown away the fundamental foundation stone of peace and happiness here and now. They deny God.

Christmas and Brotherhood

The third principle, enunciated at his birth, and applied at the moment when he said goodbye to his disciples, is that you should love your fellowmen, serve them rather than condemn. ". . . Inasmuch as ye have done it unto one of the least of these my brethren, ye have done it unto me." (Matt. 25:40.) Brotherhood involves service, not conquest. It involves confidence in man, in your brother; not suspicion and hatred. It involves truthful dealings; not chicanery and fraud. Brotherliness is but the manifestation of the spirit of Christ. Thank heaven for the spirit of Christmas that brings us closer to each other in expression of such brotherhood! It is the duty of us all to manifest brotherly love, first toward one another, and then toward all mankind; to seek unity, harmony, and peace in organizations within the Church; and, then, by precept and example, to extend these virtues throughout the world.

Love for God and for one another should be the Christmas theme. Such was the divine announcement by the heavenly host that first sang the "glad tidings of great joy."

The Heart That Loves Finds Peace

Only in the heart that loves, only in the Church of Jesus Christ where love prompts service to one's fellowmen and loyalty to God, shall we find peace.

For all the law is fulfilled in one word, even in this: Thou shalt love thy neighbor as thyself. (Galatians 5:14.)

May Christmas find love and a desire to bless others abiding in the heart of every Latter-day Saint. In all such hearts and homes, then, there will be peace and goodwill toward all men. Where peace abides, it matters little whether the possessor be rich or poor, for he will have, in addition to the peace that gives "joy unspeakable," the assurance which the Son of Man gave when he said:

. . . I am the bread of life: he that cometh to me shall never hunger; and he that believeth on me shall never thirst. (John 6:35.)

440

Chapter Sixty-eight

Philosophy of Life
Contained in Luke's Story
of the Birth of Christ

We've never seen the Father here, but we have known the Son,
The finest type of manhood since the world was first begun,
And, summing up the works of God, I write with reverent pen,
The greatest is the Son He sent to cheer the lives of men.
Through Him we learned the ways of God, and found the Father's
    love;
The Son it was who won us back to Him who reigns above.
The Lord did not come down Himself to prove to men His worth,
He sought our worship through the Child He placed upon the earth.[1]

THE STORY of the birth of that child in the old town of Bethlehem was written by a man who never met Jesus, but who studied his life and became one of his most ardent followers. He has told the story in the following words:

And there were in the same country shepherds abiding in the field, keeping watch over their flock by night.

And, lo, the angel of the Lord came upon them, and the glory of the Lord shone round about them: and they were sore afraid.

And the angel said unto them, Fear not: for, behold, I bring you good tidings of great joy, which shall be to all people.

For unto you is born this day in the city of David a Saviour, which is Christ the Lord.

---

[1]From "Thoughts of a Father," by Edgar A. Guest, *The Path to Home* (Reilly and Lee Company, Chicago, Illinois, 1919) p. 153.

And this shall be a sign unto you; Ye shall find the babe wrapped in swaddling clothes, lying in a manger.

And suddenly there was with the angel a multitude of the heavenly host praising God, and saying,

Glory to God in the highest, and on earth peace, good will toward men. (Luke 2:8-14.)

On November 2, 1921, Brother Hugh J. Cannon and I rode in a Ford car from Jerusalem down to Bethlehem. As we were going down the road, we passed Rachel's grave. We had the driver stop long enough for us to read the inscription thereon. A little farther on, we saw a man leading a herd of sheep. Our driver honked the horn and the shepherd rushed off to the side of the road and the sheep followed him; and as we drove by, the sheep were standing around the shepherd who was giving them, I suppose, some kind of sweet—I do not know what it was. To me it was a good illustration of the scripture, ". . . And the sheep follow him: for they know his voice. And a stranger will they not follow" (John 10:4-5) —an example of the sheep following the shepherd.

Soon we neared an open field—it seemed to me to be off to the left of the town of Bethlehem, to which we were going. I should like to write a few incidents about that town.

O Little Town of Bethlehem

I have quoted from the scripture the sweetest story ever told. Though we may repeat it in less than two minutes, it contains the whole philosophy of life, the science of living.

The scene is Bethlehem, a city of Palestine, which, in point of historic interest, is second only to Jerusalem. It is the scene of many important events in Biblical history. Its first mention in the Bible is in connection with the death of Rachel, to whose tomb I referred, over seventeen hundred years before Christ was born. It was the home of Boaz and Naomi, and there was consummated the beautiful story of Ruth. Eleven hundred years or thereabouts before the birth of Christ, we read of Bethlehem as the home of David's house; and it was at Bethlehem that the prophet found David tending his sheep and anointed the little shepherd boy to be the ruler of Judea and of Israel.

A little later we hear of the Philistine garrison in Bethlehem, David's home city, held by his enemies. How dear that town was to his heart, I think, is shown by the wish that he expressed for a drink of water from the well of Bethlehem Many a time he had quenched his thirst at that old well. As he stood facing an enemy that held his birthplace, three of his soldiers, hearing their general's wish, broke through the ranks of the Philistines and got the water for their leader. It is a touching picture of the loyalty and devotion that David inspired in his followers.

The Most Beautiful Story Ever Told

In Micah, the fifth chapter, Bethlehem is mentioned by the prophet as the birthplace of the Messiah. I wonder if the shepherds, to whom the first revelation of Christ's birth was given, had not that prophecy in mind as they kept watch over their flock by night. A revelation of God does not come to man unless he prepares himself for it and lives worthy of it.

Evil influences will thrust themselves upon men, but God will be sought. Evil is always urging and tempting and promising. God asks us to put forth effort and seek—". . . Seek, and ye shall find; knock, and it shall be opened unto you." (Matt. 7:7.) But we must knock, we must seek; and I think those humble shepherds were treasuring in their hearts the hope, as all Judea was treasuring it, that the Messiah would soon come. At any rate, those humble men had opened to them the vision of God.

I have said that Luke's account of the birth of the Savior is the most beautiful story ever told. I wish now to quote the paragraph that is not often associated with this story:

And it came to pass, as the angels were gone away from them into heaven, the shepherds said one to another, Let us now go even unto Bethlehem, and see this thing which is come to pass, which the Lord hath made known unto us. (Luke 2:15.)

Note that the shepherds did not say, "I wonder if this is true." They did not say, "Let us go and see if this thing be true." They said, "Let us go and see this thing which is come to pass, which the Lord hath made known unto us"—an assurance that God had revealed his Son, that the angels had given to the world the message that he who should be King of Kings and Lord of Lords had come as a mere babe in the humblest little Jordan town.

What would you give—you who may not have that assurance—to have in your hearts that same confidence that Christ is born, that Christ lives, that God had heralded his birth, yes, and his second coming, by the angels in heaven?

All doubt would be banished, all worry concerning our purpose here in life would cease. That is what such a testimony means. If we could only say: "Let us go now and see this thing which has come to pass, which the Lord hath made known unto us."

The Spirit of Christmas

The revelation that Jesus Christ, the Savior of the world, is a divine personal being, is a wonderful thing. Is it not the most sublime in all the world? With it comes the assurance that Christmas, has a divine significance. What does it matter that it is not the season of his birth? It cannot be that. The story tells us that it is not. The shepherds in Palestine kept watch over their flocks from the month of April to autumn, so it was not in December. But what does that matter? It is the spirit of Christmas that counts; it is the feeling that we are his brethren, and that we want to live to come back into his presence so that we can go, as the shepherds went, right into the very presence of the King of Kings, the Lord of Lords. We do not want to live a life that will lead us away from the Christ.

Let us have the spirit of Christmas with the same assurance the shepherds had when they received the message of the angels, and with that spirit go to him. Therein is life.

444

Unless we can find God and Christ and know them, we shall not have eternal life, for ". . . this is life eternal, that they might know thee the only true God, and Jesus Christ, whom thou hast sent." (John 17:3.)

I stated that this sweet story of the birth of the Savior contains the philosophy of life; and to know God, to give him glory, is one of the conditions of salvation and peace among the human family.

The Great Question

Peace is promised in this simple little story, but the great question is: How can we get that peace of which the angels sang, and which the shepherds found in that humble little limestone grotto with Jesus lying there in a manger? I have heard some men say: "We do not want peace." Not want peace? Why, it is the greatest blessing that can come to man! Not lethargy, not inactivity, no, but peace; that peace which Christ had in mind when, after his resurrection, he appeared to his twelve disciples and said: "Peace be unto you." Such peace was never won by subterfuge nor argument. No peace is ever in store for any of us but that which we shall win by victory over shame and sin, victory over the sin that oppresses as well as over that which corrupts. "Nothing can bring you this peace," says Emerson, "but the triumph of principle."

The triumph of principle means also triumph over the six enemies to peace, which I name as avarice, lust, worldly ambition, envy, anger, and pride; the six things which the tempter offered in varying form to the Savior on the Mount of Temptation.

Unrestrained passion, ungoverned appetite, envy, hatred, wealth, and power, used to govern men and to crush them— these are the enemies of peace. They bring misery to the individual. They bring unhappiness in the home. They bring war and contention in the world, discontent, misery, and death. They are the opposite of the peace which Christ came to give the world. Why cannot men strive more earnestly than ever before to leave these out of their hearts, to overcome avarice, to give rather than to gain? This is life; this is true living!

The Answer

Only by the trumph of principles over evil can the world have that peace which Christ came to give to the world. No peace has ever been won or has ever been obtained by the cultivation of any of the six passions I have named. Why will the Christian world not understand this?

One cannot have peace by "getting" unless one uses what one gets for the happiness and the betterment of mankind. Only by serving our fellowmen can we obtain that peace which Christ came to establish on earth. His glory, his work, is to bring to pass the immortality and eternal life of man.

I rejoice this Christmas season with my brethren and sisters that "God so loved the world, that he gave his only begotten Son, that whosoever believeth in him should not perish, but have everlasting life." (John 3:16.) And under that inspiration he established his Church that mankind might have peace through obedience to the gospel. There is no other way. Men everywhere strive for peace, but as they attain it, they do so only to the extent that they apply the principles of the gospel. The gospel of Christ is the true philosophy of life; it is the science of living; and its essence was heralded by the angels two thousand years ago.

Chapter Sixty-nine

Moral Heroes
Needed
in the World

CHARLES A. ELLWOOD once said:

Our spiritual culture lags so far behind our material culture in its development that we have no adequate control over the latter. Our science, our education, and our government can do much to help correct this lag in our spiritual development. But in the main this must be done, if done at all, by religion and by the Church. For religion is the creator and the conservator of the social ideals; and the Church is their chief propagator.

In the same view, deprecating the decline in religion and morals, Mark Hopkins writes:

Never was there a time in the history of the world, when moral heroes were more needed. The world waits for such, the providence of God has commanded science to labor and prepare the way for such. For them she is laying her iron tracks, and stretching her wires and bridging the oceans. But where are they? Who shall breathe into our civil and political relations the breath of a higher life? Who shall touch the eye of a paganized science, and of a pantheistic philosophy, that they may see God? Who shall consecrate to the glory of God the triumphs of science? Who shall bear the lifeboat to the stranded and perishing nations?

What Motivates the Inner Man?

Nearly two thousand years have passed since Jesus of Nazareth sat on the Mount in the vicinity of the Sea of Galilee and gave instructions to a group of eager listeners

447

regarding the one way to peace and happiness. On that occasion he uttered many eternal truths, among them, "Ye cannot serve God and mammon" (Matt. 6:24); and, "For where your treasure is, there will your heart be also." (Matt. 6:21.) He summarized these and many others in that wonderful expression: "Seek ye first the kingdom of God, and his righteousness; and all these things shall be added unto you." (Matt. 6:33.)

The religion of Jesus Christ looks to the establishment of a social order in which God's will shall be done—a kingdom of God "which shall make of humanity one large family with genuine love and goodwill among its members. *But this new social order was not to be established by force, but by a new life within the individual man.*"

Communists favor the establishment of their society by force. But the Church has in mind the life within. There are three guiding principles to the realization of the establishment of the kingdom of God—

First, an acknowledgment of the existence of Deity, and a desire to know his will. Those who oppose this, deny his existence. In their godlessness they teach the young, and have taught a whole generation for over half a century to deny his existence.

Second, peace through individual righteousness,
Third, a desire to do his will.

First, *Godhood,*
Second, *manhood,*
Third, *brotherhood.*

God Lives!

The first involves *faith in God and in his Son, Jesus Christ.* It means that God becomes the center of our being, the guide to our thoughts and acts. Around and over all there is God, the Father, "Lord of heaven and earth." This universe, therefore, is not left to the guidance of an irrational and random chance, but, on the contrary, *is ordered and con-*

trolled by a marvelous intelligence and wisdom. If science says to you that it has not found a divine, personal Being, nor the soul of man, you are not justified in concluding that these realities do not exist. "There is not a single scientific specialist of repute," says Dr. Hudson, "who has attempted to prove by scientific method that what science cannot demonstrate is thereby disproved."

On the other hand, in support of this first fundamental truth in the gospel of Christ, we hear these unwavering testimonies, "God and the unseen world are not merely objects of surmise. We know them in our experience." (Charles Dunsmore.)

And again—"When the light rested upon me I saw two Personages, whose brightness and glory defy all description, standing above me in the air. One of them spake unto me, calling me by name and said, pointing to the other—*This is My Beloved Son. Hear Him!*" (Pearl of Great Price, *Joseph Smith* 2:17.)

It is to be regretted that "there are tens of thousands of bright and agreeable young people in every Christian country who do not even try to believe in Christ and would regard it as positively eccentric to do so. They would as soon believe in Father Christmas. They have no particular foundation for their skepticism. They certainly have not made a careful study of the documents, and most of them would be completely floored if you asked them to name a single passage in the Gospels which can legitimately be regarded as false. All they can say is, vaguely, that obviously the whole thing is impossible. . . . But the fact remains that the man who has even for one minute believed in Christ will never be quite the same again.

"Of course, you cannot prove the power of faith any more than you can prove the beauty of the sunset. Before you can even attempt to discuss faith, you must lead your reader to believe that the thing is, to say the least of it, possible. Otherwise, you will be in the position of a man who tried to prove the beauty of the aforesaid sunset to an audience who is probably convinced that there is no such thing as the sun." (Author unknown.)

God should be the center of our lives and the lives of all in the world, including Communists.

Become Master of Self

What about *manhood?* No outward environment alone can produce manhood. The virtues of life spring from within. ". . . The kingdom of God cometh not with observation: Neither shall they say, Lo here! or, lo there! for, behold, the kingdom of God is within you." (Luke 17:20-21.)

> Nae treasures, nor pleasures
> Could make us happy lang;
> The heart ay's the part ay
> That makes us right or wrang.
> —Robert Burns.

The development of manhood involves *self-denial.* It implies the *overcoming of self-centered self.*

A proper conception of this divine principle, the sacredness of personality, would change the attitude of the world to the benefit and happiness of human beings. It would bring into active operation the Golden Rule—"Do unto others as you would have others do unto you."

Jesus taught that from within the heart of man come evil thoughts, sexual vice, acts of theft, murder, adultery, greed. When men commit these crimes, individually or collectively, they trespass upon human rights and, of course, bring misery into the world. *Greed prompts the accumulation of wealth even at the sacrifice of human life. What a different world this would be if men would accumulate wealth not as an end, but as a means of blessing human beings and improving human relations.*

A Christian conception of the right and value of a human soul would prevent the enslavement of peoples, and the injustices that are at this moment being perpetrated in various parts of the world.

There is nothing to be lost by maintaining the ideals which Jesus taught, but everything to gain. He taught us the sacredness of the human soul, the dignity of man, instead of crushing him, and making him a part of the state.

Love Thy Neighbor as Thyself

The third guiding principle is *brotherhood,* which *involves service, not conquest.* It involves confidence in man, in your brother—not suspicion and hatred. It involves truthful dealings—not chicanery and fraud. As fundamental to brotherhood and peace, Jesus recognized the rights of every man. Thank heaven for the teachings of our Savior that bring us closer to each other in expression of such brotherhood!

All these principles have but one object in mind, and that is the fundamental purpose of the Church—*to establish peace.* The spirit of the world is antagonistic to the establishment of peace. The law of nature is the survival of the fittest at all costs. That is why moral heroes are needed in the world today. That is why the Church has erected buildings and temples throughout the world. That is why we are sending thousands of missionaries to all parts of the world.

To establish the kingdom of God means to dedicate lives, fortunes, and sacred honor to the redemption of humanity from sin and ignorance. It means an army working for human salvation; working, however, not with the blare of trumpets, but quietly with adequate knowledge, with unfaltering faith in God and with unlimited love toward men.

Holiday Thoughts

8

Chapter Seventy

Some Expressions
of Appreciation
and Thanksgiving

"Open Thou Mine Eyes"

Help me not to miss the splendor
   In the commonplace, I pray.
Lord, I ask for inner vision
   As I walk in faith today.
There are blessings all around me,
   Reaching out for me to see,
Give me sight to recognize them,
   All the good Thou hast for me.

Let my gratitude be constant,
   Let my heart respond with
     praise,
Let a prayer of thanks be given
   For the manifested ways
Thou dost show Thy daily guid-
   ance,
   Thy protection and Thy care;
"Open Thou mine eyes," my Father,
   To Thy presence everywhere.
        Della Adams Leitner.

It has been well over a hundred years since my grandfather, William McKay, and my grandmother, Ellen Oman McKay, left Thurso, Scotland, having become converts to The Church of Jesus Christ of Latter-day Saints. They settled in Ogden, Utah; and so in the same year did the Powells and the Evans families from Wales. And William McKay's second son, David, met a little girl, 16 years of age, Jennette Evans, who became David's wife.

On April 28, 1875, William McKay, my grandfather, was set apart by Orson Pratt as a missionary. Later he went back to his native land as a missionary and went up to Wick Thurso, and Aberdeen, Scotland, bearing witness that the gospel had been restored and that he knew it to be a fact.

About 1882, his son, David, my father, went as a missionary. He, too, labored in Glasgow, Dundee, Aberdeen, and in Thurso; and he was president of the Scottish Conference.

In 1897, I went as a missionary, an unmarried man, young, earnest, and eager as young missionaries are. I was assigned to go to Scotland to labor. After a few months the presidency of the European Mission, then President Rulon S. Wells, Joseph L. McMurrin, and Henry W. Naisbett, appointed me president of the Glasgow Conference.

An old lady in Thurso, whom I visited in 1898, had been the playmate of my grandmother. She remembered when they were baptized, and she said, "I remember when they dipped them i' the Burn; do ye do that noo?"

I assured her that we did.

"And are ye Willie's grandson? Ach a' me, I am gettin' auld!"

As I look back in reminiscent moods upon those events and many others that have crowded my mind, I have profound gratitude in my heart that some elder over a hundred years ago knocked at a door in Thurso, or really in Janetstown near Thurso, and bore witness that the gospel of Jesus Christ had been restored. I am thankful that my grandfather and grandmother believed that, because that was the beginning of all the events that have happened in the century to our family to this moment.

Grateful, am I? Words are too feeble.

Purpose of the Gospel

What is the purpose of preaching the gospel? It is illustrated in the song we sing, "Joy, Praise, Exaltation of the Soul"; it is expressed in the scripture: ". . . Men are, that they might have joy." (2 Nephi 2:25.)

Happiness is one of the aims of the gospel; not pain, not grief, not gloom, not pleasure. There is a difference between pleasure and happiness. Happiness is the joy of the soul, always. The Prophet Joseph Smith declared that, "Happiness is the object and design of our existence, and will be the end thereof if we pursue the path that leads to it." And this path is virtue, uprightness, faithfulness, holiness, and living all the commandments of God. But we cannot live the commandments without first knowing them, and we cannot expect to know all or more than we now know unless we comply with or keep those commandments we have already received. Our desire is to declare to the world what these commandments are, as recorded in the gospels giving the account of Jesus' teachings and those of the Twelve who followed him.

What Are the Elements of Happiness?

The first condition of happiness is a clear conscience. Daniel Webster said: "Weighed in the balance, conscience compared with the world—conscience makes the world seem but a bubble, for God himself is in conscience giving its authority."

Associated with that is the principle of repentance. Peter said, ". . . Repent, and be baptized every one of you in the name of Jesus Christ for the remissions of sins. . . ." (Acts 2:38.) He had in mind the cleansing of your spirit, cleansing of your mind of all antipathies, suspicions, and hatred, cruelties to one another.

The second requisite of joy and happiness is freedom. I do not recall who wrote it, but one person said: "God desires to make men like himself, but to do so he must first make them free."

The third requisite for happiness is a sense of self-mastery. Learn to control your appetites; learn to control your passions. You are not a slave to anything. Physical qualities are secondary to the sense that you are master of yourself. If you have a sense of mastery, you control your tongue. That is power.

The fourth condition of happiness is doing your best to keep your health by obeying the laws of life.

The fifth requisite for happiness is appreciation of blessings and possessions. You do not possess money? Yet you have the greatest blessings in all the world. You have eyes to see, you have ears to hear, you have loved ones whom you can serve, you have your children; and if you have a testimony of the gospel, you know that that loved one, that wife, that husband, that child, may be yours throughout eternity. Death cannot end love if the spirit exists. Do you know that? Then you can be happy. What if you do have a few trials? You have the possessions of the soul, and that spirit can have those possessions to continue throughout eternity if you believe in Jesus Christ and his immortality—and you must believe that. These things constitute the gospel.

Clear Conscience

It is glorious when you can lie down at night with a clear conscience that you have done your best not to offend anyone and have injured no one. You have tried to cleanse your heart of all unrighteousness, and if you put forth precious effort you can sense as you pray to God to keep you that night that he accepts your effort. You have a sense that you are God's child, a person whose soul God wants to save. You have the strength to resist evil. You also have the realization that you have made the world better for having been in it. These and countless other virtues and conditions are all wrapped up in the gospel of Jesus Christ.

You have the knowledge that your soul will live after death comes to your mortal body, and that if you have lost loved ones, you will meet them. By the power of the priesthood whatsoever is bound on earth is bound in heaven. This is an eternal promise. I referred to William McKay and Ellen Oman, my grandparents; and I referred to my father and mother. I shall meet them and recognize them and love them as I recognized and loved them here.

That, in part, is the gospel of Jesus Christ; and my heart is full of thanksgiving for it, and for the happiness and salvation the gospel brings to mankind.

Chapter Seventy-one

The Price
of a
Happy New Year

Dᴜʀɪɴɢ the next few weeks "Happy New Year" will be, perhaps, the most frequently repeated phrase in the English language. Every time it is spoken sincerely, it will throw a ray of sunshine into some life. Often it will brighten the spark of hope and give new zest to him whose spirit has been darkened. It will carry with it the message that the old year, with its failings, faults, and failures, has passed forever, and that a new year comes laden with fresh opportunities and rich promises of success.

With hopes thus renewed and ambitions stirred, we find ourselves making resolutions. Some of them, it is true, are weak, frail things that struggle feebly for existence and then die, as if prematurely born. Others are strong, vigorous, and clean-cut, destined to become potent factors in our lives.

Secret of Happiness Lies within Us

Few of us stop to consider how closely related these resolutions are to the happiness that we anticipate the new year will bring us. The secret of happiness lies within each of us, side by side with our resolutions and desires. It never comes from without. It cannot be stolen; it cannot be purchased, for it is above price. It is true wealth; and friends will make it the brighter when it is already shining within.

but when it is not in the heart, all outward contributions are like paint and powder on the sallow cheek, the mere semblance of the thing desired.

Happiness from Accomplishment

One source of happiness springs from the realization of having accomplished something worthwhile; misery, from the realization of having failed. How, then, can one be happy who sincerely makes a resolution, and then ignobly fails to keep it? The accomplishing of a fixed determination in the quest for truth and nobility of soul always produces happiness. Failure and vaccilation always bring corresponding unhappiness. One is like the godly sorrow that worketh repentance to salvation not to be repented of; the other, like the sorrow of the world that worketh death.

Too many are not willing to pay the price of a happy new year. They drift along aimlessly, hoping that peace and comfort will come to them as does sunshine on a summer day. They forget that rain, hail, snow, and the biting frosts of winter come in the same way. He who would possess happiness must pay the price of effort. It is one of the laws of life that each acquisition has its cost

A muscle can be developed only by expending muscular energy. Intellectual advancement can be obtained only by mental activity. Spiritual growth comes only by spiritual endeavor. And happiness is realized only through righteous desires and worthy accomplishments. What sublime peace, what infinite power must have filled Christ's soul when, toward the close of his earthly mission, he could say, ". . . I have overcome the world!" (John 16:33.) Oh, how great the distance between the heights of his sublimity, and the depths of the degraded soul, drifting in the slime and filth of indulgence, blindly thinking, if he thinks at all, that happiness is allied with physical gratifications!

True Happiness in Christlike Life

True happiness is found in living the Christlike life—

on Monday, as well as on Sunday. He who is virtuous only at intervals proves that his pretended virtue is but a sham. Such a person lacks sincerity, the foundation of a true character, without which happiness is impossible. He who seeks for happiness alone seldom finds it; but he who lives, that is, who loses himself to give happiness to others, finds that a double portion has come to himself.

One of the missions of The Church of Jesus Christ of Latter-day Saints is to assist mankind in overcoming evil and in cherishing the good. Repentance is an eternal principle of salvation; and the thrust of our weaknesses and sins upon the old year, to be carried into the never-returning past, is but the practical application of this sublime principle.

Membership in the Church carries with it the responsibility to overcome temptation, to battle error, to improve the mind, and to develop one's spirit until it comes to the "measure of the stature of the fulness of Christ." Habits of intemperance and sensual pleasures should have been buried in the waters of baptism. What folly to permit them to return when one realizes that not happiness but misery is allied with indulgence in sin!

The Happiest Man

Truly, the happiest man is he who not only resolves, but who, with the help of the Lord, succeeds in adding to his

. . . faith virtue; and to virtue knowledge; and to knowledge temperance; and to temperance patience; and to patience godliness; and to godliness brotherly kindness; and to brotherly kindness charity. For if these things be in you, and abound, they make you that ye shall neither be barren nor unfruitful in the knowledge of our Lord Jesus Christ. But he that lacketh these things is blind, and cannot see afar off, and hath forgotten that he was purged from his old sins. Wherefore the rather, brethren, give diligence to make your calling and election sure: for if ye do these things, ye shall never fall: for so an entrance shall be ministered unto you abundantly into the everlasting kingdom of our Lord and Saviour Jesus Christ. (2 Peter 1:5-11.)

Undoubtedly, somewhere on the scroll that the new year brings, there will be marks of disappointment, discouragement, difficulty, and perhaps sorrow; but we shall try to meet these with unfaltering determination, relying upon God to strengthen us in weakness and to give us fortitude in trial. Thus overcoming what we can, and bearing bravely what we must, we shall experience the joy of mastery akin to that which Jesus felt when he said: ". . . Be of good cheer, I have overcome the world." (John 16:33.)

Chapter Seventy-two

At This
Christmastide. . . .

AT THIS CHRISTMASTIDE, I wish to refer to an incident in the life of the Savior when people who listened to a spiritual address that he had given, walked away from him because they did not understand the meaning of that address. A brief reference to the incident reads:

From that time many of his disciples went back, and walked no more with him. (John 6:66.)

As he saw those disciples walking away and noticed that the Twelve men who had been with him remained, he said, "Will ye also go away?"

Simon Peter, true to his nature, answered: "Lord, to whom shall we go? thou hast the words of eternal life. And we believe and are sure that thou art that Christ, the Son of the living God." (John 6:67-69.)

That sermon on the bread of life followed the miracle of the feeding of the five thousand with a few loaves of bread and a few fishes. Great teacher that Christ was, he used that miracle to teach the people the *spiritual* significance of the gospel. When they could not understand that significance, but had eaten of the loaves and were filled, they walked away. Then Jesus turned to the Twelve, and asked them the question to which I have referred. Later, Jesus took the Twelve up to a mountain nearby, and taught them more about the spiritual significance of the gospel, at the conclusion of which he said, "Whom do men say that I the Son of man am?" (a grammatical error that has come down through hundreds of years). They answered: "Some say that thou art John the Baptist (who had been beheaded by Herod): some, Elias; and others, Jeremias, or one of the prophets," having in mind the return of the spirit.

Then Jesus said, "But whom say ye that I am?" Impetuous Peter was voice again, and this time after several days' communion with him, he answered unhesitatingly, "Thou art the Christ, the Son of the living God." This time he received the word, "Blessed art thou, Simon Barjona (Christ did not call him 'Peter' at this time): for flesh and blood hath not revealed it unto thee, but my Father which is in heaven." (Matt. 16:13-17.)

Today, perhaps as never before, the world needs that testimony of the divinity of the Lord Jesus Christ.

We should strive so earnestly to represent him or to follow him that our spirits may be eternally young. If thoughts affect the physical being, might it not be true that eternal truths will contribute to the eternal nature of the spirit within? On the night of his betrayal, the Savior said: "And this is life eternal, that they might know thee the only true God, and Jesus Christ, whom thou hast sent." (John 17:3.) And how may we know of the doctrine? *"If any man will do his will, he shall know of the doctrine, whether it be of God, or whether I speak of myself."* (John 7:17.)

Wisdom comes through effort. All good things require effort. That which is worth having will cost part of your physical being, your intellectual power, and your soul power— "Ask, and it shall be given you; seek, and ye shall find; knock, and it shall be opened unto you." (Matt. 7:7.) But you have to seek, you have to knock.

We cannot be true to ourselves, to our loved ones, and to our associates without feeling a determination to know more about this great truth. The spirit within bears testimony that truth exists in this old world. Through the earnest and sincere prayer of a humble heart, through righteousness and well doing Jesus may be found.

In Micah, the fifth chapter, Bethlehem, the city of David, is mentioned by that prophet as the birthplace of the Messiah. I wonder if the shepherds, to whom this revelation of Christ's birth was given, had not that prophecy in mind as they kept watch over their flocks by night, and were treasuring in their hearts the hope, as all Judea was treasuring it, that the Messiah would soon come. Those humble men had opened to them a vision of God.

And it came to pass, as the angels were gone away from them into heaven, the shepherds said one to another, Let us now go even unto Bethlehem, and see this thing which is come to pass, which the Lord hath made known unto us. (Luke 2:15.)

The shepherds did not say, "I wonder if this be true." They did not say, "Let us go and see *if* this thing be true"; they said, "Let us go and see this thing which *is* come to pass which the Lord hath made known unto us"—an assurance that God had revealed his Son, that the angels had given to the world the message that he who should be King of kings and Lord of lords had come as a mere babe in the humblest part of that little Judean town.

What would you give—you who may not have that assurance—to have in your hearts that same confidence that Christ is born, that Christ lives, that God had heralded his birth by angels in heaven? All doubt would be banished, all worry concerning our purpose here in life would cease. That is what such a testimony means.

"What seek ye?" were the first words that Christ uttered to some of his Twelve, or some who afterwards became members of the Twelve. "Master, where dwellest thou?" He didn't say over here, or over there, but He said, "Come and see." (John 1:38-39.) And they went with him that day and spent the rest of the afternoon in his presence.

I ask the youth of the Church today, "Whom do you seek?" Would you keep that youth which is yours now? Then love the Lord your God with all your mind, and with all your heart, and with all your soul; and though the body becomes decrepit and, like an old house, begins to tumble, your spirit will still be young, because your body, after all, is but the house in which you live. Even when your heart stops beating, your eyelids close, and you respond no more to your physical environment, that spirit, still young, will go into the presence of him whom you have made your ideal. Then truly will it be demonstrated that:

> The stars shall fade away, the sun himself
> Grow dim with age, and Nature sink in years;
> But thou shalt flourish in immortal youth,
> Unhurt amidst the war of elements,
> The wreck of matter, and the crash of worlds.

> (Joseph Addison, "Cato,"
> Act V, Scene I.)

As we celebrate his birth this Christmastide, I hope that the teachings and life of the Master will be more beautiful, more necessary, and more applicable to human happiness than ever before. Never have I believed more firmly in the perfection of humanity as the final result of man's placement here on earth. With my whole soul I accept Jesus Christ as the personification of human perfection—as God made manifest in the flesh, as the Savior and Redeemer of mankind. Accepting him as my Redeemer, Savior and Lord, I accept his gospel as the plan of salvation, as the one perfect way to human happiness and peace. There is not a principle which was taught by him but seems to me to be applicable to the growth, development and happiness of mankind. Every one of his teachings seems to me to touch the true philosophy of living. I accept them with all my heart!

Despite discouragement and disheartening conditions throughout the world, Christmas is the happiest season of the whole year. But let us ever keep in mind that people are most blessed whose daily conduct most nearly comports with the *teachings* and *example of Jesus Christ, our Lord and Savior*, at whose birth was proclaimed: "Peace on earth, good will toward men." (Luke 2:14.)

May the peace of our Father in heaven abide in your hearts and the hearts of people everywhere as they draw near to him in prayer and in praise this Christmastide. May the sick be restored; may the sorrowing be comforted; may the lonely have their hearts lifted; and the weary be rested; the needy be fed; may the doubting receive assurance; and may evil and designing men be confounded.

> O living Christ who still
> Dost all our burdens share,
> Come now and dwell within the hearts
> Of all men everywhere.
>
> (John Oxenham.)

INDEX

everlasting foundation, 157; an unwavering, 57

Family, divine purpose, 220; God-
ordained institution, 225; permanence
of relationship, 225; supremest happiness, 190; unit unbroken, 243

Fashions, of the world, 128

Fasting, 40 days of, 23

Father, closer to, 24; of our country,
358; communion with, 22; been disobeying, 14; Eternal, enduring as,
160; an exemplary, 264; a good example, 280; Heavenly, 12; will of, 5

Fathers, our founding, 88

Fear, not death, 57

Fellowmen, serve your, 6

Fighting, for eternal principle, 367

Foot, Emerson, 33

Forgiveness, encompasses charity, 41

Fosdick, Harry Emerson, 10

Fourier, Francois M. C., 86

Free Agency, a divine gift, 370; fundamental to progress, 365

Freedom, of choice, 81; individual
threatened, 374

Fullness, of the earth, 105

Fundamental, facts of life, 81

Future, determining your, 173

– G –

Galilee, man of, 58

Game, learn rules of, 299

Gift, God's greatest, 4

Gift, precious, 16

Glasgow, 3

Glory, man's crowning, 29; a sense of,
420; work and, 10

God, acknowledge providence of, 391;
becomes center, 15; belief in, 194;
bless leaders, 21; help us, 11; enlightens minds, 91; given revelation
of life, 193; help members, 111;
intelligent being, 170; is our stay, 95;
keep commandments of, 184; noblest
work of, 271; obey word of, 39;
relationship with, 22; seek kingdom
of, 11; to presence of, 16; was
omnipotent, 38

God's gifts, appreciate, 191; relationship to man, 198

Godliness, principles taught, 427

Good, measure to customers, 280

Goodness, God's to us, 36

Gospel, and the individual, 85; in members minds, 36; is our anchor, 68;

love of, 147; restoration of, 3, 4;
radiate in home, 226; standards of, 9

Governments, servants of people, 375

Grateful, are we, 389; for church membership, 326

Gratitude, importance of, 117

Guarantees, of temple marriage, 243

Guide, Holy Spirit will, 28

Guidance, God's, 12

Guest, Edgar A., quoted, 187

– H –

Hale, Edward Everett, 93

Hallowed, to make holy, 18

Hamlet, 23

Hand, of restraint, 209

Happiness, consider it, 183; deterrents
to, 306; elements of, 457; family is
supremest, 190; from service, 114

Harmony, in the home, 284

Harris, Martin, testimony of, 318

Hatred, fatal effects, 8; fatal effects of,
174; of neighbor, 22

Hawthorne, Nathaniel, 30

Heart, heaviness of, 81

Heritage, Christian, 197

Heroes, moral needed, 447

High Priests, 7

High Priest, Christ is, 64

High, standards, 81

Holiday thoughts, 454

Holy Ghost, inspiration of, 17; is promised, 15; message through, 61

Holy Spirit, promptings of, 114

Home, children in the, 289; and the
church, 298; basis of civilization, 228;
center of power, 267; constant influence, 269; harmony in the, 284; received testimony, 61; safeguard to
delinquency, 281; school of virtue,
198

Homes keep intact, 226; make beautiful, 301; need religion, 280; obligation to build, 228; permanent through
love, 227; radiate us, 108; set in
order, 307

Honest, easy to be, 271

Honesty, fundamental principle, 140

Hoodlum, example to teach, 338

Hoover, Herbert, quoted, 206

Hoover, J. Edgar, quoted, 277

Horizons, widening, 183

Human, guidance of soul, 336

Human nature, belief in, 196

Humanity, baser side of, 94; good in,
196; to love, 7

— M —

Man, brotherhood of, 158; a dual being, 79; the happiest, 462; may know, 126; possess testimony, 12; responsible for acts, 371; spiritual life of, 92
Manhood, honor, integrity, 96; true admirable, 271
Mankind, needs awakening, 76; service to, 348
Man's dominant quest, 179
Marriage, and courtship, 228; flippant attitude toward, 248; for higher purpose, 220; low view of, 197; ordained of God, 212; referred to by Jesus, 228; significance of temple, 233; true purpose of, 306
McKay, Charles, poet quoted, 204
McKay, Sister, 20
Meditation, communion from, 23; at sacrament, 25
Meeting, open air, 3
Members, obligations of, 305; obligation of church, 303; uphold law, 100
Membership, by baptism, 125
Men, of clear vision, 304; evil and designing, 32
Meridian of Time, 6
Merit self-respect, 176
Message, importance of, 4; of missionaries, 166
Minds, God enlightens, 91
Misled, do not be, 218
Missionaries, have heard, 13; pay way, 165
Mission own great, 23; of youth, 254
Modesty, 'diamond setting', 9
Moral, heroes needed, 447
Morality, one standard of, 218
Morrison, Dr. Cressy, 12
Mother, been disobeying, 14; deserves much, 264; love undervalued, 264; offered life, 221
Motherhood, Christlike element, 262; co-partner with God, 263; four requirements, 268; mightiest force, 261
Mothers, sow seeds, 262
Motive, of gold corrupts, 106
Mount, Sermon on, 24
Multitude, dismiss the, 24

N

Name, take Christ's 26
Nation, strength in home, 284
Nature, of man, 81; never deceived, 150; partakers of divine, 103
Neighbor, hatred toward, 22

New Year, thoughts on, 460
Nichols, Beverly, author, 54
Nobility, objectives of, 18
North Sea, 25
Nuclear, war hovering, 382

O

Obedience, to Word of Wisdom, 82
Obligation, of church members, 303; our greatest, 305; man's most important, 197; of Priesthood, 7
Order, in classrooms, 17
Ordinance, all significant, 43; this sacred, 24
Organized, perfectly, 6
Others, service to, 178

P

Parenthood, appreciation of, 310
Partnership, an eternal, 211; contemplate eternal, 222
Parents, know where children are, 226; loyalty to, 287; may guide, 174; must be sincere, 98; must live truth, 295; responsibility of, 285, 297
Participate, free to, 20
Passions, animal, 17
Paul's charge and prophecy, 276
Paul, days of, 311
Peace, be unto you, 445
Pentacost, Day of, 14
People, injure the, 4; our young, 13
Persecution, of Church, 165
Personality, after death, 171
Persuasion, influence by, 376
Perturbed, about social questions, 205
Peter, chief apostle, 54
Pharisee, 14
Pilate, 29
Pioneers, noblest ideals of, 347
Plan, of salvation, 60
Poisoning, spiritual, 94
Possession, the greatest, 145; most precious, 387
Possessions, our dearest, 224
Power, of choice, 310; of holy priesthood, 241; the greater, 341
Pray, to him, 15; teachers should, 342; with children, 300
Prayed, to God, 25
Prayer, a potent force, 300; answer your, 15; basic force, 10; is reality, 15; the efficacy of, 341; of intercession, 4; night and morning, 226; writer tells of, 48
Prayers, secret, 25
Praying, keep, 15
Preparation, by the teacher, 340

Index

Pride, supplants humility, 163
Priesthood, greatest organization, 30; holy power of, 241; men of, 167; obligation of, 7
Priests, 7
Primary, reverence in, 21
Principle, eternal, 6; faith is, 6; repentance is, 6; fighting for eternal, 367; most important, 41; of self-control, 18
Principles, Christ taught, 6; compare eternal, 41; constitute will, 5; of life, salvation, 225
Probation, purpose of mortal, 79
Prodigal son quoted, 202
Profanity, national vice, 294
Profession, choose wisely, 230
Progress, demands effort, 80, 81
Providence, acknowledge of God, 391
Punishment, suffer, 20
Purpose, Christianity's ultimate, 381
Purposes, 3 important ones, 177

Q

Quarreling, aids delinquency, 293; home evils, 306; inexcusable, 70
Quest, man's dominant, 107, 179
Question, another arises, 5
Quorums, priesthood, 20

R

Reality, of Christ sensed, 420
Reason, be your guide, 257
Redeemer, Jesus our, 4; knowledge of, 430
Reject, tempter's schemes, 433
Relations, international, 142
Relationship, a glorious, 409; God to man, 198; with God, 22
Relief Society, reverence, 21
Religion, appeals to spirit, 70; for youth, 201; in education, 304; live, not preach, 296; needed in homes, 280; purpose, end of, 29; that is true, 129; too idealistic, 179; true, 8
Renaissance, a spiritual, 102
Repent, appropriate to, 430
Repentance, is changing, 14; is turning away, 42; eternal principle, 6; salvation principle, 42
Republic, founding of American, 350
Reputation, maintain unsullied, 229
Requirements, of motherhood, 268
Resistance, is necessary, 159
Respect, for one another, 262; for others rights, 209; reverence is, 26

Responsibility, of youth, 199; refusal to bear, 306; sense of, 9; to declare Christ, 258; of state, 366; upon church, 60
Restoration of the Gospel, 3
Restored Gospel, harmony of, 172
Restraint, firm hand of, 209
Resurrection, Christ's mission, 56; Christ's real, 311; the literal, 52
Retaliate, do not, 152
Revelation, on true riches, 37; of life, 193; to Peter, 163
Reverence, attitude of, 26; basis of, 18; be manifest, 21; for God's name, 28; need of, 17; next to love, 18; religious attitude, 11
Riches, revelation on, 37
Right, stand for the, 65; value of doing, 83; to worship God, 377
Rights, cannot trespass, 20; of men, 380; of others, 10; respect for others, 209
Ruskin, 18

S

Sabbath, busy day, 24; day of rest, 81; first day, 82; law of God, 82
Sacrament, the hour, 24; impressive hour, 26; the last supper, 45; meditation at, 25; partaking of, 22; passing of, 51; sacred ordinance 45
Sacred, doors, 23
Sacredness, of marriage covenant, 245
Salt Lake City, 3, 4
Samaria, woman of, 108
Salvation, baptism needed, 41
Satan, tempts us, 19
Satan's plan, for family, 380
Savior, attributes of, 17; set example, 110
Science, belief in, 195; of living, 4
Scriptures, are so simple, 5
Sealed, for time and eternity, 242
Secret, given to us, 5
Seeds, of happiness, 218
Seek, first the kingdom, 303
Self, thoughts on, 15
Self-control, lesson of, 20; power of, 160
Self-love, mothers overcome, 263
Self-mastery, be developed, 159
Self-respect, merit, 176
Sellers, of doves, 18
Sermon on Mount, 24, 47
Serve, your fellowmen, 6
Service, happiness from, 114; render it, 130; to each other, 348; to others, 178

Index